CUPAR

CUPAR

The history of a small Scottish town

Paula Martin

BIRLINN

First published in 2006 by
Birlinn Limited
West Newington House
10 Newington Road
Edinburgh EH9 1QS

www.birlinn.co.uk

Hardback

ISBN 10: 1 84158 410 X
ISBN 13: 978 1 84158 410 2

Paperback

ISBN 10: 1 84158 512 2
ISBN 13: 978 1 84158 512 3

British Library Cataloguing-in-Publication Data
A catalogue record for this book is available from the British Library

Typeset by Waverley Typesetters, Little Walsingham, Norfolk
Printed and bound by Antony Rowe, Chippenham

Contents

List of Plates, Figures, Maps and Tables	ix
Preface	xiii
Acknowledgements	xv
Abbreviations	xvii
Maps	xviii
1. Introduction	1
2. Medieval Cupar	9
The castle	14
Churches	16
The medieval town	19
3. Cupar in the Early-Modern Period	25
Urbanisation	28
The burgh of Cupar	31
4. The Economy	37
A market town	37
The linen industry	43
Other industries	49
Travel and transport	50
Financial services	52
The role of the town council	57
5. The World of Work	65
The professions	65
Guildbrethren	70
The incorporated trades	73
Other occupations	80
Women and work	81
Changing patterns of work	85

6. **Buildings and Townscape**   89
       Building materials   89
       Building and rebuilding   90
       Suburbs   92
       Parish church   94
       Public buildings   94
       St Catherine Street   96
       Public open spaces   99
       Private houses   99
       The comments of visitors   101

7. **Material Culture**   107
       Living spaces   110
       Changing fashions   111
       New materials   115
       Conspicuous consumption   119
       Personal comfort   120

8. **Literacy and Leisure**   127
       Schools and schooling   127
       Literacy   131
       Entertainment and recreation   134

9. **Local and National Politics**   145
       The town council   145
       Local politics 1714–25   150
       Local politics 1765–71   154
       Local and national issues 1792–97   156
       Expressions of loyalty   158
       Relations with other organisations   159
       Links between local and national politics   161

10. **Poor Relief, Social Control and Public Services**   169
       Poor relief   169
       Social control   178
       Public services   181

11. **Cupar c.1820–1914**   187
       Social life and recreation   200
       Administration and public services   201

12. **Cupar 1914 to the Present Day**   207

13. **Conclusions**   213

Notes on Sources   221

Glossary   229

Appendices
    1. Parish population figures for east Fife, 1755–1821   233
    2. The financial elite of Cupar c.1790 to c.1820   235
    3. Occupational profile of Cupar 1700–1819   237
    4. List of inventories used in Chapter 7   239

Bibliography   243

Index   261

List of Plates, Figures, Maps and Tables

Plates

1a   The tower and part of the nave arcade, all that survives of the church built in 1415

1b   Detail from the fifteenth-century Fernie wall monument

1c   Detail of carving on one pillar of the nave arcade

2a   Plan of Cupar, inset in a corner of the map of Fife by James Gordon of Straloch, 1642

2b   A wall monument in the churchyard to AG, 1676

2c   Stone marking the burial-place of the heads of Laurence Hay and Andrew Pittilloch, and one of the hands of David Hackston of Rathillet

3a   Preston Lodge, Bonnygate

3b   'The Chancellor's House', Crossgate

3c   Marathon House, Bonnygate

4a   The south side of the Crossgate, c.1860

4b   Buildings on the corner of Bonnygate and Lady Wynd

5   Plan of Cupar, inset in the south-west corner of Ainslie's map of Fife, 1775

6a   Cupar parish church, with the tower of 1415, and the new church built in 1785

6b   Bellfield, a large detached house in its own grounds

7a   The buildings on North Burnside which are shown on the 1775 plan

7b   One of the two-storey houses on North Burnside which are probably part of the Newtown development of c.1790

7c   House at the corner of Crossgate and Bonnygate, rebuilt c.1790

8a   73 Bonnygate, built from a design in a pattern book published in 1778

8b   9 Kirk Wynd, built for a merchant in 1811

8c   An old house in Provost Wynd, with a doorpiece added in the early nineteenth century

9a   The Latin School, built in 1806, with the upper floor later fitted out as a theatre

9b   The new gaol, designed by James Gillespie Graham, built by Maurice Finlay 1813–14

9c   County Buildings, St Catherine Street, designed by James Gillespie Graham, and built 1811–12

10a   The Tontine Inn (or Tavern), St Catherine Street, built 1811–12

10b   The building on the left, the office of James Kyd, was the headquarters of the Fife Fire Insurance Company, the one on the right the Commercial Bank

10c   The Council House, built by Robert Hutchison 1815–16

11a   Crossgate House, an early nineteenth-century villa built for Thomas Horsburgh, sheriff clerk

11b   Ladyinch, an early nineteenth-century villa at the junction of Carslogie Road and Balgarvie Road

11c   Rosemount Cottage, Riggs Place, an early nineteenth-century villa

12a   The Mote Hill, a shady gravel walk with fine views.

12b   Tollhouse at the junction of South Road and Ceres Road, built in 1842

12c   Tollhouse at the junction of East Road and Pitscottie Road, built c.1825

13   Detail from Wood's town plan, dated 1820

14a   A door with fanlight above, Millgate

14b   Exterior fanlight, 1 The Barony

14c   Fanlight inside the vestibule, 1 The Barony

14d   The Royal Hotel, St Catherine Street, built 1854

15a   The spire of the Corn Exchange, built in 1861–62

15b   A late Victorian doorway in Carslogie Road

15c   Carving above the door of the Bonnygate Church, 1865–66

16a   The War Memorial, dominating the east end of St Catherine Street

16b   The giant silo, a silent reminder of the former sugar beet factory

16c   St Columba's Roman Catholic Church, Kirkgate

Figures

1.1.	The parishes of east Fife	2
1.2.	Population changes in the parishes of east Fife between 1755 and 1821	3
1.3.	Population of Cupar between 1793 and 1991	4
1.4.	Comparative population growth of the five main Fife burghs, 1793–1991	5
2.1.	Schematic diagram of the boundaries of the medieval liberty of Cupar	11
2.2.	Detail from the 1642 town plan, showing the medieval church	17
2.3.	Surviving medieval fabric of Cupar parish church	18
2.4.	Fernie wall-monument rebuilt into the west wall of the 1785 parish church	19
2.5.	Cupar burgh arms	21
3.1.	Detail from the 1642 town plan, showing the tolbooth, with the east port next to it	33
4.1.	Mark of a Cupar stampmaster, found on osnaburgh linen	47

4.2. Mills on the River Eden   49
5.1. Chronological distribution of identified working men in the
      burgh, 1700–1819   66
5.2. Changing numbers of doctors, writers, maltmen and innkeepers,
      1700–1819   71
5.3. Changing numbers of smiths, wrights, weavers and walkers,
      1700–1819   76
5.4   Changing numbers of tailors, shoemakers, baxters and fleshers,
      1700–1819   77
5.5   Total working males compared with total guildry and trades,
      1700–1819   81
6.1. Detail from William Roy's Military Survey of Scotland, showing
      the roads and bridges around Cupar   95
11.1. Occupational data for men, from 1851, 1871 and 1891 censuses   189
11.2. Occupational data for women, from 1851, 1871 and 1891
      censuses   190
11.3. Occupational data for managers and proprietors, from Trades
      Directories for 1867, 1889 and 1911   191
11.4. Advertisement for Tontine Hotel, c.1860   192
11.5. Advertisement for Royal Hotel, c.1860   193
11.6. The spire of the Duncan Institute   196
11.7. Kirkgate School   198

Tables

3.1. Towns paying per cent or more on the tax roll of the royal burghs   29
4.1. Surviving evidence of stock, value of stock and total wealth of
      Cupar merchants   39
4.2. Surviving evidence of contacts between Cupar merchants and others
      in Scotland and England   42
4.3. Numbers employed in the main centres of the linen industry in Fife
      in the early 1790s   45
4.4. Surviving evidence for links between manufacturers in Cupar
      and customers and suppliers elsewhere   46
4.5. Investments of over £100 in public companies   54
4.6. Submission and decreet arbitral between John Ferguson and
      James Wilson, 1814   53
5.1. Surviving evidence for the financial assets of some Cupar lawyers   67
5.2. Top ten occupations in Cupar, sampled at thirty-year intervals   85
7.1. Numbers of various household items discussed in the text   112
7.2. Increase over time of average number of certain items per
      household   122
7.3. Increase over time of numbers of households possessing certain
      items   123
8.1. Subscribers to Cupar Academy, 1823   130
8.2. Main book collections listed in inventories   132

10.1. An example of private charitable contributions 174
11.1. Attendance of non-conformist churches in 1840 194

Maps

Map 1 Mainland Scotland xviii
Map 2 Central and eastern Fife xix
Map 3 Cupar and its immediate surroundings xx
Map 4 Plan of Cupar town centre xxi
Map 5 Cupar on the first edition 6" to the mile Ordnance Survey
map, surveyed 1855, published 1856 xxii

Preface

The core material for this book is based on a thesis entitled *Cupar, Fife, 1700–c. 1820: a Small Scottish Town in an Era of Change* (University of Dundee, 2000). There is therefore considerably more detail for this period than for those before and after. But as this period, sometimes referred to as 'the long eighteenth century', represents one of the most significant periods in the life of the town, and is reflected in its surviving architecture, it is hoped that the reader will forgive the imbalance.

The thesis was enhanced by the compilation of a database, listing over 3,500 men and over 500 women. Women are included within the main narrative wherever evidence for their activities survives. It is in the main narrative that they belong, not sidelined in one separate chapter. The sources are so poor, however, that no statistical conclusions can be drawn about working women. In a study such as this, it should never be forgotten how fragmentary is the surviving evidence, and how much we do not know and will probably never find out.

The material covering 1700 to the 1820s is compiled from primary sources. To avoid excessive footnotes, indications have been given in the text as to the date and source of citations of primary sources. Footnotes have been limited to extra information, and the occasional quotation or single citation of a primary source. At the end of the book there is a Note on Sources for each chapter. Full references, and more information about sources and methodology, can be found in the original thesis, which may be consulted in Dundee University Library or the library of the Royal Commission on the Ancient and Historical Monuments of Scotland, in Edinburgh. Material covering earlier and later periods has been compiled from secondary or printed primary sources, and there is much scope here for further research. Unreferenced nineteenth- and twentieth-century material comes from newspapers or trades' directories.

The illustrations are mainly maps and drawings of buildings. Other images relating to Cupar can be found on SCRAN (www.scran.ac.uk), including several portraits, old photographs, documents, banners and miscellaneous objects. The index has been used to tie together information about individuals who may appear in several different guises, and to minimise intrusive background information in text or footnotes.

Acknowledgements

First of all I would like to thank Chris Whatley for directing me towards Cupar as a research topic, and for his patience in supervising my thesis. Many people have listened to me, encouraged me, or answered my questions, over many years, including Menzies and Elspeth Campbell, the late Ronald Cant, Barbara Crawford, Nicholas Davey, Jane Dawson, Mr Ferrier of JL Anderson, Elizabeth Gordon, Wynne Harley, Bob Harris, David Jones, Hugh Kennedy, Mike King, Maureen Lishman, Charles McKean, Sir James Morrison-Low, Bill Pagan, Geoffrey Parker, Steven Penrice, Rachel Peterkin, Marie and Peter Robinson, Hamish Scott, Iain Smith, Douglas Speirs, Simon Taylor, the late Donald Watt, the late Christine Wolfe and Marion Wood. I would also like to acknowledge all those who have listened to talks I have given or come on guided walks. Particularly memorable walking companions were David Jones, Charles McKean and Simon Taylor.

The staff of all the archives and libraries I have visited have been exceptionally courteous and helpful, but I would like particularly to mention Alison Lindsay at West Register House, Chris Fleet at the Map Library, National Library of Scotland, and Seonaid McDonald at the Bank of Scotland. Norman Reid, Christine Gascoigne and others in the Special Collections Department of St Andrews University Library have provided support and encouragement as well as professional advice.

For illustrations, and permission to reproduce them, I am grateful to the National Library of Scotland (Plates 2a and 5), and Steven Penrice (Plate 4). For access to papers in private collections I would like to thank Sonia Anderson, Steven Penrice and the Secretary of the Fife Hunt.

For the purposes of this book I have ventured further into medieval history than before, and I am extremely grateful to Richard Oram for his help and guidance through this minefield. Edward Martin provided help with computing (I am on my fifth computer and fourth set of software since this project started), and Peter Martin was kind enough to supply some of the line drawings. And especial thanks are due to my husband Colin for drawing the maps, and for his patience and support.

Abbreviations

APS	*Acts of the Parliaments of Scotland*
BS	Bank of Scotland, Archives
CRB	*Extracts from the Records of the Convention of the Royal Burghs*
DU	Dundee University Library, Archives Department
ER	*The Exchequer Rolls of Scotland*
NA	National Archives, Kew (formerly Public Record Office)
NAS	National Archives of Scotland (formerly Scottish Record Office)
NLS	National Library of Scotland
NSA	*New Statistical Account*
OPR	Old Parish Registers
OSA	*Old Statistical Account*
RBS	Royal Bank of Scotland, Archives
RCAHMS	Royal Commission on the Ancient and Historical Monuments of Scotland
RPC	*Register of the Privy Council of Scotland*
SHS	Scottish History Society
StAU	St Andrews University Library, Special Collections
TA	*Accounts of the Lord High Treasurer of Scotland*

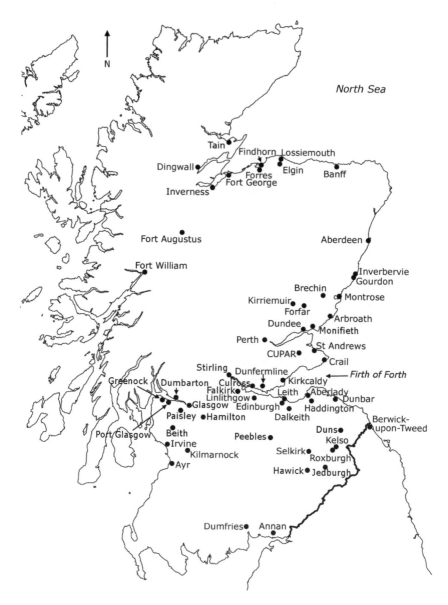

MAP 1   Mainland Scotland, showing the places mentioned in the text.

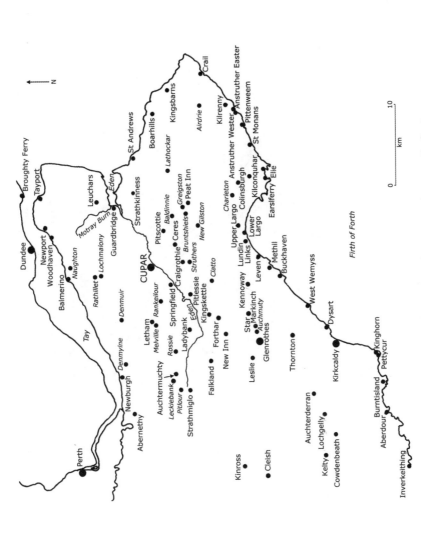

MAP 2   Central and eastern Fife, showing settlements and estates (italics).

MAP 3   Cupar and its immediate surroundings, showing settlements, road network and estates (italics).

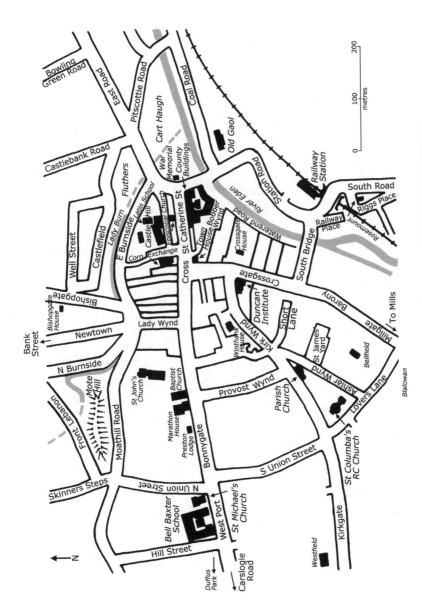

MAP 4   East Fife's parishes; the dark line divides the presbyteries of St Andrews and Cupar.

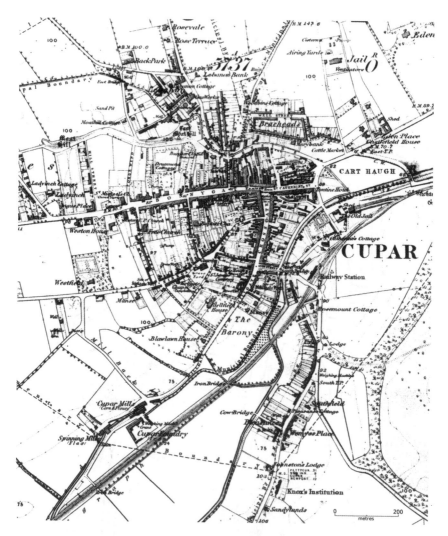

MAP 5   Cupar on the first edition 6" to the mile Ordnance Survey map, surveyed 1855, published 1856.

Introduction

A place in the middle region of the county where the rest of the people of Fife go to receive justice.

Buchanan, *History of Scotland*, 1582

Cupar has been the home of the sheriff court of Fife since 1213, though subsidiary courts were established in Kirkcaldy in 1732 and in Dunfermline in 1811. Once it became the seat of the sheriff, other developments followed, and when times were hard the town still had a continuing purpose. A royal burgh from the fourteenth century, Cupar was the county town of Fife until 1975. The name 'Cupar' is Pictish, and indicates the confluence of two rivers, the Eden and the Lady Burn. The fact that such an old name has survived highlights the importance of the town from an early date, probably the seventh or eighth century.[1]

Fife is a peninsula with a long coastline facing the North Sea (Maps 1 and 2). Within it are six medieval royal burghs: Crail, Cupar, Dunfermline, Falkland, Inverkeithing and Kinghorn. Another eight were created during the sixteenth century, all but one of them on the coast, and three more during the first half of the seventeenth century.[2] Both Dunfermline at the west end of Fife and St Andrews at the east were sites of early religious foundations and were atypical burghs, Dunfermline an ecclesiastical burgh with strong royal associations and St Andrews with the archbishop and his cathedral, and the earliest university in Scotland. There was also a later royal palace or hunting lodge at Falkland. Cupar had no strong royal or religious associations, but developed as the legal and administrative centre of Fife. Situated at the eastern end of the Howe of Fife, at the heart of the agricultural land of east Fife, Cupar was an important staging post on the road from Edinburgh to Dundee. Although in the nineteenth century the Howe of Fife was drained and a road built across it, Cupar remains the hub of the road network in east Fife (Map 3).

Land boundaries within Fife, both parish and estate, seem to have changed relatively little since the medieval period, when Fife was divided into fifty-five parishes, which may themselves reflect earlier land boundaries. In the first half of the seventeenth century several more parishes were created to accommodate new royal burghs such as Pittenweem, but this was done by subdivision, and there was no major rearranging of boundaries.[3] Because the parishes are medieval or earlier there are far more in east Fife, where there is better agricultural land, than in west Fife, where there is now a much higher population. The division into four presbyteries by the early seventeenth century probably reflects the natural spheres of influence, historical and geographical, of the four most important towns in Fife before 1700 – Cupar, Dunfermline, Kirkcaldy and St Andrews. Because this division of Fife was logical, it was also used for other administrative purposes, such as county business during the eighteenth century.

The first fairly reliable parish population figures were gathered in 1755. These were followed by the *First Statistical Account* in the 1790s, and from 1801 by the decennial censuses which continue today. At the beginning of the eighteenth century Cupar was the third-largest town in Fife, and during that century experienced perhaps its greatest period of growth. One reason for this was the movement of people from the countryside to the towns, the result of several factors including changes in agricultural practices, population growth (more births than deaths), and the development of increased employment opportunities within

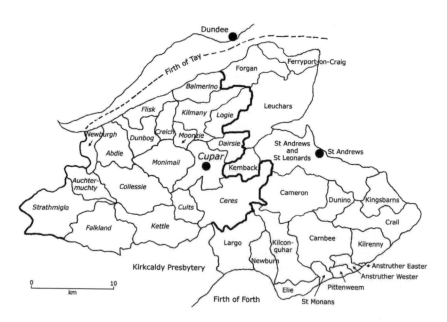

FIGURE 1.1   The parishes of east Fife. Those in regular type are in the presbytery of St Andrews, those in italics the presbytery of Cupar.

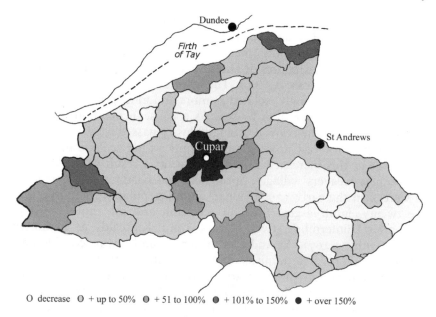

O decrease   ◐ + up to 50%   ◑ + 51 to 100%   ● + 101% to 150%   ● + over 150%

FIGURE 1.2   Population changes in the parishes of east Fife between 1755–1821.

towns. Appendix 1 shows population figures for the parishes of east Fife (Fig. 1.2) for 1755, the early 1790s, and the censuses of 1801, 1811 and 1821. It also shows the percentage changes represented by these figures.[4] Fig. 1.2 summarises these changes, and shows that the population of Cupar parish increased more than that of any other parish in east Fife.

Overall, the population figures for most of the parishes of east Fife, for which Cupar was the administrative and economic centre, fall into five categories. In the first are eight purely rural parishes (Cameron, Carnbee, Dunbog, Dunino, Flisk, Kilmany, Moonzie and Newburn) which shrank as agriculture changed and employed fewer people. Second are the seven East Neuk coastal parishes (Anstruther Easter and Wester, Elie, Kilrenny, Largo, Pittenweem and St Monans) which grew through a revival first of general maritime trade and then of the fishing industry. Third are twelve parishes (many of them close to Cupar) which, though rural, derived significant employment from the linen hand-loom weaving industry, in some cases leading to the creation of new villages within them (Ceres, Collessie, Creich, Cults, Dairsie, Kemback, Kettle, Kilconquhar, Kingsbarns, Leuchars, Logie and Monimail). The fourth group (Auchtermuchty, Falkland, Newburgh and Abdie, St Andrews and St Leonards, and Strathmiglo) contains most of the smaller towns, which also grew, mainly because of the linen industry. The three parishes on the north coast: Balmerino; Forgan, containing the recently founded New Dundee or Newport-Dundee, now Newport;

and Ferryport-on-Craig, later Tayport – show the highest decennial growth between 1821 and 1831, because Dundee provided a market for their produce, and within them the towns of Newport and Tayport were developing as satellites of Dundee. The parish which does not fit any of these categories is Crail. This medieval royal burgh seems to have become increasingly isolated as more and more goods and people moved by road rather than by sea. As a consequence both the linen industry and later the revived fishing industry passed it by.

The population of Cupar parish was only 15 per cent rural in 1793, but by 1831 this increased to 23 per cent, as a result of the creation of two new weavers' villages, Springfield and Gladney (the north end of Ceres). In the early 1790s Cupar, with a population of 3,135, was the twenty-eighth-largest town in Scotland, and the third-largest in Fife, after Dunfermline (twelfth, 5,192) and Kirkcaldy & Linktown (seventeenth, 4,267). St Andrews (thirty-seventh) was considerably smaller at 2,519. The minister of Cupar noted that 'the population has advanced rapidly of late years, owing to the extension of the linen manufacture, and to the increased demand for hands employed in erecting new buildings, and in carrying on important and extensive improvements in gardening and agriculture'. By the time of the 1821 census Cupar's overall position was little different, but the largest towns and cities of Scotland had grown far faster than the smaller ones. Many small towns experienced less growth than Cupar did between 1821 and 1831, and a few actually lost population. But by 1831 Cupar had

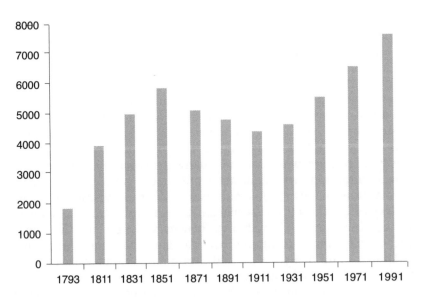

FIGURE 1.3   Population of Cupar between 1793 and 1991.

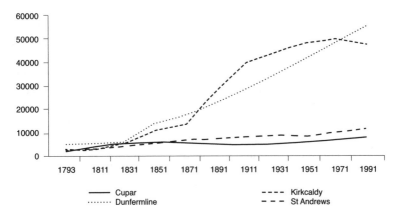

FIGURE 1.4 Comparative population growth of the four main Fife burghs, 1793–1991.

been overtaken by Arbroath and Forfar, and within Fife by Dysart. In 1755 the eastern half of Fife had 52 per cent of the population, and the western half 48 per cent. By the 1790s these figures had been reversed. Cupar may have grown more than any other parish in east Fife during the long eighteenth century, but its position within Fife and the rest of Scotland was declining, and this would accelerate during the rest of the nineteenth century.

Fig. 1.3 shows the population of the town of Cupar between 1793 and 1991, after which it has continued to grow to about 9,000. It can be seen that the town grew fairly fast between 1793 and 1851, and thereafter declined to such an extent that the population in 1921 was less than it had been in 1821. Fig. 1.4 contrasts the figures for Cupar with the slow but steady growth of St Andrews, and the far steeper rise in the population of Dunfermline and particularly of the industrial heart of Fife, Kirkcaldy. Similar population changes were experienced all over Scotland at this period. Indeed, semi-rural east Fife saw neither the extreme depopulation of the countryside nor the rapid growth of manufacturing towns which occurred elsewhere, and made contemporary observers so worried.

There was an increase in emigration in the early nineteenth century. The population seems to have become more mobile, perhaps through economic pressures, perhaps because those who served in the armed forces brought back information about other parts of Britain. There will have been many individual reasons for both emigration and immigration, which are difficult to document. But Cupar in 1820 was not dominated by the same families as in 1700. There were more government officials such as officers of excise posted to the town. Some settled, and some left behind adult children when they moved on. There was also a number of army officers, West Indian planters and East India Company employees, who retired to Cupar, for reasons which are not always now apparent. According to the *Fife Herald* the newspapers subscribed to by the Cupar Coffee Room in 1825 included the *Asiatic Journal* and the *Oriental Herald*. There were some men in Cupar of definite or presumed Highland origin, mostly after 1760, some of whom were soldiers who had married locally and set up as innkeepers.[5] This suggestion is reinforced by the absence from the record of similar numbers of Highland women. Although it cannot satisfactorily be demonstrated statistically, a strong impression gained from the database is of a gradually widening pool of surnames.

The 1850s saw emigration to Australia. The *Fifeshire Journal* in April 1854 noted that 'The shutting of Blebo Mills, the slackness of trade in Dundee and elsewhere ... will stimulate many to emigrate to a land where labour is not in excess, and every one who is able to work is sure to find plenty to do.' And there was a continuing move to the cities, particularly Glasgow. But any population movements within east Fife were dwarfed by the changes in west Fife. Between 1851 and 1951, 80 per cent of the population increase in Fife was within five parishes – Kirkcaldy, Dunfermline, Wemyss (Buckhaven and Methil), Beath (Cowdenbeath and Kelty) and Auchterderran (Lochgelly). The density of population in Cupar and St Andrews districts in *c.*1950 was sixteen people per 100 acres, in Dunfermline fifty-two and Kirkcaldy sixty-eight. From its low point in 1921, the population of Cupar gradually rose again, though it was 1971 before it overtook the 1851 figure. In the 1841 census Cupar was the fourth-largest town in Fife, after Dunfermline, Kirkcaldy and Dysart. Twenty years later it was overtaken by St Andrews; then in 1891 by Buckhaven and Burntisland, and in 1901 by Cowdenbeath, Leven and Lochgelly. While the population of East Fife between 1755 and 1951 increased by 50 per cent, that of west Fife increased by over 500 per cent. As shown in Fig.1.4, the decline in its industrial base in the later twentieth century has led to a slight decrease in Kirkcaldy's population, while Dunfermline has continued to grow.

As a royal burgh, a county town, and an inland market centre in an area of relatively good agricultural land, Cupar is a good example of a small Scottish town. A large proportion of the population of Scotland once lived in such surroundings, yet little is known about these towns and their residents. Cupar was an important medieval town, but in the early modern period failed to flourish in comparison with those royal burghs which were also ports, of which there were several in Fife. The town then experienced growth and prosperity in the eighteenth and early nineteenth centuries. New industries and financial services helped maintain the town's position in the short term, and brought unprecedented growth and prosperity, but were not sustained after the first quarter of the nineteenth century. Cupar subsequently failed to develop any major industry, and as a cultural and tourist centre was gradually eclipsed by St Andrews.

Notes

1. Pers. comm. Dr Simon Taylor. Pictish place-names date from before *c*.900 (e.g. Perth and Aberdeen), Gaelic names from *c*.950 to *c*.1150, after which Scots became the dominant language.

2. Sixteenth century: Anstruther Easter, Anstruther Wester, Auchtermuchty, Burntisland, Dysart, Earlsferry, Kilrenny and Pittenweem (and Culross but it was in Perthshire at this date). Seventeenth century: Kirkcaldy (burgh of barony of Dunfermline abbey since 1315/28), Newburgh and St Andrews (ecclesiastical burgh since 1124/44).

3. The new parishes were Abbotshall (from Kirkcaldy), Anstruther Easter (from Kilrenny), Cameron (from St Andrews), Elie (from Kilconquhar), Ferryport-on-Craig (from Leuchars), Kingsbarns (from Crail) and Pittenweem (from Anstruther Wester). At the same period Tarvit was joined with Cupar.

4. While some of the figures for 1755 seem unexpectedly high or low compared with those in the *Old Statistical Account*, only in the case of Strathmiglo did the minister question them. The minister of Abdie cited three reasons for a decrease in rural population; 'the enlargement of farms', a reduction in the numbers of 'cottagers' and 'the non-residence of the principal heritor'. Between 1755 and 1801 the population of Scotland increased by 27 per cent, that of east Fife by only 10 per cent, but that of Cupar itself by over 100 per cent. The seven largest towns in Scotland grew by over 200 per cent, some smaller ones like Cupar, Arbroath and Forfar doubled in size, while other similar-sized towns grew far less and a few even shrank.

5. Most were identifiable by surnames beginning with 'Mac', but there were others, such as Robert Munro, innkeeper, who was described by a witness as the 'long legg'd Highlandman' (NAS CS230 M3/4).

2

Medieval Cupar

Gaelic Scotland absorbed influences from its neighbours, gradually changing and adopting new ideas. England after 1066 was ruled by Norman kings who introduced European culture, and enhanced their control over their subjects by land grants to their friends and supporters This led to an administrative system with the king at the top and peasants at the bottom, each level holding land from the level above in exchange for military service when required, or payment, usually in kind (labour, or the produce of the land), depending on the landholder's social status. The kings of Scotland encouraged incomers, who not only brought with them new ideas, which gradually spread by example among the older Gaelic aristocracy, but also wanted the lifestyle they had been used to elsewhere; the demand they created stimulated the economy to produce goods which could be exchanged for imports such as wine.

The earls of Fife were Gaelic provincial aristocracy who seem to have managed to keep a balance between their traditions and the new Norman ways, becoming feudal lords under the Crown. The Crown also encouraged the Church to reform itself, and encouraged monastic organisations to set up. With their international connections, the monastic houses were a source of new ideas, as well as centres of scholarship. The machinery of government was steadily becoming more organised, centralised and systematised. The king, at the top of the pyramid, needed money from taxation, and from fines in law courts, and the machinery of government evolved accordingly. A more efficient justice system meant more income from fines and forfeitures. The country was divided into sheriffdoms, each usually centred on a royal castle. In Fife, however, from 1213, if not earlier, Cupar Castle was the seat of a sheriff, despite belonging not to the king but to the Earl of Fife.

The sheriff was responsible for defence, and for the administration of justice, though he had no jurisdiction over murder, rape, robbery and fire-raising, which were tried in the Crown Court. Justice ayres (circuit courts) were held at many places around the country, including Cupar, to reinforce the rule of law with the monarch at its head. At first, courts were held on a traditional outdoor site such as a 'moot hill'. Cupar has a Mote Hill, on the eastern extension of which stood the castle. Cupar sheriff court may well have been held out of doors on the Mote Hill until the sixteenth century, although a burgh tolbooth was in existence by the second quarter of the fifteenth century. Courts were later divided into 'head courts', held three times a year (after Easter, Michaelmas and Christmas) at the seat of the sheriff, which handled the more important cases, and lesser courts, held in various places throughout the sheriffdom, such as Falkland. By the sixteenth century courts were held in the burgh tolbooth, which also housed prisoners. By this time more and more work was devolved to sheriffs-depute.

Another device used by the Norman-influenced Scottish kings to organise the country and its economy was the creation of royal burghs. The first – Aberdeen, Berwick, Edinburgh, Perth, Roxburgh and Stirling – were created by David I in the early twelfth century. But what he was doing was almost certainly conferring formal status on already functioning communities. Numbers of burghs increased after 1130, encouraging the growth of both domestic and international trade. Early royal burghs in Fife were Crail (1150), Inverkeithing (1153) and Kinghorn (1165). Royal burghs had a monopoly of foreign trade, and were self-governing, and in exchange for these privileges paid taxes to the crown. The burghs soon developed a joint assembly or convention which sorted out the proportion of tax each burgh could afford to pay. Defence was the responsibility of all burgh residents. The Bow Butts, just to the north-east of Cupar Castle, was where regular archery practice was carried out, and Leighton in 1840 noted that 'until recently ... the small knolls upon which the marks to be shot at had been placed, were quite visible'.

Royal authority was exercised by frequent trips around the country, both for pleasure, such as hunting trips, and for the administration of justice. Cupar was often visited, as it lay on the road to the religious centre at St Andrews (and later between there and the royal palace at Falkland). Alexander III, for example, sent a letter to Edward I from Cupar in July 1277, and John Balliol also wrote to the English king from Cupar in 1293. Robert I held an assembly at Cupar in 1316. The town of Cupar seems to have just grown up naturally around the castle. It belonged to the earls of Fife rather than to the king. No founding charter survives, but among a list of properties of the Earl of Fife in 1294 is the 'burgh' of Cupar, yielding income from old mills, a new mill, a fulling mill, the earls' demesne court and the town itself.[1] Cupar appears in the list of burghs paying customs on taxable exports in 1328, for shipments the previous year. In order to handle exports it must have been a royal burgh, so it must have received its charter some time between 1294 and 1326. The burgh had a coquet (customs seal) by 1344, but the first surviving charter dates from 1381 (Robert II). The town was represented on the General Council from 1357 (the year the council needed the support of the burgh merchants of Scotland to help pay the ransom for David II). Cupar's seal came into use the same year, and the burgh was represented in parliament from 1456.

Within burghs, inhabitants were divided into burgesses ('freemen'), who paid a local tax in exchange for trading privileges, and others ('unfree'). Burgess entry, after suitable training and experience, was by payment, but much cheaper for the sons of burgesses, or those who married burgesses' daughters. Burgesses slowly came to be divided between members of the merchant guild, who tended to dominate burgh councils, and members of the trades (also known as crafts). The town was granted a 'liberty', an area within which everyone was supposed to bring their goods to sell at Cupar's markets and fairs. The boundary of Cupar's liberty, as described in a confirmation charter granted by James I in 1428, ran from where the Kemback Water (Ceres Burn) runs into the Eden, south to Callange and Dunicher (Dunikier) Law and to the water of Largo and on to the Water of Leven, and up the river to the standing stone at Miln of Forth (Milnathort), north to the church of Arngask and Cross Macduff, and descending the River Tay to the mouth of the Eden and up the Eden to Cupar, except for any lands belonging to the church of St Andrews and the monastery of Dunfermline (Fig. 2.1). Between 1363 and 1370 the merchant guild

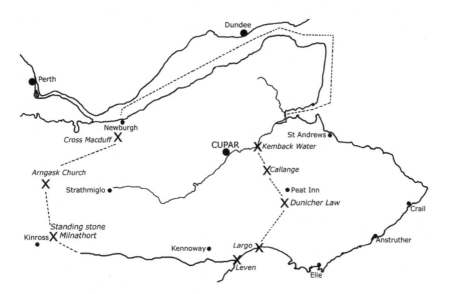

FIGURE 2.1 Schematic diagram of the boundaries of the medieval liberty of Cupar

was challenged by the bishop and burgesses of St Andrews over trading rights. The dispute was settled in favour of St Andrews, decreeing that its merchants could trade freely in Cupar's liberty in goods such as hides, wool and skins. In 1401 Robert III granted Dundee merchants the right to trade through Cupar market free of customs, and vice versa. Practical reality generally won over theoretically exclusive rights.

A document of 1363 concerning the relationship between the merchants of St Andrews and Cupar mentions the 'port of Eden' and the export of wool and sheepskins. St Andrews had its own harbour at the mouth of the Kinness Burn, but was also using the Eden estuary. Robert II in 1381 gave Cupar a charter granting a free port at the mouth of the Motray Burn (which lay within the Eden estuary, about six miles from Cupar). This was confirmed by James I in 1428, including: 'the tron, with the port of Motray and free ish [issue] and entry to the said port usual, and with full liberty within the said port and water of Eden, as the sea ebbs and flows, of livering and lading their ships with their merchandize without any impediment or obstacle whatsoever'.[2] The Motray burn runs into the north side of the Eden estuary, east of the Guard Bridge (the paper mill now stands on its west bank). In 1813, annoyed that the owner, William Haig, was setting up a distillery on the site (as opposed to grazing a few animals on the salt marsh), the town council investigated its rights and the possibility of reasserting them. Legal advice was that the rights had been abandoned so long ago that this was impossible. Although Cupar was said to have 'erected a Tron Pier or some kind of security for vessels landing in the Port of Motrie', no trace of any harbour works could be found. There was doubt as to what structures would have been necessary, given the sheltered nature of the estuary, but there were said to be old men still alive 'that remember of large stones being on the Beach with Iron rings in them for fixing vessells to'. Although some later writers claimed that there were traces of medieval quays surviving, these actually belonged to Haig's distillery.

The town had had rights to the foreshore from the mouth of the Motray burn up the north bank of the Eden 'as far as the sea ebbs and flows', but in practical terms this meant only as far as the Guard Bridge. The area was served by the 'King's Highway', but in 1396 access was improved by the purchase from the laird of Seggie of a road to the south of his house 'of a reasonable breadth by which Carts or waggons may pass'.[3] From this simple port Cupar merchants traded with countries bordering the North Sea and into the Baltic.[4] The town started paying customs in 1328, on wool and sheepskins, implying that by then the burgh economy was flourishing. Its first payment was about a quarter of the customs paid by Perth, and trade does not seem to have expanded very fast. By 1361 its contribution to burgh taxation was about the same as Peebles and Dumbarton, and more than Crail, Inverkeithing and Forfar. The goods being exported will have come from throughout Cupar's liberty, as only royal burghs could handle imports and exports. We do not know what goods not subject to customs may have been exported. Nor do we know what was imported, but it is likely to have included wheat, wine, spices, dried fruits and luxury manufactured goods. But it is possible that imports came via larger ports with better quayside and storage facilities.

Sometimes the *Exchequer Rolls* mention the number of ships the customs receipts relate to. From 1381 to 1405 there was an average of about three ships a year at 'port of Cupar' or 'port of Eden', and customs payments fluctuated considerably from year to year (partly because the date of collection varied), but averaged about £150 Scots. The taxable exports were wool, sheepskins and hides. Between 1406 and 1434 these were carried on an average of two ships (seagoing) and one boat (coastal) per year. But the records vary, and at times the customs were farmed out so no details are given. The last mention of a ship in the Exchequer Rolls is in 1481/82. In the fourteenth and fifteenth centuries Cupar exported more wool than any other town in Fife, rising from 0.6 per cent of national exports in *c.*1330 to 1 per cent in *c.*1430, but by 1500 it was overtaken by Kirkcaldy and its satellites.[5] From the 1450s there are references to using the port of Dundee as well as the Eden, and to the export of finished woollen cloth (there are references to a fulling mill in Cupar from 1294). The quantity of cloth exported fluctuated, but increased from two dozen lengths in 1460/61 to 148 dozen in 1492/93. Using a larger port would have offered a greater choice of merchants, ships and sailing times, and the timing of this development may demonstrate the growing importance of Dundee as a regional mercantile centre. How the goods were transported to Dundee is not clear, but probably either by boat from the Eden or by pack-pony and a ferry from the north coast of Fife.

We do not know how many of the ships which came into the port of Motray were Cupar-owned, but we do know that some Cupar merchants did own ships. In the early fifteenth century, for example, goods belonging to the king were transported from Flanders in a Cupar-owned ship, and in 1456 Cupar merchants were sending money home from Bruges. But the 'port of Motray' was never satisfactory, being only accessible for small ships at high tide, and six miles from the town. Its use also upset St Andrews, who had rights to the whole Eden estuary. So Cupar merchants increasingly shared ships and cargoes based in other ports. In 1582, for example, a Cupar merchant was on board the *James* of Pittenweem when she was captured by English pirates on her way back from Bordeaux.

From the beginning of the sixteenth century details are lacking, but trade seems to have declined. By 1523 an annuity to the Dominican Friary in Cupar, normally paid out of the customs receipts, had to be transferred to another source of income, because 'now through war and trouble within our realm the course of merchandise ceases within our said burgh of Cupar'. Occasionally other commodities were exported: in 1524/25 bitumen, in the 1550s rabbit-skins and a few barrels of salmon, in the 1570s oil and tar, in the 1590s oil and herring. By the mid sixteenth century the woollen cloth was of two types, broad and narrow, but by the end of the century the volume of cloth being exported fell away to almost nothing.

As well as producing these goods for export, the town would have been the base for merchants dealing in a wide range of goods, and specialist craftsmen, particularly those for whom it was advantageous to live within a royal burgh because they needed imported raw materials. Others processed agricultural produce. As well as baxters and fleshers, there were those who processed animal skins. Wool was spun and woven for home consumption as well as export, and linen as well. The hides for export were usually dried and salted, but they were tanned for the production of a wide range of leather goods for local consumption. Animal horns and bones provided objects such as spoons, buttons, combs and knife-handles. Craftsmen within the town would have included metalworkers – goldsmiths and silversmiths, pewterers, tinsmiths and blacksmiths, and lead workers for windows and roofs. In 1538, for example, the king bought two gold rings from a Cupar goldsmith. Grain was processed not only for bread but also for brewing and malting. Wood was used to make everything from houses and carts to spoons, buttons and baskets. Making a living was often a public, smelly and noisy activity.

The castle

We know there was a castle at Cupar, the seat of power and base for the king's representative, the sheriff, the Earl of Fife, although no trace of it survives. The Castlehill may be entirely natural, the south-eastern extremity of the glacial ridge known as the Mote Hill. But it is possible that it is at least partly artificial. We know nothing of the nature and extent of buildings on the hill, and whether the original wooden ones were ever replaced with stone structures. Scotland's economy was doing well in the mid thirteenth century, however, and many monasteries and castles were built or improved then. As the Castlehill is the end of a ridge, there was no lack of space for buildings. The best evidence for there being structures of some size and quality is that in February 1275 Queen Margaret, wife of Alexander III and daughter of Henry III of England, died at Cupar Castle. Alexander was back the following year, holding court. There are also references in the Laing charters to late thirteenth-century repairs to 'the houses of the castle' by the Earl of Fife.

Because of its castle Cupar played a small part in the Wars of Independence. Edward I of England claimed wardship of the lands of Duncan, Earl of Fife, who was a minor. Early in 1294 he appointed Walter de Camehou (Cambo) as keeper of Cupar Castle. In 1296, after John Balliol refused him homage, Edward attacked Scotland, and during his campaign captured the castle at Cupar. The Prince of Wales (the future Edward II) was there in 1303, and there was still an English garrison in 1306, but it was recaptured for the Scots by Bishop Wishart of Glasgow in 1307. Retaken by the English soon afterwards, it was seized by the supporters of Robert Bruce in 1308. At this point the defences may have been slighted to make the castle indefensible.

Edward I (the 'Hammer of the Scots') had died in 1307, but English aggression continued under his much weaker son, Edward II. His defeat at Bannockburn in 1314 allowed Robert Bruce to exploit Edward's weakness and in 1328 Robert finally obtained recognition as an independent monarch. But the following year Bruce died, and was succeeded by his son, David II, aged five. Edward III renewed his attempt to control Scotland through a rival claimant to the throne, Edward Balliol, who invaded Scotland, defeated the pro-Bruce Scots and was crowned in 1332, after which the young David was sent abroad for safety. Driven from Scotland by David's supporters, Edward Balliol returned in 1333 with Edward III and an English army and routed the Scots at Halidon Hill outside Berwick. Scottish resistance effectively collapsed and Balliol and his English allies set up a network of garrisons to establish their control, including Cupar, Leuchars and St Andrews. In autumn 1333 Balliol's chamberlain, William Bullock, was appointed keeper of St Andrews, Cupar and 'various other fortresses'. Between September 1334 and May 1338 Edward III paid for an engineer, a mason and a smith at Cupar Castle. There are records of supplies of food and wine being sent from Berwick in February 1336, and in June and August 1338. Oak and pine planks, iron and lead, salt and sea coal were sent from Hull and Newcastle in August 1338 and January 1339.

Duncan, Earl of Fife, seems to have gone over to Balliol's side after the battle of Dupplin in 1332, but to have changed sides again by 1336, taking part in attacks on Cupar Castle. In 1336 Andrew Murray laid siege to the castle of Cupar, and the 'many Anglicised Scots' inside it, but then agreed a truce. The following year he managed to take back all the eastern castles except Perth and Cupar, 'which had been defended by the strong courage of Sir William Bullock'. During the winter of 1337/38 the garrison numbered about sixty, plus their horses. After Murray's death his successor, Robert Stewart, went on the offensive in the spring of 1339. Bullock surrendered Cupar Castle, in a deal rewarding him for changing sides and supporting the Bruce cause. After that date nothing more is heard of the castle, and it is said that David II ordered its demolition. The earls of Fife seem to have had their main residence from the mid thirteenth century at Falkland, and had no need to rebuild Cupar. So, as in other Scottish towns, the castle hill remained as public open space. It was probably the 'Playfield' on which Sir David Lindsay's *Ane Satire of the Three Estatis* was performed in 1535.

Churches

The earliest known church in the parish stood to the north of the town (NO 3670 1525). Its foundation date is unknown. Between 1154 and 1178 (probably after 1163) the patronage of the church was granted by Duncan, Earl of Fife, to the priory church of St Andrews. In 1240 the church itself was granted to the priory by David de Bernham, Bishop of St Andrews, and it was subsequently served by a perpetual vicar. After a new church was built in 1415, the old building became a chaplainry, with four acres of land, called Maryfauld, which seems to have included the old cemetery. This had gone out of use by the mid sixteenth century and eventually came to be used as a small glebe for the first minister. The nearby clinkmill may also have been established by the priory of St Andrews. The site of the old church has long been known, because farmers have ploughed up bones and worked stones, a few of which can be seen built into later walls. Field-walking in 1995 and excavation in 1997 uncovered remains of an apsidal building, and burials, but also hints of earlier burials under the building, suggesting an earlier church somewhere nearby. The dedication seems most likely to have been to Our Lady.[6]

In 1415 a new church was built within the town. This was probably because it seemed a more sensible location in the growing town, but also implies wealth and people willing to give up burgess plots in order to create the large space necessary. Although the site is not in either of the main streets, it is in the highest part of the burgh, and the church tower still dominates the town. The parish church of St Andrews was moved in 1412 from the cathedral to the town centre, and there may have been a desire to emulate this. One source says it was 'for the dignity of said burgh (which is notable)'.[7] It may also fit in with general rebuilding after 'the town of Cupar was accidentally burned' in 1410.[8] The new church, 'planned on an ambitious scale and where cost was apparently not a limiting factor', was consecrated by Bishop Wardlaw of St Andrews, and dedicated to St Christopher.[9] It certainly had a Lady chapel, and also altars dedicated to St Andrew, St Columba and St James.[10] As well as St Mary, saint's names attached to places or properties in Cupar include St Michael (the old church bell), St James (the graveyard extension, originally St James' Yards, and the Episcopal church), and St Catherine of Sienna (the Friary and its land).

FIGURE 2.2 Detail from the 1642 town plan, showing the medieval church.

The 1642 town plan includes the only surviving picture of the church (Fig. 2.2). It consisted of a nave with a clerestory, with aisles either side. The minister in 1793 described it as 'in the best stile of the times, of polished freestone, in length 133 feet, by 54 in breadth. The roof, supported on two rows of arches, was of circular 'oak couples ... lined with wood, and painted in the taste of the times'. The tower and part of the nave arcade survive (Plate 1a, 1c, Fig. 2.3). Also surviving, though relocated, is the mid fifteenth-century effigy of a knight, in an arched recess, with the arms of the Fernies of Fernie (Plate 1b, Fig. 2.4). The oldest bell, 'Big Michael', was cast in 1485, enlarged in 1610 by the minister, William Scott, and re-founded in 1747. The graveyard once extended further out into Kirkgate. Its level has also been built up considerably, as can be seen by the blocked arch in its south wall.

Cupar had a Dominican Friary (Blackfriars) at the foot of the Castlehill, founded in 1348 at the instigation of Duncan, Earl of Fife, and dedicated to St Catherine. It was barely functioning by 1517, and closed in 1519, the two remaining friars being transferred to St Andrews. This almost certainly was a direct result of serious economic recession. After the Reformation, in 1572, James VI revoked all alienations of property by the Dominicans since the Reformation and granted their

South Elevation

Tower   *Part of North Aisle*

Ground Plan

FIGURE 2.3   Surviving medieval fabric of Cupar parish church. Source: Walker, *Pre-Reformation Churches in Fifeshire*.

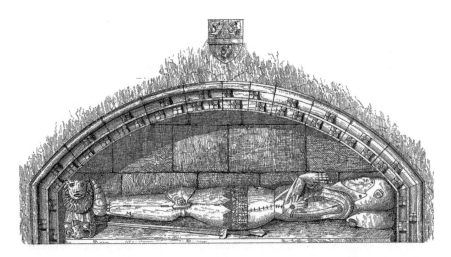

FIGURE 2.4   Fernie wall-monument rebuilt into the west wall of the 1785 parish church. Source: Walker, *Pre-Reformation Churches in Fifeshire*.

possessions in Cupar, including St Catherine's Haugh, to the burgh as a charitable foundation. By 1579, however, the buildings were in the hands of the laird of Balgarvie, and the chapel was extended to form a mansion-house, whose footprint can be seen in Ainslie's plan of 1775 (Plate 5). A watercolour survives showing the fragmentary remains of the monastery within the kitchen garden of Balgarvie House in 1798, and there are accounts of burials being accidentally uncovered.[11] The present episcopal church is probably on or close to the site of the friary chapel.

The medieval town

The earliest meeting place and probable court site is the Mote Hill. It is not known when either a mercat cross or a tolbooth was first erected. The first reference to a tolbooth is in the Laing charters in 1434, and the earliest of many documentary references to it having a forestair is in 1516. There was a school in Cupar by 1357, when Nicholas, the rector, gave surety that the town would pay part of the ransom for David II, but nothing else is known about it. There are no surviving medieval houses. We know that there were four tenements belonging to the Knights Templar, two in Crossgate (76–78, marked on the 1855 OS map, Map 5), one in Bonnygate and one in Kirkgate. There was also a Templehill just outside Cupar. But these were lands yielding rent to the Knights Templar and their successors, not properties which they occupied.

The medieval street-plan can be seen in the town-plan of 1642 (Plate 2a). Each entrance to the town was guarded by a gate, and the gates linked by high garden walls. These were not proof against attack, but provided protection from animals and undesirable people, and served to channel all traffic through the gates, where customs were charged on goods coming in to market. The bridge is shown with a gate at both ends. The outer one may suggest that a toll was charged to cross the bridge. At the heart of the town was the market-place – here a typical triangular one, created by widening the northern end of Crossgate. In or near the market-place would have stood the tolbooth and the tron (public weigh-beam). Each 'rig' or burgess plot was probably between 18 and 25ft (5.6–7.6m) wide, and ran a fair way back. The land behind was for the disposal of rubbish, gardens or workshops, and keeping animals. Most families would have kept a cow for milk, and poultry for meat and eggs. Some kept a pig, and some kept the horse they needed to transport themselves or their goods.

Ordinary houses were probably mostly built of timber-framing infilled with wattle and daub, or of clay (mud-brick). Larger houses may have had a stone vaulted ground floor. A few of the grandest houses may have had clay roof tiles, but the majority of houses would have been thatched, with whatever material was most readily available, including reeds, straw and heather. Thatched roofs would have overhung considerably to protect wood or clay walls from the rain. There would have been little furniture, mainly chests of various sizes which served as storage, but also as tables and seats. Beds were often just bags or loose heaps of dried vegetation on the floor. Food would have been stored in ceramic, wooden, leather or cloth containers, cooked in metal or ceramic pots, and eaten off wooden plates, using knives, spoons of wood or horn, but mainly fingers. Pottery became increasingly important for cooking and storage vessels, although many domestic items continued to be made of wood, either turned on a lathe or assembled from staves. Drinking vessels were generally of horn, wood, pottery or pewter.

A common find on medieval archaeological sites is combs, the size of the teeth suggesting that they were not just for tidying hair, but for removing lice. Sanitary arrangements were primitive, and open sewers ran along urban streets. Much of our understanding of medieval town life comes from the excavation of cess-pits and middens in the backlands. Life expectancy was short. The Black Death came to Scotland in 1349, and there were three more outbreaks of plague in the following fifty-two years. Further epidemics occurred in the 1430s, 1450, 1475, 1499–1500, 1514, 1530 and 1539, though each one was less devastating, as people developed immunity. But even the fear of plague disrupted trade. During the fourteenth century the merchants became more powerful, perhaps because, as the most wealthy non-landowning citizens, they bore much of the burden of the ransom for David II. It is after this that they gradually came to dominate town councils, diminishing the influence of tradesmen. An Act of 1496 established the presence of trades deacons on councils, but they remained generally a minority with little effective power compared with the merchants. The tradesmen also became more organised, and more separate from the merchants, making efforts to establish their place in burgh society. 'During the summer of 1554 the craftsmen of Cupar ... staged a violent demonstration in which they threatened the bailies, disregarded an order of the burgh court and formulated a bond amongst themselves to defend their common interests.'[12]

Cupar was an administrative and trading centre, and also a place people travelled through. To the south-west was the shrine to St Margaret at Dunfermline, while St Andrews to the east was a national centre of pilgrimage and after 1472 the seat of Scotland's senior archbishop. Royal visits continued. And the burden of garrisoning troops, to be a long-running source of unhappiness, became an issue,

FIGURE 2.5   Cupar burgh arms. Source: Porteous, *Town Council Seals of Scotland*.

as for example in 1549 when the inhabitants of Cupar and Leuchars were expected to provide lodgings and food for the French troops who had been brought in to counter the English invasion of Scotland in 1547/48. Royal authority had to be exerted by the use of troops, and by demonstrating the effects of justice. In 1551 and 1554, for example, the heads of murderers were sent to Cupar to be displayed.

By 1560 the senior members of the clergy and monastic orders had become corrupt and lazy, while parish clergy were underpaid and therefore of low calibre. Landowners resented paying taxes to the Church, and there was general resentment against the French, Roman Catholic influence of Mary of Guise. With the support of England, French influence was reduced and the Protestant church established. One of the actions which led up to this was in June 1559 when the troops of the regent, Mary of Guise, on the Garlie Bank (the northern side of Tarvit Hill), faced the Lords of the Congregation on Cupar Muir. Battle was averted and a truce signed. Tradition has it that Cupar's burgh crest of three myrtle wreaths dates from this event (Fig. 2.5).[13]

Notes

1. *Documents Illustrative of the History of Scotland*, i, 415–56, 16 Feb 1294/95, 'Extent of the Lands of the Earldom of Fife, delivered to Walter de Cambo by Richard de Daringtone'.
2. Other towns with outports included Dunbar (Belhaven, 1 mile) Edinburgh (Leith, 1½ m), Elgin (Lossiemouth, 5½ m), Forres (Findhorn, 5 m), Haddington (Aberlady, 5¼ m), Inverbervie (Gourdon, 1¼ m), and Linlithgow (Blackness, 3¾ m).
3. The road was still in use in 1498, when the town successfully prosecuted the laird of Seggie for 'impeding the landing and transport of merchandies'. It is shown on Ainslie's 1775 map of Fife but by 1855 it had reverted to private access.
4. Ditchburn, 'Trade with Northern Europe', 163, Cupar merchants were trading with Danzig (Gdansk) in 1444; 174, Cupar protested about German piracy in 1445.
5. It is not clear how long the harbour remained in use but in 1519 St Andrews was challenging Cupar's rights, poinding cargoes destined for Cupar as payment for anchorage dues, which may mean Cupar ships were using the Eden rather than the Motray Burn.
6. Most people have assumed a dedication to Our Lady because of nearby place-names including Lady Burn and Ladyinch. The suggestion that it might have been Holy Trinity seems to have been based on a misreading of an old seal, and the suggestion of St Christopher (Hall & King, 'Field Survey at the site of St Christopher's Church') is unlikely, given the date and the lack of associated place-names.
7. *Calendar of Scottish Supplications*, 27. There is no evidence that the old church was ruinous, though in 1418 that of the neighbouring parish of St Michael of

Tarvit was. Medieval churches generally stood on rural sites, but were either relocated, as at Cupar, or the burgh expanded to include them, as at Dundee and Crail.

8. There are other references in 1411, 1412 (destruction of the tron) and 1418 (renewal of weights destroyed in a fire), but it is not clear whether these were separate fires, or continuing consequences of the 1410 one.

9. St Christopher is the patron saint of travellers, and specifically associated with river crossings, so he is very appropriate to Cupar.

10. Holy Trinity in St Andrews (1412) is said to have had more than thirty altars, founded in three phases, the 1430s, the 1460s and 1490–1510. The Cupar references to St Mary and St Colm are from 1505, and St Andrew 1510 (*RMS*), so it is likely there were earlier dedications, perhaps to the patron saints of some of the trades.

11. NLS Adv MS 29.4.2, f.212r, 'Remains of the monastery of Cupar in Fife sketched by Lt. Pryor[?], 25 Decm 1798'.

12. Verschuur, 'Merchants and Craftsmen in Sixteenth-Century Perth', 44.

13. Porteous, *Town Council Seals of Scotland*, 'the myrtle garlands on the Seal appear to commemorate the bloodless or moral victory gained by the Lords of the Congregation over the Queen Regent, Mary of Guise, in 1559 ... The Romans crowned themselves with myrtle after a victory, but only when blood had not been shed'.

3

Cupar in the Early-Modern Period

The years between 1560 and 1700 were unsettled, with politics and religion inextricably entwined. In the Protestant Reformation of 1560 the Scottish parliament legislated to replace Catholicism with an independent Scottish Protestant church. The most obvious impact of the Reformation was on the organisation of the church and the nature of services. The basic unit remained the parish, but the old hierarchy of the medieval system of bishoprics, archdeaconries and deaneries was swept away, along with Roman Catholic worship centred on the Mass. Another key change was the greater role played in the management of the parishes by the laity, with influential local lairds and burgesses serving as 'Elders' to oversee the smooth running of the parish and aid the minister to impose moral and religious discipline. Such dramatic changes took time to become firmly established. Fife, which had been an early and active centre of Protestant dissent, suffered less disruption than elsewhere in Scotland, but there were still problems.

However, James VI reintroduced episcopacy, and Charles I, who had been brought up in England and was more familiar with the Anglican church, tried to move further back towards Catholicism, reintroducing bishops and Anglican-style services. The situation was made more complicated by the union of the crowns, and Charles tried to rule two countries with different forms of Protestant worship and church organisation. Hostility in Scotland to his changes led to the drawing up in 1638 of the National Covenant, a document which denounced Charles's religious policies and called for a return to the simpler style of church government of the sixteenth century. Many of the leaders behind the Covenant were clergy and landowners from Fife.

The catalyst which drove these men into drawing up the National Covenant was the king's plan to introduce a new prayer book. A few burghs, including Cupar, had protested about this and presented individual petitions to the Privy Council objecting to the imposition of the new prayer book. The town signed the National Covenant soon afterwards. This began a process which led to the fall of episcopacy, civil war, the execution of Charles I, and the creation of a Commonwealth led by Oliver Cromwell. In theory this involved parliamentary union with England, but in effect it was a virtual dictatorship with Scotland occupied by English forces.

Despite having promised not to interfere with the church in the way his father had done, Charles II restored episcopacy when he regained his throne, and clergymen who did not conform were forced out of their livings. John Makgill, first minister of Cupar since 1654, refused to accept episcopacy, and left the church, as did the second minister, Thomas Arnot. Makgill retrained as a doctor. Some ejected ministers (including Arnot) defied the government and continued to hold services, often out of doors, known as 'conventicles'. In 1674 the former ministers John Christieson and James Wedderburne were prosecuted for holding conventicles in Cupar, and in 1676 the magistrates were forced to take further action, and troops were quartered in the town. In 1677 some of those imprisoned for holding conventicles escaped from the tolbooth. Two of the bailies were accused of negligence and fined £50 Scots, but they claimed the tolbooth was properly locked and guarded, and the prisoners 'did dig and break through the wall ... in the night time'. Despite the risk of imprisonment and death, James Wedderburne continued to hold conventicles.

'1679 saw a virtual military occupation of Fife, which had become one of the chief centres of conventicle activity.'[1] Many of these troops were billeted in Cupar. James Sharp, appointed Archbishop of St Andrews in 1661, was one of the key figures in Charles II's efforts to impose episcopacy on Scotland. In 1679 he was murdered at Magus Muir (south of Strathkinness). He was dragged from his coach and shot by a group of men led by David Hackston of Rathillet. To demonstrate central authority after the murder a circuit court was held in Cupar. The incident also provoked a military response, and the Convenanters were defeated at Bothwell Bridge. The Government, however, then became more tolerant, isolating the more extreme ministers. In 1680 Hackston was tried and condemned to death for the murder of Sharp. His head was fixed on the Netherbow Port of Edinburgh, and parts of his body sent to various places including Cupar. A monument in Cupar churchyard marks the spot where one of his hands is buried, along with the heads of Laurence Hay and Andrew Pittiloch, Covenanters condemned to death in Edinburgh the following year (Plate 2c).

Charles II died in 1685, and was succeeded by his brother, James VII and II, a Roman Catholic. The cruel treatment of men such as Hackston further reduced support for the King and central government. In 1689 the parish minister, Alexander Lundie, was ejected for refusing to renounce episcopacy. He and his congregation met in premises in the Bonnygate. After three years the King was forced into exile. His daughter, Mary, and her husband William of Orange, accepted the separate offers of the English and Scottish crowns in 1689. The

'Revolution settlement' abolished episcopacy, and established a system whereby taxation could not be imposed without the consent of parliament. William was unpopular in Scotland, and there were various plots to restore the Stuarts to the throne. But the Presbyterian church became firmly established.

It was not just the church which was in turmoil over this period; there was also political instability. In 1583, for example, the fencibles (soldiers only liable for service within Scotland) were called to readiness to guard the king if he came to Fife 'in respect of the unquiet practizes and bisiy travellis of sum of his unnaturall and disorderit subjetis'.[2] Further upheaval came in 1603 with the union of the crowns, which meant that ambitious aristocrats had to spend some time at court in London, and therefore less time at home, reducing their influence on local affairs. But the other side of the coin was that Scotland became further from the centre not just of politics but of cultural trends.

To cap all these more national problems which affected Cupar, the seventeenth century saw the burgh's economy in decline. As ships became larger its port declined and fell out of use. St Andrews, too, had become less active in overseas trade, in contrast with the booming East Neuk ports. All along the southern coast of Fife coal and salt works were being developed, while inland towns were struggling to compete. Cupar had no special natural resources to be exploited, and was nine miles from the coast, but survived better than some other inland towns because of its role as a legal and travel centre. Agriculture had changed little since the medieval period, and Cupar remained an important market centre for the interchange of agricultural produce and manufactured goods. Documentary evidence survives of merchants travelling from places such as Perth to attend the weekly market in Cupar, and presumably coming from further afield to fairs.[3] But there was no dramatic increase in the volume of trade. Wars in the middle of the century imposed a heavy burden of taxation, but were probably less disruptive to agriculture than to maritime trade, which was further hindered by wars with Holland (1665–67 and 1672–74), and France, from 1689, and by impositions of tariffs on Scottish goods by England. On top of this came the last serious famine, the 'Seven Ill Years' of 1695–1700, which hit the small towns of eastern Scotland hard. The end of Scottish dreams of an overseas trading empire with the collapse of the Darien scheme in 1700 was the final blow, as many Scots had sunk huge amounts of capital into the venture, though Cupar does not seem to have been particularly badly affected.[4]

Trade was often disrupted by wars and political instability, exacerbated by crop failures and several epidemics of 'plague'. One unidentified epidemic, carried round the country from 1644 by the Covenanting army and its opponents, was the worst for over a century. In June 1647 the presbytery was very concerned 'anent the preventeing of the further spreading of the Plague'. Towns were more susceptible to epidemics than the countryside, as people lived closer together, with inadequate water supply and waste disposal. The 1640s epidemic is thought to have killed as much as a fifth of the population of Edinburgh, and its effects must have been complex and long-lasting. Religious instability led to excesses such as witchcraft trials. War brought extra taxation, plus the burden of quartering troops, and occasionally the depredations of armies as they passed through. Individuals and burghs became impoverished and their way of life disrupted.

Among all the political and religious upheavals, however, culture flourished, and science began to develop. Sir Robert Sibbald, son of the laird of Rankeilour, was educated at Cupar grammar school before going to university in Edinburgh and Leyden. With Archibald Pitcairne he founded the Royal College of Surgeons in Edinburgh, and with Sir Andrew Balfour of Denmylne, near Newburgh, established the botanic gardens in Edinburgh in 1667, as well as commissioning the first chart of Scotland's coasts from John Adair. In 1682 he was appointed Geographer Royal for Scotland, and in 1710 published the first *History of Fife*.

Another feature of the post-Reformation period was the establishment of a fresh wave of royal burghs, and a far greater number of burghs of barony. Each new burgh had a 'liberty' carved out of those belonging to the older burghs, which was greatly resented as it reduced potential income at markets and fairs. Rural markets and fairs proliferated after 1660, and in 1672 royal burghs, which were now seen as too restrictive, and hampering economic development, lost their monopoly of foreign trade. By this time, too, the focus of trade was beginning to shift from the North Sea to the Atlantic. Few burghs of barony were established in Fife in the seventeenth century, but that was because it was already a highly populous county, with a large number of existing burghs.[5] Many burghs had long been battling to retain their independence in the face of attempts at control by neighbouring landowners. Cupar had no powerful close neighbours, but as the county town it attracted attention from more distant landowners. From the sixteenth century the town had been controlled to varying extents by the earls of Rothes, whose estate was 15 miles away at Leslie.[6] The 6th earl had been a leading Covenanter. The 7th earl became rich and powerful after the Restoration of Charles II, and spent most of his time outside Fife.

Urbanisation

Like many European countries, late medieval Scotland had very few medium-sized towns (with populations of between 5,000 and 10,000).

TABLE 3.1   Towns paying 1 per cent or more on the tax roll of the royal burghs

	1535		1597		1612		1649		1670		1690		1705	
	%	rank	%	rank	%	rank	%	rank	%	rank	%	rank	%	rank
Aberdeen	9.5	3	8	3	8	3	6.66	3	7	3	6.5	3	4.9	3
Anstruther Easter					1.7	12=	0.8	–	0.2	–	0.2	–	0.1	–
Ayr	2.4	10	2.2	8	2.2	8	1.4	13=	1.7	11=	1.7	13	1.06	14
Brechin	1.7	12=	1.2	15=	1.2	16=	0.6	–	0.55	–	0.55	–	0.5	–
Burntisland					0.83	–	1.1	15=	1.15	14	0.8	–	0.3	–
Crail					0.8	–	1.1	15=	0.9	–	0.3	–	0.2	–
Cupar	2.7	7=	1.5	13=	1.5	15	1.1	15=	1	15=	1	17	0.75	16
Dumfries	1.2	15	1.7	10=	1.8	11	1.66	12	1.7	11=	1.9	8	1.9	6
Dunbar					0.51	–	1.1	15=	0.6	–	0.5	–	0.4	–
Dundee	9.7	2	10.75	2	10.75	2	7	2	6.1	4	5.3	4	4	4=
Dysart					2	9	1.4	13=	0.8	–	0.5	–	0.15	–
Edinburgh	25	1	28.75	1	28.8	1	36	1	33.3	1	33.3	1	35	1
Elgin	1	16=	1	18	1	18=	0.66	–	1	15=	1.35	10	1.4	9
Glasgow	2	11	4.5	5	4	5	6.5	4	12	2	15	2	20	2
Haddington	3	5	1.9	9	1.9	10	1.8	10=	1.8	8=	1.6	14	1.3	12
Inverness	1.7	12=	1.7	10=	1.7	12=	2.5	7	1.8	8=	1.8	9=	1.45	10
Irvine	1.4	14	1.2	15=	1.2	16=	1	19	0.9	–	0.5	–	0.55	–
Jedburgh	1	16=	1.1	17	1.1	17	0.9	–	0.9	–	0.9	–	0.95	15
Kirkcaldy	1.5		1.5	13=	1	18=	2.4	8	2.3	6=	2.6	6	1.51	8
Linlithgow					0.9	–	1.8	10=	1.7	11=	1.5	15	1.35	11
Montrose	2.7	7=	1.6	12	1.6	14	2	9	1.9	7	2.4	7	1.66	7
Perth	7.4	4	6.2	4	6.2	4	4	5	3.85	5	3.85	5	4	4=
St Andrews	3	6	2.8	6	2.7	6	3.33	6	2.3	6=	0.9	–	0.35	–
Stirling	2.5	9	2.3	7	2.3	7	1.1	15=	1.8	8=	1.8	9=	1.25	13

Source: CRB.

There were the four largest burghs, which were also regional centres –
Edinburgh, Glasgow, Aberdeen and Dundee – and then a large number of
towns such as Cupar with populations of under 2,000. The seventeenth
century saw this contrast increased, with growth concentrated in the
largest towns. With much prosperity related to overseas trade, most
inland towns in Scotland declined in relative importance. Some older
royal burghs were gradually being replaced or overtaken by new
burghs of barony, many of which, such as Dalkeith and Hamilton, were
satellites of the four major cities. Scotland experienced a remarkable
rate of urban expansion from the mid eighteenth century, and because
it started later, its speed of urbanisation was all the greater.

There are various sources from which tables comparing Scottish
towns can be produced, but the interrelationship between prosperity,
population and growth is difficult to understand, and it is therefore hard
to know what these bald figures can really tell us. In 1639, when burgh
rental figures can allow estimates of population, Cupar was the twenty-
first-largest royal burgh in Scotland, with a population of *c*.1,500, and
the fourth-largest in Fife, behind St Andrews (6,750), Kirkcaldy (3,000)
and Burntisland (2,250). The tax roll of the Convention of Royal Burghs
provides at various dates a ranking of all the royal burghs by wealth.
Table 3.1 compares Cupar with other towns, demonstrating that the
four main cities became more dominant, and several long-established
towns declined faster than Cupar. By 1705, while less important
nationally that it had once been, Cupar was by this measure the second-
richest town in Fife, after Kirkcaldy. Both Dunfermline and Kirkcaldy
increased in status during this period; Cupar declined gradually, while
St Andrews declined dramatically.

The Poll and Hearth Taxes of the 1690s have often been used
to measure the relative status of Scottish towns, although neither
survives for the whole of Scotland. No Poll Tax records survive for
Cupar, but there are Hearth Tax returns for 1694. Cupar parish had
672 taxable hearths, making it the 23rd-largest town in Scotland, and
the fourth-largest in Fife, after St Andrews (1,116), Kirkcaldy (1,008)
and Dysart (818). In the town there were 406 households, 67 per
cent of which had only one hearth. In Edinburgh the proportion per
parish varied between 35 per cent and 82 per cent, with an average
for greater Edinburgh of 59 per cent. The lower the percentage, the
wealthier the community. Cupar was similar to Dumfries (63 per cent)
and Linlithgow (70 per cent). The figure for households with three or
four hearths is 12 per cent, compared with 8 per cent in Dumfries,
11 per cent in Linlithgow, and between 9 per cent and 32 per cent in
Edinburgh. Houses with more than seven hearths were the preserve
of the gentry. The middle classes of Cupar, broadly speaking, as in
other towns, lived in houses with between two and four hearths.
Most tradesmen had only one hearth, while professionals were fairly

evenly spread between one and four. By far the largest identifiable middle-class occupations were those of merchant and maltman. But none of these figures can really tell us much about such towns, how they functioned, and why they prospered or failed to prosper. The reasons behind the pattern of urbanisation in seventeenth-century Scotland were complex, and detailed studies of individual towns are needed to help explain why the smaller Scottish burghs developed so differently.

In relative terms Cupar became less important within Scotland, but was helped by being on travel routes, and relatively accessible to major centres of population. The Convention of Royal Burghs occasionally met in Cupar. Indeed a Convention meeting in Cupar in July 1653 was forcibly broken up by Cromwell's army on the grounds that it had not asked for permission to meet. Charles II, before he went into exile, travelled in Scotland and in July 1650, like many monarchs before him, came to Cupar on his way between St Andrews and Falkland, and was dined by the magistrates. Inevitably local politics did not always run smoothly. Cupar failed to hold council elections in 1681, and the following year's election was overseen by the Earl of Balcarres 'to see that well-affected persons were chosen and that all is done orderly and peaceably'. One source of unhappiness was the cost of quartering troops. In 1690, for example, the magistrates and inhabitants petitioned the Privy Council, claiming that the last lot of troops had left debts of 752 merks for food and had shot dead a horse worth £4 Scots. They asked for the money to be deducted from the town's excise payments, and this was eventually agreed.

The burgh of Cupar

Before the eighteenth century there is no reliable means of gathering statistical information about the occupational structure of the town. Given the town's status, it is likely that there was a range of specialist craftsmen. From analogy with other towns, however, it is reasonable to assume that the guildry was dominated by merchants and maltmen. There was, however, still a blurring between what we would consider 'urban' and 'rural' activities in the burgh, with many inhabitants involved in agriculture as well as in crafts and trade. As in other small towns, many of the inhabitants would have kept chickens, a pig and often a single cow, for milk. The town paid a 'common herd' who each day, for a small fee, would walk through the streets to gather up all these cows and take them out across the Cow Bridge (Map 5) to graze beside the Eden, returning them at night. The streets would have been bustling with life. Much business was carried on out of doors. Markets and fairs were held in the street, and some tradesmen spilled out from their small workshops, even to the extent of saw-pits in the street.

The earliest depiction of Cupar was published in 1642 (Plate 2a), and shows the medieval street plan.[7] The main streets are Bonnygate, leading from the Cross to the West Port and out towards Perth, and Crossgate, running from the Cross to South Bridge and out towards the Forth ferries ('gate' is a corruption of 'gait', meaning street). Crossgate, occasionally referred to as the High Street, is widest near the Cross, forming a triangular market-place. Bonnygate is narrowest at the Cross but widens to the west, probably implying that it was built up gradually, and later than the Crossgate. The road east towards St Andrews ran along a narrow street at the foot of Castlehill, while the road north to Dundee went down Lady Wynd and up Bishopgate. There are a few buildings shown across the Lady Burn, including one called the Well Tower. By the time of Ainslie's plan in 1775 these have disappeared (Plate 5). All traffic entered through the six town gates, where access could be controlled. While it is not possible to see much detail, we know from later documents that at least one of the gates had a stone arch. The grandest gate seems to be the Bridge Port, with an arch at both ends of South Bridge, and a tower associated with the outer one, if not both. All the gates had been removed by 1775.

The 1642 bird's-eye view shows some two-storey houses with chimneys in the town centre, but most houses, particularly away from the main streets, look like single-storey thatched cottages without chimneys. Even the larger buildings may have been wholly or partly constructed of wood. There are records of major fires in 1616, when the town appealed to the Convention of Royal Burghs for help with repairs as it was 'desolate through the accident of fire', and 1669, which 'spread so fast and with such violence' that twenty 'considerable' families were made homeless and 'a great part of that ancient burgh … [was] annihilat and turned to desolation'. It is generally assumed that much of the rebuilding after 1669 was done using stone and slate. Because of the danger of fire, the town council periodically inspected chimneys, checking they rose high enough above the roof line and were not blocked.

Cupar parish boundary was the River Eden, and across the river was the smaller parish of St Michael of Tarvit. We know there was a church there in the early thirteenth century, as it was rededicated by Bishop de Bernham in 1245. The exact site has never been identified, but bones were dug up when the railway was built, and it seem to have lain near the former east lodge of Tarvit House, now just across the railway bridge on the Pitscottie Road. In 1618 the two parishes were merged, and this was marked by the minister, William Scott, by the addition of a steeple to the medieval tower in 1620.[8] His fine monument in the churchyard is said to be of Dutch workmanship,

FIGURE 3.1 Detail from the 1642 town plan, showing the tolbooth, with the east port next to it. Also shown are the mercat cross on its stepped base, and the tron.

though now badly weathered. In 1689 a second bell was hung in the tower.

The old tolbooth can be seen in the 1642 town plan (Plate 2a, Fig. 3.1). This seems to show a tower with turrets, facing the cross, with a rectangular two-storey building extending eastwards. A forestair juts out towards the cross. It is likely that the tower dates from the late sixteenth or early seventeenth century, its turreted form most closely paralleled by the tolbooths of Edinburgh Canongate or Tain. It would have consisted of at least three floors, with a debtor's prison at the top, the weighhouse in the middle, and a cell for criminals in the vaulted ground floor. The council meeting-room to the east may have been an addition. The burgh and royal arms of seventeenth-century character, built into the later Latin School, may well have come from the old tolbooth. The shaft of the mercat cross is dated 1683.[9]

Many of the local nobility and gentry had town houses in Cupar. These included the Earl of Crawford, whose house was finally demolished to give access to the Bonnygate Church manse; Lord Balmerino, the site of whose house is recorded in the name Balmerino Place; the Earl of Rothes, in the Barony; the laird of Logie; Sir George

Morrison of Dairsie; and David Sibbald of Letham. Many Fife lairds had once had town houses in Cupar, but during the seventeenth century most were given up. The Earl of Rothes, for example, sold his house in the Barony in 1657. The hearth tax of 1694 recorded town houses belonging to Lady Denmuir and Sir John Preston. The only clearly seventeenth-century building surviving is Preston Lodge, built in 1623 by James Williamson and Isobel Heggie (Plate 3a). The original house was probably U-shaped. In 1690 it was bought by James Preston of Denbrae, who added a large extension in 1702, making a new entrance in the new north façade. The house was further altered in c.1765, but retains its late seventeenth-century staircase and some panelling. A few more possibly seventeenth-century buildings survived into the age of photography (Plate 4a and b), and others may date from the late seventeenth or early eighteenth century, notably the Chancellor's House in Crossgate (Plate 3b).

The second half of the sixteenth century saw the growth of Calvinism, and gradual tightening of church control of morals. The Sabbath had to be strictly observed, and there were aspects of cultural life, such as theatrical performances, which were thought frivolous by the Presbyterian authorities, and strongly discouraged. During the 1650s Cupar races were banned for several years. Kirk sessions kept a close eye on morals, and investigated any reports of 'pre-nuptial fornication', illegitimate children, adultery, and drunkenness, and tried to extort confessions, impose fines, and demand public humiliation and repentance.

There are records of a music or 'sang' school, which probably just gradually changed its name to the English School. Together with the Latin School, this made up Cupar grammar school, which seems to have had a good reputation. It usually employed at least three teachers, who between them taught reading, writing, arithmetic, music and Latin for the brighter or more ambitious pupils. Teachers were paid a small salary by the town council, and received fees from parents for each pupil, depending on the subjects taught. Teachers often boosted their meagre salary by holding other posts such as precentor, or parish clerk.

Cupar grammar school served a wide area, with laird's sons sent there as boarders. Lamont's *Diary*, for example, mentions John Lundy, who was sent to Cupar at the age of ten or eleven in 1654, and boarded in the schoolmaster's house. Various national and local statutes during the seventeenth century had tried to impose compulsory schooling, but the fact that they were repeated shows that they did not succeed. In 1677 a quarter of the boys of school age in Cupar were not attending school. Poor scholars often attended for two years or less, enough to acquire an ability to read the Bible, but not long enough to learn to write. From 1678 a summer holiday of four weeks was instituted, as well as occasional whole- or half-day holidays and times set aside for exercise. Most towns were impoverished after the disruptions of the middle of the century, and Cupar cut down to one master at the grammar school in 1667/68, and found it hard to pay its teachers in 1689. Religious controversies also disrupted the careers of schoolmasters, as they did those of ministers, though in Cupar the schoolmasters managed to retain their posts after 1688.

Life in Cupar in the seventeenth century must have been hard for all but the most wealthy, living in small houses, with the risk of starvation, epidemic disease, or losing one's few possessions in a fire. The church kept a close eye on social activities, and was the self-appointed guardian of morals. Even the elite were not free from surveillance, but did at least have a slightly more comfortable life. The records of a Kirkcaldy merchant in the 1680s include supplying barrels of French wine and brandy to the bailies of Cupar. The end of the century, however, brought the beginning of a new era. The eighteenth century saw religious stability, an end to famine, fewer major epidemics, a more stable economy which could better ride out any problems, and parliamentary union which opened up the English market, and with it wider colonial markets. The consequence would be rapid modernisation and urban growth, and for Cupar perhaps its greatest period of growth and prosperity.

Notes

1. Oram, 'From the Union of the Crowns to the Union of the Parliaments', 71.
2. *RPC*, 3rd series, iii, no. 587.
3. In 1628, for example, a Perth merchant was attacked in Abernethy on his way to Cupar, robbed of £200 Scots, and deprived of 'the occasion of the mercat at Cowper to my great hurt and prejudice' (*RPC* 2nd ser ii, 594).
4. John Barclay, surgeon, invested £200, Thomas Bethune of Tarvit £200, and the burgh of Cupar £100.
5. For the new royal burghs see chapter 1, note 2. Burghs of barony included St Monans (1596), Elie (1599), Ferryport-on-Craig (Tayport, 1599), Leven (1609), Ceres (1620), Methil (1662), Kennoway (1663) and Markinch (1673).
6. Lynch, 'The Crown and the Burghs 1500–1625', 56–57, in the sixteenth century Rothes had to be firm in his control of Cupar because Lindsay of the Byres lived closer, at Struthers. *Calendar of State Papers Scotland*, v, 564; in 1580 'the boroughs and burgess towns are wholly at the devotion of some nobleman or other ... as Cupar in Fife at the Earl of Rothes' command'.
7. Royal burghs tend to have plans simple in concept but ambitious in size and street width. Some have one long, wide street with a dominant public building either at one end (Pittenweem) or both ends (Edinburgh, Elgin), or the centre (Montrose, Newburgh); others have two or more main streets, usually parallel (Arbroath, Crail, Perth, St Andrews). Cupar's plan is less elegant than some, but its triangular market-place is typical.

8. The combined church is known as 'Cupar Old and St Michael of Tarvit',
leading to modern misconceptions that the church is dedicated to St Michael.
This may be compounded because St Christopher was a saint particularly
rejected during the Reformation.

9. It is possible this replaced a simpler one – the cross erected at Wemyss in 1666
had a wooden shaft (Lamont, *Diary*, 139–40).

4

The Economy

This chapter brings us to the beginnings of modern Cupar, and looks at five main aspects of the burgh's economy, and how they changed during the long eighteenth century. These are its role as an agricultural market town, the development of industries, the importance of its role as a travel town, the growth of banking, and how the town council managed its resources, and the part it played in the economic development of the town.

A market town

'Couper is a small town in which there are about 2000 Souls, who chiefly subsist by shops and Marketts for Cattle Corn, etc.', wrote Pococke in the middle of the eighteenth century. The minister in 1793 described Cupar as 'the store-house, to an extensive tract of country, for iron, tar, ropes, bricks, tiles, wines, spirits, grass seeds, soap, candles, tobacco, tea, sugar, fruits, and all kinds of groceries'. Cupar had long held weekly markets for butter and cheese, general goods, and at certain times of year for horses, cattle and sheep.[1] Its grain market was the largest in Fife, and there were eight annual fairs.[2] At the beginning of the eighteenth century farmers were producing enough surplus to feed the town's non-agricultural population. Changes in farming practice during the century produced larger surpluses, for which there was a market beyond the town's immediate hinterland, in the fast-growing cities of Edinburgh and Dundee, and, after the opening of the Forth and Clyde Canal in 1790, Glasgow as well. The price of cattle quadrupled over the century, most of the increase being after 1740. The growth of the production of black cattle is a constant theme throughout the *Old Statistical Account*. As it made little sense to walk cattle to a market in the opposite direction from their intended destination, markets for cattle and, to a lesser extent, sheep, grew up or expanded in other communities within the orbit of Cupar. Some, such as Lochgelly tryst, were held outside burghs and charged no customs.

In the case of grain, Cupar gradually lost trade to the coastal ports. While remaining the main market town in the area for the exchange of goods for local consumption, by the end of the century Cupar had lost much of its export trade in agricultural surpluses to towns and villages better placed geographically. The minister of Abdie, for example, in 1789, reported that 'great quantities of wheat and barley' were shipped from Newburgh, 'chiefly for the Edinburgh and Glasgow markets'. And in Balmerino shipping of wheat and barley had expanded when 'the merchants began to buy from the farmers at the weekly market in Cupar, and received their grain at Balmerino'. Cupar was thus developing as a financial centre, dealing in goods which no longer necessarily passed through the town. The parishes on the north coast were now selling direct to Dundee. In Ferryport-on-Craig 'as there is a constant weekly demand for all kinds of country vivres in Dundee, some persons make it their business to go through this part of the country, and gather them up for the Dundee market'. The minister of Kilmany noted that the purchasing power of the elite of Dundee had increased the price of food in north Fife.

Cupar found it increasingly difficult to exert its traditional rights to supervise and control markets and fairs within its 'liberty'. In 1722 the town of Auchtermuchty refused to allow Cupar's dean of guild to 'survey their mercat', as he had traditionally done. A compromise was eventually reached, but the bailies of Auchtermuchty had demonstrated the weakening power of Cupar over its hinterland.[3] While some rural parishes such as Moonzie continued to rely totally on Cupar, other communities were increasingly holding their own markets and fairs.[4] In 1775 it was reported to the council that the proprietor of Pitlessie had advertised two markets, which was an 'encroachment on privileges' and 'very detrimental' to the customs income of Cupar. But Cupar was powerless, and the fair at Pitlessie, only four miles away, became a regular feature, immortalised in 1804 in a painting by David Wilkie.

The horizons of Cupar merchants seem to have narrowed during the long eighteenth century. The latest evidence for participation in seaborne trade is in the testament of David Clephane of Carslogie (1721), who owned 'ane pairt of the good ship called the *David* of Kirkcaldy'. In 1798 the guildry bemoaned the fact that 'forty, fifty or sixty years ago the merchant guildry of this burgh had great commerce and traffick abroad'. However, they failed to understand why things had changed, and that reinstating outdated practices would not turn the clock back. Various schemes to build a covered market came to nothing, perhaps showing a lack of enterprise or direction among the merchant community.

The table of customs drawn up by the town council shows what goods were coming into the town, and their approximate order of importance, and can therefore demonstrate changes in the pattern of

TABLE 4.1 Surviving evidence of stock, value of stock and total wealth of Cupar merchants

	Date	Equipment	Stock	Stock value (£ sterling)	Total estate (£ sterling)	Source
William Mortimer	1700	Balance and weights	Linen and woollen cloth, leather gloves	21		NAS CC20/2/8
Peter Birrell	1701	Merchant shuttles				NAS CC20/2/8; CC20/4/16
Andrew Douglas	1725–31		Paper, wine, spirits			StAU Cheape of Rossie
Alexander Barclay	1730		Chamber pots, crockery, groceries			StAU Cheape of Rossie
David Williamson	1738		Wine corks, thread, raisins, vinegar, hops, spices, cotton wool, muslin, soap, stoneware decanters, scissors, gloves, lamp black, silk, cambric, chamber pots, earthenware basins, needles, buckles, whalebone			StAU Cheape of Rossie
Robert Bell	1740–53		Tart pans, tea pot, milk pot, stoneware ashet, raisins, hops, sugar, orange peel, cotton wool, silk, wine corks, besoms, earthenware bowls and trenchers, tea, thread, ribbon, cambric, lawn, muslin, stockings, handkerchiefs, buttons, velvet, writing paper, soap, whips, hair powder, scissors, hats, gloves, chamber pots, besom, prunes, potash, hair cloths			StAU Cheape of Rossie, Hay of Leys
Margaret Peat	1747	Shop table and shelves	Merchant goods in shop and cellars	56	90	NAS CC20/4/20
John Mathie	1754	Tobacconist's tools, tobacco press, spinning table, shop shuttles	Tobacco, snuff, hops, pearl ashes, soap, sugar, logwood, brimstone	56	93	NAS CC20/4/22; CC20/6/35
John Thomson	1751–53		Claret, French wine, tea, sugar			StAU Hay of Leys
John Gordon	1756	Sign above door, weights	Hair, paper	4	18	NAS CC20/4/22; CC20/6/34
James Chalmers	1765				106	NAS CC20/6/46
William Geddie	1768				15	NAS CC20/6/46
John Brabiner	1768	Scales and weights, pestle and mortar, copper for melting tallow, tallow press, etc., tobacco table and shuttle case, hand barrow	Besoms, pens, horn buttons, thread, paper, nails, lead shot, indigo, ginger, aniseed, logwood, starch, brimstone, thimbles, brassware	9		NAS CC20/6/46

(Table 4.1 continued overleaf)

TABLE 4.1 (continued)

	Date	Equipment	Stock	Stock value (£ sterling)	Total estate (£ sterling)	Source
James Davidson	1770	Soap boiler, press, tubs, tools, scales and weights, counter, *Merchant's Companion*	Tallow, wicks, candles, cotton and tow			NAS CC20/4/23
David Sibbald	1773	Shop counter, set of shop shuttles	Merchant goods	12s	8	NAS CC20/6/51
Alexander Young	1784		Merchant goods, various linens			St AU B13/7/5
Robert Duncan	1803		Drapery; muslins, stockings, etc.	87	Bankrupt, owing 1,172	NAS CS96/3996
Henry Inglis	1816		Shop goods	1081	3,618, inc. share of tannery c.500	NAS CC20/7/9
Robert Guthrie	1818–20	Table, packing boxes, writing desk, mirror, scales and weights	Assorted fabrics, gloves, fur trimmings, handkerchiefs, hats, lace, buttons, thread, stockings, night caps, parasols, ribbons, gum flowers, feathers, shawls	1818 1,682 1820 389	Bankrupt, owing over 4,000	NAS CS96/359
William Thomson	1822	Writing desk and 4 chairs in the shop		640	1446	NAS CC20/4/31
Betty Hugh	1823	Shop furniture	Butter, cheese, coffee, sugar, pepper, starch, tea, pins, peppermint drops, worsted, tobacco, candles, soap, salt fish, gingerbread	258	1134	NAS SC20/50/1
Robert Fernie	1824		Nails, locks, hinges, knives and forks, saws, spades, shovels, razors, scissors, screws, spoons, chisels, trays, snuff boxes, watch chains, pins, needles, brushes, coffin mountings, fire irons, spectacles, weavers' shears, bolts, casters, toys, shoe heels, riddles, sash pulleys, scythes.	150		NAS SC20/50/1
James Watson	1826		Cloth, hose, corsets, fur tippets, muffs, mantles, neck and pocket handkerchiefs, sild, worsted and cotton shawls, muslins, trimmings, gloves	2047	Bankrupt, owing 3289	NAS CS96/1261

trade. Tables published in 1713 and 1744 still show the dominance of agricultural produce. A revision in 1789, however, shows linen more prominent, and additions included potatoes, wheaten bread and foreign spirits. By 1792 a cartload of merchant goods was in second place, and wood (for building) had also moved up the list. Items of furniture and bed coverings were specified, as were various agricultural tools, demonstrating agricultural changes, a building boom and increased demand for consumer goods.

Table 4.1 shows that traditional merchants such as Robert Bell (1740) stocked a wide range of goods but by the early nineteenth century most merchants specialised in either drapery, grocery or ironmongery. However, because of the increasing range within these categories, each merchant probably had more capital tied up in stock than his predecessors. Specialisations were not exclusive. Betty Hugh (1823), for example, though a 'grocer', stocked pins and worsted. Table 4.2 shows links with merchants outside Fife. Groceries were mostly bought from Edinburgh or Dundee; drapery from Glasgow and the Borders, and later from the north of England. As a major market centre, Cupar by the early nineteenth century attracted a growing number of specialist merchants such as earthenware-dealers, leather-dealers, and seedsmen, and specialist tradesmen such as coach-makers, gunsmiths, rope-makers and snuff-grinders.

For most of the eighteenth century merchants ran their businesses from home, and the term 'shop' meant no more than the room from which the business was run. Towards the end of the century, however, merchants were increasingly trading from separate premises, 'shops' in the modern sense. The Shop Tax of 1787/88, levied on premises with a valued rental of over £5 per year, was paid by only one Cupar merchant, Robert Geddie. By 1793, however, there were thirty-one 'shop-keepers', and by the time of the first trades directory in 1825 most of the eighty or more people selling food, clothing, furniture, books and hardware seem to have been trading from shop premises.[5] Others took goods to their customers; Robert Guthrie, for example, sold from a hired cart around Kennoway, Markinch and Largo.[6] Small merchants relied on middlemen to acquire goods as required by customers. Correspondence survives from 1772/73 in which Young and Trotter of Edinburgh were pursuing Alexander Brown in Cupar for payment for goods supplied to a middleman. Brown claimed that he had given McNaughton 'an order to buy for me in Edinburgh one Bed cover with several other Articles'. His wife had given £2 on account to McNaughton, who had disappeared.[7]

There were also itinerant salesmen within the town. The guildry in 1806 complained that 'haulkers and peddlers are a great nuisance to the Inhabitants and very hurtful to the Tredders in this Burrow', and ordered their officer to stop such people selling in the town other

TABLE 4.2. Surviving evidence of contacts between Cupar merchants and others in Scotland and England

Merchant	Date	Scotland	England	Source
James Oliphant, merchant and vintner	1702	Dundee (1) Montrose (1)		NAS CC20/2/8
John Mathie, merchant and tobacconist	d.1754	Edinburgh (1), + more		NAS CC20/4/22; CC20/6/35
James Chalmers, merchant	d.1768	Aberdeen (1), Beith (1), Dalkeith (1), Dumfries (1), Duns (3), Edinburgh (1), Falkirk (2), Glasgow (6), Greenock (1), Hamilton (4), Hawick (2), Irvine (1), Jedburgh (1), Kelso (1), Paisley (1), Port Glasgow (1), Stirling (4)		NAS CC20/6/46
William Young, merchant	1798	Dundee, Edinburgh		StAU B13/7/5
James Culbert, merchant	1800	Leith, Perth		StAU B13/7/5
Robert Duncan, merchant	1803	Aberdeen (2), Dundee (4), Edinburgh (3), Glasgow (3), Perth (3)	Birmingham (1), Leek (1), Leicester (1), London (1), Manchester (1), Newcastle (1)	NAS CS96/3996
Thomas George, merchant	1814	Dundee, Edinburgh, Glasgow, Leith		StAU B13/8/1
Robert Guthrie, merchant and manufacturer	1818	Edinburgh (2), Glasgow (4), Perth (1)	Birmingham (3), Leeds (4), Manchester (4), Oldham (1), Rochdale (1), Wakefield (1)	NAS CS96/359
William Thomson, merchant	d.1822	Edinburgh (2)		NAS CC20/7/14
Betty Hugh, merchant, grocer	d.1823	Dundee (1), Edinburgh (1)		NAS SC20/50/1
Andrew Hain, Draper	1824	Glasgow, Paisley	Leeds, London, Manchester	*Fife Herald* 6/5/1824
James Watson, merchant, draper, haberdasher	1826	Aberdeen (1), Edinburgh (8), Glasgow (13), Perth (1)	Beith (1), Huddersfield (1), Leek (1), Manchester (2), Nottingham(1), Rochdale (1)	NAS CS96/1261

than on market days. The growth of suburbs increased the problem. In 1817 the guildry protested at the 'great injury' caused by the public auctions held in St Catherine Street, 'it being well known that at all these Sales very inferior and often damaged articles are sold by which the purchaser is often taken in and a higher price paid in ready money than the Articles can be bought for in the Shops as a regular Credit'. But as the sales were held outwith the town boundary the town council was powerless.

The linen industry

Scotland experienced steady economic growth up to 1780, then the rate of increase accelerated. Linen took over from wool early in the century as the main manufacturing industry in Scotland, but was itself overtaken by cotton in the 1790s. Angus, Perthshire and Fife were the three areas where linen production was most dominant. The cotton industry never really took off in east Fife, and linen remained a significant product well into the nineteenth century. Cupar was prominent in the linen industry, and agents based in the town controlled much of the production in the surrounding area. As in many Scottish towns, early attempts to industrialise aspects of the linen industry met with limited success. During the 1740s, however, the industry began a period of rapid expansion, which lasted, despite a few setbacks, into the early nineteenth century, absorbing surplus labour, boosting exports, and contributing to a national increase in spending power (see Chapter 7).

The first 'linen manufactory' in Cupar was established in 1727, initially for nine years, with a stock issue of £2,000, in 160 shares. By 1729, twenty-six shareholders had subscribed over £1,500. But in 1733 the weaving part of the enterprise stopped when a main customer in London went bankrupt. The more important facility was the bleachfield, one of the earliest in Scotland. The 'undertakers had been at a great deal of pains and charges' laying it out, and in April 1728 they asked the council for permission to cut a small canal through the town's common to bring more water to it. Bleachfields were capital-intensive, and support was necessary. In 1729 the Board of Trustees for Fisheries and Manufactures in Scotland gave a grant of £225 to John Riddell for setting it up.[8] At the annual general meeting of 1736 it was proposed to renew the tack of the bleachfield for another six years.[9] Riddell received another payment of £100 from the Trustees in 1741 to fit up the 'New field', but when his lease expired in 1742 the bleachfield may have closed or sold.[10] A flax mill had been set up in the 1730s at Hospital Mill by Thomas Hope of Rankeilour as a training centre, but it is not clear how long it lasted.

The Cupar linen manufactory failed just when the industry nationally was beginning to take off, stimulated by the introduction of a bounty on the export of linen in 1742. In 1759 the Managers of the British Linen Company discussed the possibility of 'establishing a house at Dundee and Coupar Fife for promoting the linen manufacture and the sale of flax'. But developments from the 1740s seem to have been led by local entrepreneurs. In 1727 the first stampmaster was appointed. A succession of stampmasters appear intermittently thereafter in the records, including John Foulis, dismissed for drunkenness in 1775, and Alexander Wilkie (Fig. 4.1), dismissed in 1800 for 'stamping cloth unproperly made as good as sufficient', as well as being 'almost continually intoxicated'.[11] The Trustees also supported several women, and by 1731 had established a spinning school in Cupar.[12]

The linen industry was so fundamental to the town that its importance was sometimes taken for granted in the records. At various times the town was prompted by the Convention of Royal Burghs to write to its member of parliament on matters relating to linen manufacture in Scotland. In 1761 the weaver trade petitioned the council, suggesting that 'making all the yarn and linen that come to your mercats custom free' would be a 'great encouragement' to all in the industry, and 'would not much harm the customer as it would certainly increase our merkates'. In 1771 there was an application for permission for a private bleachfield, to be managed by James Ferguson, bleaching master. Its layout can be seen on Ainslie's 1775 plan of Cupar (Plate 5). In 1776 the Trustees paid £30 to James Hill, bleacher, 'for a Drying House', and a £10 premium for three consecutive years before 1783. A newspaper advertisement in 1778 announced the prices charged at Cupar bleachfield, and places in Edinburgh, Fife and Kinross where cloth could be collected for bleaching. Some of these agents also had 'the printing-books to shew; to which are added this season a considerable number of patterns'.[13] This, together with evidence from inventories of Cupar linen at other bleachfields, implies that customers did not automatically use the local field, but were prepared to pay transport costs if price and quality were right. In 1793 the bleachfield was said to be 'in good repute'.

Nationally the numbers of weavers more than trebled between 1780 and 1810, and reached a peak in about 1840. Traditional home-based handloom weavers, however, declined both in numbers and incomes after 1815. While the linen industry in Scotland grew throughout the eighteenth century, particularly from the 1740s, there were periods of stagnation or depression in the 1730s, 1750s and the early 1770s, while in the early nineteenth century the Napoleonic wars had complex effects. Some weavers left to become soldiers, output fluctuated, and flax supplies were disrupted, but military requirements led to an increased demand for the coarse linen produced in east Fife. Cupar seems to have experienced the same peaks and troughs as the industry nationally, including a general economic slump following the end of the war in 1815.

Durie has estimated that while the number of weavers increased three- or fourfold between the 1730s and 1790s, the output of cloth increased sevenfold. In Cupar the number of identified weavers increased from 63 to 195. David Loch in 1778 described 'the immense quantities of yarn bought and sold ... almost exceeds the bounds of credibility, demonstrating that Cupar is a town of much importance, and in a very prosperous way with regard to commerce and manufactures'. According to the *Old Statistical Account* fifteen years later the area had 'a considerable manufacture of coarse linens', consisting mainly of 'yard-wides, as they are commonly named, for buckram', glazed linens, Osnaburghs,[14] tow sheetings, and Silesias. As well as the linen stamped in Cupar, another £20,000 worth of brown linen came in to market from the surrounding countryside. 'All these are purchased with ready money, and sent to London, Glasgow and other markets'. The linen sold through Cupar was, therefore, as much as a fifth of the total produced in Fife.

TABLE 4.3 Numbers employed in the main centres of the linen industry in Fife in the early 1790s.

Town	Population	Weavers	Looms	Manufacturers/ merchants	Flax-dressers	Bleachfields
Dunfermline	9,550	862	800+	21		
Dysart	4,862		700–750			
Kirkcaldy and Abbotshall	4,809		550		9	2
St Andrews and St Leonards	4,335	52 +				
Cupar	3,702		223	6		1
Markinch	2,790	160			8	1
Falkland	2,198	231 + apprentices	c.200			
Leuchars	1,620		90			
Auchtermuchty	1,439	205				
Ceres	2,320		138		7	
Kettle	1,759	60 masters, 18 apprentices	170		5	
Newburgh	1,664	270				

Source: *OSA*.

TABLE 4.4. Surviving evidence for links between manufacturers in Cupar and customers and suppliers elsewhere

Manufacturer	Date	Fife	Rest of Scotland	England	Other	Source
Thomas Bell	d.1803		Glasgow			NAS CC20/4/28
David Melville	c.1803	Auchtermuchty, Crail, Kinghorn, Kirkcaldy, Leven, St Andrews	Dundee, Leith, Perth		Rotterdam, Riga	NAS CS96/707
Goodsir, Adamson & Co	c.1805	Auchtermuchty, Kirkcaldy, Leven	Brechin			NAS CS96/1166
David Birrell	d.1813	Ceres, Chance Inn, Cleish, Falkland, Forthar, Kennoway, Largo, St Andrews, Springfield, Star, Strathkinness	Dundee, Perth			NAS CC20/7/5
Robert Scott	1826	Kirkcaldy, Leven	Dundee	Halifax, London	Archangel	NAS CS96/785
William Kyd	1826		Dundee	London		NAS CS235 seqK1/26
William Smith	c.1826				W Indies, S America, Hamburg	NAS AD58/339

Table 4.3 shows the extent of employment in the linen industry in Cupar and its neighbourhood, and in the other main towns of Fife. Linen from Falkland, Kettle, Largo, Leuchars and Newburgh was brought to Cupar to be sold. Some was handled in Auchtermuchty. Newburgh also dealt direct with Perth and Dundee, and the north-eastern parishes supplied merchants in Dundee. Laurence Adamson, second minister of Cupar, in his edition of Sibbald's *History of Fife*, claimed that between £60,000 and £70,000 was paid by merchants to the linen manufacturers and weavers, slightly more than half stamped in Cupar, the rest produced in the surrounding area. If his figures are correct, they demonstrate a 99 per cent increase in volume and a 75 per cent increase in value in just ten years. Cupar's output of linen between 1777 and 1802 shows a more than threefold increase in both volume and value, compared with considerably less than a doubling of the national figures.

As well as an increase in the numbers of weavers, the later eighteenth century saw a rapid increase in the number of men described as 'manufacturers'. As the industry grew, so its organisation became increasingly complex and demanded greater capital investment. Manufacturers organised the supply of yarn to individual weavers, or to groups employed in weaving sheds, and then sold the finished webs. Of the ninety-seven manufacturers identified in Cupar, fifty-two were also described as weavers, and ten as merchants. Whatever their background,

FIGURE 4.1 Mark of a Cupar stampmaster, found on osnaburgh linen.

they acted as merchants, and built up a network of contacts throughout Scotland and further afield (Table 4.4). David Loch in 1778 named Robert Geddie as 'the principal merchant ... supposed to purchase six or eight thousand pounds sterling worth of the linen and yarn on his own private account'.[15]

Later manufacturers were even more ambitious. William Smith, in partnership with others including Ebenezer Anderson of the Fife Bank, and William Fleming of the Commercial Bank, sent linen to the West Indies, Hispaniola (Haiti) and Cartagena (Colombia). One deal in 1824 involved the proceeds from the sale of linen in Hispaniola being sent in the form of coffee to an agent in Hamburg. Such deals seem to have been common in the early 1820s, with merchants from Cupar sending linen which they could not sell in Britain to a variety of agents in the Caribbean.[16] Several manufacturers went bankrupt after 1800, particularly around 1810. In 1823 George Moon, a spinning-mill owner, said in evidence to a House of Lords Committee that very few manufacturers ran only family businesses, most employed extra hands, with 'a Workshop below, with Two or three Rooms, and their Dwelling House above'. According to the 1825 trades directory Cupar had the sixth highest number of linen manufacturers in Scotland.[17] Manufacturers increasingly needed space for buildings and machinery. John Chalmers in 1790 petitioned the town council for a piece of land 'for the purpose of erecting thereon a boiling and dying house' rather than 'carrying on his manufacturing business' in his house. David Melville owned a boiling house on the Lady Burn, and employed about twenty weavers. One of the reasons for his bankruptcy in 1803 was that he 'lost considerably by purchases of flax, yarn and cloth made at the time of the Russian embargo about three years ago'.[18] In 1799 Anderson, Birrell & Company applied for land to extend their premises at Ladyburnside, which consisted of 'a washhouse, a dying house and a boiling house'.[19]

The earliest process to be mechanised was the preparation of the flax fibres. In 1772 there were eleven lint mills in Fife, but none near Cupar. By 1775 there was one at Hospital Mill, and by 1791 ten between Cults and Lydox Mill (Fig. 4.2). The next stage to be mechanised was spinning, with mills at Leven by 1788 and at Kinghorn soon after 1792. In 1799 Thomas Anderson, William Anderson, James Carstairs and George Hog converted Tarvit Mill to a spinning mill. By this time there were eleven in Fife, another being Blebo Mill, run by John Walker (the water power on the Ceres Burn was more powerful than any closer to Cupar). A spinning mill was built at Cupar Mills between 1800 and 1809. Russell's Mill was converted by Anderson, Birrell & Co. in 1803, and in 1809 had twelve spinning frames and four carding engines. George Moon, who took it over in about 1812, 'built for himself a fine new mill, giving himself plenty of room and daylight' and acquired

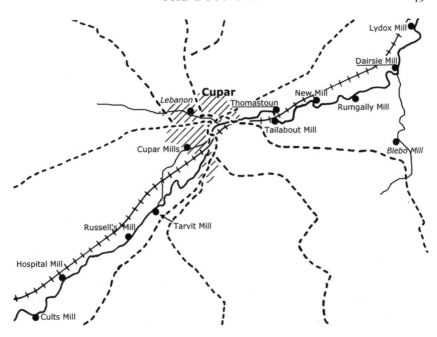

FIGURE 4.2 Mills on the River Eden; those in normal type were converted or extended as lint mills between 1775 and 1791. Lint mills not on the site of earlier grain mills are in italics, and those underlined remained as grain mills only.

'half a dozen of New-Carding Engines', made in Dundee. Lebanon Mill was converted from a wash-mill in 1813, and Hospital Mill converted to a tow-mill in 1821. By this time the coarse linen industry in Fife was becoming centralised in the Kirkcaldy area, with its growing port facilities, and larger pool of labour. The first working power-loom in Fife was established there in 1821.

Other industries

The leading medieval industry of woollen manufacture survived in a small way. Some correspondence survives between Cupar merchants and a firm in Bannockburn manufacturing plaiding, discussing finished cloth, and the supply and transport of wool. The only industrial premises shown on Ainslie's town plan of 1775 (Plate 5) are the bleachfield and the brick-works. Cupar had good local clay, and the brick-works had been set up in 1764, on the hill just across the South Bridge. In 1793 'the brick and tile work has long been profitable to the proprietors, and still continues to thrive, but is not yet able to answer the great demand for tiles'. In 1807 a new owner, James Wilson, expanded the works.

The *Old Statistical Account* also listed two tanneries. One, probably the older, was behind the Crossgate, on Waterend Road, and can be seen on Wood's town plan of 1820 (Plate 13). The other was near the foot of Lady Wynd. There were also tanneries in Inverkeithing and Kirkcaldy. The minister of Kirkcaldy in 1795 explained that local hides and skins were used, supplemented by 'a considerable quantity ... from the North of Scotland, from Ireland, and sometimes from Holland'. The oak bark used to come from England 'excepting only a small proportion from the Highlands of Scotland', but since prices had risen bark was now imported from Germany and the Netherlands.[20] A gazetteer of 1817 mentioned 'two large breweries'. Other industrial premises shown on Wood's plan of 1820 are 'Mr Thomson's Brewery' beside the Lady Burn, and, just south of the gaol, the 'Coach Work'. In 1807 permission was given for a rope-walk at the Cart Haugh. Although there was reasonable water-power in Cupar, it was not ideal. When Robert Tullis wanted to guarantee a supply of good-quality paper for his printing works he bought a bankrupt paper-mill at Auchmuty. The water power was good, there was plenty of manpower in nearby Markinch, and it was nearer to a port and to Edinburgh.

Travel and transport

It seems that the port of Motray had stopped being used by some time in the sixteenth century. Some goods came via Dundee, often through its outport at Newburgh. By the mid eighteenth century Newburgh had the great advantage that it had plenty of space for storage, and it became the main port for importing timber to the eastern part of Fife. Being inland, Cupar could not hope to compete with ports, particularly Kirkcaldy, which was growing fast. The minister in 1793 noted 'the great expence of land carriage'. As the nearest ports, Leven and Newburgh, were both nine miles away, 'the manufacturer must bring to Cupar the raw materials he uses, at a very heavy expence', and the finished goods cost as much to export. He suggested that 'to rise superior to this natural disadvantage ... a navigable canal might be formed' to the Eden estuary. It was one of many similar schemes in Scotland which were never carried out. Even a simple canal involved a large capital outlay, there were a large number of mills to be bypassed, and the volume of trade into and out of Cupar simply did not justify the expense.

Road transport, as for example between Cupar and its outport, had been used for centuries, whatever the condition of the roads. Cupar's role as a travel town was an important factor in its economy, as the town lay on the 'Great Road' from Edinburgh to Dundee and Aberdeen, at a long-established crossing point over the river Eden. During the eighteenth century travelling conditions improved enormously. Roads needed to be better engineered than could be achieved by statute labour, and in 1774 this duty was converted to a financial contribution. In some places new roads were built with shallower gradients, for example one between Cupar and Newburgh in 1790. That same year the first Turnpike Act for Fife listed seventeen roads, including six radiating out from Cupar.[21] As a consequence the number and variety of wheeled vehicles increased, and several Cupar innkeepers offered chaises for hire. Increasing numbers of people were able to travel to the town for markets, fairs and special events. According to the minister in 1793 the new turnpike roads had at first met with 'almost universal opposition' from farmers, but they soon 'entirely changed their opinion ... they pay chearfully at the toll-bars, and seem ... convinced of the vast importance and utility of the roads'. But once the novelty wore off and the number of improved roads increased, tolls were unpopular, and the distribution of toll bars was erratic and unfair. In Cupar's case there were toll houses on East Road at the junction of the road to Pitscottie (Plate 12c); on South Road where a road branches to Ceres (Plate 12b); at Carslogie, and on the Perth road near Balgarvie.

Not only people needed to be transported to and from Cupar, but letters. Before 1715 all post in Scotland was conveyed on foot. For much of the eighteenth century mail was carried north from Edinburgh via Queensferry and Perth, at first on foot, but by 1763 all the way to Aberdeen by horse, and increased from three times a week to five. Soon afterwards the mail was carried by stage coach as far as Perth, and after a new bridge was built there in 1771 coaches carried on to Aberdeen. Mail for anywhere else was carried sideways from this one route, in stages. Letters for Cupar were brought by a 'runner' from Falkland. The use of the postal system grew rapidly, and the revenue from Cupar post-office increased from £20 per quarter in 1763 to £90 in 1793. In 1795 the town petitioned the Postmaster General for a 'Horse Post', worried how in winter 'the present runner could get through ... the one half of the Road being in a very bad state'. The following year Cupar joined in petitioning for a dedicated mail coach between Edinburgh and Aberdeen, which would 'give the inhabitants of Cupar an hour or two longer to answer their letters', as well as carrying passengers. In 1800 and 1802 they lobbied their MP to back plans for a mail coach from Kinghorn to Woodhaven via Cupar. In 1805 'several individuals in the town and neighbourhood' proposed 'to establish a coach from Woodhaven by Cupar through Kirkcaldy to Queensferry'. If this could carry the mail, 'the whole towns upon the road would have their letters two hours sooner' a 'particular advantage' for Cupar and St Andrews, 'whose posts at present arrive at a very late hour'. But it was 1813 before a postal route through Fife was established.

The first passenger service across Fife was a two-horse diligence from Pettycur to Newport via Kennoway in 1805. In 1810 Mr McNab of Cupar ran a larger four-horse coach from Pettycur to Newport via New Inn. Such vehicles were 'constant sources of interest and excitement, watched and waited for by the public of Cupar'.²² In 1821 it was suggested that the post should be transferred to the steam boats 'now established on the Forth and Tay'. It was only with the coming of steam ferries, which ran to timetables, that coach services across Fife between Edinburgh and Dundee really became viable. But despite the obvious advantages, improvements in transport reduced the numbers who had to stay in Cupar overnight. In 1828 Alexander McNab, manager of the Tontine Tavern, petitioned his landlords for a reduction in rent, explaining that he had believed that 'business would considerably increase from the erection of Low Water Piers on the Forth', but in fact it had decreased for several reasons, including the 'general depression of business everywhere', and local competition: 'formerly when the passages across the Forth were irregular ... the hiring of chaises formed the greater part of his profits ... every [commercial] traveller had his own gig or horse, came to Cupar and generally remained a Day and Night at least. Now, however he arrives by one [stage] coach, transacts his business ... and departs on the same day by the next coach, thus often not calling for a single article at the Inn'.²³ The 1820s saw three stage coach services through Cupar each day in each direction, two run by McNab of the Tontine Tavern, and one by Samuel Player of the Blue Bell Inn, each picking up passengers at their own inn.

Financial services

One aspect of the economy of Cupar which changed substantially over the long eighteenth century was the amount of capital accumulated and the way it was invested. For most of the century there were two ways to invest money: the purchase of property to let; or, more risky but presumably potentially more profitable, private money-lending. Evidence for both types of investment can be found in dispositions, testaments, inventories and bankruptcy records. By the early nineteenth century, however, more people were depositing their capital in banks, both national and local, or holding shares in banks and insurance companies. Table 4.5 (p. 54) shows evidence for investments of over £100. An example of the extent and variety of investments and speculations being undertaken by the elite of Cupar in the early nineteenth century can be seen in an arbitration in the burgh court in 1814 between John Ferguson and James Wilson. Both men were involved in many aspects of life in the town, and would perhaps be best described as entrepreneurs. The deals are summarised in Table

4.6. The outcome, after much acrimony, was that Ferguson owed Wilson £30.

The most successful of the writers (solicitors) in Cupar had always been among the wealthiest inhabitants, involved in lending and borrowing money. In 1769 William Robertson, writer and town clerk, was involved with proto-banking in Dundee. By the time of the *Old Statistical Account* there were two bank offices in the town, the Bank of Scotland (from 1785) and the British Linen Company (from 1792).[24] In about 1800 John Gray of Paddington Green, London, wrote 'a Proposal for promoting the Advantage & Prosperity of the County of Fife'. 'In my late tour to Scotland', he noted, 'I was very sorry to observe, that the progress of industry & manufacture was much less considerable in the County of Fife, than in the neighbouring Counties of Perth and Angus'. As the soil was good, and Fife was richer in coal, freestone and lime than its neighbours, he tried to identify the reasons for the county's failure to develop. He highlighted 'a want of Stock, – A want of enterprizing Directors to turn the Stock to productive purposes' and 'a want of working hands'. As the last two were generally consequences of the first, he suggested that what Fife needed was its own bank. This would 'render money more plentiful' and lead to lower interest rates. When interest rates were low, he claimed, land prices rose, and manufacturers were inclined to invest more in their businesses.[25]

TABLE 4.6 Submission and decreet arbitral between John Ferguson and James Wilson, 1814

Amount Owed (£)	Wilson to Ferguson	Amount Owed (£)	Ferguson to Wilson
930	'upon a joint insurance account'	321	⅓ share of Cupar Brickwork
259	⅓ share of purchase price of 'Templelands'	68 68	share of 'loss upon an adventure in flax'
107	⅓ share of speculation in corn	16	commission on 'a former coin speculation'
200	loan	104	owed from insurance account
50	share of profits of land sale, in a bank in London	658 658	balance of a bill, Perth
110	borrowed from Benevolent Society of Cupar	533 533	balance of a bill, Dundee
Total 1670		Total 1700	

Amounts are given to the nearest £.

TABLE 4.5   Investments of over £100 in public companies

	Occupation	Date	Deposits	Shares	Source
Thomas Bell	Manufacturer	d.1803		£500 share, Fife Bank	NAS CC20/4/28
Lady Elizabeth Anstruther		d.1804		21 shares, Bank of Scotland (£21,000 Scots)	NAS CC20/2/28 CC20/6/75
James Wilson	Writer	b'rupt 1810		£300, Fife Bank; £500, 1 share, Cupar Bank. £500, Fife Insurance Co	NAS CS96/1734/1
William Millie	Shoemaker (retired)	d.1811	£138, Bank of Scotland £10, Fife Bank		NAS CC20/4/29
David Tod	Writer	d.1812	£80, Fife Bank,	1 share Fife Bank	NAS CC20/7/5
David Wilkie	Minister	d.1812	£120, Bank of Scotland		NAS CC20/7/5
Alexander Melville	Baker (retired)	d.1813	£375, Bank of Scotland £340, Fife Bank £100, British Linen Co		NAS CC20/4/29
David Birrell	Manufacturer	d.1813		5 shares, Commercial Bank (£750) shares, Fife Insurance Co (c.£60)	NAS CC20/4/30
Walter Henderson	Bookseller	d.1815	£1,448, British Linen Co; £175, Fife Bank		NAS CC20/4/30
Peter Gray	Militia sergeant	d.1815	£20, Dundee Bank; £108, British Linen Co (Dundee + Cupar)		NAS CC20/7/8
John Annan	Residenter	d.1816		1 share, Fife Bank (c.£320)	NAS CC20/4/30
Henry Inglis	Merchant	d.1816		10 shares, Commercial Bank (£1,300); Fife Insurance Co c.£60	NAS CC20/4/30 CC20/7/9
Henry Walker	Writer	d.1818	£220+, Commercial Bank		NAS CC20/4/30
James Reekie	Wright	d.1820	£113, Fife Bank		NAS CC20/4/31
Betty Heugh	Merchant	d.1823	£200, British Linen Co £200, Fife Bank		NAS SC20/50/1
John Smith	Baxter	d.1824	£345, Fife Bank		NAS SC20/50/1
Ebenezer Anderson	Banker, corn dealer, linen merchant	b'rupt 1829		shares in Edinburgh Life Assurance Co, Scottish Union Insurance Co, and 5 shares in Fife Insurance Co	NAS AD58/339

He therefore proposed that 'sixty Gentlemen, Merchants & others' including himself, should set up a bank in Cupar with a capital of £20,000, and a minimum subscription of £100. So in 1802 the Fife Bank was established, despite the opinion of a Fife-born banker in Glasgow that no-one in the Cupar area had 'either money or sense to conduct a Bank'.[26] Founded with sixty shares of £50 each, and forty-seven partners, it set up its headquarters in the Bonnygate. By 1808 it had branches in Kinross and Kirriemuir, demonstrating its close involvement in the linen industry. In 1808 the Kinross branch closed but another opened in Kirkcaldy. The bank also had one or more agencies in Glasgow. The partners who lived or worked in Cupar included eight writers, three gentlemen and one minister.[27]

The Cupar Bank was also established in 1802, by John Ferguson, Henry Inglis and David Allan, though it was 'never of any real significance'.[28] At least one writer, James Wilson, had shareholdings in both banks (Table 4.5). It was quite a feat of organisation to set up a new bank. Wilson claimed expenses from the Fife Bank for two trips to Edinburgh, one 'staying several days ordering plates to be made, paper, locks etc' and consulting with agents, the other 'waiting three days for the Company's Guinea notes'. He also went to Dundee to order 'iron chests, doors etc' and get books made.[29]

The national banks had problems managing local branches or agencies. They had to employ prominent local men, or they would not get custom, but such men tended to have their own agendas. The first Cupar agent for the Bank of Scotland was linen merchant Robert Geddie. But in 1802, partly because of the challenge from the two local banks which opened that year, Geddie was forced to resign on the grounds of age, and was replaced by Thomas Horsburgh, writer and sheriff clerk (and probably a supporter of Henry Dundas, a major political figure). Horsburgh, however, let far too many bills run over time, and his record of recovering money owed was poor. In 1812 the bank received an anonymous accusation of irregularities and sent inspectors. They found no proof, but suspicions remained. In 1814, therefore, they decided that 'none of the Objects of the Bank have been adequately attained by means of the Cupar Agency; and the labour and difficulty of superintendance have been disproportionately great', and the office was to be closed. Branch banking involved the risky transport of notes. In 1811 it was noted that 'in Summer the Cupar Office might be supplied by means of the Dundee Coach Guard' but not in the winter because landing at Newhaven in the dark the risk of attack was too great. When the branch closed, its contents consisted of 'one counter, a Bills Box, two Brace of Pistols and a pair of Saddlebags'.[30]

The Cupar Bank closed in 1811, paying all its debts but losing money for its partners. The Fife Bank failed in 1825, but did not close its accounts until May 1829.[31] Litigation lasted until 1850 and the fourteen surviving solvent shareholders 'had paid up £5,500 on each share, in addition to the original £50'. Andrew Christie, writer and agent for the British Linen Company, wrote to his son Charles in Bengal, in November 1826, that 'Fife has been in a sad state for these last twelve months on account of the failure of the Fife Bank', which had 'given a complete shock to credit, no person being willing now to trust his neighbour a shilling'.[32]

For much of the first two decades of the nineteenth century there were four banks or bank agencies in Cupar, compared with one in St Andrews. Also based in Cupar was the Fife Fire Insurance Company, established in 1806 with capital of £50,000.[33] Its £15 shares seem to have been quite widely owned. In December 1814 a meeting was held to discuss the founding of a 'Savings and Loan Bank'. It was established the following year by subscription, with the second minister, Laurence Adamson, as its secretary, and an office open one hour a week. This was not a rival bank, but part of a national moral campaign to encourage the working classes to save.

Some merchants and manufacturers invested in banks and insurance companies, but few not directly involved seem to have invested in industrial enterprises. David Allan, John Ferguson and James Kyd made long-term investments in Robert Tullis's Auchmuty paper mill. But other transactions appear to have been more concerned with short-term profits. In 1810 Ferguson bought 18 acres at Prinlaws, Leslie, including the spinning mill. The following year he sold part of the mill, but, in partnership with James Kyd and Andrew Christie, bought the nearby Walkerton Haugh bleachfield. He sold his remaining share of the mill two years later. Not all industrial investments were profitable. Among the debts owed to David Birrell, manufacturer, at his death in 1813, for example, was £135 'advanced ... to Mr Alexander Mitchell for carrying on a manufacturing concern, of which the deceased was to receive half of the profits but which yielded none'.[34]

Of the nine men known to have owned or held shares in the brick-works between 1764 and 1816, six, mostly merchants, had no other known investments, but the other three, John Ferguson, James Kyd and James Wilson, all writers, were part of a small group with a range of financial interests in the town and beyond. Appendix 2 tabulates the interests of this small but influential group of men, some of whom were also responsible for some of the finest architecture in Cupar, and were officers in the Cupar Volunteers. It was men such as these who were responsible for many of the economic developments in Cupar throughout the long eighteenth century. There were setbacks when one or more went bankrupt, but viable enterprises such as the brick-works seem to have continued despite several changes of ownership and management. The building of St Catherine Street (see Chapter 6), possibly the largest financial undertaking in Cupar before 1820, also survived the bankruptcy of its instigator, though it took many years to complete.

The role of the town council

'The town of Cupar is the most wealthy community in the county of Fife'. When the minister wrote this in 1793 it had probably been wishful thinking for over a century, though much depends on how wealth is defined. The annual income of Cupar in 1793 was £420, and that of Kirkcaldy only around £260. But Kirkcaldy was a port with customs revenues of £10,340 (paid to the Crown but a sign of economic prosperity). Cupar town council minutes present a succession of financial problems and setbacks, although over the long eighteenth century the town's financial situation improved. The common good consisted mostly of pasture land, mainly to the west and south-west of the town, beside the Eden and liable to flooding, or on Cupar Muir. Cupar seems to have had little or no arable land, and being inland had none of the extra income to be derived from maritime trade. Its most reliable source of income was its mills. In 1692 its 'milns, smal customes, ground annuities, and common pasturage' yielded £2,100 Scots (£175 sterling) per annum. Its regular expenditure was £1,772, or 84 per cent of income. However, if interest payments on debts were included, the fixed outgoings rose to 98 per cent of income. In 1742 the town borrowed money to pay its debts (instead of ignoring them). But national events soon disrupted commerce. In August 1746 the tacksman of customs petitioned the council, trade 'having suffered greatly this last year by the Intestine War', 'particularly on the Michaelmas market last when the rebels came into the town'. Not only did he make no money, but he incurred a loss 'through the breaking of his stands and dealls'. The fear of Highlanders seizing horses meant that no horse market was held, 'the passages [ferries] were all stopped', and fewer travellers meant that 'the consumpt of bread, ale and corns were very considerably lessened'.

In 1716 the town council complained to the Lord Lieutenant of Fife about the cost incurred during 'the late rebellion' in 'keeping guard both at Dundee water side and in this place', claiming that the town's patrimony was 'so encumbered' that street repairs were out of the question. There were ever-increasing demands for public services, but the town's income was not sufficient to finance them. Minor economies were often proposed but seldom implemented, or if they were, did not last long.

It is often claimed that during the eighteenth century corrupt burgh magistrates feued property cheaply to themselves or their friends. Cupar town council started to sell feus of Cupar Muir in 1698, but this was poor land yielding little income, and feuing was presented as encouraging enclosure and tidying up boundaries.[35] The town was scrupulous about always feuing by public roup (auction), and usually with an upset (reserve) price, but did not always manage efficiently the land it retained. In 1721, for example, it belatedly realised that many tacks (leases) had expired, and some land had been illegally sublet. In future the treasurer was to keep better records, and all roups were to be public and well advertised. In 1774 some of the town's pasture land was to be feued, in plots of between three and four acres. Feuing pasture, however, left less for communal use, at a time when the population was increasing, and soon there were complaints that the grass of the Common was being 'eat up and destroyed in spring and autumn by bestial belonging to people in the town, who had no right to pasture there, whereby the grass was rendered totally useless for pasture in the summer season'. As a result fewer cattle were sent to it, and 'the grass meall of the beasts sent was barely sufficient' to pay the common herd, so it was decided in 1786 to roup the rest of the Common and stop employing a herd.

The 'low state of the town's funds' was highlighted again in 1779, and a list of regular outgoings drawn up. Income amounted to about £272 sterling, and fixed outgoings to 83 per cent of income. This did not allow enough for 'extraordinary expenses' or the 'failure of tenants', and 'without some saving scheme bees adopted by the Council the Town must yearly contract more debt'. As a result a number of economies were implemented, such as stopping paying for the ringing of the church bell. An attempt was made to limit the amount spent on entertainment, and some charities were suspended. In 1781 the council even managed to get the provost to repay his debt to the town. But the potential for unplanned expenditure was infinite, ranging from 'the soldiers etc. who were active in the late fire' (1783) to 'new Presses for holding the Town's Records' (1784). Controlling the cost of council entertainment had always been a problem. In 1741 the election dinner, march stone inspection, and completion of repairs to the tolbooth had accounted for 13 dozen ale, 7 mutchkins of brandy, 3 bowls of rum punch, 10 bottles of rum and 29 of wine (plus a little food), at a cost of £6 11s.

Various schemes were adopted to stop matters getting worse. In November 1785, for example, it was decreed that no-one with outstanding debts to the town could bid for the tack of the customs. The building of the new parish church that same year, however, was a financial disaster for the town (see Chapter 6). In 1786 a list of income was again drawn up and suggestions made for economies. These included dispensing with both piper and bell-ringer and merging the posts with that of gaoler, being 'cautious in the annual occasional debursements', and feuing the Common Braes 'in lots for houses and gardens'. In 1798 another list was drawn up – rental of about £458, and fixed expenditure of about 61 per cent of income. On the face of it this was a considerable improvement on twenty years earlier, but the true position depended on how much of its rents the town managed to collect, and how much it owed to others.

In 1811 some of the town's tenants asked for a rebate, claiming that when they had taken on their leases there was 'a great abundance of money' due to 'the flourishing state of our manufactures and commerce', but now trade was bad and 'a general distress for want of money now prevails'. In 1819 foreign trade was stagnant and demand for manufactures very low, and 'the agricultural interest is in a languishing state'. In the second decade of the nineteenth century the town was regularly being pursued for payment of its debts, and banks were refusing to accept the town's bills. The problem was exacerbated by the town's inability to collect money owed to it, or the inability of its debtors to pay. In 1820 money owed to the town amounted to £3,510. In 1825 'it was a notorious fact that the debts of the Town were every year increasing while the rental was decreasing'.

A new source of income from the late eighteenth century was the sale of annuities. It was a gamble, but it yielded cash in hand. The first approach was made in 1785 by 'a lady in town', who wished to lend £150 in exchange for an annuity. In 1808 the postmaster's widow wished to invest £200. She 'had advertised her intention in the Newspapers and had received different offers'. The highest was £42 per annum; she was seventy-seven and 'would prefer the security of the Town of Cupar to an individual'. The town agreed to pay £40 a year in two instalments, and after that annuities became a regular feature, accounting for annual expenditure of £269 by 1820.

There were very few financial high-points. The first was the payment of the Equivalent in 1708,[36] but unfortunately that just prompted a number of the town's creditors to come forward to demand payment. In 1791 the mills were feued. Much to the council's surprise, the purchaser paid in full and on time. They lodged most of the money with an Edinburgh bank, which paid 4 per cent interest, while looking for people prepared to borrow at 4½ per cent. The town at various times considered or adopted schemes to improve its property and therefore its finances. In 1718 the tacksman of the coal at Charleton, near Colinsburgh, was 'of opinion that there is a coal in Cupar Muir' and offered to do 'experiments to find out' at a cost not exceeding £100 Scots (£8 6s 8d), and the council agreed that work should go ahead. The bill, finally presented in 1722, was £33 16s 8d. No coal was found, but the prospect remained alluring, and there were further attempts in 1732 and 1765. Gradually the council seems to have preferred to feu some of its assets for ready cash, or arrange annuities and other loans, rather than undertake practical schemes which involved capital expenditure.

By the end of the eighteenth century wartime inflation was becoming a problem. In January 1797, for example, Robert Wiseman, English teacher, asked for a rise in his salary because of 'the great rise of every necessary of life, which is nearly doubled' since he came to Cupar in 1785. In 1799 the guildry officer pointed out that his dues had not risen 'for a century back', and hoped for 'an augmentation'. In 1806 the town officers petitioned for salary increases 'more especially as the prices of necessaries are very much advanced'. No source suggests that Cupar did not feel the effects of the economic booms and recessions felt by the whole of Britain, though it does not seem to have experienced some of the more dramatic consequences such as riots. By the end of the eighteenth century the economies of communities all over Britain were no longer so fragile. After the 1720s Cupar, despite its problems, was never at serious risk of bankruptcy, and by the early nineteenth century was increasingly able, despite its debts, to finance some of the public services demanded by both residents and visitors.

The linen industry made an early start, faltered, but recovered momentum, showing a greater increase in production in the last quarter of the eighteenth century than Scotland in general. Other industrial enterprises flourished in the town, mainly due to a few 'able, energetic, and public-spirited' individuals.[37] Various sources, both contemporary and modern, have suggested reasons for the failure of Cupar, and particularly its linen industry, to develop after 1820. These are threefold. The first is that the industry was undercapitalised. George Moon of Russell's Mill in 1823 said that, 'there is probably less Capital in Cupar and its immediate Vicinity, in the Linen Trade, than in any other Part of Scotland', because 'the Way in which the Trade is carried on requires little or no Capital, and it is reduced so low in Profits that no Capitalist would engage in it'. The system could survive on credit provided the linen produced could be sold quickly.[38] It is clear from other sources that some manufacturers were undercapitalised. In 1803, for example, John Walker of Blebo Mills had to borrow his fare to Liverpool from James Wilson.

The second reason suggested is that Cupar was too dependent on coarse linen. Any town whose industry had to bear the added cost of transport to and from the coast had to offer something extra to justify its prices being higher than those of competitors nearer the coast. Forfar was further from the sea, and further from coal supplies, which delayed the introduction of steam power, even though, as in Cupar, the available water power was less than ideal. Like Cupar, it concentrated on the weaving of coarse linen, and its population grew even faster during the second half of the eighteenth century. William Don, one of the town's main manufacturers, seems to have survived by concentrating on quality, by becoming a shareholder in a shipping company and by building close contacts with London merchants. Though none of these measures stopped him going bankrupt in 1817, the family continued in business. There is no evidence that his contemporaries in Cupar took such sensible measures.

The third reason seems to have been that while there were several successful manufacturers, there were few if any large merchants. For many centuries royal burghs such as Cupar had been dominated by merchants. The long eighteenth century saw the decline in influence, if not in numbers, of merchants, and the rise of financiers, most of whom were writers. Lawyers had for a long time acted as financial intermediaries before the development of formal banking. This in the short term helped merchants to expand, but in Cupar the development seems to have gone so far that the lawyers took over from the merchants. Dealing and speculation were carried out by lawyers, who in general invested in banks and insurance companies, or land, rather than manufacturing industry.

Cupar, like most towns, ended the long eighteenth century with an economy more stable and more flexible than in 1700. Towns provided a regular pattern of work compared with rural areas, while the gradual weakening of the closed system of burgess-entry helped stimulate development. In addition, Cupar, unlike many burghs, did not face competition from any neighbouring burgh of barony. But change was inevitable. The need for water-power had meant that mills were often established 'in the most inland parts of the county, remote from a sea port, and with all the inconveniences of long carriages, bad roads, and scanty population'. Changing to steam power, however, meant that factories could be built 'in any populous town or village, where there is a shipping port, or where hands can be got in plenty, and at easier wages'. Cupar was too small, and too far from the coast, to be a natural place for industry to develop.

Secondary exchange had continued throughout the period but did not expand in the way contemporary commentators hoped, because Cupar's hinterland was shrinking. The north-coast parishes were increasingly looking to Dundee for employment and markets. The south-western parishes may similarly have come within the orbit of Kirkcaldy. St Andrews was also growing faster than Cupar, and overtook it by 1861. Perhaps because of its position as the county town, Cupar was determinedly independent, in an age when the small towns which grew most were often those which were satellites of larger towns or cities. Both local banks may have failed, but they were important symbols of the development of Cupar as a financial as well as a legal centre for Fife. The long eighteenth century saw Cupar changing from a traditional market town to a financial centre dealing in goods which did not necessarily ever physically pass through the town; from a town run by merchants to a town run by bankers. But it is possible that the leading part played by lawyers in the economic life of this small town acted in the long term as a hindrance to development.

Notes

1. Gradually during this period animal markets were moved out of the centre of town for reasons of nuisance and public safety.

2. Thomson, *Agriculture of Fife*, 297. Candlemas, 1st Weds in Feb (3rd Thurs in Feb); March, 1st Thurs (2nd Thurs); Pasch/Lintseed, 1st Weds (2nd Thurs) in April; Tenth O'May (1st Thurs in May); Whit, last Weds in May (1st Thurs in June); St James, 25 July (1st Thurs in Aug); Michaelmas, 1st Thurs in Oct, moved 11 days later in 1752 (2nd Thurs in Oct); Martinmas, 11 Nov (2nd Thurs); Yule (1st Thurs in Jan). In 1825 farmers petitioned for all fairs to be held on Thursdays, and on 5 June 1827, to achieve this and to avoid confusion between Old and New Style dates the dates of the fairs were fixed as shown in brackets.

3. The following year the dean of guild and his assessor claimed they were attacked 'in a most violent and riotous manner' by the bailies and councillors of Auchtermuchty. Harassment continued in subsequent years, and in 1729 it was agreed to collect money 'from the haill inhabitants' of Cupar to finance action in the court of session (NAS CS 234 L5/28, the dispute was related to wider local politics – see chapter 9). In 1776 Auchtermuchty bought the right of inspecting its own market. By the 1790s the weekly market had been discontinued, though four fairs were still held, including in July 'one of the most considerable in Fife, for the sale of black cattle, horses, sheep, wool etc'.

4. Ceres had two fairs in the 1790s, the June one 'one of the principal markets for cattle in the county'; Falkland had a weekly market and four fairs 'now increased to six', where 'very considerable numbers' of horses and black cattle were traded; Leuchars had two fairs in April and October; Letham one in June.

5. Some shops had specialised interior fittings, *Fife Herald,* 6 Jan and 24 Feb 1825, for example, one shop was advertised as a 'cabinet wareroom', and another as 'fitted up as haberdasher and clothier'.

6. NAS GD164/454, declared bankrupt in 1818, his main creditor was a merchant in Edinburgh.

7. NAS SC20/5/35, Brown to Young & Trotter, 16 Sept 1772 and 2 June 1773, 'The fellow went off both with my money & your goods. I never will pay that article unless I be oblidged by Law. For I am Certain that not a man in great Britain would pay it were he in my place'.

8. The four partners were John Riddell of Grange, Alexander Melville of Balgarvie, Andrew Douglas and David Rutherford, both merchants in Cupar. It probably used the more expensive but better quality Dutch system of bleaching.

9. NAS GD242/40/9, it was proposed to pay both the clerk, Alexander Barclay, and the master bleacher, David Barclay, reduced salaries because of the company's losses. Dr George Bethune argued that the company should be wound up, as it had run its intended nine years, 'to the great loss and prejudice of most of the proprietors'. But the majority voted to continue.

10. No payments for bleachfields in Cupar were recorded between 1756 and 1772.

11. There were also stamp offices in Kettle, Crail and Elie in 1766, and Pittenweem in 1772.

12. In 1775 the Trustees gave £20 to Catherine Maxwell, threadmaker; in 1785, Mrs Lethangie (Jean Wright) was provided with a 'hand Machine for Spinning Cotton'; in 1793 Marcia Wiseman was allowed £12 to buy a twisting mill and 'necessary utensils' for thread making.

13. *Rudiman's Weekly Mercury*; the places in Fife were Kirkcaldy, Dysart, Elie, Barnyards (near Kilconquhar), St Monans, Pittenweem, Crail, Anstruther, Kingsbarns, St Andrews, Leuchars, Ferry-Port-on-Craig (Tayport), Dundee, Falkland, Leslie and Balbirnie Bridge (near Markinch).

14. Osnaburgh linen was often used by upholsterers. When a chair made by Thomas Chippendale junior in London around 1815 was stripped prior to restoration, on the inner linen cover was found the stamp 'Alex Wilkie, Cupar-Fife' (Fig. 4.1).

15. He also named John Webster, Alexander Young and James Preston who 'deals very extensively in yarn, and employs a considerable number of spinners all along the east coast of Fife, as well as inland'.

16. NAS AD58/339, sequestration of Ebenezer Anderson, 1829. This was a period when the South American market opened up, and many people rushed in, most of them unsuccessfully.

17. Dundee had 113, Arbroath 49, Dunfermline 47, Forfar 30, Kirriemuir 26 and Cupar 24.

18. NAS CS96/707.

19. In 1801 the company was run by William Anderson, William Geddie and David Birrell; in 1802 it was sold to Robert Geddie, who sold it in 1809 to John Adamson, Alexander Goodsir and George Landale. After they went bankrupt it was sold in 1812 to John Galloway, then to Andrew Christie (NAS CS96/692/2) who had been one of the trustees for the creditors. The firm was still trading as Goodsir, Adamson & Co in 1820.

20. The leather produced was mainly for shoes, saddles and harnesses, and was sold 'in the neighbouring towns and country, in the north of Scotland, in Perth, Glasgow, Edinburgh, and occasionally in London'. By 1800 there were also tanneries in Auchtermuchty and Falkland.

21. Further Turnpike Acts for Fife were passed in 1797, 1802, 1805, 1807, 1809, 1810 and 1829.

22. Keddie, *Three Generations*, 68–69.

23. NAS GD164/897, 'Petition of Alexander McNab of the Tontine Tavern, Cupar, to the Noblemen and Gentlemen Proprietors of that Property'.

24. The Commercial Bank opened an office in 1810, and the National Bank in 1825.

25. NAS GD26/12/28. Hardcastle, *Life of Lord Campbell*; 32, Gray, son of a Cupar schoolmaster, 'had been in the profession, now obsolete, of travelling tutor, who had repeatedly made the grand tour with young English noblemen', and his last pupil had arranged for him the post of 'Secretary to the Lottery, with handsome apartments in Somerset House'.

26. This was a year in which a number of other local banks in Scotland were founded.

27. NAS IRS 1/1, a list of forty-two shareholders when the bank closed in 1825 included four writers, two clergymen and one accountant from Cupar.

28. BS (BL) 6/6/8, 15 Mar 1802; NAS GD26/5/726/5; David Allan in 1816 was also involved in one of Cupar's two tanneries. The Cupar Bank was managed

by Ferguson's father-in-law, Robert Geddie (who had just been removed as agent by the Bank of Scotland).

29. James Wilson held at least five shares in the Fife Bank from its foundation, and paid John Ferguson £500 for one share in the Cupar Bank in 1807. In 1812–13 Wilson was involved in fitting out the offices of the Commercial Bank, buying desks and two iron columns.

30. Horsburgh's other failings included conducting the bank business in the same room as all his other activities, which the bank did not regard as satisfactory, so in 1810 they paid for a separate office.

31. RBS, Minutes of National Bank of Scotland, I, 1825/26, 378; the British Linen Company came to its aid, to avoid 'creating that alarm which would have arisen from ... stopping payment'.

32. NAS CS96/692/3. Similar references to the effects of the Fife Bank failure can be found in other memoirs.

33. Several provincial insurance companies were established at this time. The Fife Fire Insurance Company was wound up in 1834.

34. NAS CC20/7/7 700–01.

35. Feuing was very profitable in the short term, yielding a one-off payment plus continuing rental income, but in the long term inflation reduced the value of the rent.

36. The Act of Union included the payment to Scotland of the 'Equivalent', mainly in compensation for losses incurred by the Darien disaster.

37. *Fifeshire Journal*, 15 Sept 1859, 4; obituary of John Ferguson.

38. NAS NG1/64/38, pp.38–39. He also said 'In Kirkcaldy, it is impossible for any Man to carry on Business without having a very considerable Capital, or a very considerable Credit, because the Yarns require a longer Progress, and the Goods have not such a regular Sale'.

5

The World of Work

Until the end of the eighteenth century almost everyone in Cupar, whatever his or her status or occupation, lived close together within the old town (Plate 2), and was woken by the communal alarm call of the town piper.[1] But economic changes during the period affected the occupational structure of the town and the working lives of its inhabitants. Like many other Scottish and English towns, Cupar saw a growth in the professions, increasing specialisation within occupations, the decline of some long-established industries, rapid expansion of the linen industry, and new jobs in transport, hospitality and domestic service. This chapter looks at working men (and occasionally women) during the long eighteenth century in four categories: professionals; guildbrethren; members of the incorporated trades; and other workers. The evidence is mainly derived from the author's database, with information on 3,513 working men and 523 women. Fig. 5.1 shows the distribution of identified working men, by decade, and a suitable fraction of these totals is used in subsequent graphs as a control line, helping to distinguish between genuine long-term trends, and fluctuations due to the erratic nature of the evidence. Appendix 3 contains the occupational data on which this chapter is based. The sources for women are so fragmentary that no chronological analysis has been attempted. It must always be borne in mind how incomplete the evidence is, and how subjective its interpretation.

The professions

The professional class in Cupar consisted of doctors, lawyers, ministers and teachers. The number of ministers was small. There were two incumbents of the parish church, the first minister having a higher status and a larger stipend. There was no manse – each man rented a suitable property. At the beginning of the century ministers were often from the landed classes. But later incumbents were mostly sons of ministers, the majority educated at St Andrews University. From the mid-eighteenth

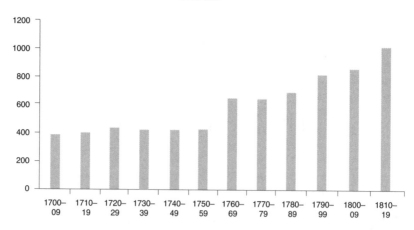

FIGURE 5.1   Chronological distribution of identified working men in the burgh,
1700–1819.

century there was also a growing number of nonconformist ministers.
By the early nineteenth century a few ministers were investing in local
banks and insurance companies. Laurence Adamson, second minister,
was involved in various financial deals and, despite having married an
heiress, went bankrupt in 1827. Teachers, like ministers, were often
appointed from other parts of Scotland, though generally from the east
rather than the west. There were usually three at the grammar school,
increased to five with the establishment of an academy in 1823, but by
the early nineteenth century there was also a growing number of private
teachers.

Lawyers, as now, represented clients in the local criminal and civil
courts, bought and sold property, and drew up and executed wills.
Some acted as agents for landed gentry and clerks for public bodies and
the growing number of other organisations such as the hunt and the
subscription library. Some held appointments such as procurator fiscal,
town or sheriff clerk, notary public, messenger at arms, collector of
cess, or surveyor of window tax. After 1790 ten writers (lawyers) were
also described as bankers. Writers had a wide network of contacts, and
often acted as links between the town, the county gentry and the wider
world, both political and financial. One example is the correspondence
which survives between Henry Walker, writer in Cupar, and Henry
Dundas in London. As well as writers and their apprentices and clerks,
there were also several advocates and Writers to the Signet, who
worked in Edinburgh but had close links with Cupar, or who served as
sheriffs-depute or substitute. There was a dramatic increase in lawyers
and trainees around 1810, presumably due to the building boom,
the growth of banking, and a general increase in disposable income,

creating more work related to property and inheritance. Perhaps the buoyant economy led to over-supply, and recession after 1815 caused a reduction in their numbers, as well as several bankruptcies.

Many writers served a local apprenticeship, usually between three and four years, and a clerkship for another two or three. Others perhaps worked in family offices without ever being described as a trainee. At the end of their training they would apply to the sheriff for permission to represent clients in his court. A few men did not progress from traineeship to become writers. It is not clear whether this was because of lack of intellect, ambition, social status, or capital. Some, such as James Carstairs, later town clerk, went straight from grammar school to an apprenticeship at the age of about fifteen. For others, such as James Kyd, there seems to be a gap between leaving the Latin school and being first recorded as an apprentice, but no evidence has been found for any writer attending university.

By the 1820s most legal trainees seem to have left Cupar, while writers trained elsewhere set up there. Presumably it was while serving as clerks in Edinburgh that contacts were made and career paths defined. William Drummond, for example, was educated at Leuchars parish school, served a four-year apprenticeship in Falkland, then worked as a clerk in Edinburgh before setting up in Cupar in 1815. William Pagan served his apprenticeship in Dumfries before coming to Cupar in 1826. The inventories of ten lawyers survive (Appendix 4). Three include significant collections of books, mainly legal. Testaments and inventories also provide information about wealth at the time of death.

TABLE 5.1 Surviving evidence for the financial assets of some Cupar lawyers (£ sterling)

	Date	Investments	Personal property	Total value of estate at death	Source (NAS)
John Thomson	1689			4	CC20/4/15
John Malcolm	1709			36	CC20/4/18
Andrew Glasford	1710		16		CC20/4/17
James Spens	1711		4	7	CC20/4/17
William Bevereidge	1749			207?	SC20/27/1
Thomas Thomson	1751		12	16	CC20/6/30
Primrose Rymer	1779			16	CC20/4/24
John Stevenson	1795		105		CC20/6/66
David Tod	1812	4,714	296	5,363	CC20/7/5
Robert Johnston	1812		403	1,127	CC20/7/7
Henry Walker	1818	786	470	1,286	CC20/7/10
Andrew Christie	1827	22,500	6,550	bankrupt	CS96/692/1
James Kyd	1827			bankrupt	CS230 seq

Table 5.1 shows a dramatic increase in the wealth of Cupar writers after
c.1800. Some were over-ambitious, and some were unlucky, caught up
in the domino effect of bankruptcies. Between 1815 and 1830 almost
all the leading lawyers in Cupar went bankrupt except for the sheriff
clerk and the town clerk. Many lawyers were active in local politics,
with lawyer-provosts for twenty-eight years between 1781 and 1827.
As the home of the sheriff court, Cupar served as the legal centre for the
county. The *Old Statistical Account* noted one writer in Auchtermuchty,
one in Crail, one in Kilconquhar, and five in St Andrews, compared
with twelve in Cupar, plus twenty clerks and apprentices. In the parish
of Moonzie there was 'no occasion for any lawyer, attorney, physician,
or surgeon ... as the town of Cupar supplies its environs with legal and
medical aid'.

Traditionally in Scotland physicians, who treated internal ailments,
were more respectable than surgeons, who treated external damage
such as wounds, broken bones and skin diseases, and extracted teeth.
During the seventeenth and eighteenth centuries the status of the
surgeon rose until it equalled that of the physician. Over the same
period the less-qualified surgeon/barbers and surgeon/apothecaries
disappeared. The latest record of an apothecary in Cupar was 1726,
and of a surgeon-apothecary, 1762; after 1814 druggists appear. Two
doctors also served as postmaster, and James Dempster was physician,
druggist, house painter and organiser of illuminations for special public
occasions. The practice of medicine often ran in families. Seven Cupar
doctors were probably sons of doctors; other fathers included two
ministers, two writers and a teacher. They were all fairly local until
the early nineteenth century, by which time doctors were coming to
the town to fill perceived vacancies created by death or retirement.
The *Dundee Advertiser* in 1814 commented that after the death of Dr
Grace, 'no fewer than four physicians or surgeons are on the point of
commencing the practice of the healing art in Cupar'.[2]

In the first half of the eighteenth century most seem to have received
their training by apprenticeship. In 1740, for example, George Makgill
of Kemback was bound to James Rigg for four years, during which he
agreed not to 'Reveall or Devulge any of his said master or Patients
Secrets Intrusted to him'. George Bethune, however, son of a local
physician, was described in 1730 as a 'Student of Medecine', who for
his 'Improvement in the Science of Physick' was 'designing to go abroad
to take the several Colleges proper to fit and qualifie' him.[3] From the
1760s the initials MD appear after the names of ten physicians. The
first, Robert Menzies, gained his MD at St Andrews by examination in
1760, and in 1770 was short-listed for the post of professor of medicine.
The later MDs would mostly have been acquired from St Andrews by
submission of references and payment of a fee, after years of successful
practice. By the early nineteenth century at least six Cupar doctors

had received a formal university training, two at St Andrews, three at Edinburgh and one in Dublin. Charles Grace junior not only trained at Edinburgh University, but is described as a physician whereas his father, also Charles, with no formal training, was described as a surgeon. These two epitomise the changes taking place in the medical profession in the early nineteenth century. Both, however, had purchased MDs.[4] The Fife Chirugico-Medical Society was formed in 1825. By this date there was also a dentist who visited the town.[5]

Some inventories include medical equipment. Andrew Scott, surgeon (1769), possessed two mortars, a plaster pan, 'a parcel of drug pipes and bottles', two small scales and weights, a *History of Surgery*, Cockburn's *Gonorrhoea*, and Monro's *Anatomy*. As well as having to purchase instruments and books, most doctors would have kept a horse to visit rural patients. George Bethune, physician (1775), left a chaise and three horses, and James Hislop (1783) a saddle, bridle, whip and spurs.[6] Cupar doctors served quite a wide rural hinterland. In the *Old Statistical Account* none of the surrounding rural parishes had doctors, while Cupar had five, and four midwives.[7] Bethune's inventory included a list of money owed to him, amounting to £313 1s 8d sterling. Most of these 493 patients lived in Cupar or adjacent parishes, but some as far afield as Auchtermuchty, Balmerino, Leven and Strathmiglo, though there is no evidence as to whether he travelled to them or they called on him in Cupar. The amounts owed ranged between 1s 6d and over £8, and his patients covered the entire social spectrum from the Earl of Crawford to domestic servants. Dr Bethune was also active on the town council, serving as provost for eight years. His partner, Robert Arnot, surgeon and landed proprietor, was a councillor for thirty-eight years. Most doctors seem to have made a comfortable living, and, perhaps because the growth of the profession in the early nineteenth century was not as dramatic as that of the writers, no Cupar doctor is known to have become bankrupt.

The inventory of one midwife survives. She was comfortably off, though this may be because she was the widow of a merchant. Her inventory contains nothing specifically medical, but includes a large number of coats and cloaks, and a 'riding skirt', suggesting that she, like the doctors, travelled on horseback to visit patients outwith the town. She would have had to go out in all weathers, and was the second recorded person in Cupar to own an umbrella. Given the lack of any hospital in Fife, it might seem unlikely that local midwives received any formal training. But Janet Scott, another merchant's wife, who set up as a midwife in 1822 after her husband's bankruptcy, advertised in the *Fife Herald* that she had 'been regularly educated by Dr Hamilton of the University of Edinburgh, whose certificate is in her possession'. By the time midwives began to gain formal qualifications, men were moving into this traditionally female role, in line with enlightenment theory of replacing folk medicine with science. In 1825 James Moffat 'surgeon and accoucheur' announced in the *Fife Herald* that he was setting up in the town.

Towards the end of the long eighteenth century a few men had other occupations which could be described as professional, including three land surveyors (from 1770), and four auctioneers (all after 1800). Almost all those involved in the growing world of banking and insurance were already writers, but the early nineteenth century saw the first professional accountant. David Mitchell, son-in-law of a Cupar merchant, spent seven or eight years as a merchant's clerk in London before settling in Cupar as an accountant in the Commercial Bank. Apart from one period of political unrest in the early 1720s, teachers and ministers seem to have kept out of local politics. Lawyers and doctors, however, did not. Unlike larger towns where there were incorporations of surgeons and physicians, in Cupar they had no separate organisation, but were welcome to join the guildry if they wished to serve on the council.

Guildbrethren

The distinction between guildry and trades was not related to social status, degree of training or amount of capital needed. It was simply that only guildbrethren could handle imported goods. Merchants bought and sold anything; tradesmen made and sold goods from raw materials which if not local, such as spices and dried fruit for the baxters, had to be bought from merchants. Tradesmen who wished to buy direct from merchants outwith Cupar had to pay to join the guildry. Any tradesman could join the guildry, but was expected only to be active in one organisation. Some joined the guildry in order to buy imported goods direct, but took no active part in guildry affairs, while others, though still carrying on their trade, joined the guildry and served on the town council. Records of burgess tickets and guildry membership are fragmentary, though membership can be assumed when a man held office. As well as merchants, others who were expected to belong to the guildry because they dealt in imported goods included vintners and innkeepers, barbers and wig-makers, and dyers.

Merchants faced a period of change during the eighteenth century. They had increasingly to defend themselves against challenges to their privileges by 'unfree traders' (non-burgesses, who paid no local taxes and therefore had lower overheads), and at the same time were developing more specialised roles. It is not clear how closed the merchant class was. It was claimed by a hostile witness in the burgh court in 1749 that it hardly ever admitted outsiders, and that whereas all craftsmen had to serve time training and learning their trade, 'any person of common sense without undergoing a regular apprenticeship may deal in paper, indigo, pens and other small branches of merchandise', and few Cupar merchants served apprenticeships, but learned by experience 'while they travelled with goods through the country'. The change from merchant to shopkeeper, and the usurpation of some merchant roles by writers, was noted in the previous chapter. Specialist descriptions of merchants include forty-eight grocers (from 1770), fourteen tobacconists (one also a snuff-maker), nine drapers, six hatters, six ironmongers (from 1794), six 'shopkeepers' (from 1792), four confectioners, four spirit-dealers, four haberdashers (from 1818), two corn merchants, two earthenware dealers, two leather merchants, a book-agent, a linen dealer, a nurseryman, a porter merchant, a salt merchant and a seedsman. Candlemaking seems until about 1760 to have been a separate trade, but after that the merchant guild included four candlemakers. Occupations carried on concurrently by merchants included vintners, brewers, manufacturers (from the 1770s), weavers, bankers, dyers, writers, baxters, tailors, a flax-dresser, a hosier, a tanner and an umbrella-maker. Some held posts such as keeper of the correction house, guildry officer, postmaster, stampmaster, or tacksman of customs. Some merchants' wives clearly played a part in their husbands' businesses or ran related enterprises. In 1822 James Staig, merchant, was working as a 'painter, gilder, and paper-hanger', while his wife advertised in the *Fife Herald* a shop selling glass and stoneware. There are records of twenty-seven women merchants, ranging in date from two cadgers in 1711 to several shopkeepers in the 1825 trades directory.

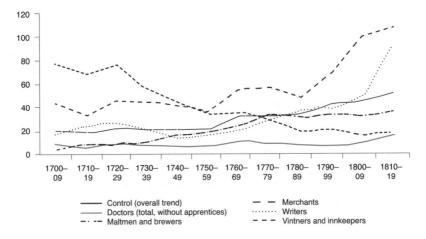

FIGURE 5.2 Changing numbers of doctors, writers, maltmen and innkeepers, 1700–1819.

Perhaps the dominant group in seventeenth-century Cupar had been the maltmen and brewers (the terms were interchangeable). Their numbers declined gradually during the first half of the eighteenth century, and thereafter rapidly, presumably because the brewing process had become more industrialised. The inventories of five brewers or maltmen survive. Robert Philp (1742), for example, left wort buckets and other brewing tools, a cart and horses. There are records of eight female brewers. As the numbers of maltmen and brewers decreased, the numbers of vintners and innkeepers increased (Fig. 5.2). Several of the innkeepers hired out horses or chaises, and there were also nine horse-hirers, seven stablers, five horse-dealers and a breaker of horses. Jobs held at the same time as innkeeper included merchants, manufacturers, carriers, writers, a coachmaker, a shoemaker and a wright.

Many soldiers were billeted in Cupar, and several left the army, married local women (sometimes the widows or daughters of inn-keepers), and set up as innkeepers. John Hislop (1770), almost certainly a former excise officer who married locally, had a house with five rooms containing ten beds, fifty-one chairs, twelve tables, six candlesticks and four pewter chamber pots. John Anderson (1775) had a smaller house, with only one bed, but eighteen chairs and two oak tables, one of them large. He had eight candlesticks, 'a Dozen China Cups and Saucers of different Sorts some Cracked', earthenware, stoneware and pewter dishes for serving food and plenty of drinking vessels. But the main proof that this was an inn is probably the 'China punch bowl and three delph ones all crack'd'. Private houses rarely had more than one punch bowl. Bartholomew Cockburn (1795) was also an incomer. Both his wives were from innkeeping families, and his widow continued to run the business after his death. In ten rooms and garret he had fourteen tables, thirty chairs and four forms, eight beds and large amounts of damaged crockery and glass. He had eleven candlesticks, five coffee pots, thirteen 'Dalcanters', seven meat covers, five china and three stoneware punch bowls, forty-two dram glasses and over a hundred plates. Entertainment was provided with a card table and a 'Backgammond Table', and he had a chaise for hire. His stock included gin and whisky. His inn, the Blue Bell, seems to have been the best in town, having several bedrooms with carpets and one with curtains and washing facilities.

As well as greater numbers of some items, vintners' inventories show other differences from domestic contexts (see Chapter 7). There was a high proportion of relatively hard-wearing and cheap items, such as spoons of pewter and tin rather than silver, and plates and bowls of stoneware rather than earthenware or china. There are records of twenty female vintners or innkeepers, at least eight of them widows of innkeepers, and the inventories of two of them survive. Katherine Ross (1797), had twenty-five chairs, eighteen stone plates, fifteen decanters and three punch bowls. Mary Anderson (1797), former innkeeper, and mother-in-law of Bartholomew Cockburn, left five decanters, twenty-one horn spoons and three punch ladles. Some of the best inns seem to have been run by women. When it is recorded where the town council held its annual election dinner, in twenty-five years out of sixty it was held at an inn run by a woman.[8] Mrs Cockburn's was also the venue for meetings of the council sub-committee in the second decade of the nineteenth century. Even presbytery meetings were sometimes held in inns. Innkeepers were central to the development of leisure in towns, and their social status grew as they provided increasingly elaborate travel and entertainment facilities, as well as accommodation.

Dyers were normally members of the guildry, as were barbers and wigmakers. Both occupations declined in the second half of the century (wigs went out of fashion c.1770). There were other workers of whom a proportion but not a majority can be shown to have been members of the guildry. This may be because by the time the occupation became common the power of the guildry was waning – as, for example, booksellers. Alternatively it may be because only certain individuals within that occupation were dealing with imported goods. Only a few gardeners, for example, sold seeds. But there was a third group, including carriers and labourers, who seem to have belonged to the guildry because it gave them the freedom to handle imported goods when the situation arose. In Edinburgh, by contrast, gardeners, candlemakers and tanners, though not incorporated trades, regarded themselves as craftsmen, as did stablers.

The incorporated trades

The order of ranking of the eight trades – smiths, wrights, weavers, waulkers, tailors, shoemakers, baxters and fleshers – may be due, as in other towns, to the order in which the incorporations were founded, but it does appear also to reflect a natural hierarchy based on the degree of skill and training needed.[9] The trades divide into four pairs: smiths and wrights, including all the building and fabrication trades, and perhaps the most skilled; weavers and waulkers, producing linen and woollen cloth; tailors and shoemakers, making clothing and footwear; and baxters and fleshers, producing food. The purpose of the burgess system was protection from competition, self-regulation of quality and quantity, and in some cases sharing of communal facilities such as shambles or waulkmills. There was no need for incorporations for trades which were so small that they were naturally regulated by the law of supply and demand, such as potters or thatchers.

It has generally been assumed that achievement of the status of a master craftsman, signified by becoming a burgess, was the natural end-product of apprenticeship and work as a journeyman. But in Cupar, where a man trained under and then worked for a close family member, it seems to have been felt that there was no point in more than one member of the family becoming a burgess, and many only became burgesses just before or just after the death of another family member in the same trade. The only reason for a junior member of a family business becoming a burgess was if he had political ambitions, and if so he often entered less than a week, sometimes only a few hours, before being elected a deacon. A few men became burgesses in more than one town. Two Cupar saddlers, for example, joined the St Andrews hammermen in 1784.

The training structure in such a small town seems to have been quite loose. There are some records of formal apprenticeships, but others seem to have trained informally among family or friends.[10] The description 'journeyman' appears infrequently. More common is 'servant' or 'servitor', which, when relating to tradesmen, almost always appears to mean paid help with work rather than the family, in effect a journeyman. To become a burgess before the age of twenty-one was not uncommon, though theoretically impossible within the formal training structure. In Edinburgh the distinction between apprentice and journeymen was becoming blurred by the eighteenth century. In Dundee journeymen were fewer and therefore less organised and powerful than in larger cities; in Cupar apparently even less so. One wright was a burgess in Cupar but 'works as a journeyman in Edinburgh all the year round, except about a fortnight, when he comes over to Cupar to serve a job'.[11] The only large groups of journeymen were those in weaving sheds. One manufacturer in 1803 employed twenty journeymen weavers.[12] In other trades, however, things were less clear, though the journeymen shoemakers were organised enough to join a national strike in 1825. It is not clear how far Cupar served as a training centre for the surrounding area. There are references in the Old Statistical Account to apprentices and journeymen in neighbouring parishes, and to young people going to Dundee and Perth 'to learn handicraft trades'.

Many burgess tickets were dispensed. Some were awarded to legal and military figures whom the magistrates of a county town felt obliged to honour. There was also wastage through death or emigration. It is impossible, given the limitations of the surviving evidence, to calculate the proportion of the male working population which held burgess tickets. But a strong impression is gained that by the early nineteenth century there was both an increase in occupations outwith the traditional incorporations, and an increasing number of men who deliberately chose not to become burgesses. And it is clear from council and burgh court records that, as happened in England slightly earlier, the trades found it increasingly difficult to protect their privileges, and eventually the possession of a burgess ticket and membership of a trade become optional, unless one had political ambitions.

General blacksmithing and building trades were provided in a number of the smaller communities around Cupar, whereas for the more specialised trades such as saddlery, and the top end of the clothing and footwear market, Cupar may have served quite a large hinterland. The only period for which there is direct evidence is the 1790s, when the *Old Statistical Account* provides comparative data for a few parishes. In Ceres the minister noted that the inhabitants were 'supplied with butcher meat from Cupar'. Cupar had more of every trade per head of population than the surrounding area, including the larger town of St Andrews, and this would suggest a specialist market. St Andrews had one saddler, for example, whereas Cupar had five. And as well as thirty-four tailors, Cupar offered two hatters, six milliners and ten mantua makers.

Smiths (Fig. 5.3) included thirty-one saddlers, fifteen clock or watch makers, nine blacksmiths, seven tinsmiths, five cutlers, four farriers, three gunsmiths, three pewterers, two ironmongers, two jewellers, a lorimer and a nail-maker. Rachel Robertson, the widow of a nail-maker, was described as a tinsmith.[13] Two female smiths in the 1820s were widows carrying on their husbands' saddlery businesses. The smith trade did not increase as fast as other occupations, particularly after the 1790s, whereas the wright trade grew faster, particularly from the 1760s. Wrights included all those who worked in stone or wood. Within the building trade this included one hundred and thirteen masons, eighteen slaters, sixteen plasterers, nine glaziers, two builders, one architect and one harler. Another group was the thirty-four millwrights (by the 1820s some were called 'engineers'), and other specialisations included cabinet-makers (a few also described as upholsterers), coopers, wheelwrights, sawyers, sievewrights, carpenters, coachwrights, a cartwright, a highway-maker, a quarrier and a joiner. Several men were identified by more than one of these descriptions, for example 'mason and slater', 'cooper and wheelwright', 'cabinet-maker and upholsterer'. The mainstay of most of the general wrights was the funeral business, making coffins and sometimes offering other related services such as the provision of drink.

The inventories of five wrights survive. William Baldie (1779) left saws, a rabbet- and three sash-planes, a glue pot, a brace and bits, a plasterer's trowel, augers, an adze and an axe. David Greig (1787) left a stock of glass, mirrors, tin foil (for lining tea caddies), leaf gold and wallpaper; and saws, and astragal-, rabbet-, sash- and 'picture frame' planes, most of which were bought at his roup by other wrights. He seems to have framed pictures and mirrors, and made small items such as tea caddies and dressing glasses, and possibly also windows. William Cockburn, cabinet-maker (1819), was the son of an innkeeper who owned a hearse, so perhaps undertaking was a family enterprise, with

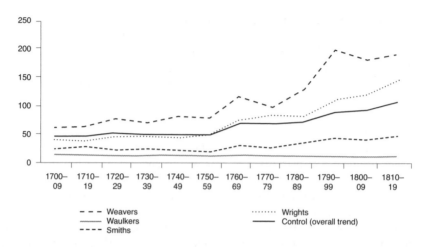

FIGURE 5.3   Changing numbers of smiths, wrights, weavers and walkers, 1700–1819.

the son making the coffin and the father providing refreshments and transport.

The job of weaver changed over time. Some became employers, or 'manufacturers', some remained independent hand-loom weavers and some worked for manufacturers, either from home or in a loom-shed. Fifty-two weavers were also described as manufacturers; a few others were described as merchants, labourers, brewers, innkeepers, a bleacher, a carrier, a heckler, a mason and a wright. Several held official posts such as beadle, bellringer, drummer, gaoler, keeper of the town clock, precentor and town officer.[14] There were also a number of weavers who changed occupations. Some did well and became merchants or ran inns; others became soldiers or labourers. The inventories of two weavers survive, demonstrating that the capital investment needed in tools and materials was less than for some other trades.

Fig. 5.3 contrasts the growth in numbers of weavers, peaking in the 1790s, with the decline of the waulker trade (processing woollen cloth). At least some of them worked at the town's waulkmills, outside the town. The numbers of waulkers were particularly low because, in contrast with other burghs, the trade did not generally include dyers, who in Cupar were members of the guildry.

The main specialisation among tailors seems to have been glover, but there was also a breeches-maker, and in 1825 a 'Habit and Pelisse Maker'.[15] Fig. 5.4 demonstrates that while the numbers of shoemakers relate quite closely to the control line, tailoring was clearly in decline after c.1760. This was presumably because of the growth of ready-made garments sold in the new drapers shops, and the increasing numbers of women making clothes, including two mantua-makers from the 1770s and three dressmakers after 1806. The shoemakers of Cupar do not seem to have had any particular reputation for quality, unlike their counterparts in burghs such as Selkirk and Forfar. Nor were any shoemakers rich enough to leave an inventory.

Of the baxters, six were also millers or mill-masters, and five brewers. There were no recorded female baxters before the 1820s, when two baxters' widows were running bakers' shops. In Edinburgh arrangements for sharing or renting bakehouses were organised by the baker trade, but there is no evidence whether this happened in Cupar, and some definitely had their own bakehouses. A few inventories survive. John Stark (1769), deacon and convener, died insolvent, whereas John Inglis, who feued the town's mills in 1791, ended up a country landowner. Alexander Melville (1813), had in his bakehouse three troughs, five peels, two shovels, six bread baskets, two hair brushes and 'some books', four flour measures, weights and scales, baking tools, two barrows and '7 wood Gantrases for Sacks'. John Smith (1825) left stocks of flour, baskets, scales and a slate, and in his bakehouse a table, shuttles, trough, scales and weights, and books.

There was always tension between the town which owned the mills, the millers who charged multure (a percentage of the flour they ground), and the bakers who used the flour. Building and maintaining mills was capital-intensive, and the town sought assurances from the baxter trade before investing money in new buildings or equipment, as for example in 1750 when the town asked the baxters to agree 'to pay dry multure for all the flour they shall buy and bake within this

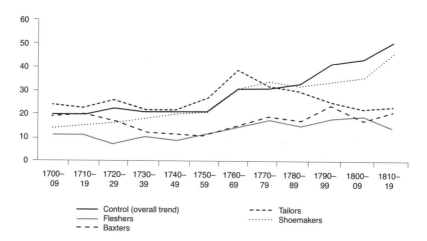

FIGURE 5.4 Changing numbers of tailors, shoemakers, baxters and fleshers, 1700–1819.

burgh' after the new flour mill was built. But the town sometimes went too far. In 1754 there were protests that recent feu charters insisting that all corn for the family's use was to be ground at Cupar Mills were unreasonable because 'were they to remove to Edinburgh, London or Jamaica ... what an intolerable burden it would be for them to send all their corns ... to be grind at Cupar mills'. As all corn grown on burgh land was thirled anyway, the clause was unnecessary, and the council backed down.

In 1769 the baxters asked for the multure to be converted to money, arguing that 'most of the mills in Fife and universally in Lothian grind wheat and dress flour at the rate of 1s per boll', and 'the payment of multure in wheat when the price ... is high is a peculiar hardship'. They threatened to take their wheat to be ground elsewhere. The millers understandably would not give way, and the argument simmered on. In 1790 the deacon of the baxters presented the council with a list of grievances, including the state of the mill machinery, and having to pay multures in kind, particularly when the grain was kiln-dried in winter, and weighed less, and the council finally agreed to feu the mills to John Inglis for £1,015. Those who held tacks of the town's mills were sometimes millers, sometimes baxters and sometimes investors who employed millers.

One of the traditional functions of the burgh court had been to fix the price of bread. The effect was to avoid competition between bakers on price, and presumably therefore to encourage competition on quality. By the eighteenth century this practice was dying out all over Britain, but continued in Cupar until at least 1815. The court which met in Cupar to fix the fiars (grain prices) for the whole of Fife each year consisted of five local landowners, five tenant farmers, and five maltmen or baxters from Cupar, and was one of the ways in which Cupar's position as the county town gave status and experience to some of those working in the town.

Fig. 5.4 (p. 77) also demonstrates the relative decline of baxters and fleshers. Like waulkers, fleshers were supposed to work in specialised communal premises. It is not clear where the shambles was in Cupar, how many times it was rebuilt, or whether it was paid for by the town or the flesher trade. But many fleshers preferred to butcher and sell meat on their own premises. In 1744 there were protests because 'the butchers ... kept mastive and bull dogs which were very dangerous to ... schoolboys and girls', and the council decreed that each flesher should only keep one such dog, which should be chained 'to a post or other secure place within their houses or shambles after sun sett'. Such dogs were obviously necessary to protect carcasses from theft by people or animals. In 1752, despite the provision of a new shambles, one flesher continued to 'slaughter and sell some of his butcher meat at the door of or within his dwelling house', and the burgh court proposed to fine him and ban this practice because of the danger of 'enraged beasts breaking from his doors'. He replied that the provision of a shambles did not mean that he had renounced his right to trade where he pleased, and some of his customers preferred 'to see and buy their meat in a private house rather than in so public and noisome a place'. He only killed small animals in his house, so there was no danger to the public.[16] In 1760 the council decreed that 'no flesher ... shall hang or sell any meat within their houses or at their doors but in the public market only'. Such edicts had to be repeated frequently, so were clearly never fully observed, and complaints continued at least until 1800.

There does not seem to have been any problem in Cupar with the trades encroaching on each other, but there was an increasing problem of overlap between trades and guildry. Challenges, however, were not always made as soon as infringements were noted, but only when the guildry felt its privileges threatened. In 1749, for example, James Bell, glover, was prosecuted by the guildry for 'selling merchant goods tho' he was no guild brother but only a simple burgess'. He was selling books, but that was acceptable for two reasons: there was no other bookseller in the town, so he was not threatening the livelihood of a member of the guildry; and as agent for a bookseller in London, he was not technically breaking any rules. But selling paper was a different matter, as many local merchants stocked it. Tradesmen were allowed to sell not only their finished goods but a limited amount of spare raw materials. Bell could sell wool, as it was related to his trade. If he had owned a paper mill he could have sold paper, but buying it for resale was illegal. It was explained that surgeon-apothecaries did not have to be members of the guildry, so long as they sold only an agreed limited range of medicines. The case dragged on to November 1751. Bell tried to claim that paper was all right so long as it was British made, and that in other royal burghs such as Perth, Dundee and Dunfermline, tradesmen were allowed to sell merchant goods and 'pay a trifle to the guildry yearly', but Cupar guildry seldom admitted any outsiders to its ranks. By the early nineteenth century such distinctions were becoming increasingly irrelevant.

There were occasional problems the other way round. In 1710, for example, the deacon of shoemakers reported a guildbrother to the council for 'selling of common shoes to their great hurt and prejudice'. And in 1751 the guildry appealed for increased mobility between guildry and trades, claiming it would be good for the town if 'guildbrothers' sons who are or shall be educate and brought up to mechanic trades' could pay reduced admission dues at the end of their apprenticeships, otherwise the outlay rendered them 'so poor as never to be able to carry on their trades to any advantage'. If guildbrethren produced too many sons, a small town could not absorb them, and they needed to diversify.

What united guildry and trades in all burghs was the threat of unfree traders. Some burghs introduced a system of licensing. But in Cupar it took longer for the guildry and trades to admit that prosecution could not stem the tide, and that licensing was the only practical way to extract money from unfree traders and control their numbers. Visiting tradesmen at markets and fairs began challenging the right of the trades to check the quality of their goods and charge a 'gate penny' for doing so. Eventually the town council had to admit defeat, for if outside traders boycotted markets the takings of the customer and the brewers were reduced. The same was happening in every other town and city in Scotland. In 1791 the guildry introduced licences costing 5s per annum. But they were soon backtracking, trying to enforce burgess entry until finally admitting defeat in 1817.

Visiting traders were supposed to be restricted to markets and fairs, but this proved harder to enforce as consumer demand and population increased, and as houses were built outside the burgh boundary, where the council had no direct control. The Napoleonic wars also caused problems, as discharged soldiers were allowed dispensation to trade, but claims were difficult to check. Chapmen were small-scale itinerant merchants, sometimes sub-contracted to burgh merchants, and were not expected to join the guildry of any town. However, by 1764 a Fife-wide Chapman Society had been formed. Its rules included a ban on excessive drinking or swearing, and fines for false weights and for travelling with goods on the Sabbath.

Other occupations

Fig. 5.5 plots the total numbers in the professions, guildry and trades against the control line, and demonstrates an increasing gap, particularly from the 1760s, between these men and the total of working males. This is accounted for by the gradual increase in non-incorporated and non-traditional occupations, generated by the sheer number of people in towns, such as gardeners, painters (of houses, carriages, shop signs, etc.), those who built and mended roads and pavements, and an increasing number of town, county and central government officials.

By far the largest body of unincorporated workers was domestic servants. The servant tax levied between 1777 and 1798 produced clear definitions, such as house servant, and specialists such as butlers, grooms, huntsmen, postillions and one 'valet de chambre'. Servants, both male and female, received some of their wages in kind, in the form of food, accommodation and clothes. The account book of Lady Elizabeth Anstruther includes entries such as 'To a beaver slouch hat postillion', and 'To flannel for the groom's waistcoat lining'. She also recorded payments to the servants of others in the town for delivering

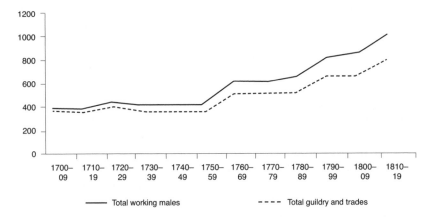

FIGURE 5.5 Total working males compared with total guildry and trades, 1700–1819.

gifts or messages to her. As well as clothing and tips, servants could also receive gifts and legacies. After the death of her master in 1824, Jean Tod was given twelve shirts, a large amount of bed linen and towels, old clothes and shoes, five plated teaspoons, a tea caddy, twelve table cloths and a cupboard.

Another group, which grew with improvements in transport, was carriers and others associated with horse-drawn transport. A list survives in the town council minutes for 1756 of all the carts in the town 'for driving the soldiers baggage'. Thirty-two 2-horse carts were owned by thirty-eight men and one woman. The Cart Tax charged between 1786 and 1792 was paid by between twenty-five and thirty individuals in Cupar. The number of carts was almost the same as in 1756, but more of the owners were dedicated carriers. By the 1780s there was a specific Dundee carrier and in 1792 the town appointed an official carrier to Edinburgh. There were at least two female carriers.

Women and work

Evidence for working women is scarce, and sometimes hard to interpret, but it is clear that many women in Cupar, both single and married, did work. The only times women appear in the records of the guildry or trades in Cupar is as recipients of charity. In some other towns women were allowed some form of membership of guildry or trades. But whatever the precise arrangements, women were in general excluded from full membership, and encouraged to work in specialist areas such as domestic service and nursing, casual or seasonal work, the selling of drink and some areas of retail trade.

While the evidence is slight, there were female merchants and traders, and not all were widows continuing their husband's business. As in Edinburgh, women could work in different jobs to those of their husbands, though there was often some link, as for example the wives of brewers running inns. Women also often worked informally for a family business. Christian Robbie, for example, an innkeeper's daughter, attended 'the Companies who come to her father's house'. The few unmarried women who went into business on their own seem to have been tolerated. By the end of the eighteenth century, however, with the increase in demand for consumer items, keeping a small shop became an increasingly attractive option for women of any marital status. A shop based in the home could be started with relatively little capital, and combined with caring for children or elderly relatives. Eventually the guildry began to regard such shops as a threat, but they could not prosecute women for not joining the guildry, as they were not eligible to do so. After some discussion they identified the problem as not the principle of women trading, but a fear that married women might be used as a front for non-burgess husbands to trade. All they could do was issue temporary licences, deciding in 1784 to charge 5s per annum to freemen's daughters and 15s to 'stranger women'. Ten years later the guildry decreed that all unmarried guildbrethren's daughters could open shops without any payment. If any of them married a non-freeman, the husband could join the guildry at a reduced rate, provided he was 'of good character'. But this was rescinded in 1796, returning to a system of annual licences. When licensing for unfree male traders was withdrawn, it had to be kept on for women because they did not have any other option.

Apart from occupations which threatened the monopoly of the male guildry and incorporations, women in other Scottish towns in the eighteenth century worked in all-female occupations such as bonnet-maker, butterwife, fruitwife, lodging-house-keeper, mantua-maker, midwife, schoolmistress, seamstress, lace-worker and wet-nurse. Contributors to the *Old Statistical Account* often failed to mention working women apart from school-mistresses, but the minister in Cupar listed mantua-makers, milliners and midwives. Working women recorded in the town council minutes included a billet-mistress, carriers, mill-mistresses, washerwomen and a tackswoman of dung. The four mill-mistresses serve as an illustration of the differing experiences of women and work. It is often said that the main opportunity for a woman to work was after the death of her husband, either physically carrying on his work, or managing employees. But not all women could cope. When David Barclay, millmaster, died young in 1733, his widow Elizabeth Forster was left with 'a numerous family', and petitioned the council to release her from the remaining term of the tack, because 'my sons being at employment or school ... I am left destitute of any help' to oversee the mills, and she was herself 'entirely unfit and ignorant of the way of managing them'. The other three millmistresses, however, were clearly competent. Helen Osburn, the daughter of a soldier and widow of a writer, took on the tack of the mills in about 1742. In 1746 she petitioned the council, claiming that the 1745 rebellion had affected her business. Her petition was eloquent, and she presented it herself, not, as some women did, through a male friend or relative.

There were some occupations where the wife was expected to share in her husband's work. In 1826 after the death of the gaoler the council gave his widow 10 guineas in recognition of 'her humane treatment to the prisoners under her husband's charge'. As well as the occupations already mentioned, records survive of fourteen teachers, seven milliners, three dressmakers, two mantua-makers, a mealmaker, a musician and two brothel-keepers. Millinery and dressmaking seem to have been generally acceptable for a woman to carry on after marriage, though in Cupar the main evidence is for unmarried women, sometimes two or more sisters working together, as is also the case with private teaching. Another respectable occupation was letting rooms. The inventory of Jean Wright, midwife (1797), included money owed by a merchant and a writer for bed and board.

A major female occupation was domestic service, with perhaps a quarter of households in Cupar employing female servants by about 1800. It is often suggested that a proportion of the female domestic servants in towns had come in from the countryside to work, and this was one reason why there was so often a higher number of females in towns than males. But the evidence from the *Old Statistical Account* for east Fife does not bear this out. The explanations offered were that the young men were going away to serve in the army, navy or merchant marine, or 'to those towns where manufactures flourish'. One minister actually stated that 'the females are generally stationary'.[17] Between 1785 and 1792 a tax was levied on the employers of female servants. The numbers of taxable servants in 1785/86 ranged from 1,584 in Edinburgh, through 232 in Dundee, to 15 in Cupar, Dysart and Burntisland, and 11 in Dunfermline. In 25 per cent of the cases where there were two female domestic servants in one household, their surnames were the same, and they were probably sisters. Specific job descriptions included chambermaid, cook, cook maid, housemaid and housekeeper. Apart from tax records, domestic servants only appear in official accounts when they got into trouble. In January 1724, for example, Isobel Clark, servant to a surgeon-apothecary and his wife, was given leave to nurse her mother 'upon her promise to return to her service so soon as her mother died'. But after the funeral she refused to return, and went into service with another family. It was put to the burgh court that if this 'base practice' were encouraged, 'masters and mistresses might be cast destitute upon every trifle that should displease servants saucy nodles'.

A further picture of working women can be gained from Lady Anstruther's account book. Some payments, such as 'to Mrs Davidson [merchant's wife] to account of cotton yarn', or 'to Mrs Carnegie [carrier's wife] account of things sent over the watter', imply that some guildry wives were active partners, or at least in charge of keeping the books. In the case of professionals and tradesmen, however, she seems to have dealt only with men. She also paid women working in their own right, as for example 'Miss Gray mantua-maker', but her stays were made by a man.[18] There are also entries such as 'to the gardiner's wife for milk', and 'washer woman'. She made payments to nurses, for her family and also possibly as a form of charity to others. She employed a cook and three maids, as well as a groom, plus occasional extra help in the house, for decorating or spring-cleaning. She also employed a Mrs Christie to buy things on her behalf, looking for things such as furnishing silk to match an existing item. No references have been found before 1820 to women employed in the linen industry, though it is generally agreed that it needed five female spinners to supply each male weaver, so spinning must have been a major female occupation in Cupar. There are, however, references in the 1820s to women working in spinning mills.

The general impression is that the status of women and their opportunities to work did not decrease during the long eighteenth century, and that there was a subtle balance between the need for many women to earn their living and support dependants, and the promotion of ideas of domesticity and separate spheres.[19] Many women, both married and unmarried, worked and participated in public events without comment, and women were often used by the commissary court to value goods such as napery in which they had more expertise than men. It has been suggested that after about 1780 the wives of professionals withdrew from the world of work. In Cupar there were certainly professional wives working during the first half of the eighteenth century, such as two of the millmistresses. After these the latest evidence is the billet-mistress who succeeded her husband, a writer, in 1777, and a teacher's wife in 1816 who was also a teacher. But while the wives of writers and doctors cannot be shown to have had distinct occupations towards the end of the century, they were certainly not hidden at home. They were managing their own property, and making purchases at roups. The wife of Philip Keddie, writer, did not work, but was allowed to let the house during Race Week and keep the profit for herself. When Harry Gibb, tenant farmer, went bankrupt c.1812, his wife took in boarders until he could re-establish himself as a land-valuer and auctioneer.

TABLE 5.2   Top ten occupations in Cupar, sampled at thirty-year intervals

	1700s	1730s	1760s	1790s	1820s
1	78 maltmen and brewers	63 weavers	111 weavers	195 weavers	158 weavers
2	54 weavers	55 maltmen and brewers	69 wrights	105 wrights	112 wrights
3	44 merchants	45 merchants	55 merchants	69 merchants	83 merchants
4	33 wrights	39 wrights	39 tailors	58 writers	74 writers
5	24 tailors	23 writers	35 maltmen and brewers	38 smiths	38 shoemakers
6	19 baxters	22 tailors	31 shoemakers	37 carriers	37 vintners and innkeepers
7	18 writers	18 smiths	25 vintners and innkeepers	34 vintners and innkeepers	35 smiths
8	17 smiths	18 shoemakers	25 millers	34 shoemakers	34 carriers
9	14 shoemakers	18 carriers	24 writers	25 tailors	24 teachers
10	11 fleshers	12 baxters	24 smiths	24 baxters	23 tailors

Changing patterns of work

The information presented here demonstrates how numbers in each occupation changed over the long eighteenth at a bread level to look at the top ten occupations at thirty-year intervals (Table 5.2). All the professions flourished, particularly writers; the rise of financial services started under the control of merchants, but soon became dominated by writers. Of the guildry, the merchants held their place numerically but lost their ascendancy, both political and financial. Merchants became increasing specialised, mainly as grocers, drapers, haberdashers and ironmongers. As tastes changed and demand and supply increased, merchants needed to hold far more stock, and began to work from separate shop premises, which demanded greater capital investment, though small shops could still be run from the home on a minimal outlay, and this option proved particularly attractive to women. Maltmen, dominant during the seventeenth century, almost disappeared, to be replaced by vintners and innkeepers. Dyers and waulkers, associated with the woollen industry, declined, and were succeeded by workers in the linen industry. The trade which experienced the greatest increase was the wrights, particularly those working in the building industry.

The distinction between guildry and trades became increasingly blurred. There is little evidence for social mobility, but a few top tradesmen do seem to have done very well both financially and socially. As well as changes to traditional occupations, the long eighteenth century saw the growth of non-incorporated occupations such as gardener, carter and painter. This period saw a growth of the professions, which excluded women totally, and of manufacturing, which employed women only in menial capacities. But at the same time increased consumerism and literacy led to a growing demand for shops, inns and schools, all of which could be run by women. By the early nineteenth century an increasing number of specialist tradesmen were having to be employed from outside the town. A few eventually moved to the town permanently. Abraham Middleton, for example, a plumber from Dundee, was employed on major building works in Cupar from 1791, and settled there in about 1822.[20] By the 1820s the council employed town officers who had previously worked as policemen in Dundee. Cupar was no longer self-sufficient.

As well as new workers coming in, some men from Cupar worked elsewhere, both temporarily and permanently. A chance documentary survival hints at unexpectedly broad horizons. In 1820 Alexander Arthur, slater, was prosecuted for fraud relating to a contract he had successfully bid for from the Board of Ordnance 'for slater work at Forts George, William and Augustus'. As a small contractor, 'not having a sufficient stock for carrying on such works he was much difficulted in procuring money'. He forged a bill, and was discovered when by mistake he repaid it a day late.[21] Even though as a purchaser of slates he presumably had contacts in the Ballachulish area, this evidence that a Cupar tradesman had the ambition and ability to take on work so far from home is unexpected.

The merchants and maltmen of 1700 would have had difficulty recognising Cupar in 1820, with its purpose-built shops, and a whole new street devoted to administration and banking. The power of the guildry and trades had been reduced, and, though the evidence is not quantifiable, probably fewer men were self-employed. For many people the experience of work would have been very different by 1820.

Notes

1. In 1770, for example, a new piper was appointed, to play 'through the Town every night at seven and every morning at five', for £24 Scots and a pair of shoes per annum; in 1771 he was to play at 6 am 'in time coming'. Many towns stopped employing pipers (playing a simple type of flute, not bagpipes) during the seventeenth century, relying only on drummers, but in Cupar the office of piper continued into the nineteenth century.

2. The next sentence noted that the magistrates had ordered 'a very considerable enlargement of the churchyard'. It is not clear whether this was meant as a joke, or is just an unfortunate juxtaposition. The four incomers all stayed at least two years, and one was definitely still in the town in 1825.

3. A statement made to the presbytery after having been named as the father of an illegitimate child, so perhaps there were other reasons for his being sent away to study.

4. Charles junior purchased his MD in 1814, the year of his father's death. Perhaps this parallels the way so many tradesmen became burgesses on the death of their father.

5. *Fife Herald*, 14 July 1825; he came for a three week period, but it is not clear whether this was repeated and, if so, how frequently.

6. Turner, *Anatomical Memoirs of John Goodsir*, 7–8; describes a Fife doctor in the 1770s 'hatted, coated, booted and spurred ... caparisoned for the week with drugs and surgical appliances', he would set out on Monday for five days. 'To obviate the dangers of travelling by night, he carried a lantern, fastened by a strap above his knee'.

7. There were two surgeons in Auchtermuchty, one in Crail and three and an apothecary in St Andrews, where 'several shopkeepers vend a few of the more common medicines, such as every neighbour prescribes to another'.

8. When it was held at the house of a male innkeeper, that innkeeper was always a councillor, and usually a bailie.

9. In Dundee the order was baxters, shoemakers, glovers, tailors, bonnet-makers, fleshers, smiths, weavers and waulkers, while wrights, masons and slaters formed a separate group known as the United Trades. The ranking in Edinburgh was goldsmiths, surgeons, tailors, skinners, wrights and masons, baxters, hammermen, walkers, shoemakers and weavers. In Kirkcaldy the seven trades (no waulkers) had almost the same order as those of Cupar. Inverkeithing had five trades: hammermen, weavers, bakers, tailors and shoemakers. Perth had hammermen, baxters, skinners, cordiners, fleshers, tailors, wrights, weavers and fullers.

10. One case in the commissary court (NAS CC20/3/bundle 1778/79) concerned a dispute between Thomas Thomson tailor in St Andrews and David Farmer day-labourer at Cupar. Farmer's son had been apprenticed to Thomson in 1778 for four years and 'being relations' he agreed 'to take the apprentice without written indentures to save Expence'.

11. StAU TypBX.D68X1, election of deacon of wrights, 1768. His status as burgess was not questioned, but he should have been resident in Cupar for six weeks rather than two to be eligible to vote.

12. NAS CS96/707; another weaver had 'several journeymen under him' (NAS JC26/294/3).

13. NAS CS96/1737.

14. Far more weavers than members of other trades seem to have held such posts, perhaps because weaving fitted well with other part-time work, including seasonal employment in farming, fishing and building.

15. *Fife Herald*, 29 Sept 1825; John Turpie (a local name) advertised that he was setting up in Cupar after many years in London.

16. As the fleshers' title to the shambles was dubious, 'none but a fool would quit ... a privilege that he formerly enjoyed ... for an imaginary one only'. In other towns, too, both fleshers and customers preferred the slaughtering of beasts outside shops.

17. The parishes which recorded more females than males were: Auchtermuchty, Balmerino, Carnbee, Ceres, Crail, Creich, Cupar, Dunino, Dunbog, Falkland, Ferry-Port-on-Craig, Kemback, Kettle and Pittenweem. The explanation given in Ceres was that 'The army, navy, and different pursuits in life, carry away many young men'; in Crail, 'young men going to sea'.

18. Staymaking was male work because it needed strength. Tailors did not make clothes for women, as measuring and fitting would not be decent. If stays were made-to-measure, who did the measuring?
19. NAS SC20/5/4, bundle 1749; a pursuer objected to the calling of a female witness, claiming that 'they are not by law regulariter witnesses in civil cases but only in circumstantial cases and Domestick affairs'. But the sheriff upheld the defence view that 'there was no law reprobating women to be witnesses in any case'.
20. In about 1818 he did the plumbing work for Kirkmay House in Crail. Plumbers fitted not only water pipes, but gutters and lead used on roofs.
21. NAS AD14/20/310, the sheriff-depute wrote to the Lord Advocate asking him not to prosecute, as there was no intention to defraud, and Arthur was 'a man of most unblemished character, and has a large family, and seems to have excited universal sympathy and commiseration'.

6

Buildings and Townscape

Building materials

In 1700 the town probably had stone-built houses of two or three storeys on the main streets, though perhaps a few were still of wood, and fairly simple buildings in the minor streets and closes. Slate is not found locally, is heavy and expensive to transport, and would probably only have been used before the mid eighteenth century for public buildings and the grandest private houses. Thatch was still being used in the early nineteenth century for cottages and outbuildings within the town, and in the new suburbs. Thackstanes can be seen on street-front houses built well after 1800. If such buildings had still been thatched in the early nineteenth century, one would expect there to be some surviving documentary or pictorial evidence. It is possible, therefore, that thackstanes were used out of habit, or in case thatch might later be used for temporary repairs. The price differential between thatch and slate was such that in 1734 the town chose to thatch the tolbooth as a temporary measure until they could afford to re-slate it.[1]

There was plenty of good local sandstone, but building materials were often recycled. In 1754, for example, the council donated the arch stones of one of the town's gates to the county heritors for a new stone bridge over the Lady Burn, carrying the 'Grand Road ... to Dundee Water side'. And in 1757 when the hangman's house was demolished its stones were used for coping stones and parapets for bridges. While most town-centre buildings were large and solid, some were much simpler. The house at Russell's Mill, for example, was described in 1750 as 'only stone and feall [turf]'. The new tenant felt it was not only too small but dangerous, and asked for permission to build a new house 'of stone and lime'. In 1771 a widow in the town petitioned the council for help when her house 'fell down owing to the stormy weather'.

Partly because of the high cost of imported building materials, and the availability of local clay, the town council in 1755 encouraged the establishment of a brick and tile works, though it was not finally set up until 1764. While it is known that by the later eighteenth century clay pantiles were used extensively for industrial buildings and farm steadings, it is not clear whether they were used on town houses, though both bricks and tiles were used for flooring.[2] Locally-made bricks were mainly used for internal walls, being stronger and more fireproof than the wooden partitions they replaced. Various court cases during the eighteenth century highlighted the problems of living in flats only divided by wooden partitions, in terms of both privacy and security.

Town-centre houses would have had glazed windows (as opposed to wooden shutters) by the beginning of the eighteenth century, as did the new school built in 1729. But they were fragile. In 1712 Patrick Bruce of Bunzion asked to 'build a Litle Laigh dycke befor his houss for secureing glas windous thereof' (like that belonging to the laird of Logie), and this was granted as 'reasonable and just'. Despite extensive rebuilding, there were still wooden elements on the fronts of some houses. When the town council ordered the removal of front-garden railings in Bonnygate in 1792, one owner protested because 'there is a projection in the front of their house, which is built only with laths and plaster having timber posts', and if not protected 'the first cart which should happen to take hold of it would level the whole fabric'.

Building and rebuilding

In Cupar the wright trade included all building workers – stonemasons, glaziers, plasterers and slaters – as well as workers in wood; painters, like thatchers, do not appear to have belonged to any incorporation. Occupational data demonstrates that the growth in stone building dates from quite early in the eighteenth century, with a peak in the 1760s, and a second peak in the early nineteenth century. This correlates with other documents and architectural evidence. But for most of the eighteenth century houses were fairly simply fitted out, and other building trades, such as plastering and painting, show a much slower rise from the 1760s, though the same peak between 1810 and 1820. The *Old Statistical Account* includes comments about how recently plastered walls and ceilings had become the norm. By the early nineteenth century not only would all windows have been fully glazed, but they would have been larger than earlier ones, and more numerous, as the size of buildings increased.

Rebuilding and improvements continued steadily throughout the eighteenth century. In 1748, for example, William Gregory, merchant, asked for a feu charter to extend his house which would add 'to the regularity and beauty of the town'. In June 1763 it was reported 'that there was a scarcity of houses in the town', and proposed that the town council should offer loans to 'such of the landlords or heritors of houses ... as incline to enlarge them'. According to the *Old Statistical*

Account Cupar, 'especially when approached by the turnpike road from the east, has the appearance of a neat, clean, well built, thriving town ... There are no houses in ruins, and none untenanted. Upwards of a third part of the town has been rebuilt, during the last twenty-five years, in a neat and handsome stile.' Similar comments can be found about many Scottish towns. The rebuilding of Edinburgh began after 1746, with George Square laid out in 1766 and the New Town started in 1767. In Aberdeen rebuilding gathered speed in the 1760s and 1770s. Dunfermline, too, had grown rapidly since the 1760s, with new streets at Abbey Park and Pittencrieff. The developments of this period involved far more than the simple provision of housing, being linked to 'improvement', and a new emphasis on space, light, regularity and elegance.

There seems to have been a further increase in building activity between about 1790 and 1815, with street-front tenements of three storeys and garret. Attention was increasingly being paid to visual amenity. In March 1810, for example, James Webster, writer, petitioned the council to build a new house in Crossgate in line with its neighbours 'which will ornament the street'. There are references in the council minutes to the removal of forestairs or the demolition of buildings, to be rebuilt further back in order to widen the streets, particularly at South Bridge, and Cunzie Neuk, the narrowest part of the Bonnygate. Plate 7c shows the corner house as rebuilt, one-and-a-half blocks wide. There are few references to the dean of guild and his assessors, and few records of his court survive, but there are occasional references to his acting to enforce planning decisions made by the council.

The pressure of space within the town also applied to industrial buildings. In June 1748, for example, a weaver petitioned for permission to enlarge his byre because 'when he boiled his cloth he was obliged to remove his cow which was a mighty inconveniency to him'. In January 1770 some of the 'principal inhabitants' petitioned the council to clear the streets, pointing out the nuisance not only from dunghills but from 'the manufacturers of carts, wains, ploughs, sawers of wood etc' who were 'intolerable nuisances', obstructing the street and 'depriving the neighbouring inhabitants of rest and quiet by their great noise and hammering'.

The second surviving town plan of Cupar, inset in a corner of Ainslie's map of Fife, published in 1775 (Plate 5), shows some changes. The gates have all been removed; Kirk Wynd and Dead Wynd are shown as narrower; and there seem to be fewer houses in Provost Wynd, Dead Wynd, Kirk Wynd and Bobber Wynd. There are some buildings, probably industrial or agricultural, at the foots of rigs by the Lady Burn, one large block across the Lady Burn (Plate 7a), and a new road from the foot of Lady Wynd westwards along the edge of the Mote Hill. There are more buildings to the west of the church, including a continuation of Ashlar

Wynd, known from other sources to have been called 'Clarty Wynd'.[3] Another new street, Mouse Wynd, runs from the top of Kirkgate to the West Port. Also shown is Balgarvie House, immediately outside the East Port, and the Castlehill with the school and a bowling green on top, and the river running close to its foot.

Suburbs

Soon after this plan was drawn, expansion outside the town boundary was encouraged by the feuing of plots by both private developers and the town council. The extent of the suburbs by 1820 can be seen on Wood's town plan (Plate 13). It also shows more buildings in Mouse Wynd, a few more in Provost Wynd, and extensive development in the backlands of the inner north side of the Bonnygate. There is little change south of the kirk apart from the disappearance of Clarty Wynd. The first feus were laid out on the property of Mr Low of Pittencrieff, immediately across the Lady Burn from the foot of Lady Wynd, and called Newtown, or Lowstown. In 1793 'no less than 70 houses, chiefly for manufacturers and labourers, have lately been built on ... the Lady Burn'. Evidence from the least altered of the houses in Newtown suggests that they were single-storey and thatched.[4] But if there was only one house per plot, then Newtown itself could not account for seventy houses, and the development must have included some buildings on North Burnside, probably the two-storey houses to the north-west of the pre–1775 block (Plate 7b).[5] Half the identified residents of Newtown were weavers, and another quarter were masons or wrights. The speed of development suggests that parcels of plots may have been sold to masons, who built several houses, kept one for themselves, and sold the rest.

The *Old Statistical Account* also reported that 'A street, in a better stile', had begun to be developed on the south side of the town. The feuing of this area, known as the Common Braes, 'in lots for houses and gardens' was proposed by the town council in 1786.[6] When the first thirteen plots were sold in 1787, most seem to have been bought as investments, and some changed hands within a year.[7] By 1808 this development was being referred to as Riggs Row. There were also by 1806 further feus along this road, and another batch of plots was sold by the council in 1817–18, the area being known as South Toll or Pleasance.[8] After the brick-works this ribbon development continued only on one side of the road. The first houses are two-storey and ashlar. Further out there is more variation in size and quality.

In 1800 there was a proposal to feu house stances on the west side of the Cart Haugh; and the council agreed, but the scheme did not happen. The next major development was the feuing by the town of the Bow

Butts, immediately to the east of Newtown, first proposed in 1815 (Plate 13). In 1817 plans were drawn up for regular plots and a road twenty feet wide through to Bishopgate. The following year it was agreed that the 'remaining part of the Bowbutts' was to be 'feued in small lots for gardens'. Not every plot sold quickly, and the same proposal was made in 1821 and in 1824. The houses on the Fluthers frontage may have been two-storeyed, but most of the others were probably single-storey, and some at least appear to have been thatched.

The authors of the *New Statistical Account* were able to say that the town's 'dimensions have been much extended by the suburbs called the Brae-Heads, New Town, and Lebanon' (Plate 13). Lebanon was another private development, to which there are no references in the town council minutes.[9] In April 1810 the *Dundee Advertiser* reported 'the laying of the foundation of a new street, called Mount Lebanon,' on the north bank of the Lady Burn, 'with much masonic solemnity'.[10] Further development in this area, however, seems to have been haphazard, and the result is not a true 'new town', but resembles some areas of Dundee, with a mix of industrial buildings, manufacturers' villas and workers' cottages. Although the council minutes have few references to private developments, the growth of the suburbs can also be followed through the county sasines. These show peaks of activity between 1810 and 1814 for Lebanon and Skinners Steps, and between 1815 and 1819 for Bow Butts, South Road and St Catherine Street, though Bow Butts had an earlier phase as well. It would appear that the majority of suburban developments were private initiatives, and the feus laid out by the town were slower to sell.

These suburban developments were piecemeal, and solved the housing shortage but created other problems. Being outside the town boundary, the council had no control over their inhabitants. In June 1792, for example, there were complaints that when clothes or bleached cloth were spread out to dry on the Bow Butts the 'Tenants or ffeuars of Mr Low ... wantonly, and with open violence have thrown down their foul water on the said Cloathing' and had treated demands for an apology 'with contempt' in 'language the most insolent and opprobious [*sic*]'. The council seems to have assumed that those living outside the town, while not paying cess, would work and shop in the town. But those in Newtown were mostly weavers, and after 1751 there was no obligation on weavers to join a trade incorporation. Many people moved to these areas to gain space for workshops, so they both lived and worked outside the town. Itinerant salesmen held auctions and peddled their goods in these suburban areas without having to pay customs dues. Shops in St Catherine Street were advertised in 1824 as being within 50 yards of the Cross, but the occupiers were not 'liable to enter with the Guildry'. The footprint of the town had increased dramatically. When special constables were appointed in 1817, and the town was divided into four divisions, new housing accounted for one whole division and part of another.[11] Problems continued until the town boundaries were extended.

Parish church

As in towns all over Britain during the long eighteenth century, the development of suburbs was part of a wider vision of improvement, which led to the rebuilding of town centres and public buildings. The first such target in Cupar was the parish church. In 1785 the medieval church was in a poor state, and the heritors decided to build a new one 'on a more convenient plan' (Plate 6a). The width is the same as the present church, though the overall length of the present church plus the medieval remains is about 15 feet longer, but this does suggest that the present church stands approximately on the footprint of the old. Probably the reason for rebuilding was not to achieve more floor space, but to achieve an open area tall enough for galleries to be built. The old church with its narrow nave and aisles would have been very difficult to adapt to hold large numbers, all of whom could see the pulpit. But it is interesting that they seem to have retained traces of at least one of the altars, and reset a medieval monument into the later church (Plate 1c, Fig. 2.3), suggesting respect for the medieval church.[12] According to the *Old Statistical Account* this was 'by far the most convenient and elegant structure of the kind' in Fife (Plate 6a).[13] What the account glosses over is that within a few weeks of its opening in July 1786 'the walls appeared much bulged and out of the plumb'. Although independent assessors assured the heritors that it could be put right, public confidence had been lost and major rebuilding had to be undertaken before the public would enter the church again.[14]

Public buildings

The tolbooth was repaired and re-slated between 1699 and 1703, and regular repairs continued to be necessary. In 1723, for example, the treasurer was to 'cause to mend the holes in the Tolbooth and to put up the Cock upon the Lumb'. In 1735 another storey was added, and later there were further alterations to the turrets and a 'Stone Ballusters placed betwixt these Turrets'.[15] A new clock was installed in 1789, and by 1799 the turrets again needed repairs. At some point there had been added a town house, with a 'Council House' on the first floor, reached by an outside stair, and below it a guard room and storage facilities. This was almost certainly used by the sheriff court and for county heritors' meetings.[16] In 1793 it was said that in about 1775 'the gentlemen of the county ... built on a large scale, and in the modern taste, adjoining to the town-house, a room for their use at head courts, for their accommodation at balls, etc.'. Another 'Ball Room' was proposed in 1786 and 1790.

The grammar school of Cupar stood in isolation on the Castlehill, and was a key responsibility of the town council. In 1729 a new 'plain' schoolhouse had been built on or near the site of the previous one, and in 1742 a 'House of Office' was built behind it.[17] This building remained in use until after Cupar Academy was founded in 1823, though a separate building was provided for the Latin School in 1806

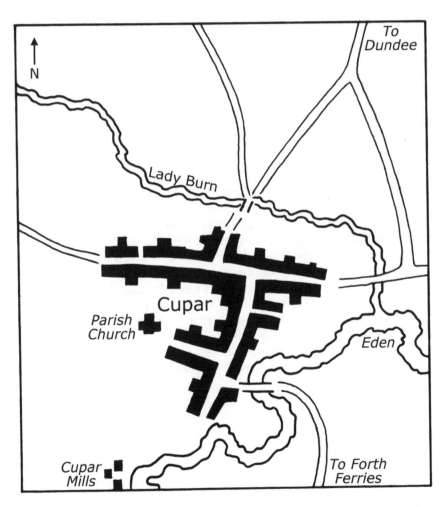

FIGURE 6.1   Detail from William Roy's Military Survey of Scotland, showing the roads and bridges around Cupar.

because of increasing numbers, and acrimony between the English and Latin teachers (Plate 9a). The siting of schools here, so close to the narrow road to St Andrews, caused road safety problems, and various building alterations and traffic regulations were introduced, until the problem was solved by the building of St Catherine Street.

St Catherine Street

George Campbell in 1793 condemned the old prison in the tolbooth as 'a reproach to the town in which it stands, a disgrace to the county which employs it, and a stain on that benevolent and compassionate spirit, which distinguishes and dignifies this enlightened age'. The cell for criminals was 'a dark, damp, vaulted dungeon ... without a fire-place', and with little light or ventilation. Though the prison served 'the very populous and wealthy county of Fife', it was paid for by the town. Campbell appealed to the county gentlemen to subscribe to the building of 'a prison on a modern improved plan'. By 1808, when three prisoners escaped by 'making a hole in the West wall next the street', the old building may have been semi-derelict.

General Roy's Military Survey of c.1750 shows the rivers and roads around Cupar (Fig. 6.1). From the eastern approach road a branch runs north to join the road to Dundee. While at first sight this looks like the first Cupar bypass, it may well be an alternative route for wheeled vehicles because the eastern approach was so narrow. First came a small bridge over the Lady Burn, then a narrow road at the foot of Castlehill, dangerously close to the school. To reach the town centre vehicles had to pass the tolbooth, at one side of which the road was 15' 9" (4.8 m) wide, on the other only 9' 9" (3 m) (Plate 5). In 1809 John Ferguson, provost, banker and 'developer', bought Balgarvie House, to the south of the Castlehill. By October he presented to the town council and the county heritors his plans for 'improving the eastern access' to Cupar, which entailed diverting the Eden, demolishing Balgarvie House, and 'throwing down the County Hall, Ball Room, weigh-house and other accommodation which blocked up the eastern access'. The new street to be laid out would be about 60 feet wide and 'run nearly in a direct line from the Cross eastwards towards the East toll bar'. The town council and county heritors agreed the scheme should go ahead, though asked for more detailed plans and estimates. What Ferguson had done was offer each of the three bodies concerned, council, sheriff and county heritors, new premises as good or better than their present ones, at no cost, in return for permission to demolish the old ones, and re-use the materials. Naturally each group agreed, not realising that each was being offered the same new rooms. Thus began a saga lasting almost ten years, details of which can be found in the minutes of the town council and of the county heritors, and occasionally in other sources.[18]

By 1810 Ferguson had diverted the river into a new cut and laid out the line of the new street, and disputes and legal actions began. The first building to go ahead was the new gaol, its site to be bought by the town, which would also contribute £300 plus the materials from the old gaol, and another £300 towards the cost of the necessary legislation. By May 1812 the Act had been passed and a suitable site identified.[19] The county heritors were being assessed for £4,000, though some still maintained that the burgh should pay the full cost. Since 1597 burghs had been responsible for holding county prisoners to be tried in sheriff or higher courts, and the town would certainly be liable for all the running costs once the new gaol was built. The council petitioned the Convention of Royal Burghs to clarify the position and ask for backing to campaign for change (see Chapter 9). In April 1814 the new prison was ready. The councillors went to inspect it and listed a number of problems – there was no water closet, in fact no water supply (although there was a well on the plans), and there was no heating for the damp ground-floor cells. They therefore refused permission for the demolition of the existing gaol. But funds were exhausted, so the council paid for water closets and well, and the new gaol was opened (Plate 9b).[20]

Meanwhile, in April 1811 the foundation stone was laid for County Buildings (Plate 9c). But the town council began to realise that it was expected to share a room with the sheriff court and the county. In addition, the old buildings had been upstairs and there had been plenty of space below for weigh-house and storage, and replacements for these had not been offered. In 1815 the tacksman of customs was withholding his rent until a new weigh-house was provided. Meanwhile, in 1812 George Aitken questioned whether the new room was within the burgh boundary. Most councillors, who supported Ferguson, did not seem concerned about this technicality, but Aitken insisted that sharing a room with the sheriff court was not viable, and if the room was outside the burgh, the burgh court would be illegal.[21] Progress on the new buildings was slow. Without the demolition of all the old buildings the new street was not viable. Some were holding out against demolition until the new premises were finished, while others realised that the project would move more quickly if demolition went ahead. One building was demolished overnight before an interdict could be served, and this 'disregard and contempt ... for lawful authority' shown by Ferguson alienated many heritors. It now became clear that the new rooms had not been handed over because Ferguson did not yet have title to the ground on which they were built, though transfer was said to be imminent. Even when title was established, no-one was happy about the allocation of rooms. The heritors received an apology from Ferguson for the demolition episode, but it was not immediately accepted.[22]

Meanwhile, Ferguson's supporters maintained that he had kept his side of the bargain; the fact that the rooms on offer were not within the burgh was a problem for the council, not for Ferguson; and the demolition of the old buildings was necessary for public safety. By now Ferguson had alienated one of his most influential supporters, Thomas Horsburgh, the sheriff clerk, and was in financial difficulties, still owing the purchase price of £3,500 for Balgarvie House. A group of investors known as the Hope Street Trustees took over the debt, forming a tontine so that if any partner died his shares went to the others.[23] By 1815 the council was split, and deprived of all its normal meeting and storage space. One of the trustees, bailie James Kyd, tried to break the log-jam by promoting Ferguson's offer to build a new council room at the Cross, definitely within the burgh. He produced plans by Robert Hutchison, a mason from Coaltown of Balgonie who had become involved in building the new street, and asked the town to contribute 200 guineas (£210). In July the council agreed to £150, and first refusal on the upper flat, before it was fitted out. Kyd would get from Ferguson a valid title to the building, and in return the town would grant him title to those old buildings which had not yet been demolished.

At the end of 1815 Ferguson was declared bankrupt. The three commissioners appointed were writers Andrew Christie, James Kyd and Thomas Walker. Negotiations began to get the street finished, and title transferred to the new owners. Six months later negotiations were still going on, and although the old 'Tea Room' had been demolished, the 'Ball Room' had not. The heritors, in frustration, demanded quite unrealistically that the new building be demolished and the old tea-room rebuilt. By May 1817 a compromise had been reached; the last of the old buildings were demolished in 1817, and the county heritors were granted sasine in January 1818 (Plate 9c). Meanwhile the town council held the October 1816 election in their new room, before discovering that Ferguson had not owned the land on which it had been built, and it was eighteen months before they finally got title to all their property (Plate 10c). The building the town council finally got, while visually impressive, was never a success. The stairs were narrow and awkward, and the belfry an afterthought.[24]

Also in 1818 the Hope Street Trustees sold the remaining house stances at public auction to Hutchison for £1,500. By 1820, when Wood's town plan was surveyed (Plate 13), the only buildings on the north side were the first two at the west end, the offices of James Kyd, writer, the Fife Fire Insurance Company and the Commercial Bank (Plate 10b). After a gap there was the episcopal chapel, built by Hutchison, possibly to a plan by William Burn.[25] On the south side were the new burgh chambers and a house belonging to James Carstairs the town clerk. After a gap came the county buildings and the Tontine Inn (Plate 10a). It took over 30 years for the street to be completed.[26]

Public open spaces

As population increased and the town expanded, public open spaces became increasingly important. Two areas close to the Cross, though outside the burgh boundary, the Cart Haugh and the Fluthers, were protected by the council from development, though both were encroached on before they were finally defined and protected by being encircled by buildings and roads. In June 1820 proposals by the turnpike trustees to put a new road across the Cart Haugh produced a petition from 152 leading citizens, protesting that public open spaces were essential, 'particularly so to the poorer classes who possess the fewest conveniences in their own houses for washing and drying their clothes and are least able to afford fuel for these purposes'. In addition, the area was attractive and set off the view of the new street. The protesters had their way, and the proposed crescent marked on Wood's town plan of 1820 was never built (Plate 13).

Private houses

Few lairds' town houses survived into the eighteenth century, as improved transport made them redundant, and after 1707 anyone active in politics had to keep a house in London as well as Edinburgh. By the end of the eighteenth century, however, new houses were being built by members of the growing urban middle class, and some local gentry, particularly those active in the county, once again built town houses. Men such as William Morrison of Naughton spent much of their time in Cupar.

The late eighteenth and early nineteenth centuries saw an increase in disposable incomes, and consequently increased expenditure on improvements, making houses larger, more elegant and more comfortable. One of the luxuries people aspired to was privacy, and all but the simplest housing was adapted to achieve this. Tenement buildings were often altered internally, with rooms opening off a central hall or corridor instead of each room opening off another. Internal partitions were constructed of brick or lath and plaster, which provided better sound and heat insulation than wood panelling, and wherever possible each flat had a secure and separate entrance.

Those who could afford it moved to discrete houses, ideally with a walled back garden. One such house is 9 Kirk Wynd, built by a merchant in 1811 (Plate 8b). The houses in the new suburbs, while humbler, were generally self-contained, with private gardens. Most opened straight off the street, but a few in South Road had small front gardens. There were very few architects in towns such as Cupar, and those who were so described were generally builders, who copied or adapted designs from published pattern books, in the same way as cabinet-makers did. The design of 73 Bonnygate can be identified in *The Rudiments of Architecture* of 1778 (Plate 8a). In some cases an owner added modern details to an existing house, perhaps replacing a thatched roof with slates, replacing casement windows with newer and larger sash windows, or adding a doorpiece (Plate 8c). Other architectural details which were introduced from about 1800 were cast-iron fanlights (Plate 14a,b,c), railings and balconies. The fashion for symmetry and the wide use of pattern books led to a decline in local vernacular details.

The elite aspired to 'villas'. In 1793, 'At various distances, buildings of a more magnificent form, elegant and stately villas, tower on the rising grounds.'[27] Gow has argued that the reason architectural historians have found the 'villa' so difficult to define is that 'It is much more a question of attitude than form or scale.' A villa was 'a house with a garden, close to town', country houses for the urban elite. Not a country estate but a house in its own grounds, usually with outbuildings for horses, carriages and other purposes.[28] In contrast to the uniformity of the New Town, Edinburgh villas 'permitted an unrestricted display of personal taste'.[29] Those in and around Cupar appear in general to have been the sole or main residence of their owners, though a few may have been town houses of local landowners. Most were built in the first two decades of the nineteenth century, and outside the burgh boundary for reasons of space. Examples can be found all around the town, including Bishopgate House, built *c.*1810 by Robert Wiseman, English master; Rosemount, Riggs Place, built *c.*1810, probably by Alexander Martin, land surveyor (Plate 11c); Westfield, built *c.*1810, possibly by Henry Walker of Pittencrieff, writer; and Ladyinch, built *c.*1817 (Plate 11b).

Some people wanted to live in this style but within the burgh boundary. The surviving large detached houses of the seventeenth and early eighteenth century such as Bellfield (Plate 6b), Blalowan, Preston Lodge (Plate 3a) and Marathon House (Plate 3c) came into their own again at this time. Winthank House, in Kirk Wynd, may be a rebuilding of an older town house of the Wemyss family of Winthank (Wemysshall, now Hill of Tarvit). Some writers from the 1790s started buying up small pieces of property as they came on the market, gambling on acquiring a large enough area to be able to demolish the existing buildings, and build a new house on a redesigned site. The foremost example of this is Crossgate House, built by Thomas Horsburgh, sheriff clerk, probably before 1815 (Plate 11a).[30] Here four rigs were acquired, one street-front building demolished, and a detached house built, set back from the street but visible from it, and with a walled garden and outbuildings to the side and behind. The effect, as well as the house itself, is still impressive. But such developers could not go too far. When some property-owners tried to close a vennel they were initially given permission but public opinion forced the council to reverse its decision.[31]

Several villas were inhabited only briefly by those for whom they were built. Some went bankrupt, others moved on to larger, rural properties. Andrew Christie bought up pieces of land to create a small country estate close to Cupar, and advertised it for sale in 1807 as a 'convenient spot for a gentleman's residence'. In 1812 and 1814, Ferrybank was described in the *Dundee Advertiser* as having a villa built on it, 'fit to accommodate a genteel family'. Soon after this, Christie seems to have given up trying to sell it, and moved in himself.[32] Some professionals like Christie may have built suburban villas as a speculation, fully intending, even if they lived in them, to sell them at a profit and move on. Such houses were often then purchased by 'residenters' (see Chapter 7), for whom the villa was an ideal home, offering comfort and privacy close to all the facilities and social life of the town. These villas are therefore more important than their numbers might suggest. They added to the elegant appearance of the town, and encouraged retired people with money to come and settle. Their construction, maintenance and staffing provided increased employment in the town, and their owners also spent money on consumer goods. These were houses in which people could live in considerable comfort, entertain visitors, hold dinner parties, read newspapers and books, and discuss literature and politics. But perhaps most importantly, as with the New Town of Edinburgh, they mark the beginning of the physical separation of the middle and upper classes from the rest of the townspeople.

A few professionals aspired to buy a country estate, however small. Several of these estates are to the north and north-east of the town, from where the houses, (often newly built or rebuilt) faced south and looked down on Cupar. Old estates were subdivided to satisfy this demand. Middlefield, built *c*.1760 by the town clerk, William Robertson, was detached from Prestonhall, and Cairnie Lodge from Hilton. One of the most elegant of such houses is Dalgairn, built *c*.1790. Some estates, especially those further from Cupar, may have been bought purely as speculations, and their owners may never have lived on them. Among the leading writers, for example, George Aitken owned Todhall, Thomas Horsburgh Lathockar, James Kyd New Gilston, and Robert Johnston Kedlock.[33]

The comments of visitors

Many visitors passed through Cupar. Defoe made no comment. Pococke noted 'a handsome Market house and Cross, and a good parish Church'. Johnson lumped Cupar together with Kinghorn and Kirkcaldy as 'places not unlike the small or straggling market-towns in those parts of England where commerce and manufactures have not yet produced opulence'. One visitor in 1791 'observed several new and neat buildings'.[34] But another in 1800 was less complimentary: 'This town has a mean and paltry appearance ... It consists of two irregular streets running from west to east, the northmost of which is called the Bonnygate, one would be apt to suppose in derision, for it is certainly the s....t place we ever set foot in ... We never before now thought it possible to build a whole town without hewing [sic] two houses alike, but here we were undeceived, for ... we did not find ten yards of uniformity in the whole place, the houses being all placed higgeldy-piggeldy ...'[35] An article in the *Scots Magazine* in 1804 also claimed that Cupar made 'no great appearance. The streets are ill paved and dirty'; and with no street lamps 'it must be a dreary place in a winter's evening'. In contrast a gazetteer of 1817 noted a 'great number of elegant houses', and streets 'clean, well paved and lighted'. Wood, in the text accompanying his Town Atlas, described Cupar thus: 'The Streets are broad and spacious, and contain many elegant houses ... St Catherines ... a new and elegant street ... may vie with some of the best streets in the metropolis. This town, taken altogether, is one of the neatest, most regular, and best built county towns in Scotland ... Cupar may almost be said to have been rebuilt within the last half century, and continues to extend its dimensions in every direction.' These dramatic changes were summed up by the ministers in 1836 in the statement 'that Cupar wears now the appearance of a clean and comfortable English town'.

Despite setbacks, St Catherine Street was ultimately a success, a street of which the town was proud and on which subsequent visitors commented favourably. It is, however, unusual in that most of the new developments on which it was modelled, such as the New Town of Edinburgh, were predominantly residential, whereas St Catherine Street was from the outset designed to house public buildings, and among its first occupants, as well as the county buildings and burgh chambers, were the offices of at least three writers, a bank, an insurance company and a hotel. It is the only such planned early nineteenth-century street in Fife.

The long eighteenth century saw major changes in the built environment of Cupar. The seventeenth century had been a great era of burgh architecture, but Cupar probably never had as much as towns with direct overseas trade such as Montrose. Space was filling up by the mid eighteenth century, but because of the ambitious way in which Scottish royal burghs were laid out, there was no need for the major alteration of town centres which happened in England. The 1760s building phase produced houses which were taller and more solid than their predecessors, but plain. The second phase, from about 1785 to 1820 produced some fine architecture, with an emphasis on elegance and privacy. By the early nineteenth century the spirit of improvement meant that many Scottish towns felt the need for new public buildings. In contrast to the villas and town-centre architecture, however, the contemporary suburbs, mostly built for tradesmen, were simple and practical, though still providing more space and privacy than town-centre tenements or cottages in closes. Because the town did not continue to grow much after 1820, much of the Georgian public and private architecture has survived.

Notes

1. In 1734, after discovering the cost of re-slating, the council got estimates for thatching 'to keep it water tight till the spring season', and agreed to thatch the north side as a temporary measure. Similar references can be found relating to public buildings in other burghs at this period. According to Bettesworth & Hitch, *Builder's Dictionary* (1734), thatch cost about 4s for 100 square feet, tiles about 30s and slates between 40s and 60s. Thatch was also possibly easier for do-it-yourself repairs. Wilkie's painting *Pitlessie Fair* (1805) shows thatch covering the ridge of a pantiled roof.

2. While pantiles were used for roofing in the East Neuk burghs, this may be because they were used early to replace thatch, which cannot have been improved by salt spray. And even there the major buildings were slated, as were most farm houses.

3. Pers. comm. Simon Taylor, from information compiled by Geoffrey Barrow.

4. The few houses which have not been altered or rebuilt show clear evidence of having been thatched. As well as thackstanes, some have window and door lintels at different heights to reflect the slope of the ground, implying a similarly-sloping roof-line. Thatch can be put on any shape of roof, but rectilinear tiles or slates need a horizontal roof-line (though can be fitted to a slightly-sloping roof, as here).

5. This probability is enhanced by the fact that this row ends at the west end of Well Close, which runs from Newtown to a well beside the Ladyburn, thus defining a coherent block.

6. Economies were urgent because of the cost of rebuilding the new church. Feuing land for building was more profitable than letting it for agricultural use.

7. Thomas Horsburgh, sheriff clerk, bought several plots and applied to remove the access road at the back, presumably to build one large private house, but the council refused.

8. There is one reference to a Tarvit Street, which may refer to the same area. The Rigg family lived in Tarvit house, one of whose lodges stood opposite the end of the street. 'Pleasance', meaning a walled garden, was frequently at this period applied to 'garden suburbs'.

9. The derivation of the name is not clear. The area was called Snuffmill Park until *c*.1800.

10. Probably the street now called Front Lebanon. On the same day the foundation stone was also laid for the first 'new town' of St Andrews.

11. A copy of 'Instructions for the Constables for the burgh of Cupar-Fife' was kindly sent to me by Sonia Anderson. The areas covered were: the Bonnygate

and its wynds west from Lady Wynd; from Lady Wynd to St Catherine Street; Crossgate and Riggs Row; and 'Burnside, Lebanon, and New Town'.

12 *NSA*, 6; 'in the east end of the outside of the present church there is a niche shewing where St James's altar once stood'.

13. This claim meant little, the only real comparison being with Auchtermuchty, built in 1779. By 1836 there were numerous new churches, and Cupar's was described as 'a large and commodious, though by no means an elegant building … plain and unattractive' (*NSA*). *Fifeshire Journal* (25 Mar 1875) described it as having 'no greater pretension to architectural beauty than a brewer's malt barn'.

14. The first doubts about the quality of the timber-work were reported to the council in February 1786. By September 'the roof was raxed, three of the cupples split from top to bottom and the fore and back walls off the plum'. Edinburgh architects Alexander Reid and James Salisbury inspected the building, and reported that strengthening the roof beams and buttressing the side walls should suffice. But buttresses would disturb graves, so the walls and roof were rebuilt (it may be at this point that the walls were heightened and the windows in the north wall changed). The problems were noticed only ten weeks after completion, and the local architect, Hay Bell, was sued (NAS CS237 Misc/1/28, 1787), but a compromise had to be reached because Bell had had no formal contract, and repairs were urgent before the expensive interior fittings were damaged. The north porch was added in 1811.

15. In 1737 John Douglas, architect from Edinburgh, produced an estimate for just over £88 sterling; in 1742 the council received 'a Plan or Draught how the Turrets of the Tolbooth are to be altered drawn by Mr Mercer architect in St Andrews', who was paid 1½ guineas.

16. In May 1724, the council asked for a contribution from the commissioners of supply for 'repairing and plastering the room or court hall where the meetings of this shire uses to sit', and the county helped to pay for repairs in the 1770s. In 1782 repairs to the west room were discussed, and George Paterson, architect, was to be approached.

17. In 1729 the old building was so ruinous that 'neither masters nor school boys could venture themselves therein without eminent danger and hazard of their lives'. The new building cost £1,861 12s 5d Scots (about £155 sterling).

18. In 1810 the heritors chose a site at the centre of the north side of the new street for the new county rooms, but on 24 Dec 'Mr Gillespie architect recommended changing to the south side'. The old county property consisted of the room in which the sheriff court and town council met (38¾ × 18¼ ft), the large ball-room and the area below (35 × 48 ft), the Tea Room and the area below it (21¼ × 22¼ ft). Provost Ferguson was offering a ballroom of 50 × 30 ft, a tea room 25 × 20 ft, 'a retiring room for the ladies' 16 ft square with a water closet, and a sheriff court room or town house of the same area as present, 'with water closet adjoining', all on the first floor, with 'a proper stair case'.

19. In October 1810 the council agreed that 'an alteration to the gaol is absolutely necessary both for the security of the prisoners and for their comfort while in confinement'. The first design by James Gillespie Graham was for eight cells for criminals and two for debtors, at a cost of £1,200, on the site now occupied by the war memorial, but it was felt that a bigger building was needed, so the

present site was chosen. Arbiters were appointed to value the site (owned by the provost). Iron beds, cooking-range and water-closet would add another £300 to the cost. A plan of the gaol can be found inside the front cover of B13/21/2, minutes of the prison committee. The only other gaol in Fife was in Dunfermline.

20. *NSA*; it was not long before the new gaol was condemned as unsuitable; 'the lodging is bad, and reckoned unhealthy', there was no chapel, and no attempt to separate hardened criminals from minor offenders.

21. When the river (the original town boundary) had been diverted no-one thought to record its position. In early 1815 the council proposed meeting temporarily in the new gaol, but it was also outside the burgh, so for the next 33 months it met in one of the schools.

22. The problem was exacerbated by the need for access to the new Tontine Inn. In October 1815 Ferguson's apology was finally accepted. As an interim arrangement all the rooms should be conveyed to the care of the sheriff-depute. Once everything was sorted out, he would get the west room, the JPs and Commissioners of Supply the east room, the heritors the ballroom and the adjoining small room. The heritors shower no interest in the town council's requirements.

23. The major shareholders were George Johnston, writer, William Smith, manufacturer, Patrick Pearson, writer; others were John Dingwall, tenant of Ramornie Mill, Walter Dingwall, saddler, William Jack, merchant, James Kyd, writer, James Smith, manufacturer, and Thomas Walker, writer in Edinburgh (*Sasine Abridgements*, 3 Aug 1818). The 'New Street' was clearly intended to be called 'Hope Street', probably in honour of Sir John Hope of Rankeilour, who played a prominent part in the Peninsular War. But by the early 1820s it was being referred to as 'New Street' or 'St Catherine Street', as the friary over whose site it was built had been dedicated to St Catherine.

24. The design recalls Robert Adam's 1771 alterations to Kinross townhouse, and the roof would presumably have been similar had the cupola not been added. By early 1821 everything was sorted out, and by the end of the year the clock and bells finally installed, but the roof had already started leaking.

25. The episcopal meeting room in Crossgate was destroyed by the Duke of Cumberland's troops in 1746, and they moved to another building nearby. The trustees for the subscribers to the episcopal chapel bought the ground opposite County Buildings in May 1819. The building, shown on Wood's town-plan of 1820, 'had a portico supported by pillars over the entrance, and was lighted by a cupola in the roof, and a large window in the north wall' (Innes, *Historical Notes*, 125). A letter book in private hands records payments made for the building and its fittings on 22 August 1820 (including to a Mr Burn of Edinburgh), amounting to £1,678 11s 7d. The episcopal chapel in St Andrews was built by Burn in 1824/25.

26. The original Tontine was in the eastern end of the central block, and in 1817 its committee of management bought the land to the east. On the north side, the third part of the terrace was built *c.*1825 for Christie & Pagan, writers, followed by the Clydesdale Bank in 1840, and the Royal Hotel in 1854.

27. If you stand in the right places, such as the Mote Hill, the same is still true today, both of suburban villas and rural ones such Dalgairn and Hilton.

28. The lack of space to store wheeled vehicles was a problem in old burghs, and the reason for several manses (e.g. Pittenweem and Newburgh) being rebuilt outside towns.

29. Gow, 'The Edinburgh Villa', 34. While they can sometimes be difficult to distinguish, the villa has stables and coach-house, whereas the estate or improved farm will have some form of farm steading as well.

30. The design of the house is distinctive. The closest parallel is perhaps among the published designs of the Scots architect William Hastie (Shvidkovsky, 'Classical Edinburgh and Russian Town-Planning').

31. In 1802 Thomas Horsburgh, John and David Young, merchants, and Peter Frazer, flesher, applied to buy and close 'a narrow vennel that runs through the petitioners properties to the water side'.

32. It had dining and drawing rooms, 'six good bedrooms, with suitable dressing closets, large kitchen etc.'.

33. It is not clear whether mansion houses were ever built on some of these estates, or whether they were only ever intended as investments and acquiring the right to be addressed as 'Esquire'.

34. StAU msDA855.A9T7, *Tour Through Scotland and the Borders of England made in the year 1791 and 1792*, 141.

35. Anon, *Notes of a Tour*, 10.

7

Material Culture

Every man is rich or poor according to the degree in which he can afford the
necessaries, conveniences, and amusements of human life.

Adam Smith, *Wealth of Nations*

T he study of material culture can do much to enlarge our
understanding of how people chose to spend their money and live
their lives. 'We are surrounded by things, and we are surrounded
by history. But too seldom do we use the artefacts that make up our
environment to understand the past'.[1] Spending power increased during
the eighteenth and early nineteenth centuries. Adam Smith commented
in 1776 that, 'the wages of labour' seemed to be 'more than what is
precisely necessary to enable the labourer to bring up a family'. It was a
'common complaint that luxury extends itself even to the lowest ranks
of the people, and that the labouring poor will not now be contented
with the same food, cloathing and lodging which satisfied them in
former times'. This meant, he concluded, that 'it is not the money price
of labour only, but its real recompence, which has augmented'.[2]

The minister of Cupar in 1793 also commented on 'an immense
additional consumption of fish, poultry, etc.', and, despite the high
cost of provisions, and essentials such as 'leather, soap, salt, candles
... the labourer at present is better lodged, better fed and clothed, and
can give a more decent education to his children, than his father'. He
attributed this to three causes: wages had risen in relation to prices; the
cultivation of potatoes provided extra food for the family, as well as
for pigs and poultry; and thirdly the labourer could 'depend on being
employed during the course of the whole year'. While it is clear that
prices rose as well as wages during the second half of the eighteenth
century, factors such as increased job security led to an general increase
in disposable incomes. There are plenty of contemporary comments
on the consequent increase in consumer spending. Once there was
money to spare, there were choices to be made about how to spend it.
McKendrick has suggested that it was the increased use of female and
child labour which made the difference to family incomes, and that

women consequently decided what to spend the money on, and that areas of increased production such as fabric, china and cutlery reflect women's choices. Records of purchases at roups confirm that middle-class women in Cupar were active consumers. Nenadic, however, has made the point that too much emphasis has been put on fashion and emulation of social superiors as reasons for acquiring goods. Human motivation is more complex, and by matching inventories with contemporary accounts, it would seem that consumer choice in Scotland was highly selective, and founded on very specific cultural agendas.

There are three reasons why people buy new objects for their homes. The first is fashion, in the broadest sense, as for example the adoption of tea-drinking, which changed social habits. The second is the introduction of new materials. And the third is the increase in disposable income. All three are interrelated. New fashions often employed new materials; new materials and new fashions tended to be more expensive, needing a greater disposable income. Most studies have used examples surviving in the homes of the gentry, but little work has been done to examine how quickly fashions moved out to the provinces and down the social scale. Thomson in 1800 wrote that 'as the people become more wealthy, a taste for refinement will, of course, spread and be more generally indulged'. Once this trend starts, it cannot be reversed, and 'not satisfied with bare necessaries, men will look out for the elegancies and delicasies of life'.[3] This chapter shows how this manifested itself among the middle classes of Cupar, based on material from ninety-one inventories, dating between 1689 and 1827, listing the property of seventy-two men and nineteen women. Appendix 4 lists their names, dates and occupations, and the locations of their inventories. These inventories provide an extremely small statistical sample, and clearly do not represent a cross-section of the community. No evidence from within the town has been excluded, but people from the surrounding area have been included if they were active in the life of the town.

The inventories present two major problems. The first is that not all are complete lists. One, for example, only lists those goods not sold at the roup. It is also clear that some goods did not get inventoried, but were presumably given away before death. It is rare to find family bibles or jewellery listed unless there were no near relatives. The same may be true for watches, clothes, and perhaps other items. We have no way of knowing how much was not inventoried.[4] The second is that the objects and the way they are documented change over time. In early inventories kitchen utensils can form two-thirds or more of the goods listed, and are usually described in detail. Later, when people had more possessions, kitchen utensils were described in far less detail. This is probably the reason for an apparent decrease in numbers of some items between the periods 1795–1814 and 1815–27. Other problems stem from lack of specific information in the descriptions. Although the wood from which some furniture is made is mentioned, presumably because of its quality or value, it cannot be assumed that all unspecified furniture was made of pine. By the 1820s mahogany is hardly mentioned, perhaps because it had become standard, particularly for dining tables.

In the early eighteenth century goods were listed even if they only had a scrap value. Examples include 'two old Timber beds whereof one was made use of for mending a horse Manger' (1743), and a horse 'only worth the skin and the shoes' (1752). In other instances an explanation was provided for items which were not in the same condition as when the owner died, as for example 'fyve bed sheets one of which was made use of for the minor when her running sores were dressed' (1743). Later inventories ignore items of no value, and contain fewer such personal details. There is evidence, however, of objects which retained some value despite damage. Delftware is a soft tin-glazed earthenware, and many Delft bowls were recorded as cracked, but presumably still kept as ornaments. In one house in 1827 a chamber pot whose handle had broken off was listed in the servants' bedroom.

Household goods were often listed room by room, and the number and use of rooms described. In some later inventories the order in which items were listed within a room appears to be a guide to their relative cost, status or novelty value. The inventories do not in general list any fixtures, and they cannot tell us whether items were new, second-hand, gifts or inherited. While the means by which an object was acquired does not affect its usefulness to the owner, it does affect theories of consumer behaviour. Scottish inventories become more useful for comparative purposes from the third quarter of the eighteenth century, as they were often compiled by professional valuers or appropriate tradesmen, and were therefore more standardised.

Although very few inventories survive, it is possible by looking at a number of different aspects of material culture to build up a pattern which may have some validity. Unfortunately the inventories do not survive evenly over the 139 years covered by this study, and the choice of time-frame is itself subjective, its two ends fixed by surviving inventories which are of interest. The latest inventory, that of Andrew Christie, is included because he was an important figure in the town, and because the house he built c.1812 survives. Although his bankruptcy was attributed to 'various misfortunes in his banking transactions and otherwise', one cannot help but suspect that the building and furnishing of his new house may have been a contributory factor. The inventories have been divided into five chronological groups.[5]

Some writers have divided items in inventories into 'necessities' and 'luxuries', but this is too simplistic, and one generation's 'luxury' may be the next generation's 'necessity'. The material here is divided into four main sections, considering living spaces, changing technologies and fashions, conspicuous consumption and personal comfort. The items chosen for discussion are those which appear in a wide range of inventories, and which show change over the period. In a few cases the inventories can be linked to surviving buildings.

Living spaces

The names rooms were given, and the way they were furnished and used, changed significantly during the eighteenth century. The number of rooms gradually increased – space and the increased privacy it could bring were 'luxuries' to be aspired to. In the earliest inventories, rooms were designated simply by their position within the house, for example 'back chamber'. The first room other than the kitchen to develop a separate identity was the dining room, holding a large table or tables, and the best crockery and cutlery. At first it was the only room in the house not to contain a bed, and often served as a general family living-room as well as for formal entertaining. The next specific room was the bedroom, for sleeping and for privacy. In larger houses a second public room was designated for entertaining. A drawing room was a formal reception room; a parlour less formal. Where there was also a dining room (or drawing room), the parlour was an informal family living-room, often housing a dining table which could be moved to the formal dining room when guests were present. A parlour could therefore be a public room used for entertaining, but was generally a private part of the house.

Looking at the inventories for evidence of specific rooms other than kitchen, cellar and garret, the first dining room belonged to the minister William Dick in 1736. After 1795 half the thirty-eight households definitely had a dining room. Most of the houses advertised in the *Fife Herald* after 1822 had both dining room and parlour, and very few did not have a dining room. After the middle of the eighteenth century the dining table took over from the bed as the single most expensive item of furniture. As well as the table, and a set of chairs, dining rooms often had ornamental mirrors with sconces over the fireplace, the earliest listed in 1749; sideboards; and later a few wine coolers and plate warmers. There were other luxury items such as pictures, clocks and barometers, and displays of the best china and glass, varying from 'a Large Delphic Bowel Cracked', and 'a Black Japaned Decanter' (1749), to 'punch bowel, silver ladlle' (1818).

The drawing room took longer to become standard in middle-class houses in Scotland. Only one is recorded in Cupar before 1800 (Captain Hay, 1792), followed by one in 1813 (Katharine Skene, possibly Marathon House, Plate 3c), one in 1822 (John Anderson) and one in

1827 (Andrew Christie). The drawing room, like the dining room, was designed for formal entertaining, and for display of the best furniture, pictures and ornaments. All three rooms contained sofas, two had tea tables, one a card table. By the early nineteenth century newspaper advertisements of houses for sale can tell us about the arrangement of rooms. Bellfield, for example (Plate 6b), in the *Dundee Advertiser* in 1811 had parlour, kitchen and servants' quarters on the ground floor, large drawing and dining rooms on the first floor, and three bedrooms and two dressing rooms on the second. Most villas seem to have had an upstairs drawing room, even if this meant some bedrooms being on the ground floor. Ladyinch (Plate 11d) (*Fife Herald*, 1825) had a dining room and two bedrooms on the ground floor, and a drawing room and two more bedrooms (with dressing rooms) on the first floor. Some of those who did not have a drawing room had a parlour. One was listed at Bunzion in 1758. Three more inventories from 1813 (Alexander Melville; William Cockburn, 1819; and John Smith, 1825) had parlours which were clearly used as a combination of dining room and sitting room, with tables, chairs, sideboards, pictures and clocks, as well as china, glass and cutlery. Two households (David Tod, 1812; Robert Wiseman, 1822) had a parlour as well as a dining room; Henry Walker (1818) had two. The minister of Cults, David Wilkie (1812) had a parlour and a dining room, but when the inventory was made the dining table was in the parlour, presumably for everyday use.[6] This parlour also had a pantry off it where china, glass and cutlery were stored. Robert Wiseman, a teacher who probably took in boarders, had a crumb cloth (see below) in the parlour as well as the dining room, another indication that the room was used for meals.

Other rooms specified in inventories include six lobbies, two nurseries and two libraries. Lobbies in the late eighteenth and early nineteenth century developed a character of their own. In Edinburgh, great importance was attached to the lobby in the design of houses in the New Town, as it 'provided an opportunity for a display of fashionable but dignified taste before the visitor was shown by a servant to one of the main reception rooms'.[7] Of the six lobbies listed, five had 8-day clocks on display; Andrew Christie (1827) had a table, an umbrella stand, a shoe-scraper and a boot-jack. The first umbrella had appeared in Edinburgh in 1782.[8] The only one in a Cupar inventory belonged to Jean Wright, midwife (1797).

Changing fashions

In the seventeenth century good-quality furniture was often imported from Holland. The one example from Cupar is the 'holland wand [wicker] cradle' in the home of a merchant in 1700. Furniture at the beginning of the eighteenth century was generally simple, consisting of free-standing beds, often enclosed, and plain tables and chairs, the commonest wood being pine. Oak was used occasionally for almost every item of furniture, but most frequently for tables. Inventories list a 'great Wainscot table in the Kitchen' (1723), and 'An Bigg Oak Table' in the dining room (1743). By 1758 Bunzion had a mahogany dining table but also 'a wainscot Dyning table' in the 'vestable'. William Beveridge (1749) had a mahogany dining table, and 'a Very Large Winscot Table' in the cellar. It would appear, therefore, that those who could afford it had dining tables made of oak, but when mahogany became fashionable, these large oak tables were retained but relegated to a lesser position within the house.

The cheaper and commoner woods never ceased to be used, but new woods were introduced for good-quality furniture, particularly, during the eighteenth century, mahogany and walnut. Mahogany is hard and

TABLE 7.1   Numbers of various items discussed in the text with (in brackets) the number of households from which they come.

	1689–1751	1752–69	1770–92	1795–1814	1815–1827
Mahogany furniture	4 (1)	15 (3)	7 (4)	27 (9)	34 (9)
Serving and eating dishes					
Wood	63 (6)	41 (7)	29 (3)	0	0
Pewter	188 (13)	184 (11)	109 (9)	33 (4)	0
Earthenware	60 (5)	73 (7)	28 (3)	10 (3)	3 (1)
Stoneware	0	72 (5)	73 (4)	c.100 (3)	0
China	55 (2)	100 (5)	100+ (6)	c.350 (10)	c.600 (11)
Total	c.385 (14)	545 (15)	c.620 (14)	c.1200 (15)	c.1000 (10)
Drinking glasses and glass dishes	c.40 (4)	63 (5)	c.160 (6)	c.290 (9)	c.225 (7)
Carpets and Rugs	2 floor cloths (1)	0	11 (4)	64 (12)	c.65 (10)
Green cloths	0	0	1? (1)	8 (5)	8 (5)
Curtains	0	0	3 (1)	9 (3)	16 (4)
Clocks	6	3	6	7	13
Barometers	0	0	2	2	8
Prints, maps and paintings	9 (2)	29 (3)	42 (3)	51 (5)	c.60 (9)
Mirrors	13 (9)	26 (13)	26 (10)	56 (17)	40 (13)
Beds	50 (16)	64 (16)	50 (17)	66 (18)	52 (17)
Matresses	52 (14)	71 (17)	57 (15)	80 (17)	46 (8)
Lighting					
Candlesticks	28 (11)	51 (13)	61 (13)	110 (15)	50 (8)
Lanterns	2 (2)	4 (4)	3 (2)	12 (10)	1
Lamps	0	1	4 (3)	6 (6)	10 (6)
Total lighting	30 (11)	56 (13)	68 (13)	128 (15)	61 (10)

durable, with a close and straight grain and an attractive colour. It was at first imported mainly from Jamaica, later from Cuba and various parts of South America, and its use became far more common after import duties on it were abolished in 1722. Mahogany furniture presumably took some time to reach the provinces. The first recorded in Cupar was the 'Large Mahoginie Table' in the dining room of William Beveridge in 1749. Melville of Balgarvie (1756) had 'a Mahogony Table', and 'a Scrutore [escritoire] of Mahagony'. At Bunzion in 1758 there were three mahogany dining tables, three tea tables, two beds, ten chairs, two chests of drawers, a bureau-bookcase, a dressing mirror and three tea caddies. In contrast, the only mahogany items belonging to John Anderson in 1775 were two candlesticks. Twenty-six of the ninety-one inventories include mahogany furniture, sixteen of these after 1800. Counting a set of six chairs as one item (otherwise they distort the statistics), and excluding small items such as mirrors, candlesticks, tea trays and tea caddies, the numbers of pieces of mahogany furniture are shown in Table 7.1. But it is possible that by the early nineteenth century mahogany furniture had become the norm, particularly for dining tables, and it therefore stopped being specified in inventories. It seems more likely, therefore, that the majority of households before 1800 did not have mahogany furniture, but that after that date few if any were without something.

The inventory of a wright in 1787 included 'Four inch Boards of Mahogany & two short pieces' (probably to frame mirrors and pictures). In 1791 the deacon of wrights petitioned the town council about wrights outside the town undercutting burgesses. The council agreed to add to the table of customs payments for work by non-freemen, including 'a chest of mahogany drawers' and 'a mahogany clock case', both charged the highest rate of 2s (similar pieces made of oak were charged less). Clearly by 1791 there was a growing market for mahogany furniture, and some was being made locally. Apart from fir, oak and mahogany, other woods mentioned in inventories include beech (chests of drawers, 1757 and 1779; chairs, 1758 and 1792); 'plaintree' (sycamore) (table, 1812); walnut (six chairs, 1760; chest of drawers, 1783); walnut veneer (six chairs, 1758); and unspecified veneer (chests of drawers and a dressing table, 1749–60). The number of oak items remained fairly steady.

During the eighteenth century furniture became not only more varied and more elegant, but also more comfortable. Instead of being arranged formally around the walls, it began to be placed around the room ready for use. The most distinctive new item of furniture was the sofa. In Cupar a 'sattee' was listed in John Stevenson's inventory in 1795, and was bought at his roup by the incoming second minister. Eighteen sofas were listed in fifteen households between 1812 and 1827, three in dining rooms, four in drawing rooms, three in parlours, one in a 'front room' and one in a bedroom.

Most chairs had plain wooden seats, though leather seats are also found occasionally. Others were covered in a variety of materials including carpet (1709), red Turkey (1749) and yellow silk (1749). But gradually more and more chairs had padded seats. An inventory of 1775, for example, lists chairs with 'soft' seats, one in 1796 had 'hair bottomed chairs' and three more 1816–18. Cane seats were fashionable in the seventeenth century and into the first half of the eighteenth, appearing in inventories in 1721, 1743 and 1756. Late in the century rush-seated chairs became fashionable, and between 1812 and 1822 are found in five inventories. Upholsterers had been established in Edinburgh by 1750. The first three upholsterers in Cupar were all cabinet-makers, working in the first two decades of the nineteenth century. There are very few cushions in the inventories – one in 1756 had eight, another in 1796 had one, and Andrew Christie (1827) had a 'pillow' on each of his three sofas. Towards the end of the eighteenth century it became fashionable to put covers over sofas and chairs for everyday use, and only remove them for formal occasions. Such covers are recorded in six inventories between 1795 and 1827. Katherine Skene (1813) had 'Two Stripped Soffa Covers, and Twelve Chair covers' and 'A Set of white Covers for ditto'.

The first dressing table was listed in 1756 (a very early example), and then several in or after 1812. Bedside or 'night tables' came into fashion in England around 1760. The first owner in Cupar was in 1813, followed by three more by 1827. Desks are found at all periods, from a 'scrutore' [escritoire] in 1721 to 'An Oak Bevereau' in 1775. Later examples are often described as 'small' or 'portable writing desk', but the terminology is too imprecise to draw any conclusions about changes in style. However, they do seem to have been kept in the private part of the house – two were in libraries, and the rest in bedrooms. Furniture which died out during the period included forms (backless benches) which were common, especially in kitchens, in the first half of the eighteenth century, but the last example is in 1760 except in inns where they remained in use.

Inventories do not tell us where furniture was bought, or how much was made locally. Between 1770 and 1827 there were thirteen wrights who were also described as cabinet-makers. By the 1820s each man would have had a workshop with several employees, and some had a 'wareroom' in which to display their stock. At least one local ironmonger stocked 'tools and stock for wrights and cabinet-makers'.[9] There are various items of Cupar-made furniture in private collections. For those who could afford it, however, the best furniture was bought in Edinburgh.

The second-hand market operated at all levels of society, and the gentry bought second-hand when the opportunity arose. Furniture seems to have had a particularly high second-hand value because of the saving in transport costs over buying new. In 1739 at Mrs Dick's roup in Cupar Lady Rossie bought 'a bed and hangings', '6 Cane Chairs and one armed Chair' and 'a Looking Glass'.[10] Lady Anstruther bought 'a feather bed, bolster, 2 pillows at Pitlour's roup' in 1789. Seven domestic roup rolls were found. The purchasers included ministers, doctors, lawyers, the town clerk, members of guildry and trades, women and people from outside the town. A roup was useful if you were setting up home. Laurence Adamson, who was appointed second minister in 1794, bought fifty lots at a roup the following year, including a silver tea pot for £8 1s, a 'sattee' for £4 18s, a bed and curtains, three mirrors and seven chairs. Those who purchased large numbers of items include several innkeepers, who presumably found roups a useful opportunity to replace items broken or worn out. There were also second-hand dealers.

It was not just objects that were subject to changing fashions: in 1773 Boswell and Johnson 'stopped at Cupar, and drank tea'.[11] The drinking of both tea and coffee had been introduced into England around 1660, and was common in Edinburgh by about 1720. Not everyone approved, it being considered 'by many reflecting persons' to be 'expensive, wasteful of time, and calculated to render the population weakly and effeminate'. In the 1740s there were moves to discourage the drinking of both tea and brandy, 'pointing strongly to the manlier attractions of beer'.[12] Such official disapproval was probably linked to the fact that both tea and brandy were heavily taxed, and their popularity led to an increase in smuggling. In the *Old Statistical Account* the minister of Ceres claimed that 'tea is used in three fourths of the families'. By 1800 there was 'scarcely a cottager's house in the county where it is not to be found'.[13]

New materials

While fashion is often given as the only explanation for changes in material culture, changing and improving technology was also a factor. Tea-drinking, for example, would have been less attractive without its accompanying new materials. Wood, horn and pewter, the traditional materials used for drinking vessels, were unsuitable for hot liquids; and while cups and saucers could be made in earthenware and stoneware they were crude compared with china, which was not only more delicate but absorbed less heat. And so, like tea itself, expensive imports or fairly expensive British-made copies of china tea services became almost 'necessities'. As well as china cups, tea drinking required many other purchases. Tea-urns, tea-vases, tea-kettles, teapots, tea chests (caddies), tea-cups and saucers, tea-tables, tea-trays, tea-knives, teaspoons, and the related milk jug, sugar basin and slop bowl all appear with increasing frequency in the inventories; accessories for a new and complex ritual presided over by the women of the household.

Despite the substantial cost involved, the habit of drinking tea moved rapidly throughout Scotland and down the social scale. In Cupar the minister, William Dick (1736), had a silver teapot and six silver tea spoons. Inventories in 1747, 1749, 1756, 1758 and 1760 include a wide range of tea-drinking accessories. Before c.1770 tea-drinking in Cupar seems to have been limited to gentry, professionals and women. After this it became almost universal. The values of tea services varied enormously. By the 1820s the ownership of china seems to have been fairly general, and there were shops in Cupar selling glass, stoneware and china 'from Wedgwood, Spode, and the other principal manufactories in England'.[14]

Fewer households possessed specialist items relating to coffee-drinking – copper coffee pots in 1749 and 1756, and coffee cups in 1758. Six inventories between 1760 and 1800 contained evidence of coffee drinking, including two coffee mills, and an innkeeper in 1795 had five coffee pots. This, along with the existence of a Coffee House in the town in the early nineteenth century, seems to confirm that the drinking of coffee was often a public and communal activity, whereas tea-drinking was private and domestic. After 1812 eight of the twenty-seven inventories (30 per cent) have evidence of coffee drinking. One, in 1792, listed 'a chocolate pot and Skimmer'.

Developments in eating utensils seem to have taken longer to move down the social scale. The use of forks was regarded in the early seventeenth century as a curious habit indulged in by Italians. The fashion began to catch on in France in the second half of the century, but only became widespread in the eighteenth. The use of knives and forks was said to have become common among the middle classes in London by the early eighteenth century, and in Edinburgh by about 1750. While Boswell found tea drinking to be universal, he found people still eating with horn spoons rather than forks. Somerville also spoke of people in the mid eighteenth century carrying a knife and fork with them when they travelled, or went to weddings or public dinners.

In Cupar the first owners of knives and forks were two landowners in around 1720, followed by the minister William Dick (1736), and a writer in 1749. After 1750, 45 per cent of inventories specify forks. It is possible that cutlery was not listed in some later inventories because it was in drawers or cupboards. It is also possible that isolated pieces of cutlery escaped listing along with other small personal items. Keddie spoke of farm labourers in her grandparents' day (c.1800) only possessing one wooden bowl and one horn spoon. And this was true even in the early twentieth century. Horn spoons appear in many of the Cupar inventories. It could be assumed that they lingered on because they were virtually unbreakable, but Lady Anstruther bought half a dozen in 1768, so they would appear to have still been the utensil of choice for certain purposes.[15] Henrietta Keddie also described a 'silver mother-of-pearl fruit-knife – an unfailing article in the pocket of every well-bred woman of the period'.[16] But none appears in inventories, presumably yet another small personal item which escaped being listed.

Wooden dishes had been around for a very long time, supplemented by pewter in the sixteenth and seventeenth centuries. Earthenware and glass both became more widely used during the seventeenth century, but transport problems meant they were not often found outside the main cities. Somerville claimed that in the 1760s wooden platters were 'more or less in use in almost every house'. Among the country gentry, 'pewter vessels were also to be found; with a set of delft, or china, for the second course at table ... A punch bowl, and teacups and saucers of china were, however, always considered as indispensable, and were ostentatiously arranged in ... the dining room'.[17] Keddie described her grandmother's kitchen as containing 'pewter plates and mugs ... the shelves laden with an ample array of blue-and-white stoneware'.[18] 'It is difficult for twentieth-century man to understand the excitement that was generated by pottery and porcelain in the eighteenth century'.[19] While china had to be imported from a distance, earthenware had been made in small quantities in Cupar from 1760 or earlier, and stoneware was probably made in Kirkcaldy by the end of the century. Cupar's table of customs in 1713 listed earthenware; in 1789 the revised list referred to both earthenware and stoneware, charged by the crate.

The use of pewter had reached its height during the seventeenth century, but started to go into decline from the 1740s onwards. Pewter was unbreakable, easily transportable, and could be recycled, but declined in the face of competition from a wide range of alternative materials. Pewter lasted longest for jugs, tankards and large serving dishes, for which it was tougher and lighter than ceramics. The numbers of serving and eating dishes of different materials are shown in Table 7.1 above. The last inventory to list wooden dishes was in 1792; pewter dishes in 1813; and earthenware in 1820. However, it is clear that the bulk of serving and eating dishes by the end of the eighteenth century were of china. The use of wood and pewter seems to have declined through the century, while both earthenware and stoneware increased and then declined, stoneware peaking later than earthenware.

The general adoption of china by the middle classes is said to have happened in London by the 1690s, and in Edinburgh by 1750; in Cupar it would appear to have been the end of the century. The number of serving and eating dishes in each household vastly increased towards the end of the eighteenth century, and most if not all of this increase was accounted for by the purchase of china. A certain amount of stoneware was also bought, even by the most wealthy, presumably chosen for durability and use by servants. China also brought increasingly specific descriptions, such as dinner services, tea services, breakfast services, soup plates, sugar bowls, cheese plates and fruit plates. Glass, like china, had been around in small quantities for a long time, but the number and variety of glass receptacles took off at the end of the eighteenth century. Both china and glass developed increasingly specialised shapes, such as egg cups, first listed in Cupar in 1783, and jelly glasses, from 1795.

Carpets were expensive imports and had long been used as table-coverings, but in England began increasingly to be used to cover floors during the third quarter of the seventeenth century. In mid eighteenth-century Scotland, however, carpets were unknown in all but the wealthiest houses. 'Scotch Carpet' was made from the middle of the eighteenth century in Edinburgh and the Borders. It was 'double-weave', had no pile and was reversible, and was laid in strips sewn together. True carpets woven in one piece were far more expensive. It was the 1820s before the manufacture of carpets within Scotland really took off. An alternative was floor-cloth, a treated canvas, produced from the 1720s and used until it was replaced by linoleum in the late nineteenth century. The earliest floor-covering material to be listed in the inventories is a 'Cloath for the floor' in the back bedroom of a writer in 1749. The first floor carpets appear in 1783 and 1784. From this period they become quite common, and from 1812 onwards it was almost standard to have a carpet and hearthrug in dining room, drawing room or parlour, and the best bedroom(s). One house in 1813 had carpet in the upper lobby, though the lower lobby and staircase had painted cloth. At Cupar Mills in 1822 there was waxed cloth in the upper lobby but carpet on the stairs, while Andrew Christie in 1827 had a 'Stair carpet with Brass Rods'. An item which seems strange to us but which is clearly shown in the painting *The Arrival of the Country Relations* by Alexander Carse (1812) is the 'green' or 'crumb cloth' which was put under the dining table and chairs to protect the carpet from wear and spillages. This clearly became standard at the same time as carpet did, appearing in 1795, and in seven of the fifteen inventories between 1813 and 1827 which include carpets (always in the same room as the dining table).

According to Loudon's *Encyclopaedia*, window curtains gave 'an air of comfort' to any room, and gave 'the mistress of the house an excellent opportunity for exercising her taste in their arrangement'. Curtains were slow to become general; with wooden shutters fitted inside most windows, curtains were decorative rather than functional.[20] An inventory of 1792 had curtains in drawing room, dining room and one other room. The best inn had one curtained bedroom in 1795. Curtains only appear in six of the twenty inventories between 1812 and 1827. More common than curtains were blinds, presumably to keep the sun from fading upholstery. These may have been 'Venetian blinds' like those described in the *Old Statistical Account* for Newburgh 'for blunting the rays of the summer sun', or linen blinds, which were manufactured in Fife at this period, mainly in the Falkland area.

Conspicuous consumption

There are various items in the inventories which were used to symbolise the wealth and fashion-consciousness of their owner. Only nine watches appear in the inventories. Perhaps, like family bibles and jewellery, they were given away before death. Their existence must be assumed from the presence of clock- and watch-makers in the town during the whole of the period, but increasing in number from about 1760. Clocks, however, do appear from 1709, with another five before the middle of the century, and becoming more common after 1760. They were generally displayed in prominent and public positions such as dining rooms and parlours and, by the early nineteenth century, in lobbies. The first record of a barometer is in 1775. After 1812 they became more common and, like clocks, were generally displayed in public areas, three in dining rooms, three in parlours, one in a library and one in a lobby.

A number of inventories include pictures. William Dick, minister (1736), had eight framed pictures in his dining room and bed chamber. At Bunzion in 1758 there were 'eight pictures' in the parlour, and 'seven large pictures with gilt frames' and 'six framed prints' in the bedroom. By contrast Elizabeth Duncan (1760) had a single picture hung above a chest of drawers. A physician in 1775 had ten large pictures and fifteen prints, and his wife 'three glazed prints'. The reproduction of paintings by engraving was a feature of the late eighteenth century in response to a growing market. Mostly produced in London, prints were distributed unframed, through booksellers or print-sellers or by mail order, and then framed by the purchaser. In the Cupar inventories are a 'Print of the Earl of Hopetoun' in a dining room in 1827, and two prints of works by David Wilkie in 1824.[21] In the parlour at Bunzion (1758) was 'a Map of the world', and a merchant in 1760 had maps of England, Scotland and Germany. Paintings were rare. Katherine Skene (1813) had 'A portrait' in the drawing room, and in her bedroom a 'Painting of Queen Mary'. David Methven (1824) had 'Portraits of Mr & Mrs Methven' and 'Miniatures of Ditto'. Andrew Christie (1827) also had two family portraits. An invoice survives from JT Nairne, portrait painter, Cupar, in 1815 to the Earl of Leven and Melville for £17 17s, for twelve copies on vellum of 'a miniature of Buonaparte', 'two editions of drawings in Chalk of The Hon[le] Lady Lucy, Lady Jean and Lady Marianne Melville', two other portrait drawings and a painting of Crawford Priory.[22]

In the seventeenth century those who could afford it covered their walls with arras or painted cloth. Somewhere between 1730 and 1745 wallpaper started to be made in Edinburgh. A Cupar inventory of 1743 included old wall hangings, while another in 1751 had 'a piece of painted hangings' in his dining room, and 'a piece of mock Arras' in the closet. The stock of a wright in 1787 included 'Thirty nine pieces of paper for Rooms – Six pieces of borders & 2 broken Do'.[23] By the 1820s wallpaper had clearly become more common, as several painters also advertised themselves as 'paper-hangers', and Robert Tullis offered for sale new 'Washable Paper Hangings', which were less vulnerable to fading, damp or insects.[24]

As the quantity of silver, glass and china grew, the best items not required for everyday use took on an ornamental function. Keddie remembered 'A great porcelain punch-bowl, ordered and made in China' which 'lay beneath the sitting-room sideboard'. A number of inventories list one or more china or silver punch bowls, and their associated ladles. Carpets, curtains and mahogany furniture had an ornamental as well as a practical function. But by the end of the eighteenth century there were items other than pictures being purchased and displayed for no function other than ornament. There were pot plants on stands, and 'trophies of sport – foxes' brushes, stuffed birds – owls, partridges, long-tailed pheasants' as well as 'foreign coral and shells' and 'a silver cup or two, prizes gained at agricultural shows and curling matches'.[25]

It is a natural instinct to ornament and personalise one's living space. Many ornaments such as flowers or shells would have no monetary value and therefore not be listed. In a few inventories, however, can be seen the beginnings of the display of objects deliberately made or bought as ornaments. The parlour at Bunzion in 1758 had 'a Glass box with gum flowers'; Alexander Hay (1792) had four 'flower glasses'; John Stevenson (1795) and Henry Walker (1818) 'flower pots'; Katharine Skene (1813) 'Two Jars' in the drawing room and 'A pot Stand' in the dining room. At Cupar Mills in 1822 were '4 stuffed birds & 3 shells' in the dining room and 'a fruit piece, 5 birds and 2 shells' in the drawing room, while John Smith (1825) had a stuffed pheasant and 'chimney piece ornaments'.

Personal comfort

Some items were clearly bought for personal comfort, with little or no element of conspicuous consumption.[26] There are of course a number which fit both purposes. Curtains and carpets were fashion items, and conspicuous, but also served to improve heat and noise insulation. The items selected to demonstrate increased spending on personal comfort are beds, mattresses, candlesticks, mirrors and washstands.

Free-standing box beds, often with doors, 'virtually a little house within a house, providing privacy [and] increased warmth', were common in the first half of the eighteenth century and increasingly rare in the second half. From the 1740s the predominant type was the curtain bed, sometimes subdivided into tent beds and (four-)posted beds. By the early nineteenth century some of the smartest beds had mahogany frames, and the hangings matched chair coverings and curtains. It is clear that the middle classes in Cupar made the purchase of as many beds as space and money would allow one of their first priorities. There were ideally two things put on top of a bed base. One was a tight-packed mattress or palliasse, normally filled with chaff or chopped straw, but later with hair or wool. On top of this was put a 'bed', resembling a modern duvet, loosely filled with chaff or preferably feathers (Table 7.1). Like tea-drinking, the increasing comfort of beds was not always approved of. 'The indulging in down-beds, soft pillows, and easy seats ... tends to enervate the body, and to render it unfit for fatigue'. The same writer condemned the increased use of coaches rather than walking or riding, claiming that physical weakness led to mental weakness, and luxury 'renders the mind so effeminate as to be subdued by every distress'.[27]

Lighting was by candles, or cruisies, simple oil lamps with rush wicks. Everyday candles were made of tallow, needed regular trimming to make them work effectively, smelled disagreeable, and produced black smoke. Wax candles worked far better but cost about three times as much.[28] The Argand oil lamp, introduced into Scotland in 1784, used a cylindrical wick and a glass chimney, producing a radical improvement in efficiency. When looking at the count of candlesticks it must therefore be remembered that candles were increasingly being supplemented by lamps and lanterns, so the increase in comfort was greater than appears from the table. Where a material is specified, early candlesticks were of brass, and the use of brass continued throughout the period. From 1775 a few people had mahogany candlesticks, perhaps a way of acquiring something relatively affordable in this fashionable material. Silver plate was introduced in the early nineteenth century. Plated candlesticks were found stored with the best china and cutlery, usually in the dining room, for use only for formal entertaining. Everyday candlesticks were almost always listed in the kitchen, where they were kept during the day and prepared for use each evening. Another item which, although it has an aspect of display and conspicuous consumption, is also useful, is the mirror. The more there were, the higher the proportion kept in the private parts of the house. The average number of mirrors is shown in Table 7.2. This is a fairly crude measure, as there was a great difference in status and cost between a simple bedroom looking-glass and a gilt-framed overmantle mirror. This, and failure to list the more humble examples, probably explains the apparent reduction after 1815.

TABLE 7.2   Increase over time of average number of certain items per household

	1689– 1751	1752– 69	1770– 92	1795– 1814	1815– 27	% increase 1689–1751 to 1815–27
Beds	3.1	4	2.9	3.7	3.1	0
Chairs	14	16	16	22	19	36
Chests of drawers	1.25	1.7	1.6	1.6	1.7	36
Rooms	4.5	4.8	4	6.3	6.2	38
Mattresses (all types)	3.7	4.2	3.8	4.7	5.8	57
Mirrors	1.4	2	2.6	3.3	3.1	121
Candlesticks, lamps and lanterns	2.7	4.3	5.2	8.5	6.1	126
Glasses and glass dishes	10	13	27	32	32	220
Serving and eating dishes (all materials)	27.5	36	44	80	100	264

The table is laid out in ascending order of the % difference between numbers for earliest and latest time periods.

Apart from the ubiquitous chamber-pot, there is nothing in the early inventories relating to personal hygiene. Basin-stands appear in Edinburgh from 1759, but it is 1792 before there is evidence for one in Cupar, with others in 1795 (the Blue Bell Inn), 1796 and 1797 (Jean Wright, midwife). After 1812 there are references to 'bason stands' in fourteen of the twenty inventories, some on their own, others with basin and ewers. The number per household ranged from one to eight. In 1822 John Anderson had a 'corner bason stand bason and ure' in each of three bedrooms. Corner units were a fashion which started in London in the 1770s. Robert Guthrie in 1820 had a 'toilett table' as well. This was a period when all classes were becoming more concerned with personal hygiene. The inventory containing most in the way of washing facilities is that of Andrew Christie (1827). Spread through five bedrooms, three with dressing rooms or closets, and a servants' bedroom, were six basin stands, thirteen basins, ten chamber pots, eight ewers, two foot pails, two soap drainers and two bidets.[29]

One demonstration of changing ideas of what was necessary is the fittings of the prison. In 1790 the gaoler petitioned the town council because the debtors' cells had 'neither a table nor seats for a person to sit on or to set a tankard upon', and he had to lend furniture from his own house. The council authorised a wright to make two small forms and a table for each room 'at as moderate an expense as possible'. In 1817 the new gaol was supplied with blankets, and when Joseph Gurney and Elizabeth Fry visited in 1819 each cell had a straw mattress, two blankets and a rug. The council also demanded more comfort for itself. In 1781 they authorised the making of 'proper seats' for the council room, and in 1804 a cushion for the provost's seat in the magistrates' loft in the kirk.

Another way of looking at the evidence from Cupar is to consider the average numbers of each item per household. When there is spare money for extra material goods, what was it spent on first? Table 7.2 presents average numbers of various items, with the percentage increase between the first and last figures. Table 7.3 presents similar figures for the number of households in which certain items were present. It is clear that there was a consumer revolution in Cupar during the eighteenth century. Given that by the early nineteenth century there was money for a wide range of domestic goods, it could be suggested that where the tables show little change over the century it is not that expenditure on this particular item never took off, but that it took off early. Therefore the lower the percentage difference between the first and last group of inventories, the earlier that item had become the subject of increased expenditure, and the higher the priority put on it as soon as spare money was available. Tables 7.2 and 7.3 have been laid out in ascending order of this difference, beginning with beds and ending with serving and eating dishes, beginning with clocks and ending with mahogany furniture. While the numbers are small, the tables appear to demonstrate that practicality and comfort were given a higher priority than display.

The speed with which new fashions moved down the social scale is difficult to assess because the surviving inventories all represent the elite. In general terms, tea drinking caught on very fast, other items less so.

TABLE 7.3   Increase over time of number of households possessing certain items

	1689–1751	1752–69	1770–92	1795–1814	1815–27	% increase 1689–1751 to 1815–27
Clocks	6	3	6	7	13	117
Tea drinking items	5	8	11	15	11	120
Forks	4	9	7	9	9	125
Glasses and glass dishes	4	5	6	12	11	175
Pictures	2	3	3	5	9	350
China serving and eating dishes	2	5	6	13	11	450
Mahogany furniture	1	3	4	9	9	800
Carpets	0	0	4	12	10	
Wash basins	0	0	1	10	9	
Curtains	0	0	1	3	4	
Sofas	0	0	0	8	7	

The table is laid out in ascending order of the % difference between numbers for earliest and latest time periods.

Some fashions were constrained by space. One had to be very well off to have a dining room and a drawing room into which to fit furniture such as sofas, sideboards and pianos, so the purchase of such goods reflected the presence of far more money than the cost of the objects themselves. Similarly basin-stands almost certainly imply the employment of servants to carry water to bedrooms. However, within this relatively narrow middle-class group significant differences can be identified. Gentry and professionals, together with the richer 'residenters', lived in larger houses, were the first to buy new items of furniture and other domestic goods, and tended to invest in higher-quality goods than the merchant class. Success was what mattered most, and one way of reinforcing success was a display of conspicuous consumption.

Another conclusion to emerge from the study of material culture in Cupar is the importance of the 'residenters' as consumers. The terms 'residenter' and 'indweller' were used very loosely in the first three quarters of the eighteenth century. By the end of the century, however, the terms were used more specifically. A residenter was someone living in the town but not working, while indweller meant someone with no regular employment, or a non-burgess. Residenters fell into two categories: locals who could increasingly afford to retire before they died; and those with private means who chose to move to the town, such as retired colonials or tenant farmers.[30] Female residenters were usually the widows, unmarried sisters or daughters of such people. Many therefore were incomers and little is known about their backgrounds. Some had chosen to set up a separate establishment in town rather than live within an extended family on a country estate. Katherine Skene (1813), for example, the illegitimate and unmarried daughter of the laird of Pitlour, lived in Cupar with her widowed sister Helen, one of whose daughters was married to a local doctor.

As well as being a market town, Cupar was visited by many travellers, and spending by outsiders had always been important to the local economy. Income from people retiring to the town was an extension of this dependence on external finance. The contribution of residenters to the economy and to the rebuilding of the town has already been noted, and they were also major consumers of material culture and employers of servants. The evidence of the inventories alone might be taken to indicate a very small middle class, but the scale of building in and around the town during the long eighteenth century indicates a large and thriving elite. The dramatic changes in the architecture of the town between 1700 and 1820 were reflected in the interiors of the houses, with rooms designed for specific purposes, filled with more, and more comfortable, furniture. A more interesting diet was complemented by services of china and silver cutlery. There were carpets on the floor, pictures on the walls, ornaments on the mantelpiece and even a few curtains at the windows. The comment in the *New Statistical Account*, that 'Cupar wears now the appearance of a clean and comfortable English town', can be applied not only to the townscape but to the interiors of the houses. During the long eighteenth century Cupar experienced not simply a 'consumer revolution' but a revolution in domestic comfort.

Notes

1. Lubar & Kingery, *History from Things*, viii; 'too seldom do we try to read objects as we read books – to understand the people and times that created them, used them, and discarded them'.
2. Smith, *Wealth of Nations*, 176, 181.
3. Thomson, *Agriculture of Fife*, 391, claimed that farmers would benefit as well, with 'a ready market, and a high price for the productions of the field'.
4. Weatherill, *Consumer Behaviour and Material Culture*, 203–4, noticed in English inventories a lack of small personal items such as hair combs (as does Houston, *Scottish Literacy*, 166–67).
5. The more sub-divisions, the more easily averages would be affected by one particularly rich or poor inventory. It was impossible to divide them into even blocks because of the random nature of their survival, so there is one group of 19 and four of 18, covering 1689 to 1751, 1752 to 1769, 1770 to 1792, 1795 to 1814 and 1815 to 1827.
6. Dining tables were often made in several pieces so they could be expanded when necessary, and this also made them easier to move between rooms.
7. Jones, 'The Hall and Lobby', 111.
8. In 1783 Lady Anstruther bought an umbrella in Edinburgh for 14s, bought three more by 1789 and had one mended for 1s 6d in May 1797.
9. *Fife Herald*, 'Jan–Aug 1825 to let, workshop, wareroom and shades, South Bridge, occupied for the past 30 years by Mr Cockburn'; 22 Jan 1824.
10. StAU ms36929, box VIII/298; for a total of £73 12s Scots.
11. Boswell, *Tour to the Hebrides*, 195.
12. Chambers, *Domestic Annals*, iii, 613.
13. Thomson, *Agriculture of Fife*, 93.
14. *Fife Herald*, 21 Mar 1822 and 16 Jan 1823, James Staig and his wife sold 'Crystal and stone-ware from a shop'; 23 June 1825, John Methven, manufacturer of earthenware in Kirkcaldy, was opening a warehouse in St Catherine Street, selling glass, china and stoneware.
15. They still are the best utensil for feeding babies or for eating boiled eggs.
16. Keddie, *Three Generations*, 34.
17. Somerville, *Life and Times*, 335–36.
18. Keddie, *Three Generations*, 17.
19. McKendrick, 'Josiah Wedgwood and the Commercialization of the Potteries', 100.
20. Tarrant, *Going to Bed*, 21–2, suggests that curtains came into use in the mid eighteenth century; Gow, *The Scottish Interior*, 11, suggests that the lack of curtains in Alexander Carse's picture *The Country Relations* is an artistic device to emphasise the urban setting, but it seems more likely that, as the

evidence from Cupar suggests, curtains were not in such widespread use at this period as has been assumed.

21. The Earl of Hopetoun was a local hero of the Peninsular War, though there may also be a connection with patronage. The Wilkie prints suggest pride in a local artist. *The Jew's Harp* was painted in 1808, and sold without being exhibited, but a print was made in 1809. This was Wilkie's first move into print-making, and was perhaps chosen because it only had three figures so he could afford to finance the experiment. This was followed by *The Blind Fiddler* in 1811, *The Village Politicians* in 1814 and *Rent Day* in 1817, then no more before 1823.

22. NAS GD26/5/726/5, with a letter dated 15 Apr 1816 politely asking for payment.

23. A 'piece' was 12 yards long, and usually about 18 inches wide, and would therefore cover an area 3 × 2 yards; so two pieces might cover one wall, six pieces a small room.

24. *Fife Herald*, 3 Apr 1823 et seq., 21 Mar 1822, James Staig worked as 'painter, gilder, and paper-hanger'; 28 Mar, Alexander Stables, 'plain and ornamental painter' was setting up as a paper-hanger. Porter, *English Society*, 222, wallpaper sales in England were 197,000 yards in 1713, and 2,100,000 yards in 1785.

25. Keddie, *Three Generations*, 51–52, 13.

26. It is generally recognised that the 'feel-good factor' is reflected in increased expenditure not just on champagne and fast cars, but on less visible things such as expensive underwear – a mixture of conspicuous and inconspicuous consumption.

27. Home, *Sketches of the History of Man*, i, 348, 350.

28. It can take as many as 100 candles to produce a light equivalent to a 60-watt bulb.

29. Bidets were sold in Paris from 1739, and in England from the 1780s, but they never really caught on with the British public.

30. Some of the saddest inventories are of those who could not afford to retire but whose businesses obviously ran down as the owner aged. The horse 'only worth the skin and the shoes' had probably grown old with its owner who had neither the heart nor the money to replace it, hoping it would see him out.

8

Literacy and Leisure

This chapter looks at the social and cultural life of the elite of Cupar, a way of life which, like the buildings and their contents, changed and developed, particularly from the last quarter of the eighteenth century. Many English towns experienced an 'urban renaissance' from the Restoration in 1660; the same happened in Scotland, but started later. Cupar was a county town, and a travel town, and this provided a basis on which it was able to develop a new role as a 'leisure town' and cultural centre.

Schools and schooling

Much has been written about the masters, salaries, fees and management of the burgh and parish schools of Scotland. But it is harder to find out about schools from the point of view of the children and their parents, and how schooling fitted into the life of a small town. The general assumption is that children attended the burgh school for about five or six years, roughly between the ages of six and twelve. Earlier schooling was available at home, at private schools, or at a rural parish school. Universal school attendance was not achieved, particularly as the population grew during the eighteenth century. It has also recently been recognised that not only did not all children attend school, but that even those who did so often attended irregularly. Tranter has questioned the meaning of basic statements such as 'enrolled at school', and found in his particular source a record of school attendance of between one and three years. In the case of Cupar there survives a different and unusual source, a book recording quarterly payments for each child for the whole grammar school from May 1759 to February 1761, and May 1774 to February 1788, and for the English school only for November 1788 to May 1801. This provides a rare opportunity to analyse attendance figures. There are several unknown variables which make calculations difficult, but it seems that most parents saw at least a basic education as desirable.

No reference has been found to a child who never attended school, and it seems likely, therefore, that the vast majority of Cupar children went to school, even if only briefly.

For most of the eighteenth century school meant the grammar school, but gradually the options widened, with more private schools offering a cheap basic education. The minister of Monimail in 1791 pointed out that 'the number of scholars varies, according to the abilities and reputation of the teacher'. The figures for Cupar for 1774–88 demonstrate how each new teacher had a honeymoon period usually followed by a decline in numbers. The exceptions were two who were sacked before their numbers could decline, and Robert Wiseman, whose attendance figures continued to increase after 1788. In 1791 he petitioned the council because his classes were 'so crowded as to render it impossible for him to pay that attention to each which the parents … would wish, and are entitled to expect'.

It is clear that very few children stayed at school for as long as five years. For 1774–88 over 50 per cent of children attended school for one year or less, 80 per cent for three years or less. Numbers fluctuated, with both new enrolments and overall attendance being highest in the May quarter, and lowest in February, which must have made teaching difficult. Many children who did attend school for a reasonable length of time still missed one or more quarters. The reason might have been financial, illness, or perhaps, in the case of girls, staying at home to help with a new baby. While it is possible that poor attendance in August was for agricultural reasons, as is often suggested, it might also be because by the eighteenth century schools had a summer holiday of four to six weeks. The Lammas quarter would therefore have offered the poorest value for money. The figures from Cupar show that brief and irregular school attendance was the norm, and steady attendance the exception. Some children, particularly girls, attended school very sporadically, sometimes with gaps of one or even two years. By combining the school account book with parish registers it is possible to demonstrate that five or six was the usual starting age for both boys and girls at the English school. But the habit of sending siblings to school together, and the varying popularity of teachers, led to a wide range of starting ages. John Campbell, for example, was taught to read at home, but at the age of about seven was sent with his brother (aged nine) to learn Latin at the grammar school.

Those children who attended for three or more years seem on the whole to have been destined for the law, but by the 1790s were going into a wider range of occupations. The parents who stand out as choosing to pay for extended education for both sons and daughters include a sheriff clerk, two town clerks, several writers and doctors, a few farmers, merchants and tradesmen, and several innkeepers. Harry Gibb, a tenant farmer, sent all his six sons and four daughters to school, whereas George Campbell, the first minister, sent both his sons but none of his four daughters.[1] Some children were sent to school even though they were not very bright. In 1754 the schoolmaster gave evidence to the court of session that David Sibbald, merchant, a former pupil, was a 'very Indifferent Schoolar', and 'generally reputed ... to be rather weaker than the ordinary run of mankind'.[2]

As social attitudes changed, parents became increasingly concerned about the long-standing problem of excessive use of corporal punishment. In 1765 the council decreed that punishment was only to be administered by the regulation tawse, not by hands, feet or any other weapon. Only the rector could administer the severest punishment, and girls were not even to be struck on the hand, 'a reproof being all allowed to be given them'. By August 1767 'most of the Gentlemen of the Town and neighbourhood have taken away their children from the School'. The rector was persuaded to resign, but his successor, George Gray, was 'a cruel pedagogue' who 'applied the ferula or tawse with unmerciful severity'.[3] In April 1788 several prominent citizens complained 'of sundry abuses' by Gray. One boy 'was severely struck over the head ... in consequence whereof he was confined to bed for some time'; another was 'cruelly beat', took to his bed and died; another had his back broken and was dying. The petitioners were 'so disgusted ... that they propose to leave this place altogether, and take up their residence in a town where their children can receive their education without any danger of their being maimed or their health destroyed'. Within a few weeks Gray offered his resignation, provided he got a pension of £20 a year. Violence was not limited to the grammar school. In 1793 John Ewan, a relatively new private teacher in Newtown, took legal action against a parent who 'came into the schoolhouse ... in a fighting posture' and called Ewan a 'Blackguard, scoundrel, villain and rascal'. The father's defence was that Ewan had struck his eldest son 'most unmercifully upon the head and breast'.

In the *Old Statistical Account* the ministers of the surrounding parishes complained that parish schoolmasters were so poorly paid that no-one 'properly qualified ... will devote himself for such an income to the most laborious of all professions'.[4] Despite posts at Cupar grammar school being better paid and more prestigious than at many smaller schools, only six teachers died in office, while twelve chose to move elsewhere. Five retired by agreement with the town council, while nine were dismissed or forced to resign because of old age, incompetence or violence. It is not clear why young men went into teaching. In the case of George Gray, the rumour was that he had had to abandon his intended career as a minister because his first child was born less than nine months after his wedding. The chant in the playground was 'Oh! my fate sinister. Oh! my fate sinister! Jeany's eyes so bright and bosom so white Have spoiled me for a minister.'

Gray's successor, John Bayne, was a self-made man. 'While apprentice to a shoemaker he had contrived to pick up some knowledge of the Latin language at a parish school, and this he improved by a short residence at a Scotch university'. After being appointed to a country parish school 'he acquired such fame by his assiduity and success in teaching that he was elected as successor of Gray' as rector of Cupar grammar school.[5]

All over Scotland from the 1760s there was a movement to establish 'academies' with a wider, more modern curriculum than the old grammar schools.[6] In Cupar a subscription was organised in 1823 (Table 8.1), and five teachers appointed, but unlike other towns the academy took over from the grammar school in a seamless transition, using the existing buildings.[7] For much of the eighteenth century evidence for private schools in Cupar is fragmentary. Occasionally private teachers were given subsidies by the town council for teaching poor scholars or towards their rent. The number of private schools grew rapidly in the early nineteenth century, and by the 1820s there were ten or more, some approved by the presbytery and some not. Another development in towns in the early nineteenth century was the establishment of technical schools. In 1825 the *Fife Herald* reported the establishment of a 'School of Arts'; teachers from the academy offered evening classes to 'operative mechanics', and the council gave ten guineas towards its library.

Unlike major urban high schools, Cupar grammar school was attended by a number of girls, though none seems to have studied Latin. Apart from restrictions on corporal punishment, they seem to have been treated the same as the boys. However, there were alternative schools for girls. As early as 1713 the suggestion had been made that the town

TABLE 8.1   Subscribers to Cupar Academy, 1823

	Number	Total subscription	Average subscription
Gentry	4	£102	£25 10s
Lawyers	7	£137 15s	£19 13s 8d
Manufacturers, spinning mill owners	5	£79	£15 16s
Merchants	4	£51 10s	£12 17s 6d
Doctors	3	£31 10s	£10 10s
Ministers	3	£26 5s	£8 15s
Saddler	1	£15 15s	
Vintner/hotelier	1	£10 10s	
Carrier	1	£10	
Waulker Trade		£45	
Guildry		£30	
Total raised		£537 18s	

Source: *Fife Herald*, 6 Feb and 12 Jun 1823.

should employ a schoolmistress, and the council seems thereafter to have intermittently supported one or more women who taught 'sewing and other branches of education'. In 1795 the council agreed to pay for a mistress 'suitably qualified to teach plain and ornamental needlework, drawing and music'.[8] In 1812 John Gray of Paddington Green left various bequests to Cupar including £500, the interest from which was to pay a schoolmistress 'properly qualified ... in the proper branches of female education, such as reading and writing, needlework, arithmetic, geography and dancing', to be chosen from among the daughters of the clergymen and schoolmasters of Cupar.[9]

Henrietta Keddie's aunts, after they left the grammar school, studied dressmaking under the Misses Adamson, milliners and mantua-makers. While the girls sewed, the teachers' brother Laurence, the minister, 'used to ... read in his solemn sonorous church voice the portion of his newspaper containing the very last war news'. Her aunts also went to the Misses McPherson, where they studied embroidery and made ornaments 'in moulded and tinted wax'.[10] In 1810 the countess of Leven and Melville established a 'School of Industry', to teach poor girls 'useful domestic knowledge ... to fit them for becoming servants'. In 1824 the *Fife Herald* reported that it had about thirty pupils, aged between 11 and 15, who were taught needlework and bible study. By the end of the eighteenth century there were ambivalent views about female education. Some felt it should be encouraged only so far as it provided a practical training for future wives and mothers; others that academic subjects should not be abandoned. Sir John Sinclair wrote that 'society cannot be placed on its proper footing, unless the blessings of education are extended to both sexes ... when women are properly educated, they are very far from shewing any mental deficiency', and 'the education of females, when it is considered only as a preparation for fashionable life, seldom leads to a happy result'. Cupar academy continued the grammar school's tradition of co-education, and a list of prizewinners in 1824 included several girls.

Literacy

There are few sources for Cupar which lend themselves to the study of literacy. Throughout the eighteenth century almost all those active in the town appear to have been able to read and write. In 1715 the council claimed that those who had signed a controversial petition included the 'meanest of the inhabitants', some schoolboys, and even 'some who could not sign themselves'. The best surviving sources of signatures are bonds of caution in lawburrows, which provide a reasonable cross-section of society. They do not, however, yield

TABLE 8.2   Main book collections listed in inventories

	Date	No. of volumes	Types of books
William Dick, minister	1736	373 books, 132 pamphlets	overwhelmingly theological
Alexander Melville of Balgarvie	1756	over 600	a French dictionary and grammar book, law, politics, history and biography, classics, travel, literature, including works by Addison, Congreve, Fielding, Gray, Ben Johnson, Pope, Alan Ramsay, Swift, Shakespeare and Voltaire
Andrew Scott, surgeon	1769	52	3 definitely medical, 2 dictionaries
William Smibert, soldier	1776	over 40	Hume, Pope, Thomson, Young, and a book of maps
John Stevenson, writer	1795	c.20	mostly legal
David Tod, writer	1812	81	law, politics, history, including Sibbald's *Fife*, travel, 'sundry school books', and literature including Burns, Milton, Ossian, Ramsay, Shakespeare
Katherine Skene, residenter	1813	83, a parcel of pamphlets	a parcel of maps, 10 books in French, theology, history, literature including Goldsmith, Milton, Pope, Shakespeare
Alexander Swan, surgeon	1814	143	almost all medical or unspecified 'old books', plus 27 volumes of a medical journal
Henry Walker, writer	1818	175	mainly law, including Montesquieu, *Spirit of Laws*, history, geography, financial works such as interest tables, an 18-volume set of the *Encyclopaedia Britannica*, 5 books on gardening, literature including Burns, Ossian, *Pilgrim's Progress*, Shakespeare's plays
David Methven, ex-vintner	1824	21	religious, classical, and mathematical books, *Introduction to the History of Asia and Africa*, and *Dictionary of the Wonders of Art*, but no literature

Source: see Appendix 4.

large numbers of signatures, and only survive for 72 per cent of the period 1699–1820. While the figures for women are too small for any conclusions to be drawn, the number of men able to sign their names increased steadily over the century, from 85 per cent to 95 per cent. These figures for male literacy are higher than Houston's national figures, but literacy tended to be higher in towns, and the Cupar figures are similar to Houston's 83 per cent for an urban population 1650–1770. However, the ability to sign one's name is far from equating with regular reading and enjoyment of books. The impression from other sources is that few people before the turn of the nineteenth century saw reading and writing as anything more than a necessary business skill. One of the rules of the Fife Chapman Society in 1797 was that 'those that cannot read shall be obliged to learn'. In the preface to his *Arithmetician's Text-Book* in 1806, Robert Wiseman, English master, described a knowledge of arithmetic as 'ornamental to the gentleman, and absolutely essential to the man of business'. Book-keeping was one of the subjects taught at the grammar school, and continued at the academy.

'The family Bible was in a place of honour, but other books were commonly conspicuous by their absence'.[11] Books appear in only 33 per cent of the inventories. Of these, seven contained only Bibles, sermons or psalms, and a further eight gave no details. Some were work-related, for example 'A Merchants Companion' and 'A large blank Company book' (1770). Table 8.2 lists the significant book collections. Professionals had some books relating to their work (see Chapter 5), but also owned classical texts, books on history and geography, reference works and literature, particularly poetry. There was no independent bookseller in Cupar until 1756. But books were sold in other ways. In 1749 James Bell, glover, was selling books as an agent for a bookseller in London. In 1789 the town's table of customs had added to it a charge 'for every auctioneer of Books on the Street 1s'. But it is clear that books were in general not a high priority among the majority of the middle classes of Cupar. After about 1790 there were between two and six booksellers in Cupar, but at least two went bankrupt in the 1820s.

The spread of new fashions and new interests was aided by the increasing availability of newspapers, periodicals and the new genre of self-help books. William Dick, minister (1736), had one on gardening and two on health. Henry Walker (1818) had five gardening books, two cookery books and an almanac. Five inventories included copies of the *Spectator*. One had fifteen volumes of the *British Magazine*, and four years' worth of the *Scots Magazine* and *London Magazine*. Lady Anstruther subscribed at various times to the *Scots Magazine*, the *Lady's Magazine* and the *Evangelical Magazine*. In 1746 the town council began subscribing to the *Edinburgh Courant*, Edinburgh being then the nearest source of newspapers. Local coverage improved with the establishment of the *Dundee Advertiser* in 1801, and in 1822 Robert Tullis started the first Fife newspaper, the *Cupar Herald, or Fife, Kinross, Strathearn and Clackmannan Advertiser*. Newspapers were usually sold by booksellers, by regular subscription rather than casual sales. Some bought their own copies; some read them in the Coffee Room; some banded together to subscribe, for example a 'Club of twelve for procuring the *Scots Chronicle* which goes round amongst the different Members'.[12] Dramatic news, however, was still read aloud, or displayed in a public place. In July 1815 the *Dundee Advertiser* reported that news of the surrender of Napoleon to Captain Frederick Maitland of Rankeilour arrived in Cupar with the *Fifeshire Union* coach. A crowd had already gathered 'before the coach-office, where the newsroom is held; from one of the windows of which, Provost Ferguson … communicated, by reading a newspaper, the intelligence so eagerly desired'.

There had been bookbinders in the town since at least 1725, but they mainly produced blank bound volumes for record-keeping. The first books produced in Cupar were printed by Robert Tullis, who, after training in St Andrews, set up as a bookseller in Cupar in 1797, published his first book in 1800, and printed books from 1803.[13] Following the example set by the Foulis brothers in Glasgow, by 1807 or 1808 Tullis had become printer to the University of St Andrews, producing high-quality editions of classical texts. In 1809, to guarantee the supply and quality of paper he needed, he bought Auchmuty paper mill, near Markinch (now Tullis Russell).

The first circulating library in Scotland was opened in Edinburgh in 1725 by Allan Ramsay. The first in Fife was Dunfermline in 1789, followed by Cupar in 1797 and Kirkcaldy in 1800. The Cupar library was run by nine managers; the subscription was 2 guineas for the first year, and 12s thereafter. It was open every day from 12 noon to 3 p.m. in the summer, but only three days a week between October and April. The original 74 subscribers included gentry and professionals, a wright and a saddler, and 5 women. By 1813 the number of subscribers had risen to 148, and the number of women to about 10. By 1823 the membership was over 200, and the library had about 2,000 books. It is not clear where it was housed. On the evidence of the inventories, private book collections generally lacked novels, and the library seems to have filled this gap. In 1814, for example, the Earl of Leven and Melville's factor wrote to the manager, passing on his lordship's recommendation that the library should purchase *Waverley* and *Pride and Prejudice*.[14] Some people subscribed to the publication of individual books, such as the 1803 re-issue of Sibbald's *History of Fife* (421 subscribers; of whom 63 were from the town or parish of Cupar, predominantly professionals, but including 12 tradesmen and 2 women).

Entertainment and recreation

The Reformation had put a stop to theatrical performances, but by the 1780s the theatre had lost its stigma. As spending power and leisure time increased, a number of theatrical troupes toured the country, and eventually permanent theatres were built in towns all over Britain.

Edinburgh's Theatre Royal was established in 1767, Dundee's in 1800, and the fashion spread to smaller towns such as Kelso, which had a permanent theatre between 1791 and 1809. Cuparians were entertained by visiting players from about 1790. When the new Latin school was planned in 1806, it was suggested that it might as well be built with an upper floor, which could be let out as a hall. The trades and the masonic lodges turned the offer down, but eventually, rather reluctantly, a group decided to fit the hall out as a theatre. It was 1812 before it was finished, and by 1817 they were asking to give up their lease, though they did not achieve this until 1825, when the space was needed for the academy.[15] One performance was put on in 1811 by French prisoners of war who were lodged with families in the town, though it is not clear whether they used this building.[16] Only between 1823 and 1825 is there evidence for performances, as they were advertised and reviewed in the new local newspaper. Ticket prices were: Boxes 2s 6d, Pit 2s, Gallery 1s. There were also other public entertainments. In 1789 the revised table of customs included 'each public Exhibition of whatever kind whether on the Street, in the Tolbooth, or in a Private house'. And in October 1823 the *Fife Herald* advertised a 'Rhetorical Melange' in the 'Assembly Rooms'.

Music played a more important part in people's lives than is often apparent from documents. Henrietta Keddie recalled that though her grandfather could not afford a spinet or piano, his daughters sang unaccompanied, 'over their work, by their children's cradles, to relieve the dwindling gaieties at a friend's supper-table ... out in a rustic garden bower'.[17] Music was part of the general curriculum at Cupar grammar school, and by the 1820s there were several visiting teachers of dancing, elocution, instrumental music and singing, and piano and harp lessons could be had at Miss Greig's school. There was at least one shop selling musical instruments.[18] The inventories confirm national trends: instrumental music declined in the first part of the eighteenth century, and did not return until the pianoforte became fashionable in the early nineteenth century. There was a pair of virginals at Carslogie in 1721; in 1743 'Virginalls, a Flute and a Spinet' in a garret, and in 1758 a spinet in the parlour at Bunzion. There is then a gap until 1795 when an organ was bought at roup by Mr Clarkson, dancing master, and a piano in the dining room at Cupar Mills in 1822. Pianos (square, not upright) became widespread in the 1820s, taking over from the dining table as the single most expensive item of furniture, and were usually placed in the dining room. Most of Lady Anstruther's expenditure on music occurred in Edinburgh, where she regularly paid for music and music lessons for her daughters. She also had her spinet in Cupar and harpsichord in Edinburgh regularly tuned. In 1784 she bought a piano for £13 5s 6d. It cost 7s 9½d to transport it by sea from London to Dundee, and £1 5s 4d to bring it overland to Cupar.[19]

Music also played an important part in public life and ritual. The town normally employed a piper (fife, not bagpipe), a drummer and a bell-ringer, as well as occasional self-employed musicians (including one woman). In 1797 the town gave money to the Cupar Volunteers 'for Musick', and their quartermaster, James Wilson, recorded a payment in 1807 for the repair of trumpets. In the 1820s the Fife Hunt paid for drums and bugles at the races, and in 1824 the Earl of Leven's factor paid for a 'Band of Music going to Letham on occasion of his Lordship's Marriage'. In 1827 the town paid David Rattray for music at the king's birthday celebrations. Music was equally part of impromptu public events. During a disputed election in 1767, for example, an innkeeper was abducted and then 'carried down to the Council House in the midst of a large crowd of people ... with instruments of music playing before them'.

Public events also included colour and pageantry. On formal occasions the magistrates were accompanied by the town officers in livery, carrying halberds. The trades incorporations, and the masonic lodges, had banners which they carried in public processions. 'The masons' walks were the most alluring, with the glittering jewels and the leather aprons worn on the occasion to the gay lilt of: 'Hey, the merry masons, Ho, the merry masons, Go prancing along'. Floral arches were erected to celebrate the passing of the Reform Bill, and perhaps earlier as well. As today, elections involved colour, 'neckerchiefs and ribbons of the candidate's colours, bought up and lavishly distributed among the wives and daughters of the future constituents.'[20]

Dancing became fashionable in the 1770s, and from that time there is evidence for at least two dancing masters in Cupar, and in the 1780s a County Room, large enough for balls, was built next to the tolbooth. During race week there were usually two hunt balls, at which 'Gow and his band, in their best style, kept the company on each evening dancing till a late hour'.[21] There are references to a 'Volunteer Ball' between 1804 and 1808. David Rattray, a freelance musician, held an annual ball in Cupar in the 1820s, and there were probably many other subscription balls. 'Assemblies' were a feature of elite society in the eighteenth century. Major towns often had purpose-built assembly rooms; smaller towns often used inns or public buildings. In Cupar the Crown Inn, in the Crossgate, had a large public room, probably built in the 1790s, but no references have been found to its use except for dinners. The term 'Assembly Room', used from about 1825, almost certainly refers to the county ballroom.

There were other ways in which the townspeople could enjoy their increasing leisure time. Coffee Houses were established throughout the eighteenth century as places where men could meet. It is not clear when the first coffee room was established in Cupar, but there was one by 1804.[22] In the 1820s there were four masonic lodges (Plate 11a), and a branch of the Royal Arch Chapter.[23] Special interest societies also began to be formed. As well as reading, music and dancing, there is evidence for indoor games. Card tables were listed in inventories from 1749. From 1758 there were backgammon tables, a chess board and a cribbage board. The town's table of customs revised in 1789 referred to 'each Wheel of Fortune Table or other game'.

Central to social life were the inns, which provided a range of rooms for business meetings and social events. The fortunes of individual inns rose and fell with the careers of their proprietors, but there seems to have usually been one dominant one. The first such to be firmly identified is the Blue Bell, on the corner of Crossgate and South Bridge. After Bartholomew Cockburn's death in 1795 the lead seems to have been taken by the Crown Inn, in the Crossgate. In 1811 the builders of the Tontine, in St Catherine Street, clearly believing the town could only support one major inn, bought out the goodwill of the Crown, and paid an allowance to its owner to retire.[24] The Tontine was described by the *Dundee Advertiser* in 1813 as 'built, on the most approved plan, and containing every accommodation necessary for an extensive business', having a large dining room, travellers' room, five parlours, stables for forty horses and communication between the dining room and the county ballroom (Plate 10a).[25] In the mid 1820s, after the death of the owner of the Crown, 'an Inn upon a great scale' was built in its place, in competition with the Tontine, and linked to a rival stage coach company.

The tradition of gardening survived from the medieval monasteries, in the gardens of the town houses of the gentry. Many gardens can be seen in the town-plan of 1775 (Plate 5), displaying the formal layouts fashionable at the time. Some had hothouses – Lady Elizabeth Anstruther in 1769 paid for 'dung to the hot beds', and at Balgarvie in 1797 there were pineapples growing.[26] In the *Dundee Advertiser* of 1814 Bellfield had 'a hot-wall' and a garden 'stocked with excellent fruit-trees in full bearing', and Ferrybank a walled garden stocked with fruit bushes and trees 'of the best kinds'. In 1800 there was only one large market garden in Fife, and a few smaller ones. Cupar council was keen on encouraging both private and market gardens, as a way of avoiding excessive reliance on oatmeal. The building of a road on the south side of the Eden, east from South Bridge, created a plot of about five acres, lying between road and river, which was let in 1808 as 'Nursery and Kitchen Garden' with a shelter belt and 'a substantial Gardener's House in the Cottage Stile'.[27] Part of it was still functioning in the 1850s (Map 5). There were gardeners in Cupar throughout the period, and from the 1790s nurserymen and seedsmen. Lady Anstruther employed a freelance gardener, and bought seeds from him, plants from the gardener at Rankeilour and 'asparagrass' from the provost's garden.[28] The Cupar Horticultural Society was established in 1820 for 'the cultivation and improvement of the best fruits; the most choice sort of flowers; and those vegetables which are most useful in the kitchen'. In line with other developments in the eighteenth century, gardens came to be planned not just for growing fruit and vegetables but as places for recreation and relaxation. Six inventories from 1758 list garden tools, and two early nineteenth-century ones also have garden chairs.

Bird cages appear in two inventories. Lady Anstruther regularly bought dog meal and canary seed, and later a bird's cage, a 'cock bullfinch' and a 'black bird'. Witness statements relating to a mysterious death in 1816 included one from a twelve-year-old girl who had looked down into the street because she was feeding her pet bird whose cage hung in the kitchen window.[29]

The eighteenth century saw the decline of hawking and the growth of shooting, partly as a result of agricultural improvements and increased planting of trees. A variety of guns, some military and some sporting, appear in seven inventories, including a 'blunderbash' (1756), and a 'foweling piece' (1818), and there was a gunsmith in the town by 1792. There were also the inevitable accidents.[30] A few of the elite of Cupar purchased game licences. In 1808 James Wilson paid 10 guineas for a gun, £3 4s for a game licence and £2 4s 6d for 'a pointer dog'. Other outdoor sports included golf, curling, archery, fishing, horse-racing and cock-fighting. John Campbell occasionally played golf, which he considered 'much superior to English cricket, which is too violent and gives no opportunity for conversation'.[31]

Horse-racing had been popular in the seventeenth century, held at places as far apart as Banff, Dumfries, Jedburgh and Perth, and races had been held regularly in Cupar since 1621. The tradition continued into the eighteenth century, with the town providing a silver cup or plate each year. In 1741, however, the date of the annual race meeting was changed from April to October because Parliament was generally sitting in April and 'a good deal of Nobility and Gentry are out of the Country'. The following year the rules were written down. Two races were to be run, on consecutive days, with prizes of 15 guineas and 5 guineas. There had to be at least three horses competing in the first race. Without good horses crowds would not turn up, and the town would not get a boost to its economy to justify the prizes.

By the second half of the eighteenth century racing was declining in popularity, and in the 1760s seems to have died out in Cupar. The 1790s saw a revival of racing all over Scotland, both in places which, like Cupar, had a tradition of race meetings, such as Ayr, Dumfries, Kelso and Perth, and in new locations including Montrose (from 1795), Monifieth (from 1807) and Tayport (from 1822). Cupar races were revived in 1800 by the Fife Hunt (established in 1780), and the town council contributed a prize. Not everyone approved – one bailie claimed that this was 'an encouragement to idleness and dissipation'.

1a. The tower and part of the nave arcade, all that survives of the church built in 1415.

1b. Detail from the fifteenth-century Fernie wall monument.

1c. Detail of carving on one pillar of the nave arcade, two lions which once supported a shield.

2a

2b

2c

2a. Plan of Cupar, inset in a corner of the map of Fife by James Gordon of Straloch, 1642 (reproduced by permission of the Trustees of the National Library of Scotland).

2b. A wall monument in the churchyard to AG, 1676.

2c. Stone marking the burial-place of the heads of Laurence Hay and Andrew Pittilloch, and one of the hands of David Hackston of Rathillet.

3a. Preston Lodge, Bonnygate, built 1623, altered c.1700 and c.1765.

3b. 'The Chancellor's House', Crossgate, probably early eighteenth century.

3c. Marathon House, Bonnygate, probably early eighteenth century.

4a. The south side of the Crossgate, c.1860 (from *Fife News Almanac*, 1928).

4b. Buildings on the corner of Bonnygate and Lady Wynd (now demolished).

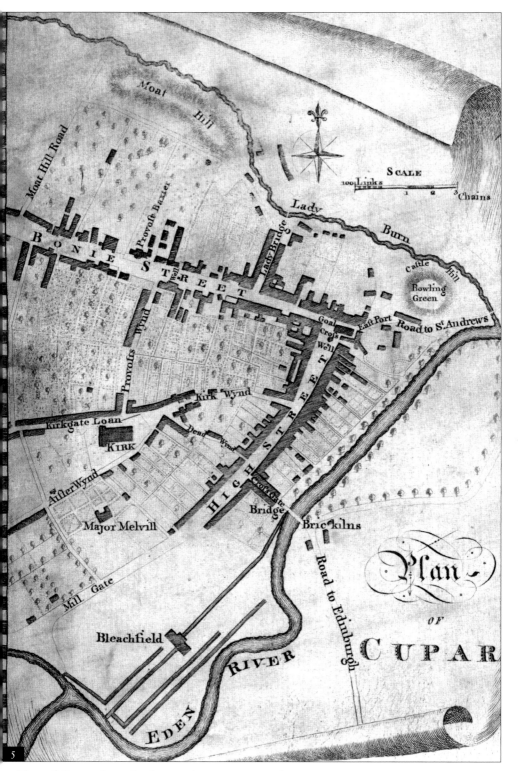

5. Plan of Cupar, inset in the south-west corner of
Ainslie's map of Fife, 1775 (reproduced by permission
of the Trustees of the National Library of Scotland).

6a. Cupar parish church, with the tower of 1415, and the new church built in 1785.

6b. Bellfield, a large detached house in its own grounds, probably rebuilt in the mid-eighteenth century.

7a. The buildings on North Burnside which are shown on the 1775 plan.

7b. One of the two-storey houses on North Burnside which are probably part of the Newtown development of c.1790.

7c. House at the corner of Crossgate and Bonnygate, rebuilt c.1790 one and a half rigs wide to allow the narrowest part of the Bonnygate to be widened.

8a. 73 Bonny-
gate, built from
a design in a
pattern book
published in
1778.

8b. 9 Kirk
Wynd, built for
a merchant in
1811.

8c. An old
house in Provost
Wynd, with a
doorpiece added
in the early
nineteenth
century.

9a. The Latin School, built in 1806, with the upper floor later fitted out as a theatre.

9b. The new gaol, designed by James Gillespie Graham, built by Maurice Finlay 1813–14.

9c. County Buildings, St Catherine Street, designed by James Gillespie Graham, and built 1811–12.

10a. The Tontine Inn (or Tavern), St Catherine Street, built 1811–12.

10b. The building on the left, the office of James Kyd, was the headquarters of the Fife Fire Insurance Company, the one in the centre, the Commercial Bank. The third was not built untill after 1820 (see Plate 13).

10c. The Council House, built by Robert Hutchison 1815–16.

11a. Crossgate House, an early nineteenth-century villa built for Thomas Horsburgh, sheriff clerk.

11b. Ladyinch, an early nineteenth-century villa at the junction of Carslogie Road and Balgarvie Road.

11c. Rosemount Cottage, Riggs Place, an early nineteenth-century villa.

12a. The Mote Hill, a shady gravel walk with fine views.

12b. Tollhouse at the junction of South Road and Ceres Road, built in 1842.

12c. Tollhouse at the junction of East Road and Pitscottie Road, built c.1825.

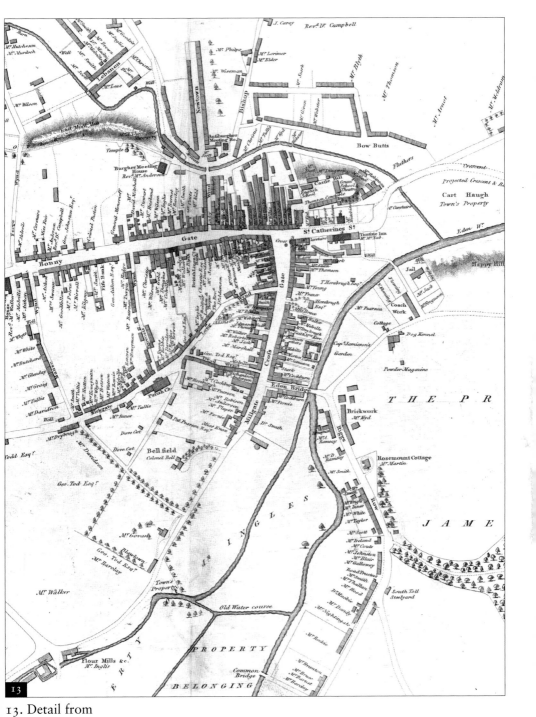

13. Detail from
Wood's town plan,
dated 1820
(reproduced by
permission of the
Trustees of the Fife
Folk Museum).

14a. A door with fanlight above, Millgate.

14b. Exterior fanlight, 1 The Barony.

14c. Fanlight inside the vestibule, 1 The Barony.

14d. The Royal Hotel, St Catherine Street, built 1854.

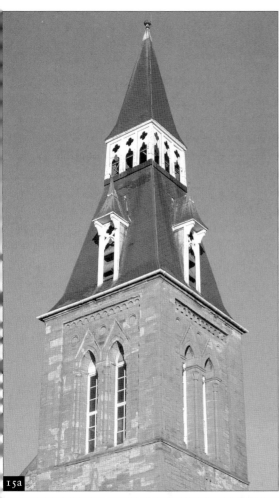

15a. The spire of the Corn Exchange, built in 1861–62.

15b. A late-Victorian doorway in Carslogie Road.

15c. Carving above the door of the Bonnygate Church, 1865–66.

16a. The War
Memorial,
dominating the
east end of St
Catherine Street.

16b. The giant
silo, a silent
reminder of the
former sugar beet
factory.

16c. St Columba's
Roman Catholic
Church, Kirkgate.

But the races were, according to the *Dundee Advertiser* in 1808, 'numerously and fashionably attended'. Traditionally the race had been run over roads or fields, but this became unsatisfactory, and in 1811 the Fife Hunt laid out a course at Uthrogle, just to the west of Cupar, with a small grandstand to provide a viewing platform and shelter from the weather. The course can be seen on maps from 1832, and the ruins of the grandstand still survive. By the early nineteenth century events in race-week were once again benefiting the town : 'there was an "ordinary" for meals in the principal hotel, where visitors, if they chose, could dine and sup together. There was a succession of balls in the handsome County Hall, for the benefit of the ladies who accompanied the gentlemen on these occasions.' But there was a shortage of 'superior sleeping accommodation', so the 'professional residents' would let their houses. In return for this they 'secured the patronage of the mighty' and a payment 'which was left to the generosity of the donors'.[32]

Fox-hunting was never as popular in Scotland as in England, but was similarly becoming more organised by the end of the eighteenth century. There were several private packs of hounds in Fife during the eighteenth century, and in 1791 the town granted a tack of land on the Bridge Hill to the Earl of Crawford, John Hope of Craighall and others 'for building a dog kennel', probably for a pack of harriers. The first subscription pack of hounds in Scotland seems to have been the Fife Foxhounds, established in Cupar in 1805. They improved the kennels, built stables and bought horses and hounds. One of the subscribers was the Fife Hunt, whose membership overlapped with that of the Foxhounds. There was also informal hunting. The minister, George Boes, when accused by the Earl of Leven and Melville of hunting on his land, replied that he no longer hunted hares with dogs, but hunting was 'an Innocent amusement and Diversion' which was good for his sore leg.

In many English towns bowling had become popular during the seventeenth and early eighteenth century, but was in decline towards the end of the century. In 1711 Cupar town council gave Dr James Bethune permission to 'cast as much green turf ... as will lay his bowling green'. In 1772 'it was proposed by some of the council that the top of the Castle Hill should be levelled and made into a Bowling Green' (Plate 5). This was done within the year, but by 1776 it was in disrepair. It limped along under a series of tacksmen until in 1799 it was offered rent-free to a suitable person.[33]

Perhaps the most popular form of exercise was walking, in private gardens where possible, but if not in public walks and parks. While public open spaces had always existed in towns for sports and markets, it was the eighteenth century which saw the development of formal walks or promenades in many towns. The Back Walk in Stirling, for example, was first laid out in 1723, and extended in the 1790s. In 1770 a suggestion was made to Cupar town council that the 'artificial bank' in the middle of the town's pasture land 'would be a good place for a summerhouse and arbor for the reception of the ladies of the Town and Gentlemen to retreat to in the summer evenings', but the land was let instead. A gravel walk was laid out around the bowling green in 1773, and the tacksman told that residents should have access 'at all times convenient', and in 1785 more of the Castlehill was planted and enclosed. The Mote Hill, a natural glacial feature running north-west from the Castlehill on the south side of the Lady Burn (Map 4; Plate 12a), was planted in 1776, and in the 1780s was repeatedly defended by the council from road contractors wishing to quarry gravel. In 1804 a better walk was laid out on it. Gradually other walks were defined, such as along the river at the foot of the feus at Riggs Place and South Road, and within the Cart Haugh (cover illustration).

Major sources of entertainment for all classes were public events such as the eight annual fairs, and race week. Some civic functions were relatively private, such as dinners held after elections, inspections of the grammar school, or the ordination of ministers. But there were other more public celebrations such as the monarch's birthday. As elsewhere in Scotland and England, such events may have had an organised civic ceremony at their heart, but often spilled over into wider public involvement. The town council was conscious of costs, and of the adverse publicity associated with excess. In 1727 they decreed that the coronation of George II should be celebrated 'with the greatest demonstrations of joy' but 'as frugally as possible'. By 1774 the council decided that because of 'the abuse that has crept in' to celebrating the King's birthday, 'which occasions an enormous expense annually to the Town', they limited numbers attending the formal ceremony, and decreed that when the party moved to the Cross they should 'drink a few healths not exceeding six without destroying the Glasses'. But it was difficult to balance economy with enthusiastic public displays of loyalty. As well as the public drinking of toasts, celebrations included bonfires, firing guns and ringing bells. The first mention of illuminations was in 1789, when Cupar celebrated the King's 'happy recovery' from mental illness; 'its brilliancy delighted me, but I still recollect my terror from the squibs and crackers which were let off round the bonfire at Cupar Cross'.[34] The *Dundee Advertiser* reported that in 1808, when news reached Cupar of military success in Spain, the bells were rung and 'the drums of the Volunteer Infantry beat to arms ... in a moment the whole town appeared transported with joy'; news of the restoration of the Bourbons to the French throne in 1814 was celebrated by illuminations, along with processions and exhibitions.[35] One unexpected public entertainment was in 1785 when Vincenzo Lunardi, who had set off from Edinburgh in a hot-air balloon, landed near Coaltown of Callange. Escorted to Cupar by the minister of Ceres and an excited crowd, he was entertained in the best inn (the Crown), invited to dine with the provost and magistrates, and presented with the freedom of the burgh.

It is clear from testimonies in legal cases that such special occasions, notably race week, were an opportunity for absentees to return, and a time where the town, packed with visitors, experienced problems with drunkenness and public order. In a case of assault in 1823 the sobriety of the two victims, one the sheriff-clerk depute, was questioned, as 'celebrating the King's birthday till twelve at night casts a doubt on this point'.[36] There were also events laid on for all classes, such as sack races. One visitor recounted how in 1817 during race week he and a friend, approaching Cupar, heard gunfire, and found a crowd of about 3,000, 'of both sexes, and of all ages, forms, and conditions ... yeomen ... squires, beggars, lairds, weavers, ploughboys, and constables', gathered for a pig-wrestling competition:

> the heroes shout, and the pig squeaks; the squires wager, and the yeomen swear; the boys huzza, and the ladies laugh; the old applaud and the children scream ... Now a desperate assailant seizes the pig by the ear, but young grumphie, by a well-timed manoeuvre of his teeth forces the enemy to forgo his temporary advantage. Now he is grasped by the tail, but fortunately his Cupar friends (by means of the razor and grease) had rendered this part of his person proof against any permanent hold ... At last ... the pig, after manfully running, and squeaking, and whirling and biting ... was beaten down, and compelled, most reluctantly, to yield, if not to superior skill, at least to superior force.[37]

The eighteenth century saw improvements in travel, and an associated increase in travel literature and geographical reference books. William Dick, minister (1736), had in his library Echard's *Gazetteer* (1704) and *Compendium of Geography* (1704). Alexander Melville in 1756 had Tournefort's *Voyages to the Levant*, Eachard's *Gazetteer*, *Accompt of Lima*, *Thomson's Travell*, *A New Survey of the American Isles*, *Zoroaster's Travels*, *Brown's Travels* and several others. Katherine Skene (1813) had a gazetteer and Cook's *Voyages* (1784), while Henry Walker (1818) had *Bowman's Collection of British Views*, a two-volume *Geographical Grammar*, an atlas, two gazetteers, *View of South Carolina* and *Campbell's Journey overland to India*.

By 1820 schooling responded to the ideas of the Enlightenment and adapted to the changing demands of parents and employers, culminating in the replacement of the grammar school by an academy in 1823. Both masters and pupils were expected to behave in a more civilised way, and the annual cock-fight at the school was banned in 1805. However, the fact that almost everyone in the town had been to the same school had been socially cohesive. Just as the building of detached villas marked the physical separation of social groups within the town, so the proliferation of schools in the early nineteenth century reinforced social distinctions. The evidence points to an increase in reading for information and pleasure as well as business. But again these developments signify a growing social divide, between those with leisure to read books, particularly novels, and those without.

There was a varied social life for the elite, from casual meetings in the Coffee House to subscription balls, theatre, music, and a wider range of sports and pastimes, as well as gardens for growing fresh and varied food and for relaxing in privacy. Society in Cupar was too small, however, for the rigid social heirarchies established in larger towns to be applied very strictly. Events such as balls needed a critical mass, and it would appear that in Cupar the top professionals mingled with the county gentry, and the top shopkeepers, tradesmen and businessmen joined in the same social activities. As noted in previous chapters, the residenters stand out as a group which made a significant contribution to the cultural life of the town. Some, particularly those from the armed forces or colonial service, brought in new ideas. Newspapers and periodicals also provided reports of events and facilities elsewhere to be emulated. Life was more organised, with the proliferation of account books, diaries, clocks and watches. And all the new organisations which contributed to urban identity, such as the library, needed management committees, offering opportunities for networking.

Despite moves towards privacy within house and garden, much life was still carried on out of doors or in public surroundings such as inns. While much of what has been described was provided by or for the middle classes, there was presumably a trickle-down effect from the wider circulation of newspapers, a wider range of schooling, a more interesting diet and the enhancement of public open spaces. Public celebrations provided illuminations, fireworks, music, banners and processions to brighten up the lives of everyone in the town.

Notes

1. Keddie, *Three Generations*, 22, 24–25; Hardcastle, *Life of Lord Campbell*.
2. NAS CS232/S/9/13, another witness described Sibbald as 'but sillie'.
3. Hardcastle, *Life of Lord Campbell*; 9, he added that 'although my brother was by no means slow or idle or mischievous it was discovered that the right-hand cuff of his coat was actually worn away by the frequent application of the instrument of punishment'. In 1775 the council had decreed that the tawse was not to be used without the approval of the magistrates, but this was rescinded at Gray's insistence.
4. Thomson, *Agriculture of Fife*, 325–26; 'an office of such high importance ... especially of the lower classes' ought to be filled with 'men of education, or prudence, and respectability of character', yet the salary offered was less that that of 'the menial servants' of the rich. Similar views were being expressed across Scotland.

5. Hardcastle, *Life of Lord Campbell*, 9–10.

6. Other academies included Perth (1761), Dundee (1786, closed 1792, reopened 1801), Inverness (1791), Ayr (1798), Elgin (1801), Dumfries (1802), Leith (1806), Kilmarnock (1807), Tain (1811), Irvine (1814), Forfar (1815), Annan (1820), Arbroath (1821).

7. The *Fife Herald*, 4 Sept and 23 Oct reported the appointment of teachers of Latin, Greek, Ancient History and Ancient Geography; Geometry, Surveying, Navigation, Arithmetic, Algebra, Mathematics and Chemistry; Writing, Arithmetic, Book-keeping, Drawing and Geography; English; and French.

8. The female teachers supported included Miss Glass (1784–1800), died in 1800, Miss Euphemia McPherson (1800–03), replaced by her sister Christian. In 1806 Miss Campbell was appointed in her place, with an increased salary and an assistant.

9. In 1815 interest on a further £50 was to provide prizes. In 1821 Ann McPherson was claiming £2 10s for several years back from Gray's legacy. Her claim was bought out, and 'Dr Gray's School for young Ladies' was run by Miss Anne Greig from 1822 or earlier. Both schools took boarders.

10. Keddie, *Three Generations*, 26, 68.

11. Keddie, *Three Generations*, 14.

12. NAS CS96/1734/1; James Wilson bought his papers in 1804 from Robert Tullis. *Fife Herald*, 5 Jan 1826, the newspapers taken by the Cupar Coffee Room in 1825 were *London Courier, Morning Chronicle, Farmer's Journal, Caledonian Mercury, Edinburgh Times, Asiatic Journal, Oriental Herald* and *New Monthly Magazine*. NAS JC26/294 examination of William Morris.

13. The first book published in Cupar was the 1803 reprint of Sibbald's *History of Fife*, with a commentary by Laurence Adamson, second minister. In 1805 Tullis published an anonymous pamphlet by Thomas Chalmers, then minister of Kilmany, and in 1806 the *Arithmetician's text-book* by the English master Robert Wiseman.

14. StAU Leven & Melville factors' books, no.7, 1813–16, f.83r. The manager was Laurence Adamson, second minister. *Waverley* was published in 1814, and *Pride and Prejudice* in 1813.

15. From details given when the theatre was converted to classrooms, we know that as well as stage and pit, it had a gallery and two dressing rooms.

16. Keddie, *Three Generations*, 40; Cameron, *Prisons and Punishment*, 71–72; ordinary soldiers were housed in the new 'depot' at Perth; officers on parole were sent to towns such as Cupar, Kelso and Selkirk, where they seem to have been regarded as a useful addition to the social life. *Dundee Advertiser*, 30 Aug 1811, reported the performance in a 'neat little theatre, fitted up by the French officers upon parole here'. The audience enjoyed it even if they didn't understand French.

17. Keddie, *Three Generations*, 27, 30.

18. *Fife Herald*, 21 Mar 1822; the bankrupt stock of Erskine Connolly, bookseller, St Catherine Street, included musical instruments.

19. She employed a piano-tuner, but whether he was resident in Cupar is not clear. The transport costs work out at less than ¼d per mile by sea and about 30d per mile overland.

20. Keddie, *Three Generations*, 85, 152–53.

21. *Dundee Advertiser*, 8 Nov 1811; the famous fiddler Niel Gow may well have played in Cupar. Gow's band, which played at many of the most fashionable balls in Scotland, was led by his son Nathaniel.

22. In 1828–29 the managers of the coffee room paid to have the 'Council Room' painted, so presumably the two rooms were the same. The managers had traditionally shut the coffee room during Sunday services. When the council proposed a complete Sunday closure, the Tontine Inn next door offered alternative facilities, which would have defeated the purpose of the ban, so the council backed down.

23. The masonic lodges were St Regulus (est. 1759, for the nobility and gentry), St John, Fifeshire Militia (est. at the same time as the militia, and mostly consisting of milita and volunteers), Thane of Fife (the newest); the Royal Arch Chapter lodge was St Michael's.

24. NAS SC20/50/1, f.479; David Methven was owed just over £9 when he died by the 'Proprietors of Tontine Inn', and he seems to have been paid about £30 per annum.

25. *Fifeshire Journal*, 1 Mar 1834: it had a kitchen in the basement, six parlours and a bar on the ground floor, a dining room 38 ft by 24 ft on the first floor, plus a parlour and a bedroom, and twelve bedrooms on the second floor.

26. Thomson, *Agriculture of Fife*, 228, 'many of the Noblemen and Gentlemen have hot-walls, hot-houses and green-houses', and fruits such as pineapples, grapes, and nectarines 'are cultivated with success'.

27. *Dundee Advertiser*, 30 Dec 1808. The house is still there, to the east of the new flats. The land later became an industrial suburb, housing two linen factories, a printing works, a foundry and the cattle market.

28. It is clear that any surplus from the larger private gardens was sold. Low, *Fifty Years with John Company*, 18; in 1822 'peaches sell in Cupar for three halfpence a pound, that is when there are purchasers, but the gardener at Hilton cannot get them sold'.

29. NAS AD14/16/32.

30. OPR 1797, death of 'a child accidentally shot by the Cupar Volunteers when exercising'; OPR 1804, Robert Wilson died 'by his Fowling piece going off by accident and lodging the contents in his head'.

31. Hardcastle, *Life of Lord Campbell*, 26.

32. Keddie, *Three Generations*, 98–9; one year her mother earned £30, and spent it on a watch for her husband.

33. In 1804 a new bowling green was laid out on a corner of the Cart Haugh, but this too failed, and by 1808 was a 'nuisance' and was to be let as pasture if no-one was prepared to maintain it.

34. Hardcastle, *Life of Lord Campbell*, 12; he was aged 9.

35. In 1810 illuminations for the jubilee celebrations cost over £25. The organiser was James Dempster, doctor and house-painter.

36. NAS AD14/23/224.

37. *Fifeshire Journal*, 31 Oct 1844, quoting from *Mentor, or Edinburgh Weekly Essayist*.

9

_____

Local and National Politics

Burgh politics ... are always pernicious to the industry of petty towns.

Forsyth, *Beauties of Scotland*

This chapter looks at how the burgh worked at a practical level during the eighteenth century, and how Cupar was affected by or involved in politics in the rest of Fife, Scotland and Britain. As the county town, Cupar had political links with the rest of Fife, its lawyers had connections with Edinburgh, and the town shared an MP with Dundee, Forfar, Perth and St Andrews. Its merchants and linen manufacturers networked within Scotland and beyond (Table 4.2). The study of local politics is frustrating, as the sources are generally uninformative or one-sided. Only when local and national issues became intertwined are sources fuller, but still often enigmatic or one-sided. Political life in Cupar appears to have consisted of periods of tranquillity interspersed with brief moments of drama, and longer periods of factional division which could paralyse normal council business, and frequently resulted in legal action. The council had to strike a balance between protecting its independence and cultivating friends in high places, while becoming increasingly overshadowed by the growing county administration to which it played host.

The town council

Each royal burgh had a slightly different sett (constitution), but all were controlled by small, self-perpetuating cliques. It was difficult, and expensive, for any individual or outside patron to control a burgh, as the nature of burgh setts tended towards a system of collective leadership. The core of Cupar town council consisted of thirteen guildry councillors. At 'election' time, each of the thirteen 'old' councillors (who had served for a year) nominated a 'new' councillor. If a councillor was absent, the rest chose a replacement, sometimes referred to as a 'half hour's

councillor', whose sole purpose was to nominate a 'new' councillor.[1]
It is clear that nominations were pre-arranged, and when someone
did not appear, a substitute was waiting outside the door. Meanwhile,
during the week before the election, each of the eight trades met to
elect a deacon, by a straight majority vote among those present. On
election day one of the eight deacons was elected convener.[2] Convener
and deacons then joined the thirteen old and thirteen new councillors,
and all thirty-four chose from among the twenty-six guildry councillors
a provost, three bailies and a treasurer. The final office-bearer was the
dean of guild. Until 1738 he was chosen by the guild councillors, and
tended to be the runner-up on the list of magistrates. After 1738 he was
chosen by a separate meeting of the guildry, and their choice did not
have to be one of the twenty-six old or new councillors.[3]

The new council thus consisted of a maximum of twenty-seven if all
six office bearers were chosen from the old council, and a minimum of
twenty-one if they were all new councillors. The provost and bailies
then each nominated one of the old council to stay on for another year
('adjoined councillors'), making a total of between twenty-five and
thirty-one. The appointment of adjoined councillors probably evolved
from a provision for absentee magistrates to nominate substitutes, but
developed into a system whereby magistrates could reinforce their
power-base and reward those who had nominated them. No-one from
the old council, whatever his office, had any say in the following year's
nominations. Cupar was one of only four Scottish burghs in which
the majority of councillors was replaced each year (this was no bar to
control by a clique – it just needed a larger clique). Cupar had quite
a high number of councillors, and the system of adjoined councillors
seems to have been unique.[4]

The only votes taken were for provost, bailies and treasurer; often
nominated as a 'list' of people prepared to work together. Magistrates
could only serve for two consecutive years, and the same rule was
voluntarily adopted for deacons, convener and dean of guild. Some
managed to serve as councillors for several years in succession, if they
were regularly chosen as adjoined councillors, but few managed this
for any length of time. As deacons only served two-year terms, there
was room for every ambitious tradesman to serve on the council. After
1725 the council established an occasional and eventually a permanent
executive committee, mainly to scrutinise the treasurer's accounts, and
the convener was one of its ex-officio members. While eight deacons
could not outvote the seventeen-plus guild councillors, it did mean that
the guild councillors had to attend meetings, or the deacons, who were
good attenders, might form a majority.

There were occasional attempts to manipulate the sett. One ploy was
for an old councillor to fail to appear at the election, whereby he lost
his right to make a nomination, but became eligible to be nominated.

There were periodic attempts to define the rules more tightly, few of which lasted. In 1702 they agreed a quorum of thirteen, to include at least one magistrate, and in 1717 instituted fines for non-attendance. Normally the provost, or in his absence the senior magistrate, called a meeting when business warranted it, or if any councillors made a reasonable request. At times of factional division this could cause problems. In 1803 it was decided that 'any two members of the Council on giving a reason, have a right to desire the Magistrates to call a council' within three days. At various times the council decreed that it should meet regularly on pre-arranged dates, but then ignored the decision. In 1816 it was finally realised that meeting regularly was a safeguard against manipulation by factional interests, and the practice was finally accepted.

Royal burghs tended to be conservative. The question of parliamentary reform was first raised in 1781, but Cupar council rejected any discussion as disloyal. Some guildry members, however, felt that all burgesses (tax-payers) should be able to vote for councillors, and in 1784 a meeting of the guildry expressed support for a degree of burgh reform, because the present system was 'most imperfect arbitrary and oppressive and repugnant to the principles of just and equal liberty'. The council minutes, however, are silent.[5] Although people were shocked by the excesses of the French Revolution, it did stimulate political debate, and burgh reform soon returned to the agenda, though it attracted less support than parliamentary reform. Early in 1817 the *Dundee Advertiser* reported a public meeting held in Cupar 'to petition for reform'; boycotted by the council, it was attended by between 700 and 1,400 people. Although their leaders were 'people in very humble life', their behaviour was 'quiet, orderly, and irreproachable', though the speeches were too long. Later that year the council rejected a proposal to alter the sett. A Parliamentary Enquiry set up in 1819 to report on the state of the royal burghs referred in its report in 1821 to 'the practice of selling seats in council' in Cupar. While rejecting universal suffrage or annual parliaments, many in Cupar wished to see a more open system for electing councillors, and the guildry drafted a petition to parliament in 1818, claiming that the thirteen annual nominations 'are so much Considered as absolute property that there has been instances of them being sold and the Individuals pocketing the money', and a few years earlier 'One hundred pounds was paid to one and Thirty pounds to another to vacate their seats in favour of the purchasers or their particular friends'. But the Government did not advocate changing the system, only tightening up procedures.

The key post was that of provost.[6] At various times Cupar, like many other towns, had an 'honorary' provost. The advantage of appointing a landowner was his access to legal, social and political contacts in Edinburgh and beyond. The disadvantage was his absence from day-to-day business, and possible lack of interest in local issues. John, Lord Leslie (from 1700 9th Earl of Rothes), an active anti-Jacobite and agricultural improver, was provost from the 1690s until his death in 1722. In 1700 it was stated that members of the Rothes family had 'these many years bygone' been provosts of Cupar 'to the great honour and credit of the town', and that the two-year limit did not apply. In 1702 the Laird of Tarvit tried to challenge Rothes, who countered with a letter advising the council that 'those who so assiduously seek after such offices are much to be suspect'. A local provost, however, could exploit his position, as for example John Ferguson who was provost while developing St Catherine Street. When the scheme began to go wrong there were those who felt he had used his position to private advantage.[7] Over 132 years there were seven honorary and eleven working provosts.

Magistrates often had to be restrained from acting beyond their authority, and, particularly, incurring expenditure on the town's behalf without prior approval, often awarding contracts to friends or political allies rather than seeking the best tender, and overspending on entertainment. Lord Kames, in 1774, claimed that 'the revenues of a royal borough are seldom laid out for the good of the town, but in making friends to the party who are in possession of the magistracy, and in rioting and drunkenness, for which every pretext is laid hold of, particularly that of hospitality to strangers'.[8]

Although the two-year rule technically applied to the treasurer, it was recognised that this was inefficient, as it was too easy for him to leave the job of pursuing defaulters to his successor. There was a limited number of men prepared or able to serve as treasurer, as it involved advancing money which often took some time to be repaid. There was a delicate balance between keeping a competent treasurer and allowing him too much power. On the whole, however, a powerful treasurer was preferable to an incompetent one. After 1725 a council committee was set up to conduct day-to-day financial business, and to check the treasurer's accounts.

The dean of guild does not figure prominently, but he was often delegated by the council to oversee the more practical parts of its business. But by the later eighteenth century the trades convener seems to have taken over this role. In England by the eighteenth century the guilds were changing into social clubs or property-owning friendly societies. In Scotland their decline was slower, but they ultimately became redundant. The guildry in Cupar may have continued to thrive in the eighteenth century because its membership (and therefore eligibility to serve on the town council) was not limited to merchants, as it was in Edinburgh and Glasgow. Professionals, and others who did not need to join the guildry to carry on their businesses, were welcome to become members in order to participate in politics, but often did so only a few days, or even hours, before they were nominated as councillors. The composition of the council demonstrates a cyclical swing between control by gentry and professionals and control by merchants, but by 1820 professionals, particularly lawyers, had taken over. In that year the fifteen lawyers on the town council constituted an effective majority.

The chances of any tradesman becoming a deacon depended on the overall numbers within his incorporation. The waulker trade was so small that not only did 67 per cent of known waulkers serve as deacon, but most served several terms. One reason for standing as a trade deacon was that the council tended to award contracts to its own members. Because voting for deacons and dean of guild was democratic, and therefore more difficult or more expensive to manipulate, those wishing to influence elections resorted to questioning the eligibility of certain members of trades or guildry to vote. The standard charges were not being of age, being a pauper, not being a resident paying local taxes, or being a 'hired hand' rather than self-employed. Other accusations included having been declared ineligible in the past, having been unburgessed, not having paid burgess entry dues, or having been nominated by someone to whom any such charges applied. In 1788 there was a debate as to whether it was signing a burgess ticket which mattered, or having paid for it. However, it is clear that many candidates who were strictly speaking ineligible went unchallenged in times of political stability, and questions were only raised when a majority was tight or a new faction trying to take control. When individual circumstances changed, men usually remained eligible to vote or be a candidate through habit or sympathy.[9]

The town clerk was appointed by the council, and the post would appear, from the bitter competition for it, to have been both lucrative and powerful, and for life. Between 1690 and 1830 there were seven town clerks, including three father-and-son combinations. Lengthy depositions survive from a disputed appointment in 1759. One deacon was summoned out of town on the pretext of work three miles away, then given so much to drink that he woke up next morning beyond Newburgh with no recollection of how he had got there. While there he was offered 10 guineas and a cartload of deals for his vote. Another voter was detained by his daughter, the wife of the sheriff-clerk, who 'got betwixt him and the Door that she might have a longer time to argue with him'.[10] When the delayed meeting to choose a new clerk was held 'a mobb gathered about the Cross and Tolbooth Stair foot'. Some councillors were too frightened to enter the tolbooth, and held a meeting in an inn. The inquorate meeting inside the tolbooth chose one candidate and the quorate meeting outside chose the other.

Sometimes political disputes provided a respectable cover for personal animosity, greed, ambition, or in extreme cases mental illness.

For ten years before his father's death in 1783 Thomas Robertson had
been joint town clerk. His enemies claimed that 'the old man knew
to[o] well the Character of his son' and refused to retire. When his
father died Thomas claimed the clerkship as 'his freehold for life'. His
opponents claimed he had been convicted of various crimes including
'throwing stones at the chief Magistrate and breaking his carriage',
found guilty, and imprisoned for 'a considerable time'. On another
occasion he had knocked down one of the magistrates 'with the butt
end of a loaded whip by which the Gentleman was thought to be killed
and lay senseless on the Ground for a considerable time'. Sent before
the court of justiciary, Robertson had 'fled the County', and would have
been banished if 'his Father and some of his Friends had not made up
matters'. It was claimed that Robertson was an alcoholic, had severe
memory loss, and could not possibly carry out the role of town clerk.
He died the following year.

For the purposes of electing an MP, Cupar was grouped with
St Andrews, Dundee, Perth and Forfar. As these burghs were in three
counties, they were difficult and expensive to control, and the seat
was unpopular. Each town nominated a delegate, usually its provost,
and the five delegates chose an MP. Meetings of delegates were held in
rotation in each burgh. The actual election was usually a formality, as
any conflict had been over getting the right people in control of each
town council the previous year, which is when instances of bribery,
blackmail or physical coercion are likely to be found. All burghs
wanted two things from their MPs. One was the promotion of the
interests of the town, in Cupar's case mainly the linen industry. The
other was patronage. If an MP was of the government party, there were
minor government offices to be distributed. Before 1747 the possessors
of heritable jurisdictions, such as Rothes, had legal offices in their gift.
And there were other sources, the main one being posts in the gift of
the directors of the East India Company. The dividing line between
patronage and corruption was, and still is, difficult to define.[11]

Local politics 1714–25

In October 1714 two councillors absented themselves from the election,
unwilling to swear the oath of loyalty to the new king, George I. In
July 1715 there was 'ground to suspect danger from turbulent people',
and the town guard was posted. They were still on duty in September,
'there being arisen in the Highlands a great number of men enemies
to the King and Government … from whom continual danger may
be expected'. On 6 October 1715 a proclamation was made at the
Cross in Cupar in the name of the Earl of Mar as representative of
James VIII, calling all men between sixteen and sixty to join the army

at Perth. A 'Party of the Rebel Gentlemen' came from Perth 'to manage the Election; who making Search that Night for the Counsellors and Deacons of Craft, severals of the Counsellors made thir Escape'. Those they found 'were threatened, and frightened ... to vote next Day for such a Set, as they named to them'.[12] There are no further entries in the town council minutes until October 1716.

Although the status quo was re-established the following year, Jacobite support had been widespread, and national events seem to have exacerbated already simmering local problems. The Jacobite administration had been led by Dr James Bethune of Kingask, brother of the Laird of Tarvit who had challenged Rothes in 1702.[13] Jacobitism locally had become linked with opposition to Rothes, who was a prominent anti-Jacobite, and problems continued.

The town council minutes tell the story of the following years, in particular the election of October 1720, while the other side's story is contained in a pamphlet published in 1721, entitled *A Vindication of the Action of Declarator concerning burghal privileges* taken out by Patrick Crombie, late bailie, against Robert Hay of Naughton, sheriff-depute. According to the author, only identified as L A, Cupar had had no political problems when run by 'such as used Trade and Traffick in the Town, and had their fixed Residence therein'. This had been the norm until 'the Inhabitants, out of the great Respect which they had for the noble Family of Lesly' elected Rothes as provost. Rothes, a powerful figure, had nominated a bailie who was not a trader. Out of respect, this encroachment on the town's privileges was not initially disputed. But 'there being no good Understanding betwixt the noble houses of Lesly and Melvill', opposition was led by the Melville faction (which had been behind the challenge to Rothes in 1702), and 'it occasioned hot Work in the Burgh some Months before Michaelmas yearly, for several Years successively'. To keep Rothes in power, his party had to resort to more and more 'Stretches'. They tried various means to influence elections, including forcibly detaining voters, paying for individuals to join the guildry, and imprisoning one councillor on election day. According to L A, the trades at the election of 1716 claimed to be challenging the eligibility of those who had supported the rebellion, but in fact decisions on eligibility were related to support for bailie John Clerk, Rothes' nominee, whose 'Testimony, as to their alledged Disaffection to the Government, was sustained a sufficient Proof'.

The administration of 1716–17 was disunited, with two bailies, William Rigg and John Clerk, ignoring the third. In 1720 when his successor's term of office was over, Clerk, backed by the sheriff-depute, tried to get re-elected, but failed. Rothes, having failed to fix the list of bailies, tried to threaten the old council, accusing some of them of Jacobite sympathies. He then suggested three gentlemen bailies; the council claimed these could not run the town 'at a Distance', and nominated three local men. As a result Rothes raided the meetings of the Trades with 'a little Army of mercenary Soldiers', abducting several tradesmen, but despite this only two deacons of his faction were elected. Rothes' party decided to stay in town until the council election, to try to persuade a few people to change sides. One man hid under a sack of lint to avoid being detained by Rothes' men. The magistrates issued a summons against one of Rothes' lieutenants, but the reply came 'to tell the Magistrates to dight their Arses with the Summons'. Rothes' presence at the election, and his removal of certain councillors, meant that his nominee bailies were elected. The dispute was probably related to the candidature of Rothes' brother as MP.

The defeated town party did not know what to do next; even if they had grounds for legal action, Rothes was the sheriff. According to L A, the new magistrates behaved vindictively against the opposition, including quartering troops on them unfairly. So they took their case to the court of session. When Rothes managed to delay the case, they approached the Convention of Royal Burghs, which offered help with legal costs. The action was led by Mr Greig 'a worthy Burgess, a tenacious Adherer to the Liberties and Privileges of the Burgh, a publick spirited and tender-hearted Gentleman'. In response, Rothes' party, claiming Greig had encroached on the town's property, insulted the bailies and disrupted council meetings, unburgessed him. L A's pamphlet repeatedly pointed out that the objections were not to Rothes as provost, but to his nominees as bailies. But one consequence of the continuing dispute was 'the Sport and Satisfaction of Jacobites, who take Pleasure to see People well affected to the Government set by the Ears'.

The council minutes, and papers sent by Rothes and Lord Advocate Dundas to London, continue the story. The two-year rule meant that it was hard to unseat an administration which had already served one year, especially with the case against Rothes *sub judice*. Despite all his efforts, Rothes had failed to dislodge three out of thirteen guild councillors, or six of the eight deacons. Rothes' death in May 1722, followed by the end of the two-year term of his nominees, encouraged the opposition to renewed efforts, including nominating ensign James Erskine to be their delegate to choose an MP rather than the official choice of Rothes' brother Charles. After six months of legal dispute William Erskine (James' brother) was declared as MP. Despite this setback the Rothes camp did not give up. After various challenges to voters, and a boycott by the six hostile deacons, the new earl was elected provost. According to his account, when he arrived in Cupar for the election of October 1722 he was warned to expect a mob. It withdrew 'after some Protestations', but did not disperse, so Rothes, as sheriff, stood on the tolbooth stair and 'order'd the Proclamation against Mobbing to be read'.

In the weeks after the ensuing riot, a number of witness statements were taken, both by the legal establishment and by a group of JPs sympathetic to the opposition. While they disagree in emphasis and detail, the sequence of events is clear. The election results were proclaimed from the tolbooth window, and Rothes' party tried to leave. They were confronted by a mob which Rothes estimated at 400–500, but all other witnesses at 100–200, unarmed except for two army officers with swords. One of the crowd threatened Robert Hay, the sheriff-depute, while others tried to drag Rothes away. Hay called for silence, and read the Riot Act twice. The response of the crowd was to throw stones at Rothes, one man even 'pulling him by the breast and shakeing him'. Rothes sent his servant to the inn, to bring back 'some Pistols, and broad Swords'. Thus armed, his party confronted the mob, who 'had a little more Respect for their own sweet Persons', and withdrew but did not disperse. The opposition held a rival election in Mistress Bogie's inn. Once Rothes and his party had left to dine in another inn, the town party, led by the deacon of smiths 'with a Hammer and Chizell in his hand', broke into the tolbooth and posted an armed guard. Only at this stage did the opposition carry weapons. According to Rothes his rivals taunted him that even if he evicted them 'the moment I leave the Town they will resume the Possession, and make my Friends in Town pay dearly for it, by burning their Houses and the like'. The absentee nature of Rothes' administration was a weakness to be exploited. The following two days the number of guards was increased, and some were 'marched ... thorow the Town in Warlike manner'. When the magistrates tried to take their seats in church the following Sunday they found the loft locked. At this point Rothes sent for some troops.

According to Dundas 'severall persons were in these mobbs who have at least the reputation of having been in the rebellion 1715'. At first the authorities in London backed Rothes, regarding opposition to him as a dangerous precedent in unsettled times. Government leniency in other instances had encouraged further challenges. He recommended that sufficient troops be sent to support the magistrates, and the 'principal Persons' be prosecuted 'with all Vigour', particular those who were 'officers in your Majestie's Troops'. Witnesses paint a vivid picture of determined opposition. Most agreed on who was in the 'mob', and between them named eighty-five men, including two army officers, three gentlemen (at least two of them JPs), four doctors, two writers, seven merchants, thirteen maltmen and thirty-three tradesmen. There were several father-and-son combinations, and a number of apprentices and journeymen. The one woman, a leading stone-thrower, was the wife of a brewer. No witness made any comment on her participation. Those opposed to Rothes played down the events on election day, and claimed that the real trouble started later when a detachment 'of General Sabine's Regiment of Welsh fuzeliers' arrived, and remained for several months. They accused the commander of imprisoning people illegally, including the gaoler, locked in his own prison for refusing to hand over the keys of the tolbooth; and of unfairly quartering soldiers on those who had been active in opposing Rothes.

Both sides could play the loyalty card. In February 1723 the anti-Rothes faction petitioned the King, arguing that the use of troops was unlawful, as there was no threat to central government. By this time the establishment was becoming increasingly reluctant to back Rothes with legal action, because of the 'bad success that all Government prosecutions have met with in Scotland for severall years'. In 1723 the court of session finally ruled that some of Rothes' nominees in the election of 1720 had been illegal. The army received instructions not to send any troops to Cupar without orders from the King. But Rothes did not withdraw, and the election of 1723 proved equally turbulent. There follows a gap in the town council minutes until August 1725, when the court of session declared the elections of 1722 and 1723 null and ordered 'a popular election ... made by all the burgesses'. Twenty-four men, all Fife landowners or Edinburgh lawyers, were named to take charge, and a new council chosen, to serve for just two months. This was a victory for the burgh's right to self-government. The temporary council settled down to sort out the finances, and the October election went ahead without incident. It was clearly stated that all councillors had to be resident and paying cess, and anyone let in under false pretences could be disqualified later.

Local politics 1765–71

The spring of 1765 saw the town council split in a dispute between the rector of the grammar school and his two assistants, each appointed by the council. The rector, refusing to work amicably with subordinates he had had no say in choosing, was suspended. In 1766 there was a disputed election for dean of guild, which paralysed council business. One candidate, the outgoing treasurer, was reluctant to have his accounts checked while the dispute was unresolved. The case went to the court of session, and a number of testimonies survive. One merchant said he had taken 'a Disgust at the Guildry' since 1760 when two rival candidates had enrolled 'a parcel of low kind of people, which were a Disgrace & an affront to the Guildry'. One candidate was accused of issuing free guildry tickets to his supporters. Others testified to having been bribed or threatened. John Foulis, the stampmaster, was warned that the provost 'could have as much Interest with a Member of Parliament as Turn out one Stampmaster & put in another'. Some voters were objected to as minors, but one witness testified that 'he has known Guildbrethren's Sons admitted Guildbrethren and have a

Vote for Dean of Guild before they were Twenty one years of age', and one man in particular had been a member of the council before he was eighteen. The reaction of the guildry seems to have been increasingly to distance itself from the council.

Both candidates for provost were accused of 'corrupt and undue practices to influence this election', which immediately preceded a general election and so affected the fate of George Dempster, the sitting MP. Two weavers were said to have been offered bribes to influence the election of a deacon, while the deacon of waulkers was said to have received £60 'which bank notes now lie in the sheriff clerk's hands'. The losers named a rival administration, took legal action, and made a nuisance of themselves for the next few months. When the next election came round, the protesters tried to stop it, claiming that the previous dispute was still *sub judice*. Once again there were disputes over the elections of deacons. The general election of 1768 involved similar problems throughout the country. Although the town council minutes tell the story of the party in power, there are hints of widespread unrest. In March 1769 councillors and magistrates had 'frequently been insulted in walking the streets by stones and dirt thrown at them'. In April there were reports of legal action naming the dean of guild and the council as accessories 'to a mob assaulting the Provost and throwing stones at the Earl of Leven's coach when it was driving him and the provost home after the election of the Magistrates' (a rare glimpse of the presence of the provost's patron).

Whether in response to local unrest, or national events, in April 1769 the council sent a loyal address to the king, expressing 'their disapprobation of the late riotous and unlawful meetings'. The next election saw further disputes over trades deacons. One unsuccessful candidate claimed he had been told that even if he had had fifty votes he would not have been enrolled as deacon because he was 'not of their way of thinking'. One bailie proposed that the magistrates should ask 'for a party of the Military to lie in the Town to keep peace and good order'. George Dempster, MP, had been re-elected unopposed in 1765, but soon afterwards Robert Mackintosh started manoeuvring to unseat him. Just before the council elections of 1767 Dempster was accused of bribery, but got bail; his supporters won the election (although Mackintosh was elected a councillor in Cupar), and Cupar declared its support for him. Robert Geddie, the main local backer of Mackintosh, offered a reward of 100 guineas 'to any person who shall swear bribery against another'. No-one came forward, but it was claimed that the election of one deacon had cost 'Lord Clive's party' (Mackintosh) £200. At the election of 1771 there was a protest that the provost, John Baxter, was ineligible because of previous bribery charges: he responded with a range of arguments but no denial. Things went quiet for a while, and Baxter failed to turn up to the 1776 election.

This episode illustrates the down-side of the network of patronage which so influenced politics. A dispute between two factions within the directors of the East India Company led to an attempt to unseat George Dempster as MP, which in turn entailed attempts to manipulate town council elections in Cupar and presumably other burghs in the group. As in the 1720s, those whose jobs depended on patronage, such as the stampmaster, could become pawns in political disputes. Once again the elections of deacons took most effort to influence, giving them more importance within the council.

Local and national issues, 1792–97

National politics once again impinged on Cupar in the 1790s, but from the available sources it does not seem that national issues were quite so intertwined with local ones as in the 1720s and 1760s. The council was determined to demonstrate its loyalty to King and Parliament, but there seem to have been elements among the trades, particularly the weavers, who had more radical aspirations. Cupar as county town was in the public eye, frequently visited by the county gentry, and with soldiers regularly billeted in it. In 1792, in response to the setting up of Trees of Liberty at various places in Scotland including Perth, Dundee, Auchtermuchty and Strathmiglo, and to the King's Birthday Riot in Edinburgh, Cupar council instructed the magistrates to draw up a loyal address, expressing 'their warm attachment to the King and our present Happy Constitution, their detestation of all riotous proceedings, and their firm purpose to suppress every thing of that kind', adding that, 'nothing disorderly has made any appearance in this Burgh or neighbourhood'.

Most of the unrest for which evidence survives seems to have been caused by long-standing resentment against the burden of quartering soldiers. In 1717, for example, the council had complained that the town was 'much harassed by the frequent passing of the King's troops, by their taking free quarter and by furnishing baggage horses, for which rarely there was any hire paid'. The problem of fairness within the town was addressed by the appointment in 1749 of a billet-master, who was to quarter troops first on 'Tapsters of Ale, Brewers who keep changes, fleshers, baxters, chandlers and mealmakers'. If further accommodation was needed, private families were to be used, but in rotation. The 1790s saw a number of protests about both the numbers of troops quartered in Cupar compared with other burghs, and perceived unfairnesses within the town. The post of billet-master (billet-mistress 1777–79) was a thankless task.

The burgh records generally only mention matters which impinged on the administration of the town, brought it unfavourable public attention, or threatened its prosperity. The minutes of 28 November 1797 referred to 'sundry illegal and seditious practices' in the town, and congratulated the magistrates on their efforts in 'detecting those concerned', but gave no details. The written record of the next meeting, on 11 December, stands out because it is in the form of a statement presented and signed by Thomas Horsburgh, sheriff-clerk and bailie, and a powerful figure: 'It is Melancholy to think that throwing off all regard to Religion or Morality, they by Secret Machinations, both expose the State to danger and the Subject to private depradation'. He called on townspeople to stand together 'in the defence of their private Rights and public liberties', referring to 'house breaking and theft', and to two arson attacks. He proposed an amnesty for informers, but also recognised that the quartering of soldiers, while necessary, was 'a peculiar Hardship on the poorer Inhabitants, and has for these three years past been severely felt by the sober, honest and vertuous Householders', whose burden would have 'been relieved had not the Wickedness and disaffection of other Inhabitants rendered the assistance of Military indispensably necessary'. This suggests that problems had been simmering for a while, and that the disaffected 'other inhabitants' were fairly numerous. He continued with resolutions to apply to the government for the erection of barracks in Fife; to borrow £200 to subscribe 'for the support of the Government'; and to buy a fire engine.[14] The following September William White, wright, was given a free burgess ticket 'in consideration of his services in discovering and assisting in bringing to light the United Scotsmen', and being probably responsible for 'preventing the spreading of that business in this part of the country'.

The Society of United Scotsmen started in Glasgow, and spread to Dundee and Fife in the autumn of 1797. There seems to have been a branch in Cupar, but its secrecy made information difficult to obtain at the time, and even harder now, and it is not clear what really went on. One witness claimed to have heard 'that there are Societys formed in England, in Scotland and in this very Town with a view to overturn the present Established Government'. He had been invited to join the Cupar branch, but when he asked to see 'the articles of their association', was told he could not 'untill he Should take an oath of Secrecy', which he refused to do 'it being against his principle as a Quaker'.[15] He had heard that there were branches in other Fife towns, but had no details. Fifty-one men were listed by the authorities as suspected of membership of a secret society. At least 80 per cent were tradesmen, nearly two-thirds of them weavers. A few were found guilty of membership of the United Scotsmen, and sent for trial at a higher court.

The autumn of 1797 also saw over forty major disturbances across Scotland in opposition to the Scottish Militia Act, and many more minor protests, including some in Leuchars and Auchtermuchty. In some places the United Scotsmen seem to have been involved in local campaigns against the raising of a militia. The Cupar weaver John Aitken, for example, who later admitted to being the secretary of the Cupar branch of the United Scotsmen, was involved in a committee to petition against the Militia Act in Fife. Generally, however, opposition in Cupar seems to have been directed not against the principle of raising the militia, but against the quartering of soldiers, though the two were closely related, as the Fife militia was based in Cupar and added to the numbers of soldiers needing accommodation. The long-term effect of these events seems to have been the complete control of the town council by lawyers, including the sheriff-clerk, who was clearly powerful behind the scenes, and perhaps in the most regular contact with the county heritors.[16]

Expressions of loyalty

Cupar, like most burghs, had regularly sent loyal addresses to the monarch. In 1708, for example, they thanked the Queen for her 'tender care of our safety by sending your Royal Navy ... so seasonably to our assistance when this part of your Kingdom was in so great danger from ane invasion by a pretender ... threatening Popery and slavery' (a French fleet with the Old Pretender on board had approached the Firth of Forth). After the events of 1797 the council took every opportunity to express its loyalty to the King and his ministers. One address in February 1817, referring to another wave of radical protest in Scotland, expressed 'detestation' at attempts 'to delude and mislead the populace', taking advantage of recession and unemployment to incite 'disaffection, sedition and violence'. In 1820 when the provost called a special meeting to send a loyal address, one of the councillors claimed 'the loyalty of the inhabitants of Cupar was not to be called into question', but was outvoted. The text expressed the town's 'deep regret' at 'the daring attempts ... by artful and designing men, to alienate the affections of your Majesty's subjects', and pledged to oppose 'every attempt to inflame or delude the Public mind'. A rejected amendment expressed regret at the action being taken against the Queen, which was 'degrading to the Crown and prejudicial to the best interests of the Empire'. With more information and faster communications, Cupar was increasingly aware of and affected by events far away. In 1821 there was 'riot in the Burgh of Cupar occasioned by the Queen's acquittal'.[17]

The King's visit to Scotland in the summer of 1822 prompted both a loyal address and an extra effort at his birthday celebrations. The town was to be 'splendidly illuminated', and it was 'recommended to the inhabitants, to vie with each other in showing their loyalty and affection'. A public dinner, chaired by the provost, was to be held in the Tontine Tavern, and a dinner provided for 'the Poor of the Burgh at the expense of the Community, that they may be enabled to participate in the general rejoicing on this happy occasion'.

In the seventeenth century, Cupar, like most towns, had an active town guard, but 1715 seems to have been its last major mobilisation. In 1735 most of its guns were sold, and thereafter the town would call on government troops if necessary. When men were needed for military service, towns were expected to respond, often by offering a bounty to encourage enlistment. In 1759, for example, Cupar offered 40 shillings to any volunteers for the navy. Later such offers were usually limited in numbers and time, and sometimes to specific regiments. According to the minister in 1793 'the youth of Cupar' were 'at all times forward to engage in the military life'. This applied at all levels of society. Major James Horsburgh of Mayfield was adjutant at Gibraltar, and Captain Charles Bell of Pitblado was before 1789 Inspector-General of the Military Roads of Scotland. Recruiting was also carried on in the rural hinterland, particularly where landowners were themselves serving officers.[18]

Another way loyalty and patriotism could be expressed in the 1790s was by service in the various militia and volunteer regiments. By far the most important to the town was the Cupar Volunteers, formed in 1797. Few men in steady employment chose to enlist and leave home, but many were willing to demonstrate their loyalty by joining the Volunteers, who seem to have been keen and active.[19] The officers were mostly professionals and guildbrethren, and the rank and file may have been predominantly tradesmen. There was a distinction in the minds of the general public, if not the Establishment, between willingness to serve one's country in the face of a foreign enemy, and acceptance of the status quo within the country, and some of those accused of membership of the United Scotsmen were Volunteers. In 1801 'in consequence of the melancholy accident ... with Gun Powder' at Inverness, the council decided to stop keeping powder in the townhouse, and to build a proper store 'at some distance from the town'.[20] In 1803 the council offered to help 'the three Cupar Companies of Volunteers in purchasing their accoutrements'. By 1817 the burden of troops in the town had eased, and the salary of the billet-master was reduced as he had 'now little or nothing to do'. In 1825, however, the militia was back exercising on the Cart Haugh, and the billet-master was instructed to draw up a new list to 'make the burden bear equally'.

Relations with other organisations

As the county town, Cupar was expected to be a generous host to those other bodies which met within its boundaries. The town regularly provided coals for the sheriff court. In 1718 when a court of oyer and terminer was to be held it was decided that 'the present bench is too little for holding the judges' and the treasurer was to buy timber to enlarge it. Many visiting dignitaries were presented with the freedom of the burgh, at considerable expense in parchment, clerical time and the inevitable alcoholic refreshment. The responsibilities of JPs and Commissioners of Supply gradually increased, and many of their activities were based in Cupar. There were occasions when the town council felt that it was being taken for granted or dominated by the county gentlemen. In 1780 the road trustees asked the town for some gravel from the Mote Hill, and were grudgingly permitted to take a small amount. The following year permission was again granted 'in regard the Council wish to lie on a friendly footing with and to show every respect to the Gentlemen of the County'. By the early nineteenth century the council was increasingly torn between asserting its independence and showing due deference to its superiors, who wielded social and political power. In 1820, for example, the town council, despite financial problems, agreed 'to purchase a piece of plate to be presented to the Noblemen and Gentlemen of the Fife Hunt as a mark of the respect and esteem' in which the council held them. The county increased its infrastructure in the town during the eighteenth century, culminating in the building of St Catherine Street from 1811 (Chapter 6); County Buildings is central to the new street, while the burgh chambers were an unsatisfactory afterthought.

The Convention of Royal Burghs provided its members with a networking and lobbying system. At the beginning of the eighteenth century, however, Cupar felt unrepresented, perceiving the Convention as too occupied with maritime trade. In 1717 'being an inland town ... without import or export and very much harrassed by the frequent passing of the King's troops ... they are not able to pay the cess that the Royal Burghs has laid upon them'. In addition, 'the bridge and streets are become ruinous' and the mills were so dilapidated that 'with difficulty will any person venture to be in them for fear of their falling'. The council repeatedly complained about the amount of tax for which they were assessed, and the cost of sending a delegate to the annual meeting.

Relations between the council, the county heritors and the Convention came to a head in 1812 over the question of the running costs of the new gaol, most of whose inmates would be from the county, not the town. The county heritors had raised £4,000 for the new building, the town about £1,300 in money or kind. The council petitioned the Convention, pointing out that while county towns had traditionally provided prisons for the whole county, the principle was unjust, and most burghs could not afford it, particularly as the prison population was increasing. The county heritors, by raising the bulk of the capital, had tacitly admitted they had some responsibility, and set

a precedent which could save other burghs money. Cupar was granted
£400. By 1821 the county heritors refused further help, asserting that
the town was 'bound to maintain a gaol' in return for its privileges as
a royal burgh. The council felt that once prisoners had been convicted
the Crown should pay for them, but both the Lord Justice Clerk and
the Lord Advocate replied that prisoners should not suffer while the
cost of their maintenance was under discussion. The sheriff refused to
contribute, so the prisoners were maintained by a local subscription,
and the town again wrote to the Convention 'to draw their attention
to this important subject'. The Convention was supportive, but in 1824
the court of session finally ruled that 'the liability is upon the Burghs'.

Links between local and national politics

Given the inadequacy of the sources, it is impossible to calculate what
proportion of the town's adult male population was actively involved
in politics, though it will have been a higher proportion than in larger
towns. What is clear is that there were many who regarded politics as a
spectator sport. In 1759 a witness explained that 'it is usual when any
thing extraordinary happens in the Council about Elections for young
boys to run up [the tolbooth] Stairs and endeavour to go in'. Most of
the 'mobb' on that occasion was not hostile but simply curious, and in
the background, watching the action, were old men, women, children
and servants. All the sheriff-clerk's maids, for example, 'went along ...
to the head of the Closs to see the Croud and to know what they were
about'.[21] In all the episodes described above, even where the crowd was
clearly partisan, and there was intimidation, the most violent action
was stone-throwing, and no-one appears to have been hurt.

The problems created by politics were financial rather than physical.
One councillor in 1777 said that Cupar, 'like most of the other Royal
Burghs has been all along ruined by violent [intemperate] parties in
politics'. Those actively involved tended to be leading figures in the
economic life of the town, and if they were diverted by politics, business
and trade could suffer. In 1789 the Bank of Scotland instructed its
Cupar agent to take care that the Bank's interests in Fife should not
'suffer Injury by your Interference in the political contests within the
Burghs of the County. The Bank knows no parties, and discountenances
their Agents and officers meddling in them'.[22] The minister in 1793
claimed that a succession of contested elections had led members of
the trades into: 'habits of idleness, dissipation, and vice ... seduced
by the flattering attentions and promises of the great; accustomed to
the plenty and conviviality of the tavern ... the tradesman learns to
despise the moderate profits arising from the regular performance of
his accustomed toil ... he seldom visits his work-house or his shop, and

when the election has at length taken place ... with extreme difficulty, can prevail on himself again to enter on the rugged tasks of patient industry.' In other words, political involvement was bad for business. This was not an isolated example.[23]

Most of what has been described was not as parochial as it may initially appear. External forces were at work, sometimes for obvious reasons such as the election of an MP, sometimes for other reasons which are now hard to understand. The main feature of political life in Cupar in the first half of the eighteenth century was the struggle for control between the families of Leslie and Melville. This was linked with questions of loyalty to the Hanoverian monarchy, but was also part of a wider unhappiness within Scottish burghs.[24] Even since the Act of Union unrest had been breaking out at intervals in Scotland: the 1715 rebellion; food riots in various east-coast towns in 1720; electoral unrest in several burghs in the early 1720s; and the Malt Tax riots in Glasgow and elsewhere in 1725. Whatley has demonstrated the importance of the food riots in 1720, and argued that these had no direct link with Jacobitism. Any organised defiance was seen by the authorities as a threat to the as-yet-insecure Hanoverian monarchy, and therefore automatically linked to Jacobitism. Even where there was some link, as in Cupar in 1720–23, the issues were wider and more complex. Whatever the immediate cause, protests could easily be joined or even taken over by those seeking an opportunity to upset the government.

Cupar's citizens did not participate in the grain riots of 1720, and the town council rather smugly invited to the King's birthday celebrations that year 'the Lords of Justiciary presently sitting here for judging the persons guilty of the late Mobbs and Tumults'. The Tayside grain riots of 1772–73 swept through Cupar. On 7 January 1773 a 'great mob' of 900 or 1,000 'assembled at Cupar upon the sound of a horn; plundered several houses of potatoes and meal', then went to Seggie. It sounds as though the rioters came from a wide area. Only one resident of Cupar, and a couple who had recently lived in the town, were among those tried and transported.[25] The mob concentrated on places such as Newburgh and Balmerino, where grain was exported.

It could be argued that Cupar was fairly introverted for the first half of the eighteenth century, mainly concerned with holding on to its privileges as a royal burgh in the face of a changing world. It has been suggested that contests for control of towns, such as that between the earls of Rothes and Leven, was caused by the reduction of parliamentary seats after the Act of Union, but their antagonism was of longer standing. During the second half of the century the town gradually became more outward-looking and less conservative, enjoying increasing prosperity and contact with the wider world. Although the merchants of Cupar were no longer involved in foreign trade, newspapers and other reading matter, military service and increased population mobility all broadened the horizons of the town's inhabitants. Sheriff courts became more important after the abolition of hereditary jurisdictions in 1747. However, although the third quarter of the eighteenth century saw local politics becoming more liberal and outward-looking, it was also the period when bribery and corruption appear to have been most prevalent. By 1800 the effects of war and inflation, fear of revolution, threats to the linen industry, and a burgh sett which allowed lawyers to dominate the council, led to an increasingly conservative attitude to national politics. Perhaps this is reflected in the strength of the episcopal church. Long linked with conservatism and loyalty to the Hanoverians, episcopal worship in Cupar was at its weakest towards the end of the eighteenth century, and then revived quickly, to the extent that a new chapel was built by subscription in St Catherine Street in 1819–20.

The three main episodes of political unrest in the town can perhaps be seen as symbolic of the way life was changing. The disruption of the early 1720s involved force on both sides, with buildings broken into and people intimidated. The problems of the 1760s involved the use not of physical force but of money and manipulation to achieve control. The third episode involved physical violence, in the form of arson, though force was not met by force, but by political action. Tactics such as the kidnapping of voters had by the 1790s been replaced by more cerebral tactics, and more reliance on the power and authority of the ruling elite.

If it is the case that the town was at its most outward-looking and liberal between about 1760 and 1790, this is perhaps reflected in its choice of MP. Although it was one of a group of five burghs, many of the same factors will have influenced each burgh. After the Act of Union the burghs at first chose the same sort of people to represent them in London as they had chosen for the Scots parliament – respectable citizens, often present or former magistrates, or minor landowners. Joseph Austin was a former bailie of Perth. His successor, George Yeaman, was a Dundee merchant, followed by Patrick Haldane, provost of St Andrews. This cycle was broken by the disputed election in 1722 of Charles Leslie and William Erskine, followed by the choice of two government supporters, the second of them another Leslie. George Dempster, MP from 1760 to 1791, was the most radical and the most conscientious MP Cupar had in the eighteenth century. He was unusual among Scottish politicians in his support for American independence, for electoral reform (in counties, not burghs), and for freedom of the press, but his main interest was in the development of agriculture, fisheries and industry, including the linen industry. An improving landlord, he treated his tenants with respect, and encouraged them to stay on the land. He could not be bribed, but he bought votes just as others did. His parliamentary career, though active, was probably less important than his other interests. His election marked the end of the influence of the Rothes family in Cupar.[26] In the general election of 1767 Robert Mackintosh of Auchintully stood against him, supported by the Clive interest in the East India Company.

The next MP, from 1796 to 1805, was David Scott of Duninald; also a director of the East India Company, with the backing of Henry Dundas he had introduced changes whereby the Company was run more like a business than a colonial power, and became more profitable. In April 1796 he informed Patrick Rigg of Tarvit, a Cupar councillor, that he had obtained 'a Bengal appointment' for John Elder, and for Robert Methven 'an appointment of a clerk in the India House'. He explained how sought after the posts were, 'that our friends of Cupar may know that we don't do things by halves'. Later that year he wrote to St Andrews, pointing out that he had to share his patronage between five burghs, and if they were all as demanding as St Andrews 'they would require more patronage than the whole East India direction have in their gift'.[27] It was a thankless task keeping even the small number of voters in five burghs happy. Scott and his successors were government supporters, placed in the seat by and related to the ruling aristocracy. They were providers of patronage rather than supporters of local industry. Patronage, however, was very important to the electorate, both burgh and county, and without it election as an MP was unlikely.

Local politics are perhaps the hardest aspect of life in the town to interpret and understand today. There was certainly corruption, but for most of the time those running the burgh of Cupar were concerned for the good of the town as well as their own interests, and in such a small town the two were necessarily closely linked. The only firm evidence for corruption relates to events surrounding the election of George Dempster in 1767–68, and the later account of payment for nominations to the council. There was certainly favouritism shown in the awarding of contracts. Unlike smaller burghs such as Pittenweem, with many absentee councillors, Cupar councillors had to be seen to be active in order to keep in control of people and events. There was always a risk of radical elements, and a town council too full of 'honorary' members, or too complacent, risked disaster. This was why suggestions of burgh reform, which seem so mild and logical now, provoked such extreme reactions at the time. As the middle classes acquired property, and a more comfortable lifestyle, their fear of threats to the political stability they had come to enjoy increased. The arson attacks in 1797, attributed to the United Scotsmen, provoked a conservative reaction which may well have led to the control of the council by lawyers by 1820, and perhaps contributed to the town's subsequent lack of industrial development.

Notes

1. By virtue of co-option to the 'old' council, he became eligible to be chosen as a magistrate. Sometimes, therefore, a substitute was deliberately introduced to allow more members of a clique to take over the council, and occasionally this led to disputes about the eligibility of substitutes.

2. Cupar was one of the few burghs where all trades deacons served ex-officio. This was more democratic than in some other burghs, where guild councillors chose deacons from a short-list provided by the trades, or councils where there were fewer seats than deacons.

3. This seems to have been a reversion to an earlier practice. The advantage was that the guildry gained an extra member on the council, who could be outside any ruling clique. The disadvantage was that the choice was made before the election of magistrates, so candidates ruled themselves out as bailies.

4. There were 29 or more councillors in Glasgow, 29 in St Andrews, 27 in Linlithgow, 26 in Perth, 25 in Edinburgh, Haddington and Dumfries, 24 in Dysart and Pittenweem, 22 in Dunfermline, 21 in Stirling, 20 in Dundee and Dunbar, 19 in Aberdeen, Montrose and Forfar, 17 in Irvine, 15 or more in Inverkeithing.

5. Perhaps the fact that this reform movement was led by merchants would have attracted little support from a town council already dominated by lawyers. The movement nationally died in 1792 after a major defeat in Parliament, and the burgh reformers joined forces with the parliamentary reform movement.

6. It was usually the provost who was chosen as delegate to the meeting of the five burghs to choose a member of Parliament. Great political power could also be wielded by town clerk and particularly sheriff clerk, both of which were effectively appointments for life.

7. He went bankrupt just after being re-elected in October 1815, which gave his opponents, apparently led by the convener of trades, Thomas Horsburgh and George Aitken, writers, and James Rigg and John Russell, local landowners, plenty of time to plan openly, 'with infinite activity and zeal'.

8. Home, *Sketches of the History of Man*, ii, 494–95.

9. In general the rule taken most seriously was that to be eligible to vote a man should have been resident and a member of the trade for at least six weeks – to avoid last-minute creation of burgesses for political reasons.

10. There were no comments in any of the testimonies as to the right of a woman to hold or express political views. The imprisonment of opponents in disputed elections was a common practice in Scottish towns.

11. Fergusson, *Letters of George Dempster*; in a rare glimpse of an MP's real view of his constituency, Dempster wrote from Abergavenny (Wales) that 'The girls are all debauched and the men drunkards. It beats in that respect Cupar of Fife, and Cupar of Fife rivals Gomorrah'.

12. *A Vindication of the Action of Declarator* ..., 1721, 8–9.

13. The other bailies were James Oliphant, merchant, and Richard Applin, vintner (one of those who withdrew rather than swear an oath of loyalty in 1714); George Douglas, merchant, was treasurer; James Baxter, surgeon; and James Hepburn, maltman, were councillors; and John Smith 'Collected the Land Tax for the Pretender's use'.

14. The purchase of a fire engine by subscription had been proposed in Nov 1783, with the town offering £100, but nothing happened. By 7 Apr 1798 an engine had been bought for £114, and six men chosen to man it, testing it once a month for £1 a year. It did not get much use, and the hoses were expensive to repair, so in Oct 1806 the town handed it over to the new Fife Fire Insurance Company, with £4 a year for maintenance.

15. NAS GD20/7/222; the same witness referred to troops being sent to a riot at Crawford Priory, about 2½ miles south-west of Cupar, property of the Earl of Crawford. Nothing more has been found about this incident.

16. Horsburgh, who had only just become sheriff-clerk in 1797, on the death of his father, served as clerk to several other bodies such as the JPs, Commissioners of Supply and Turnpike Trustees.

17. Caroline had married the prince of Wales in 1795, but they had separated. When he became king in 1820 she tried to take her place as queen, but the Government introduced a Bill to exclude her. She had popular sympathy, and the Bill was withdrawn, but she was forcibly excluded from the coronation, and died soon afterwards.

18. Pers Comm. Professor Nicholas Rodger, University of Exeter, Captain Frederick Lewis Maitland, for example, gathered most of his crew during the American revolutionary war from the Cupar area.

19. The Volunteers were particularly popular in Scotland, and in towns, although their usefulness in an inland town was limited. After 1808 their status was changed to local militia.

20. The 'Powder Magazine' can be seen on Wood's town plan of 1820 (Plate 13) near the gaol and hunt kennels to the south of the river.

21. NAS CS234 R4/1, testimonies of James Tod, town treasurer, and Janet Goodfellow, maid. When Mrs Horsburgh finally let her father out she found the house deserted.

22. BS Letterbook 1/30/25, 15 Dec 1789; Banks were closely linked to the government interest, and it was in reaction to this that the non-political Commercial Bank was founded in 1810.

23. Other towns experienced similar problems. The minister of Kirkcaldy deplored the divisive effects of burgh politics, and linked it with the fact that the adjacent burghs of barony of Linktown and Pathhead had 'for 30 years back increased in more than a double proportion to the royal burgh of Kirkcaldy'. Similar comments were made by the minister of Inverkeithing, while the minister of Scoonie commented on the benefits of Leven not being a burgh, with the consequent problems of 'corporation or borough politics, which … are attended with such bad effects upon the industry and morals of the people'.

24. There were problems in 1722 at Dingwall, Haddington and Montrose, and in 1725 elections at Dysart had to be externally supervised.

25. *Scots Magazine*, 1773, 14–20, 332.

26. Fergusson, *Letters*, 50–51, 56: Dempster to Fergusson, 3 Sept 1760, Dempster described Cupar as 'long entail'd to the Lessly family', simply because of 'that awe and respect which the inhabitants of a little burrow naturally feel for a man who lives in splendor and makes a parade in their neighbourhood', Dempster would have to 'play the frog and endeavour to puff myself up to the size of this mighty court fed ox'. The seat is said to have cost Dempster up to £10,000.

27. Philips, *Correspondence of David Scott*, 285–86, Scott to Patrick Rigg, 23 Apr 1796, Scott to Alexander Duncan, 13 Nov 1796, he explained that he couldn't transfer posts from one burgh to another 'as the patronage of every burgh is sacred to it'.

10

Poor Relief, Social Control and Public Services

Poor relief

The sources for the nature, extent and relief of poverty in Cupar are fragmentary. We know a bit about those who tried to deal with the problem, but little or nothing about the personal experiences of poor people. The lack of evidence in Cupar is exacerbated by the absence of kirk session records. However kirk sessions in Scotland generally grew weaker during the eighteenth century, and in towns the council seems to have been more active than the session in poor relief, particularly from *c*.1750. At times this is the result of problems such as food shortages or unemployment. It may, however, also be because the growing urban middle class began to distance itself both physically and psychologically from those less fortunate, and consequently grew to fear the poor as both a financial burden and a threat to social stability.

There was a difficult relationship between the kirk session and the town council, which was a leading heritor. As the result of a long-standing financial dispute each felt the other was not contributing its fair share. In April 1765 it was claimed that the town had owed 800 merks to the kirk session since 1701, and, having paid no interest since 1714, now owed £1,839 6s 8d Scots (about £150 sterling). Despite deducting a number of items of expenditure such as founding a new bell, and 'victual for the poor' (it was spending over £20 sterling a year on poor relief), the town still owed £1,227 6s 8d, and the kirk session used this as an excuse for inactivity. The council started stipulating that it would only go ahead with any approved charitable donation if the amount were matched by the kirk session. In 1779 the council decided to suspend all charitable payments until the savings amounted to the sum owed to the kirk session, which would trigger future payments from the session. Those who received no help protested, the council partially relented, but the problem was still not resolved.

The only other source of information about the kirk's role in poor relief is the *Old Statistical Account*, where Cupar can be compared with neighbouring rural parishes whose sessions were the sole or lead organisations in poor relief. Ceres, Cults, Monimail, Moonzie, Logie, Dairsie and Kemback had poor funds gathered from church door collections, mortcloth dues and other sources including interest on loans and rent from land or church seats. Poverty in rural parishes was generally on a scale which could be handled at a local level. According to the minister of Kilmany, the rural poor showed a 'reluctance, not merely to solicit, but often even to receive aid', showing a dignity which was lacking 'amongst the lazy, dissipated, importunate beggars of large towns'. In Cupar in 1793 there were between four and seven licensed beggars, fifteen regular pensioners of the kirk session, and many more received occasional help. Between £70 and £80 per year was collected at the church door, and £16 more received in interest. There were also alms houses where 'a few aged and infirm women are lodged'. In addition, the poor were 'indebted to the liberal spirit of public bodies, and to the compassion of individuals, for essential and seasonable support', as well as to the town council who 'greatly to their credit, give liberally out of the revenue of the burgh, to the indigent and distressed'.

The town council itself recorded few charitable donations before 1740, though it is possible that they were contributing in a way which is not obvious in the surviving documents. The permanent poor are hardly ever mentioned, but from the 1740s there are increasing references to help distressed former councillors or town officers or their dependants, often one-off payments for clothes, house rent or funeral costs. In 1745, for example, they gave 20s sterling to a former bailie 'on account of his low circumstances'. The council occasionally gave money to other townspeople for specific purposes such as to help a man 'put on the roof of his house' in 1757, as well as more regular payments to those in indisputable need, as in 1777 to a man whose son was 'deprived of reason'. As the century progressed, class distinctions seem to have developed in the amounts given. In 1767 Andrew Scott, surgeon, in 'distressed circumstances' was given £10 sterling, and a further £26 the following month to prevent him and his family becoming 'a burden on the Town and parish'. On the other hand in May 1768 the charity of 3s 6d a week to a former councillor was reduced to 1s 6d because 'there are many in the Town who are greater objects'.

The council could agree to adjust rents or defer payments if it felt individuals were genuinely unable to pay. In 1792 they were petitioned by a widow because the treasurer had seized her cattle and agricultural tools in part payment for rent owed by her late husband. She could not pay the rest without selling her house, but she was 'unable by reason of old age to earn her livelihood' and was also looking after a seven-year-old illegitimate son of her husband's. There are also references to charity as a result of disasters such as a fire in 1756, when the council gave £3, the general inhabitants £6 17s, the wrights 12s, the bakers 12s, the weavers 10s 6d, the tailors 10s and the shoemakers 5s (the other three trades claimed they could afford nothing). The charity roll grew imperceptibly, and when times were hard the town's income from rents was reduced, and it had less to spare. Regular payments to individuals during 1768 amounted to £16 13s 4d over the year (£200 Scots), almost 6 per cent of the council's annual income. In 1779 a list of the town's regular expenses included £5 13s in house rents 'for poor objects', £33 16s in weekly charities, and £3 in incidental charities, 19 per cent of total committed expenditure. The result was a campaign to reduce the amounts given to individuals by a third, and to remove some people from the charity roll altogether. But implementation was delayed. And, while the town's contributions to the relief of the poor were helpful, the sums involved should be compared with the expenditure of £15 17s on the annual election dinner in 1785, and £13 7s 6d spent on 'entertaining the Aerial Traveller Mr Lunardi' the following year.

Although there were several unsuccessful proposals by individual councillors to reduce expenditure on entertaining, the magistrates did eventually realise that self-indulgence was inexcusable in times of hardship. In 1799 it was decided that the election dinner should be paid for by those who participated, because the council had had 'to shorten their allowances to the poor, at a time they most require it'. And in May 1801 it was agreed to give £25 to the poor instead of spending it on celebrating the King's birthday. In 1803 a number of poor people had to be removed from the billeting list, though a plea for all single women and widows to be removed was unsuccessful, because with 500 men of the Fifeshire Militia 'besides recruiting parties ... almost every home in Town has soldiers quartered upon them'. In February 1805 the council decided to limit its charities to £40 a year while at the same time agreeing once again to spend £15 on the annual election dinner. In 1812 it limited its casual charities to £5 per year, but while wishing also to reduce its longer-term commitments, found it difficult to do it in practice: 'the poor upon the Town's list are so destitute that the committee cannot at present recommend them to be struck off until some more appropriate mode of maintaining them can be devised'. Another action the council took by the end of the eighteenth century was to organise, co-ordinate or simply endorse public subscriptions for charitable purposes.

In 1757, during a national grain shortage, the council gave £10 for the magistrates to bestow 'in meal or otherways as they shall think most proper', and agreed to draw up lists of those most in need. Meal was bought jointly with the kirk session, and the charity roll continued until at least October, with a maximum outlay of £14 Scots per week. Meal was bought in bulk by the council from 1782, this being presumably more efficient than giving money to individuals to buy it. In 1799 its distribution was better organised, with tickets to be issued to the 'real poor' entitling them to a specific quantity at a reduced price. In April 1800 there was no meal at all in the market, and the town agreed to buy in what it could. In 1805 the council petitioned against the Corn Laws, claiming that the effect 'must be to keep the price of wheat much higher than the manufacturer or tradesmen are able to pay'.

In 1811 the town received a legacy of £500 from John Gray for the magistrates to buy oatmeal, to provide a permanent rolling stock to be sold to the poor, though 'in case of a dearth or great rise of price in the markets the whole store may be disposed of and the money ... kept until the market fall'. The town fixed the price of bread until at least 1815, later than in many other burghs, and this would have helped to avoid profiteering in times of shortage. A constructive response to food shortages was to ensure that as broad a range of food was available as possible. In February 1803 the town subscribed 10 guineas 'for bringing fishermen from Shetland to St Andrews, as their fishermen have mostly died out, and on that account, fish have become exceedingly scarce and dear'. In 1809 a vegetable market was established, and part of the reason for encouraging the building of new suburbs was to allow more space for gardens, specifically for growing vegetables. From November 1792 there are also regular references to the town buying coal in bulk for distribution to the poor.

From the turn of the century the lead in charitable schemes was increasingly being taken by the county heritors. As well as serving as Justices of the Peace and Commissioners of Supply, the heritors were accumulating other responsibilities such as the management of turnpike roads. They perhaps had a better overview and a less parochial attitude than town councils. In 1800 they set up a 'public charity kitchen', with contributions of £21 each from the town and the kirk session, and subscriptions from other bodies such as the guildry, trades and Volunteers. It was still running in 1807. Another aspect of poor relief originally instigated by the town council but later organised by county heritors was job creation at times of high unemployment. Increasingly after 1800 the council asked for subscriptions from other bodies and individuals so that a realistic sum could be raised. Everywhere in the country the end of the Napoleonic wars led to mass unemployment which was alleviated wherever possible by public works schemes. In 1816 local heritors formed a committee for 'devising means for the relief of the labouring and manufacturing classes now suffering from the want of employment and dearth of provisions'. They decided to ask coal-works with local connections to provide cut-price coal, and farmers to lend carts to transport it. They also devised a scheme to top up the earnings of weavers according to the number and ages of their dependants. One of the other suggestions was 'to give as much employment ... as possible by making footpaths along the different roads entering to the Town'. They raised over £300 in the first month and paid men 'of every trade and of all ages' between 8d and 10d per day for labouring. In January 1817 the heritors decided to re-establish the soup kitchen. They defined the reasons for poverty as twofold – unemployment or reduced wages, and the high price of food, which hit the poor hardest. As grain and potatoes were in short supply, the use of vegetables was to be encouraged. A soup of meat and vegetables seemed the best way to provide a cheap and nutritious addition to the diet of the poor. As in 1801, the price of the soup was to be 1d per English quart. Their estimated price for ingredients for 40 quarts of soup was:

	£	s	d
34lb good beef at 3d per lb	0	8	6
16lb barley at 3d per lb	4	0	
turnips, carrots, cabbage and onions	1	6	
salt and pepper		6	0
Total	0	14	6 (1.07d per qt)

The loss on 300 quarts per day, three days a week, for twenty-six weeks worked out at £18 0s 6d, mainly accounted for by fuel and labour.[1]

By March 1817 the subscribed funds had risen to nearly £500, with a further £30 raised from a charity ball, and £7 from a lecture. Of this, £187 16s 6½d had been spent on subsidies to weavers, winders and spinners, £142 14s 6d on general charities, £96 1s 10d on footpaths, £23 5s 9d on coal and £14 10s 5d on general expenses. But the need was great. In April the heritors asked for a special church collection which raised almost £30, and in June launched a new subscription. By August, however, the worst seems to have been over. The subscription was closed, the soup kitchen equipment rouped, and the minutes of the committee cease. But public works continued. In 1819 over sixty people were being employed, and the town agreed to subscribe a further £50.

The other churches which were established during the long eighteenth century, such as the Boston church, made special collections for their own poor. Though few records survive, it must be assumed that, as in other towns, the guildry and trades did their best to support their own members. During the 1790s expenditure by the guildry on charity fluctuated between a quarter and a half its overall annual expenditure. By 1817 it was more regularly half. But this was not particularly generous, as guildry income, including interest from investments, was increasing faster than its outgoings. The guildry also contributed towards general schemes, such as £30 for subsidised meal and £20 for the 'public kitchen' in 1800 (while pointing out that the kirk session was failing to contribute). In 1817 it was noted that 'all the incorporations with the exception of the Waulkers have given their mite towards the general Improvements', and 'the Guildry should not be backward', so they agreed to contribute 15 guineas. The trades were less well off, but did what they could. With an increasing number of workers no longer members of guildry or trades, a general friendly society had been founded in Cupar 'in order to lay a found for the support of distress and old age', and in March 1790 their numbers were 'increasing daily' and they petitioned the council for a place to meet. Later other friendly societies were formed, such as the Carters' Society, and the 'Society of Gardners'.²

The minister in 1793 also noted that 'The ladies of several of the principal heritors' each had 'their list of weekly pensioners, to whose wants they kindly and regularly attend'. The council always welcomed private contributions towards its charitable schemes. In January 1818, for example, a number of the heritors and gentlemen had 'agreed to drive coals for the benefit of the poor inhabitants', the town and others to pay for the coal itself. In 1817 Mr Rigg of Tarvit was given the freedom of the burgh in recognition of his generosity to the poor over the previous winter. The account book of Lady Anstruther records many donations both through the church, and directly to individuals. Her expenditure in four sample years is shown in Table 10.1. While it is clear that she could easily afford what she gave, her charitable contributions are quite high compared with the total charitable expenditure of the town council of £16 13s 4d in 1768 and £42 9s in 1779. Her individual charities varied. Occasionally as she travelled to and from Edinburgh via Kinghorn she recorded payments to 'the women on the road' or 'to the women through Fife', presumably referring to beggars. Her charity to those not personally known to her was nearly always to women.

The town council, through its teachers' salaries, subsidised the education of poor scholars. The general impression given for most of the eighteenth century is that bright children were never denied education, and that each master was expected to teach a reasonable (though unspecified) number of poor scholars as part of his salary. Teachers occasionally asked the council for recompense for books provided for poor scholars; the school account book notes, in 1795, payments from kirk session and town for individual poor scholars. There seems to be no pattern of amounts paid or numbers of children supported, though possibly the kirk session supported fewer girls than the town did. By

TABLE 10.1   An example of private charitable contributions

	Church collection	Charities	Total expenditure	church and charity as % of total expenditure
1768	£2 10s	£0 12s 2d	£347 1s 2d	under 1%
1778	£4 10s	£1 16s 10d	£746 5s 2d	under 1%
1788	£7 11s 2d	£1 12s 1d	£601 4s 10d	about 1.5%
1798	approx £3	£2 12s 6d	£442 12s 1d	about 1.3%

Source: Lady Elizabeth Anstruther's account book, StAU msCS479.A8.

the early nineteenth century, however, attitudes towards educating poor children were changing. When, in 1812, Robert Wiseman, English master, asked the council for a refund of £16 15s 2d, a committee was set up to consider whether they should discontinue providing books to poor scholars and to 'bargain' with him as to what he should be paid for teaching poor scholars. They agreed that 'in future no poor scholars shall be sent to the school without a recommendation from the whole magistrates'. They examined the scholars, decided that two were good enough to leave school, and none of the rest had any claim to support 'being all strangers or bastards', and agreed that 'no books ought to be given to poor scholars'.

In December 1816 the convener and six deacons petitioned the council, because some families were so poor they were 'unable to give their children any education even to read the Bible', and suggested that, as the private teachers could not afford to teach them free, some 'should receive a salary from the Town' in return for teaching 'a certain number of Freemen's children'. They suggested six children per teacher, and that the three teachers at the grammar school should also educate a certain number of children 'gratis'. But the council apparently did not agree, for the following year one of the private teachers petitioned the council for an allowance for teaching poor scholars. He was offered 2 guineas, but the council decided no further grants would be made 'until the Town's funds are in a more flourishing condition'. Another private teacher, however, asked for help with his rent as his pupils' parents were 'trades and labouring people', and in these difficult times his quarterly fees 'must be small and many times not paid at all'.

Once more the local heritors became involved. In January 1817 they agreed to pay the school fees for some poor families, dividing the town into three areas to share the children out between the grammar school (eighteen) and two private schools (twenty-four and twenty-nine), and twenty-five girls at a private female school. In 1819 the council contributed three guineas to a subscription 'for the education of poor children in this Town', and another subscription was raised in 1825. The problem was exacerbated when the grammar school became an academy in 1823, with a large increase in fees to reflect the wider curriculum. The trades petitioned the presbytery for the provision of a parish school, because the higher fees would 'preclude many families from obtaining the usual course of instruction in Reading, Writing and Arithmetic for which our county has so long been distinguished'.[3] But with the kirk session weak, and the heritors already contributing in other ways, a parish school was out of the question.

In 1740 a collection had been made in Cupar for the Edinburgh Royal Infirmary. In 1760 there had been a proposal for an infirmary in Cupar, recognising the links between ill-health and poverty: 'To view the Distress of our Fellow-creatures, groaning under Sickness, heightened

by Poverty, must raise a strong Fellow-feeling, and excite Compassion
... How many spin out a wretched Life, painful to themselves, and
useless to Mankind, by Diseases that might be cured if properly treated,
and taken in Time? How many, who are now a Burden and Nuisance,
might, by proper Assistance, be brought into a Condition to support
Themselves, and become useful to Society?' A site was earmarked, but
nothing came of the scheme.[4] There was no official provision in Cupar
for medical care to the poor. Doctors' fees to the rich were so high that
they must have been accepted as a form of subsidy to the poor. Lady
Anstruther appears to have paid for medical attention for others as
well as herself.[5] When Dr Charles Grace occasionally asked the council
for money towards his care for the poor, and for prisoners, he was
usually reimbursed.[6] A 'surgeon and accoucheur' setting up in Cupar
advertised in the *Fife Herald* in March 1825 that he would 'dedicate a
part of his time to attend poor lying-in women, and the sick in indigent
circumstances gratuitously'. By the early nineteenth century there was
some concern for the care of the mentally ill. In February 1807 the
council decided that the sum raised 'for the lunatic Finlay now dead'
should be used to pay the keeper of another sufferer. In 1812 they gave
£5 to the kirk session for help in boarding an 'idiot' in Edinburgh,
and in 1818 offered up to £7 a year towards the keep of a 'deranged'
woman, so that she could be removed from Cupar gaol and sent to a
lunatic asylum.

From the 1780s there was a national debate about whether there
should be a more formal system for dealing with the poor. Both
emotionally and financially, limited numbers of poor in rural parishes
or small towns could be supported from local resources. But the
vagrant poor represented both a financial problem and a threat to the
stability of society. The town council regularly expressed its concern
about unknown incomers. In 1777 the heritors blamed the council
for the increasing numbers of poor, because of 'people in town letting
houses to strangers who are not able to support themselves', and asked
for this practice to be banned. According to the minister in 1793 there
were still several houses 'that harbour the idle and the profligate'. By
day 'they prowl in the neighbouring country ... and beg or plunder by
turns'. At night they returned to Cupar, 'dispose there of their spoils,
and riot and carouse, at the expence of the simple, the sober, and the
industrious'.

In 1723 the Commissioners of Supply, concerned about the 'great
number of vagabonds and sturdy beggars and other idle persons
going up and down this shire', decided that 'correction houses' should
be built, and asked for contributions from kirk sessions. In 1725
vagrants were blamed for 'thefts and breaking of houses' which would
increase 'if some remedy were not speedily provided', and the heritors
again urged the building of a correction house. Cupar offered land on

the Bridge Hill; by June 1730 it was almost finished, and by 1733 a keeper had been in post for a year (but had not been paid). However, by 1779 it had 'for these many years past never been used ... but remains unoccupied and useless'. The decision to sell the building was finally taken in 1786, because it had never 'answered the purpose for which it was Built', and even if restored it 'would not let to families for dwelling houses, as the lower people have a prejudice against it'. With its abandonment, vagrants again took up valuable space in the tolbooth cells. In 1790 there was a proposal for a Bridewell to be built on the Calton Hill in Edinburgh, to hold 'the vagrants and delinquents ... in the five contiguous counties', to be financed by a tax on every householder. The Commissioners of Supply agreed. The Bridewell was built, but does not seem to have included space for vagrants from Fife.

In 1793 one of the town officers was paid extra 'to keep the Town free from all vagrants and stranger beggars', and the minister commented that 'there is no town perhaps in Scotland, of the same extent, where a greater number are daily seen infesting the streets'. Because Cupar lay on 'the great turnpike road leading through the county of Fife', and there was no 'plan being steadily followed' to deal with vagrant beggars, 'the inhabitants are daily subjected to their importunities and extortions'. He regarded a Bridewell like that being built in Edinburgh as a 'pressing necessity', without which Fife would face an 'influx of pickpockets, swindlers, etc.', threatening economic development. In 1801 all the town officers were to exert themselves 'in keping the town free of vagrant beggars' or risk dismissal.[7] When a new prison was proposed, there were suggestions that it should incorporate a Bridewell 'where vagrants, disorderly persons and criminals for triffling offences could be committed and kept to hard labour', particularly as the magistrates had recently searched 'some suspicious houses' and found vagrants, 'some of them from Ireland'.[8] But town and county had to finance an expensive new prison, and neither wanted to pay for a Bridewell for which they had no legal obligation.

By the early nineteenth century the sheriff officer was also being referred to as a constable, and in lieu of a Police Act the town recruited volunteer constables. *Instructions to the Constables for the Burgh of Cupar-Fife* from 1817 survive. The duty of the constables was to report any breach of the peace, to apprehend any suspicious 'night-walkers', to arrest 'all idle persons whom they know to have no means to live upon', any criminals, or anyone carrying weapons, and 'inform of all Houses suspected of receipting of thieves, vagabonds, and idle persons'. The chief constable was Robert Tullis, printer, the heads of the four divisions of the town were a manufacturer, a merchant, a doctor and a brewer, and their four 'orderlies' tradesmen.

Social control

By the second half of the eighteenth century, as was generally the case in Scotland, the hold of the kirk session over public life and private morality was weakening. In Cupar there were several successful challenges to its authority. When in 1778 the session accused Thomas Robertson, a writer, of immorality, he responded by suing it for slander.[9] Not only was life becoming more secular, but the number of townspeople attending the kirk was declining as a range of non-conformist churches became established. The first Relief or Boston congregation was formed in 1770, a Secession church built in Burnside in 1794–96, and a Baptist congregation formed in 1815.

Inevitably the wider range of places of worship, and the increasing numbers who did not attend any church, made social control by the kirk more difficult. In 1744, for example, two residents of Cupar, and others outside the town, were prosecuted in the sheriff court for not attending church on a day decreed by royal proclamation as a fast day. Instead 'They wroght Publickly att their ordinary Trades ... in the most open and Contemptuous manner'. Their defence was that they meant no disrespect, but a different fast day had been decreed by the Associate Presbytery, of which they were members, and they had a few days earlier 'joined in publick acknowledgement of the Sins of the land and age wherein they Live and offered up their fervent Supplications to the Almighty'.[10]

Much has been written about the social control exercised by the kirk sessions of Scotland in the seventeenth century. However, not only was such control waning by the eighteenth century; it has also become increasingly apparent that the situation was different in towns and cities, where there was a civil system of social control alongside the religious one. The burgh court dealt with cases of slander, and could banish those who refused to conform to social norms. Although the kirk session records of Cupar are missing, the most intractable cases were referred to the presbytery, whose records do survive, and give a general indication of the problems which arose and how they were dealt with. Fornication or adultery were frequently alleged to have occurred, in a wide range of locations including shops and barns, and in 1738 in the minister's garden 'while pulling onions'. There were also several events linked to one of the eight annual fairs, or race week; occasions where outsiders came to town, and locals drank more than normal. Kirk session and presbytery were all-male institutions, and their judgements were biased. Prostitutes might be condemned, but their clients were not. Men were generally believed rather than their female accusers. In 1776 a pregnant unmarried girl claimed that Charles Grace, then apprenticed to Dr Young, had given her some pills to procure an abortion, but she showed them to her mistress, who advised her not to take them. Grace denied the whole story, and was believed. Accusations of rape were in general not believed unless the men involved confessed. When in 1762 John Carnegie, flesher, was accused by his servant Mary Ritchie of rape and of infecting her with venereal disease, he admitted the rape but denied the venereal disease, and was sentenced to lesser excommunication.

Evasion of discipline or defiance of the church was frequent. Those who were recalcitrant enough for their cases to have been referred to the presbytery had a tendency to stick to their story, or fail to appear, giving a range of excuses, or change their story so that each new version had to be investigated, and many cases were never satisfactorily resolved. In 1782, for example, Helen Alison, 'whose Husband has been abroad for several years, and who is now believed to be with Child', refused to appear, and was eventually excommunicated. Later she named John Stevenson, writer, who also refused to appear and was sentenced to lesser excommunication. Some women accused the real fathers of their illegitimate children of bribing or threatening them to lie about paternity. Christian Matthew, who 'had brought forth several children in fornication without finding Fathers to one or other of them', named bailie James Tod as the father of her latest child in 1768. Several witnesses, however, named Thomas Elder, servant to a flesher, while she herself changed her story to 'a Recruit, whose name she did not know, and who is not now in the country', and claimed that she was bribed to name Tod by 'some people in the town'. This was a time of political upheaval in the town (see Chapter 9), and her story may well have been true.[11]

At the beginning of the eighteenth century the kirk session was not afraid to criticise gentry for antisocial behaviour. In 1701 Sir William Hope of Craighall and Sir James Hacket were reported to have 'drunk to excess and in Mistress Bogie's house [inn] had used some abominable expressions about taking rooms in hell'. And in 1708 both George Clephane of Carslogie and Sir John Preston of Prestonhall were under scandal. In 1768, however, Betty Lorimer named as the father of her baby Captain Peter Rigg, and claimed that when the baby was born Rigg's brother George gave her 40 shillings. Peter Rigg claimed that she was by 'habite and repute an infamous woman and common strumpet'. This was not a direct denial, but appears to have been accepted as one, given his social status. Towards the end of the century most of those dealt with by the presbytery were servants or journeymen.

One issue which worried the kirk considerably was prostitution. In the seventeenth century there was apparently little organised prostitution in Fife, though there is evidence for prostitutes working singly or in pairs, from either their own homes or alehouses. In England garrison towns from the eighteenth century onwards attracted prostitutes, and this may well have also been the case in Cupar. In 1768 the session reported to the presbytery that they had 'once again applied to the Magistrates to have Janet Thomson or Leckie and other disorderly persons expelled from the town but without success'. Later that year the session received another complaint that Leckie was 'a person of a most scandalous behaviour, who keeps an infamous bawdy-house'. Several other witnesses endorsed this, describing her house as a 'humping school' and accusing her of 'entertaining in her house women of bad fame, and admitting Soldiers and other men to such women and shutting them up in beds together', and even of 'dragging her own Daughter to be corrupted by a man in the house'. The session had petitioned the provost to expel her from the town, but no action had yet been taken 'to rid the town of her and other such pests of Society'. Leckie failed to appear before the presbytery, and when visited by the moderator uttered 'such indecent and obscene language as is improper to be recorded'. She was excommunicated, but that was all the church could do. No explanation was given as to why the magistrates refused to act.

Though the evidence is slight, there seems to have been a decrease in action taken by the church authorities against Sabbath-breaking, perhaps indicating the increasing secularisation of society. The last case reported to Cupar presbytery was in 1728, when the session accused the overseer of the bleachfield for leaving webs out on Sundays. He replied that to interrupt the bleaching process would be harmful, and other bleachfields did the same. The presbytery decided the practice was 'highly offensive and scandalous', but it is not clear whether it managed to stop it. Another symptom of the decreasing hold of the church over society is that several otherwise respectable citizens, such as John Stevenson, writer (see above) were sentenced to lesser excommunication during the 1780s. Presumably they were confident that this would not harm their status or adversely affect their business.[12]

As in other towns, Cupar burgh court by the eighteenth century dealt mainly with debts and evictions, though it did handle a few cases of theft, slander and other forms of antisocial behaviour (criminal cases were dealt with by the sheriff or higher courts). A female thief in 1699 was branded on the cheek, scourged through the town by the hangman and banished from the town. A young male thief in 1731 gave security for good behaviour, under the threat of banishment if he re-offended. By the 1740s the threat of banishment was dropped. In contrast to the kirk session, the burgh court seems to have dealt with the sexes more even-handedly. One volume contains bonds of caution and arrestments for debt between 1699 and 1757, involving 448 men and 103 women (19 per cent), most of whom were being protected rather than prosecuted. It also contains eviction orders from 1699 to 1744. Of the 75 people evicted, 11 (15 per cent) were women; the 69 on whose behalf the court was acting included 12 women (17 per cent). Presumably the evictions were for non-payment of rent, and the court was protecting the livelihoods of those who let property. It is not clear whether the proportion of landladies in these cases reflects the numbers of women letting property, or whether women found it harder to evict tenants without resorting to legal action.

Some cases in the burgh court dealt with matters which might just as easily have come before the kirk session. In 1754, for example, a burgess had to bail out his two sons who had been imprisoned 'for their breach of Sabbath'. This had involved attacking a servant girl 'upon the open fields in a most rude and debauched graceless and profane manner by turning up her petticoats and discerning her nakedness and using towards her other wicked practices'. Their father gave a guarantee that from now on his sons would 'live Christianly soberly and circumspectly free of all debauchery such as drinking to excess, whoreing, profane swearing' and would observe the Sabbath.

In general Cupar's position as county town, with the consequent regular presence of lawyers, justices of the peace and commissioners of supply, the quartering of troops in it, and the large number of travellers who passed through the town, seem to have made the town conscious of its public image, and to have kept its inhabitants generally well behaved, though the council does not seem to have been inclined to close brothels. Perhaps they were seen as part of the service the town provided to travellers, or perhaps their presence was regarded as inevitable, and closing one would only encourage another to open.

The predictable effect of soldiers stationed in or passing through the town was a number of illegitimate children and a few deserted or maltreated wives.[13] But on the credit side were those soldiers who chose to settle in the town, several of whom became prominent citizens. As well as several innkeepers, from the second half of the eighteenth century the town's pipers and drummers tended to be former soldiers. And in the words of the minister in 1793, the presence of retired 'Gentlemen of the military profession', had 'contributed to diffuse an elegance of manners'. The only mention of industrial unrest is in 1825 when the journeymen shoemakers went on strike for 'more per pair'. According to the local (liberal) newspaper the employers at first stood firm, but after failing to find replacement workers, gave way, only to be faced with further demands. But the report emphasised that the leadership came from outside the town. When some commentators blamed increased education, the editor stoutly defended the principle of a better-educated workforce.

Public services

Many visitors came to Cupar for markets, fairs and law courts, and the council was conscious of the public image of the town, making regular attempts to tidy up and repair the streets. By 1754 the old town gates had been removed to improve access.[14] The following year the council ordered 'all carts and middens to be removed off the streets'. Two years later came the first proposal to light the main streets. Lamps were installed but not always lit, depending on the state of the town's finances. In the 1760s the council decided to pay to have the streets cleaned and dung regularly removed, rather than relying on individuals. Other developments at this time were the beginning of parking regulations, with a ban on carts being left on the street overnight, and the employment of a professional street paver from Edinburgh rather than local casual labour. By 1769 work had also begun on providing proper pavements.

The first 'Boards to point out the Roads' were erected in 1785 'at the different outlets from the Town'. The brightly painted mercat cross had by 1788 lost its symbolic importance and become a nuisance which 'greatly incommodes the street'. It was decided to remove it and sell the stones. In 1806 the town council threatened to prosecute 'the people that go with carts and wheel barrows on the forelands [pavements]'. Three years later the council suggested that the dean of guild should be 'more vigilant ... in preventing carts and other obstructions from standing in the streets during the night' and to prevent the deposition of 'coals or other loads' which might damage the pavement. In March 1810 came the first speed limit – those coming to the kirk in carriages were 'required to walk their horses' because of the inconvenience and even danger caused to the inhabitants, particularly the elderly, by chaises being driven too fast down the narrow wynds. Although the roads were greatly improved, they were far from perfect. In 1828 the council authorised temporary repairs to the Crossgate 'to make it passable during the winter'.

By 1796 the council could not afford to light the streets, and 'many disagreeable accidents ... happened both to the inhabitants and strangers ... on dark nights'. One solution was a Police Act, but the town could not afford this, unless they could get it appended to a Turnpike Act. This scheme failed, and in 1803 a subscription was raised to buy new street lights. The council agreed, once they were installed, to pay for the oil and the lamplighter. In 1809 the council again considered applying for a Police Act, including extending the boundaries of the town, so that services could be supplied and 'nuisances and obstructions' removed. Again nothing happened, and in 1813 another voluntary subscription was raised to pay for lighting the street lamps. A Police Act was proposed again in 1821, but rejected by the inhabitants, so another subscription had to be raised for street lighting. Special constables had been introduced in 1817 as a cheaper alternative to a Police Act.

The removal of rubbish was always a problem. As dead horses are difficult to move, it had been customary to take dying horses to specific pieces of waste ground were they were killed and left to be scavenged.[15] As the number of horses increased, this practice was no longer socially acceptable. In 1780 there was a formal complaint by residents that the smell 'had become most noxious and might be detrimental to the lives of the inhabitants' and the council decreed that it future all dead horses should be buried. Live horses were also a problem, as numbers increased while the available grazing decreased. In 1787, for example, there were complaints that 'enclosures and gardens were of late broke into, and their sown grass cut and carried off', and that a number of people 'had no land, or any visible way of maintaining their horses'. The problem was exacerbated by the troops billeted in the town bringing horses with them.

The town council was regularly petitioned about pollution of both the Eden and the Lady Burn. In 1792, for example, there were complaints that the huntsman at Blalowan had 'of late thrown the Bones of the dead Horses and ... Dogs into the Water of Eden; Whereby the water is much Spoiled'. As the population grew and more industries developed the problems increased. In 1818 there was an outbreak of typhus, and concern about the possibility of rabies spreading from Dundee. The council subscribed five guineas to help the 'poorer classes' get their houses cleaned and fumigated, and ordered all dogs to be quarantined for three weeks, and any found loose to be killed. Wells were also polluted. The stables of the Tontine Inn, for example, regularly polluted a well near Bobber Wynd in the 1820s.

The town struggled with poor relief and the control of vagrants, but its experience was little different from that of other towns. It is not clear from the available sources to what extent vagrancy was a real or only a perceived problem. Over the long eighteenth century the authority of the kirk session weakened, while both it and the burgh court grew increasingly unwilling to prosecute the middle and upper classes. Social control was becoming the responsibility of the national civil and criminal courts rather than local courts and the established church. The long eighteenth century also saw a decline in generosity to poor scholars, part of a national debate on the education of the poor and of females.

As the town grew richer, with more money invested in industry, buildings and financial institutions, the middle classes grew increasingly concerned about crimes against property. And as newspapers brought increased awareness of events elsewhere in the country and abroad, they grew more nervous of radical ideas and civil disorder. The purchase of a fire engine by the town council in 1798, and the establishment of the Fife Fire Insurance Company in 1806 both symbolise this. Whatever the sympathies or intentions of those involved in the management of the town, there was a limit to the amount of money either heritors, council or other bodies were willing to spend, and poor relief, health care, social control and the provision of public service were still dealt with, as they always had been, in a piecemeal and short-term way.

Notes

1. NAS HR31/10; the ration was 1 quart for small families and 2 quarts for large ones.
2. Carters, *Fife Herald*, 19 Aug 1824 and 18 Aug 1825; Gardeners, StAU B13/11/1, 6 May 1729, and *Sasine Abridgements*, vi/2, 20 Feb 1813.
3. This was probably part of a wider movement, led by Thomas Chalmers, for more schools under church control, making the parish more central to an increasingly secular Scottish society.
4. NAS GD26/12/23/1, printed *Proposals for Erecting an Infirmary in Fife*, 20 Aug 1760. No hospital seems to have been established in Fife until well into the nineteenth century. Infirmaries were established in Montrose (1782) and Dundee (1794); lunatic asylums in Aberdeen (1800), Edinburgh (c.1812) and Dundee (1813).
5. She paid 1 guinea per visit for the doctor, and between 5s and 1 guinea to nurses for unspecified services. The birth of her first grandchild cost her 1 guinea for the midwife and 3 guineas for the doctor.
6. For example in May 1800 one of the town officers had a leg so bad that he would have died 'if Dr Grace had not given him attendance every day, for at least 7 months past', for which the council gave him £5.
7. The implication is that while the authorities were frightened of both the cost and the risk to public order, many ordinary people had some sympathy for vagrants.
8. NAS GD26/12/32/1, 31 Jan 1810.
9. NAS CC20/3/6, bundle 1778–79. Robertson was a very difficult character, but there were others who also challenged the right of the church to govern their lives.
10. NAS SC20/5//2, bundle 1744–45.
11. It seems to have been quite common for guilty men to try to persuade women to name another man. In Feb 1769, for example, two women named James Farquharson, brewer, and both claimed he had offered financial help provided they named an unknown stranger. In the end he confessed and was rebuked.
12. James Hall, private teacher (1780); John Stevenson, writer (1783); Alexander Smith, writer (1789); this seems to coincide with the 'sudden deterioration in the system of church discipline' identified by Mitchison and Leneman c.1780 (*Sexuality and Social Control*, 38).
13. For example in Feb 1710 Isabel Chalmers admitted fornication with 'one of the Dragans of the troop lying for present at Cupar'. As he was Irish it was not possible to check whether he was married. In Aug 1716 Marjory Stewart named as the father of her child 'William Johnstoun one of the Rebells that was at Cupar before Martinmas last', and it could not be established whether Johnstoun was married. Such births also appear in the OPR, e.g. 16 Oct 1723, baptism of Robert Peage 'begot in ffornication ... by Robert Bevens soldier in the Regiment of the Welsh fuzleers'.

14. Many towns removed their gates in the mid to late eighteenth century to allow easier passage for wheeled traffic, including Irvine (1756), Dumfries (1764) and Elgin (4 between 1783 and 1792).
15. StAU B13/14/6; 27 Aug 1764 a piece of waste ground at the foot of Castlehill was 'of no use ... but as a receptacle for dead horses and other vermin'.

11

Cupar *c.*1820–1914

There was a general agricultural depression in the early 1840s, but just as the linen industry had been stimulated by the wars with France, so 'a particularly prosperous period in the history of farming in Fife was that occasioned by the Crimean War [1853–56]. Money was plentiful, and many of the farmhouses and steadings that exist today were built at that time'.[1] Cupar prospered when agriculture prospered.

The linen industry gradually became mechanised and concentrated in larger factories. In 1836: 'Though there are ... no power looms, yet the manufacture of linen is carried on to a considerable extent, and the number of weavers and others employed is great ... there are employed within the parish not less than 600 weavers. And as every two weavers require one person to wind for them, the number employed and earning a comfortable subsistence from this trade may be reckoned at 900 ... The linen manufactured is of various kinds and qualities, and is exported to the East and West Indies, as well as to all parts of ... Europe and of America.' There were three spinning mills. George Moon of Russell's Mill employed eighty, had a 20 hp water-wheel and a steam engine for when the water power was not adequate, and made thread for sailcloth and bagging. William Smith's flax mills (part of Cupar Mills) had 336 spindles, a 9 hp water-wheel, and employed thirty-three people. Mr Glenday at Lebanon used steam and employed seventy. Smith and Glenday both had associated plash mills for washing the yarn. The supplies of flax mostly came from Kirkcaldy and Dundee, and the yarn was sent back there to be woven in power-loom factories. By 1851 Smith's flax mill was employing fifty men and thirty women.

Between 1864 and 1871 three power-loom factories were set up in Cupar. Leadbetter, McCaull & Co., at Front Lebanon, had forty looms, 'a neat, clean, roomy, and well-ventilated establishment' employing fifty 'females of a highly respectable class, who by industry and attention can earn excellent wages'. Stenhouse and Westwater built the Stratheden Linen Works in Station Road in 1866, and in 1871 Honeyman moved from Kirkgate to a new factory at South Bridge, with seventy looms driven by 'a large powerful condensing engine, with crank overhead'. In 1884 a finishing-house was built next to the factory. That year there was a strike at the Lebanon factory for higher wages. It was settled quickly, and working hours reduced from 60 to 57. The other two workforces followed suit, with the same result. These factories marked the end of hand-loom weaving.

The nineteenth century saw diversification at old mills and the building of new mills for sawing wood and processing raw materials. In the 1830s there were five water-wheels working at Cupar Mills, as well as corn mills at Thomastoun and Tailabout just downstream. There was a snuff mill belonging to William Smith. Sharing a wheel with his plash mill, it processed tobacco 'from all parts of Fife, but also from the counties to the north', making about sixty thousand pounds of snuff every year. It did so well that in 1836 it was reported that a steam engine had recently been added. In 1847 the Stratheden Foundry, another new venture at Cupar Mills, was reported in the *Fifeshire Journal* to have plenty of orders, including 'an iron steam-yacht, which they are furnishing complete with hull and machinery to the order of a continental nobleman'. By 1848, despite the small size of the site there was also saw-mill and a dye-works.

In 1836 there were also three breweries, a rope-works and three foundries making machinery. The long-established tannery on Waterend Road processed hides, while one at Skinner's Steps produced sheepskins and glue. A third tannery was opened in the 1860s at Burnside. Closed in 1951, it was converted into flats (Tannery Court). When the railway was built the brick-works moved out to Cupar Muir (Brighton), where a second works was set up by 1871, by which time the main product was probably field-drainage tiles, reflecting the land improvements being made at the time. Another small industry was clay-pipe making. James Burton set up in about 1835 in the Bonnygate, and by 1862 was working from premises in Back Lebanon. When his grandson retired in about 1945, he was the last pipe-maker north of the Forth.[2]

According to the *Third Statistical Account*, 'The latter half of the nineteenth century and the beginning of the twentieth saw the passing of a dyeworks, three small breweries, a flax factory, a linen factory, two carriage works, several joiners' shops, three tinsmiths, a cooperage, a snuff mill, and an aerated water factory.' In 1862 there were twelve smithies in the parish, but by 1948 only two remained. 'A quarry and a brick-works at Cupar Muir, a quarry on the old road from Ceres, and a meal-mill and saw-mill at Tailabout, all ceased operations round the turn of the present [20th] century.'

'Being the principal seat of business in connection with county matter, the town is always inhabited by a number of practitioners of the law.'[3] By 1836, 'There are no less than 28 procurators before the Sheriff-courts, who reside and carry on a respectable business, and hold a

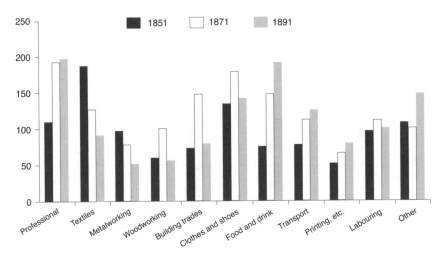

FIGURE 11.1   Occupational data for men, from 1851, 1871 and 1891 censuses.

respectable rank in the town ... Allowing to each of them 2 apprentices or clerks, there are no less than 84', despite the establishment of a sheriff court in Dunfermline. This compared with eleven in Dunfermline, ten in Kirkcaldy and four in St Andrews. In 1878 there were sixteen firms of solicitors, compared with fourteen in Kirkcaldy, but by 1893 there were more in Kirkcaldy. In 1840 the British Linen, Commercial, and National banks were joined by the Clydesdale (in the building it still occupies), and in 1857 the City of Glasgow Bank. Soon afterwards the Royal Bank also opened, but in 1878 the City of Glasgow Bank collapsed.

The nineteenth century saw many changes in occupations. Fig. 11.1 is derived from the census returns for 1851, 1871 and 1891.[4] For men, the number of jobs in the professions, management, finance and administration increased, as did the selling of food and drink, and occupations related to travel and transport. The production of clothes and shoes changed, with more being imported ready-made and sold in specialist shops, rather than being made-to-measure locally. The increase in the 'other' category was mainly due to other retail occupations, such as ironmongers, jobbing or market gardeners, and a general broadening of the range of occupations in the town. The population fell slightly over this period, but there were also by 1891 more people listed as retired or unemployed.

Fig. 11.2 shows similar occupational data for women. As the processing of flax and cotton, and particularly linen weaving, became mechanised, men worked as overseers, but women did the basic monotonous work, in factories rather than in the home. Dressmaking and millinery (mostly

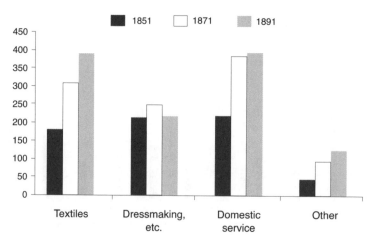

FIGURE 11.2   Occupational data for women, from 1851, 1871 and 1891 censuses.

based at home) continued longer than tailoring and shoemaking did for men, demonstrating a reduction in the number of households making their own clothes, but also a desire for privacy and individual fitting for women's dresses, rather than buying them ready-made. Domestic service seems to have reached a peak. The growth under 'other' is mainly due to a gradual increase in women working in shops. There were also more women doing washing for others, and also cleaning, not as domestic servants, but independent 'charwomen'.

Figure 11.3 is derived from Trades Directories for 1867, 1889 and 1911. These list only owners or managers rather than everyone working in the business, but they demonstrate the same trends. Given the relatively static population, numbers of professionals and specialist tradesmen changed little. The biggest change is in shops, particularly a reduction in the number of little grocers' shops, presumably replaced by a smaller number of larger shops. More foodstuffs were being sold from shops rather than market stalls. The 1889 directory lists fishmongers, and the 1911 one fruiterers. This chart also demonstrates the decline in tailoring, and particularly in dressmaking.

Because of its status as county town Cupar has remained at the centre of a web of travel routes. By 1829 there were five competing coach services to Edinburgh in the summer via the steam ferry from Kirkcaldy. In 1836 there were three coaches in each direction, six days a week, and also coaches to St Andrews and to Largo, 'where there is now a steam-boat ferry to Newhaven' (the Largo coach may not have been a success, as it stopped in 1839). Although after the drainage of the Howe of Fife a new route between the Forth and Tay ferries was built via New Inn and Melville Gates, bypassing Cupar, stage and mail

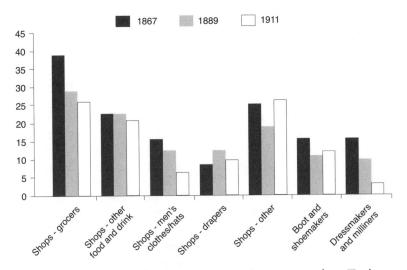

FIGURE 11.3 Occupational data for managers and proprietors, from Trades Directories for 1867, 1889 and 1911.

coaches continued to take the longer route through Cupar because of the availability of refreshment, accommodation and stabling.

The authors of the *New Statistical Account* hoped that when the railway 'now talked of' happened, 'it seems impossible to conceive the advantages that would accrue to the town of Cupar and the neighbourhood'. But far from stimulating industrial development, the coming of the railway may well have ended Cupar's hopes of growth. If goods could move in and out faster and cheaper, so could people. Thomas Rodger in 1861 wrote that like many other Fife towns which had flourished 'in the halcyon period of the Scottish monarchy', Cupar had 'come down in the world'. He identified the coming of the railway as the factor which had 'quenched the last sparks' of activity.[5]

Mad financial speculation in railways developed in 1845, and there were several rival local schemes. The Edinburgh & Northern Railway company was mainly financed by landowners from the Cupar area, keen to boost the fortunes of local agriculture and industries. But there were differences of opinion as to the route, and whether it should go from the Forth to Dundee, Perth or both places. Cupar naturally wanted a line going through it and on to Newport, rather than being at the end of a branch line. The Edinburgh & Northern merged with the Edinburgh, Leith & Granton railway, to form the Edinburgh, Perth & Dundee Railway, and in 1847 bought the Granton–Burntisland ferry. The same year it opened a line from Burntisland to Cupar, with four trains a day each way, and the following year completed the line from Ladybank to Perth. The first train ferry, or 'floating railway', in the world, between

Granton and Burntisland, designed by Thomas Bouch, opened in 1850. The following year the company established another train ferry from Tayport (as the railway company had renamed Ferryport-on-Craig) to Broughty Ferry. In 1851 'it is yet in remembrance, when the carrier left Cupar in the beginning of the week, and returned from Edinburgh on Saturday evening. And now by the aid of steam-power and locomotives, half of Europe may be traversed in the same period of time'.[6]

A branch railway to St Andrews from Leuchars opened in 1852, and two years later another, from Thornton to Leven opened, extended in 1857 as far as Largo, and reaching Anstruther in 1863. Meanwhile in 1861 the Edinburgh, Perth & Dundee Railway had merged with the North British. The line from St Andrews was extended to Boarhills in 1883, and the loop to Anstruther completed in 1887. Both ends of the line changed with the opening of the Tay Bridge in 1878 (it fell down in 1879, but a new bridge was opened in 1887), and the Forth Bridge in 1890. The coming of the railways reduced the income from tolls on turnpike roads. In 1878 tolls were abolished, and in 1889 the new county council took over responsibility for maintaining the road network. Increased mobility meant an increasing need for the services of hotels and inns. In 1854 the Royal Hotel was built opposite

FIGURE 11.4   Advertisement for Tontine Hotel, c.1860.

CUPAR-FIFE.

ROYAL HOTEL.

JOHN BUIST.

COMMERCIAL AND FAMILY HOTEL.

POSTING ESTABLISHMENT.

WINES, LODGINGS, BATHS, &c.
AN ORDINARY EVERY MARKET DAY.
LARGE HALL FOR PUBLIC MEETINGS, &c.
BILLIARD TABLE.
POST and JOB HORSES and CARRIAGES of all descriptions.
MARRIAGE EQUIPAGES, CARRIAGES for PIC-NIC
PARTIES, &c.

HEARSES
WITH ONE, TWO, OR FOUR HORSES,
AND
MOURNING COACHES
TO ALL PARTS OF THE COUNTY.

SUPERIOR STABLING AND COACH HORSES.
HORSES KEPT AT LIVERY.

J. B. has built this Large First-Class Hotel for the accommodation of the Public, without which there would have been no choice in Cupar. He has also the largest Posting Establishment in Fife; and was the first to introduce fashionable Carriages for Hire into the County.

FIGURE 11.5 Advertisement for Royal Hotel, *c.*1860.

the Tontine, and soon claimed to be 'The Largest Hotel and Posting Establishment in Fife' (Plate 14d, Figs 11.4 and 11.5). By the 1860s there were six hotels, by the 1890s seven.

After the crash of 1815, building projects already in hand were finished off. But from 1820 to 1860 architecture in Cupar stagnated. While some houses were built during this period, it was by individuals, and there were no further planned suburbs until the provision of council housing in the early twentieth century. Comparison of Wood's 1820 plan (Plate 13) with the first six-inch Ordnance Survey map of 1855 (Map 5) shows more individual suburban houses, and some infilling of town-centre sites, but little further development apart from a few more houses on the south side of South Road. The Georgian character of Cupar is therefore enhanced by the fact that most houses built between about 1820 and 1860 were unambitious and conservative, and were it not for their absence from Wood's town-plan, many could easily be dated stylistically to before 1820.[7] Perhaps the most dramatic example is the Royal Hotel, dated stylistically by architectural historians to the 1830s, though it was actually built in 1854 (Plate 14d).

The 'fine stone bridge of four arches' over the Eden, shown on the 1642 plan and described by Sibbald, had been replaced by 1803 by a single arch. When the railway came in 1847 South Bridge was rebuilt at a higher level to link with the new railway bridge, leaving the old street far below. This railway also caused the realignment of the first part of South Road, leaving the old road, split by the railway line, as Railway Place and Riggs Place. The *Fifeshire Journal* recorded the raising of a subscription in August 1851 to build a new bridge near the prison, to allow animals to be herded from the railway station to the cattle market at the Fluthers without 'the unseemly and dangerous necessity of driving the bestial along the main streets of the burgh'. This was replaced by the Victoria Bridge in 1901. There were several changes or standardisations of street names. Mouse Wynd became South Union Street, Fogage Wynd became North Union Street, while Dead Wynd (Short Kirk Wynd) became Short Lane.

There had been various non-conformist churches established in Cupar during the eighteenth century, but none of their buildings survive.[8] The earliest surviving structure is probably the Kirkgate Chapel, built in 1821 by the Baptist congregation established in 1815. Numbers attending the various churches in 1840 are shown in Table

TABLE 11.1   Congregations of non-comformist churches in 1840

	Site	Attending	Communicants
Episcopal chapel	St Catherine Street	82	50
United Associate congregation		340	260
First Relief chapel	West Port	600	500
Second Relief chapel	Provost Wynd	559	380
Burghers	Burnside	360	240
Baptists	Kirkgate	300	120
Congregational (Glassite)		20	7

Source: Leighton, *History of Fife*, ii, 32.

11.1. After a split in the Relief congregation (at the West Port), a Relief Chapel was built in Provost Wynd in 1830 (now Age Concern). In 1847 the congregation dispersed and the building was sold to the Baptists. St Michaels, at the West Port, was built as an overflow for the parish church. Designed by James Gillespie Graham, and completed in late 1837, it had an efficient heating system and the *Fifeshire Journal* reported that 'an ordinary voice will be heard throughout without any effort'.

In 1843 came the Disruption, a major split in the Church of Scotland. The dissenters, including the first minister of Cupar, Mr Maitland-Makgill-Crichton of Rankeilour, and Mr Rigg of Tarvit, formed a Free Church congregation. They tried to buy St Michael's church, without success, but were allowed to share the Relief Chapel at the West Port until they built a church in Union Street, a plain building, which lasted them until 1878. It then became a hall, and in the 1920s a cinema. The Relief Chapel was rebuilt in 1849, and called the Boston Church, for a congregation of the new United Presbyterian Church, formed through the merger of the Secession and Relief churches. The 1860s and 1870s saw much new church building, with the United Presbyterian Church, successor to the Burnside Chapel, built 1865–66 on the Bonnygate, to a design by Peddie & Kinnear (Plate 15c). In 1864 a Roman Catholic mission church was established in Millgate in the upper floor of a house. In 1866 St James' Episcopal Church in St Catherine Street was rebuilt to a design by Robert Rowand Anderson. In 1867 the extension to the churchyard was filling up, and a new cemetery was established out on the Ceres road. A fine new home for the Free Church was erected in the Bonnygate between 1875 and 1878, designed by Campbell Douglas & Sellars, and financed by a legacy from Sir David Baxter of Kilmaron. In 1890 St James' Church Sunday School was built in Castle Street. There were also changes to the established church. In 1878 a Sabbath School hall was built in Kirk Wynd. The interior of the church was renovated In 1882, including new seating. Between 1875 and 1915 all the windows on the east, south and west walls were filled with stained glass, mostly memorials. The quality is variable, but the overall effect is attractive. In 1910 a clock was added to the tower.

The Municipal Reform Act of 1833 imposed tighter financial scrutiny, and few burghs indulged in major building projects until the new system had become well established. Cupar also took a while to recover from recession, and what little new building there was before the 1860s seems mainly to have been financed externally. The sheriff soon found sharing the county rooms unsuitable, and in 1836 the Tontine Hotel was gutted and converted by William Burn to form a sheriff court, and a new Tontine Hotel was built next door. The prison had never been satisfactory. In 1839 responsibility for prisons was transferred to County Boards, and in 1841 a field was bought for a new prison. Opened in 1844 at a cost of over £5,000, it was described as 'a splendid edifice of the kind, and contains fifty cells, with kitchen, washing-house and store', and housing for governor, matron and warders. The Old Gaol became the militia headquarters. In 1889 the new prison closed, and the building later became the headquarters of the Fife and Forfar Yeomanry.

Cupar had a county ballroom, and at least two inns had a large room for dinners and balls. In 1840 the Bonnygate Masonic Hall was said to be 'often used for concerts and exhibitions, by companies of strolling actors, and for meetings of the working classes'. But there was no public hall. Eventually in 1861/2 a group of shareholders built the Corn Exchange, at a cost of just over £3,000 (Plate 15a). Designed by Campbell Douglas & Stevenson, it was used both as a covered market and a hall for public events. To achieve a large open area without the use of pillars it was roofed with semicircular iron girders. There was no suitable vacant site in the town centre, and even by demolishing an existing building

FIGURE 11.6 The spire of the Duncan Institute (Peter Martin).

only a partial frontage on St Catherine Street was achieved. It was not a great success as a hall, and most people preferred the former Free Church building in Union Street. In 1862 a statue of David Maitland-Makgill-Crichton of Rankeilour, by John Howie of Ceres, was erected overlooking the station.[9] In 1870 the Duncan Institute was built in Crossgate (Fig. 11.6), and the new cemetery opened. The mercat cross, which had apparently been moved in 1789, but not demolished, had ended up on top of Tarvit Hill in c.1812. In 1897, to celebrate Queen Victoria's diamond jubilee, it was brought back and reinstalled on a new base.[10] Although there was an architectural renaissance from the 1860s, work was by local architects, rather than the Edinburgh architects used fifty years earlier, and by this time the range of styles had expanded. There is no coherence to Cupar's Victorian architecture, nor much of real quality.

Some of the most impressive nineteenth- and early twentieth-century buildings in the town centre were built for banks. The oldest is the Clydesdale, in St Catherine Street, built in 1840 and still in use. The British Linen Company agency was run by Christies, then Pagans or Osbornes until 1964. In 1862 it moved from the Bonnygate to 14 St Catherine Street until it merged with the Bank of Scotland in the 1970s. On the other side of St Catherine Street stood the Royal Bank, from the 1860s until merger with the National Bank and a move to premises at 18–20 Crossgate, occupied by the National Bank since 1878 (and presumably built by them). The Commercial Bank had started at 12 St Catherine Street when the street was built, moving to number 10 by the 1860s, and staying there until merger with the National Bank. Cupar Savings Bank, established in 1837, was for many years based at 108 Bonnygate, until it moved to new premises at 46 Crossgate in 1902 (and was later taken over by the Trustee Savings Bank). The Bank of Scotland, having closed its Cupar branch in 1815, did not come back until 1963, through merger with the Union Bank at The Cross.

The second quarter of the nineteenth century saw a few more villas, including Marybank (East Burnside); Southfield, c.1835; Blairneuk, on the corner of Carslogie Road and Balgarvie Road; Weston House; and Eden Park. By the first detailed Ordnance Survey map of 1855, Castlefield House and Eden Place had been built on East Road, along with more houses up Bank Street, including Rosevale and Rose Terrace, the first few houses along the east side of South Road, a few isolated houses along the west side of Kirkgate after Provost Wynd, including one marked as 'Manse', a few along Carslogie Road and a few along Balgarvie Road. There are several on a new street, Hill Street. Westfield House had gained an impressive approach with a driveway from just east of Weston House (you can still see the pillars).

By 1895 the *Ordnance Gazetteer* reported that 'the erection of numerous villas, both at the east and west ends of Cupar and on

FIGURE 11.7   Kirkgate School (Peter Martin).

the south side of the river, has added considerably to the extent and architectural beauty of the town' (Plate 15b). Comparing the 1855 map with the 1894 edition it can be seen that there are more villas up Castlebank Road, along Bishopgate, and along Barony, and more houses along Skinners Steps, and the road to Ceres. Campbell's Tower, in the Bonnygate, is an eccentric building of 1913, providing the shopkeeper with a fine view across the town, but hard to spot above the traffic in the narrowest part of the Bonnygate.

In 1831 Dr Andrew Bell established a trust: 'to promote and encourage the education of youth in Cupar, the metropolis of his native county of Fife, and more especially of exhibiting therein a model and exemplar of the new and momentous system of education, fitted, by its stupendous powers, when duly administered (on which all depends), to give a new character to society at large.' Known as the Madras (or monitorial) system, it used older pupils to teach the younger. Bell wished the academy to continue, with 'an amalgamation of the old and new school, so obviously advantageous to all concerned'. By 1836 'besides the academy, Dr Bell's trustees have opened three schools in the town, for the benefit of the industrious classes, at which education is to be had at the most moderate rates', or free for the poorest parents. There were also 'four female schools, and one promiscuous [co-educational] school'. In 1844/46 the Madras Academy on Castlehill was extended, with a south range which also housed the library and the 'guildhall'. In about 1860 the old English school was demolished, and in 1867 the north block built. Also in about 1860 the Kirkgate School (Fig. 11.7) was set up, for pupils whose fees were paid by local charities.

The Reform Acts of 1832 and 1867 both stimulated discussion about the need for citizens to be educated to fulfil their responsibilities. In

1871 Lady Baxter, wife of Sir David Baxter of Kilmaron, established the Baxter Educational Institution for Young Ladies in a new building at the West Port. The following year the Education (Scotland) Act was passed, establishing compulsory education between the ages of five and thirteen, school boards, and certification of teachers. As a result, the Baxter Institution merged with the Madras Academy to become Bell-Baxter High School. The West Port buildings were extended in 1889/90.

In 1840 there was 'a public news-room, supported by yearly subscription, where a well selected supply of the leading London and provincial journals is received, besides a few monthly publications. A mechanics' reading room has also been recently instituted, in which the working classes are accommodated with newspapers at a very cheap rate.' As well as the subscription library there was a circulating library run by one of the three booksellers in the town. In the 1840s the managers of the library shared in the building of premises on Castlehill. Ten years later only half the cost had been paid, and there were moves to raise funds to clear the debt and create a library worthy of the town. In 1847 Cupar New Reading Room opened above a shop in the Crossgate. Unlike its rivals, it was closed on the Sabbath. In 1851 two rival groups bid for the use of the Town Hall as a reading room, one proposing Sunday opening, one excluding it. But all they succeeded in doing was bidding up the rent, and there was no moral benefit in closing on Sundays if people went to pubs instead.

The *Fifeshire Journal* reported in 1853 that 'the Coffee and Reading Room for the working classes has been so far successful beyond all expectation': 'To the working man, who heretofore had no alternative but to eat his bread, butter and cheese, at the dykeside or in the shade of a hedge, this room will be an immense advantage, enabling him to procure even for less money, a more nutritive and refreshing meal, with greater comfort. We are not without hope, too, that the pamphlets, periodicals and newspapers, of the reading room ... will engender a habit of reading, and excite a desire for information, which in their turn will enable many to pass an hour without having recourse to the beer-shop for excitement.' The library on the Castlehill, described in 1867 as 'well stocked with books, in the various branches of literature and science', and providing evidence of the 'polished taste of the inhabitants' was replaced by the Duncan Institute. Opened in 1870, it was designed by John Milne of St Andrews, and described by Millar in 1895 as 'one of the most elegant of the public buildings in Cupar' (Fig. 11.6). Miss Duncan of Edengrove, who died in 1867, left money for the complex, for the benefit of 'the working classes of Cupar, Dairsie and Kilconquhar'. It contained a library, two reading-rooms, a recreation room, a lecture hall and a billiard-room.

The printer and publisher Robert Tullis died in 1831, and was succeeded by his son George. The *Fifeshire Journal* was established in 1833 by Tories upset by the radical coverage of the Reform Bill in Tullis's *Fife Herald*. At first based in Kirkcaldy, it was moved to Cupar in 1836 by its new owners William Pagan and James Moore Graham. After passing through various hands, in 1893 it was acquired by J & G Innes and merged with the *Fife Herald*. During its life the *Fifeshire Journal* press is also known to have published 133 books, many of purely local interest, such as lists of voters, annual reports of organisations, lectures and regulations. Alexander Westwood published a monthly newspaper, the *Stratheden Advertiser*, from 1853–55, then the weekly *Fifeshire Express* for a further year. Between 1855 and 1922 Westwood & Son published over a hundred books and pamphlets, including directories, valuation rolls, poems, sermons and guide books, and Millar's *Fife Pictorial and Historical*.

In 1848 George Tullis died, and the following year Whitehead & Burns took over the *Fife Herald*, and in eight years also produced thirty-five publications. From 1857 to 1869 the press was run by John Cunningham Orr. Robert Tullis, George's son, bought back the *Herald* in 1863; Orr continued as editor, but went bankrupt in 1869 and left Cupar. Between 1857 and 1869 Orr published over sixty books, including Farnie's *Handy Book of St Andrews*, Rodgers' *The Kingdom of Fife Calotyped*, and Connolly's *Biographical Dictionary of Eminent Men of Fife*. In 1879 Tullis sold the *Herald* to John Innes, who had been the editor since 1870, the year in which he had also founded the *St Andrews Citizen*. Innes became the largest printing firm in east Fife, and took over the *Fifeshire Journal* in 1893. As J & G Innes, they took over Westwood's Edenside Printing Works in 1923. The firm sold its newspapers in 1974 to the Fife Free Press Group, and sold the Edenside Printing Works in 1981. The Cupar shop remained for a little longer, and the shop in St Andrews survives. Between 1869 and 1982 Innes produced over six hundred publications, including the usual guide books, directories, catalogues, cash books, annual reports, the *Fife News Almanac* (1872–1917 and 1923–42), *Historical Notes and Reminiscences of Cupar* (1884), and works by David Hay Fleming, the St Andrews historian.

Social life and recreation

The Fife Agricultural Society, established in 1821, was followed by the Fifeshire Agricultural Association in 1834. The Fifeshire Literary, Scientific and Antiquarian Society was founded in the 1830s, and began to assemble a museum collection in a room in County Buildings. After 1870 this was moved to a museum in the Duncan Institute, which continued to receive donations, mostly of ethnographic specimens. There was also a Phrenological Society, established in 1835, with 'a small library and a good collection of casts for the use of the members'. Cupar Philharmonic Society was established in 1853, and Cupar Amateur Musical Association (now Cupar Choral Society) in 1865. A number of new societies seem to have been formed from about 1870. The Fifeshire Medical Association first met in 1882, and still survives as the Fife branch of the British Medical Association.

The Cart Haugh lay on the east side of the Lady Burn (now in a culvert). Two plots of land lay on the west side. One of these was presented to the town by Provost Hood in 1869, and called Hood Park. A cricket club was established in 1833, which first played on the Haugh, but in 1884 moved to Bonvil Park. A golf club was set up in 1856, and they built a clubhouse in 1908. In 1884 there were clubs for curling, golf, cricket, bowling (from 1859), bicycling and lawn tennis (from 1882), tricycling and highland games. A curling club was in existence by 1822, when it was given permission to flood the Cart Haugh instead of the Fluthers. A curling pond on the Tarvit Estate was in use from 1844 to the 1870s. The Cart Haugh was flooded for skating in the winter from the 1870s to at least 1930, and there was another curling pond at Ladyinch. In c.1871 a new pond was constructed near the former site of Thomastoun mill, on the north bank of the Eden between the town and Tailabout (its earth banks can still be seen). Racing continued at Uthrogle until 1841. After that Cupar races became point-to-points, held on suitable farms, including Bruntshiels (just above Baldinnie) and Greigston (near Peat Inn). There was a pack of foxhounds, and a pack of harriers.

Administration and public services

The Municipal Reform Act of 1833 established a slightly more democratic town council: twenty-six councillors elected 'by persons paying £10 of yearly rent, resident within the burgh'. These councillors elected from among their ranks provost, bailies and dean of guild. There were actually two deans of guild, one the leader of the guildry, and one on the council, responsible for planning. Complaints about elections distracting men from their work were still being made in 1842. Since the Reform Act of 1832 Cupar had been joined with St Andrews, Crail, Anstruther Easter, Anstruther Wester and Pittenweem to elect an MP. In 1885 Fife was divided into just two constituencies, East and West, while the University of St Andrews, combined with the University of Edinburgh, also returned an MP. From 1918 there were four constituencies, East Fife, West Fife, Kirkcaldy Burghs and Dunfermline Burghs, with St Andrews sharing an MP with the other Scottish Universities. The 1868 Reform Act gave women ratepayers a vote in local elections for town councils, and school boards. Married women, who did not have a vote, could still stand for office on school or poor law boards, though not town councils. Many women found this a satisfying way to get involved in local affairs. The first meeting to discuss female suffrage was held in Cupar in 1873. A Conservative Association and a Liberal Association were both started in 1879, perhaps in response to Gladstone's active campaigning in Scotland.

While burghs were self-governing, the administration of the rural areas of the county grew too burdensome for the landowners who had long filled posts as Commissioners of Supply, Turnpike Trustees and other similar roles. In 1889 Fife County Council was established, composed of sixty councillors, seventeen from the royal burghs, and forty-three from the rest of the county. For most administrative purposes Fife was divided into four districts – Cupar, St Andrews, Kirkcaldy and Dunfermline – similar to the seventeenth-century presbyteries. The county council took over responsibility for many pre-existing organisations such as Commissioners of Supply, School Boards and Parish Councils.

By 1840 there were three lodges of Free Gardeners, all of which 'are formed into benefit societies'. There was no need for a compulsory rate to support the poor: fifty-six regular and sixty-four irregular paupers were supported by church collection, a proportion of the fees paid for the registration of births, marriages and deaths, and 'a poor's box carried through the town on Saturday'. The old almshouses at St James' Yards had been rebuilt on a new site, housing ten to twelve poor people, the old site becoming the extension to the churchyard. In 1836 the town received a legacy to build Knox Cottages, providing a chapel and six cottages for poor women over fifty. And there was a Ladies Society for 'relieving aged and decayed females'. The Disruption of 1843 was disastrous for poor relief, as kirk sessions lost people and money to the Free Church. As a result the Poor Law (Scotland) Act was passed in 1845, establishing parochial boards with the power to levy compulsory rates to help the poor, overseen not by individual kirk sessions but by a new Board of Supervision in Edinburgh. Each parish appointed an inspector to handle applications and assess the amount which should be granted in each case. There were proposals for a Poor House in 1849 and 1855, but it was never built.

In 1833 the town adopted the General Police Act, appointing commissioners to oversee public services, and levy rates for street lighting but nothing else. The next Police Act of 1850 was adopted in 1861. The Cupar Gas Company was established in 1830, with seven retorts and two gas holders at Back Lebanon. 'The streets, shops, warehouses, and other places of business, are all lighted with it; and it has also been introduced into the greater portion of the houses of the more respectable inhabitants'. Prisons and policing were increasingly the responsibility of wider authorities than burghs. Cupar finally established its own police force in 1858.

In 1836 it was claimed that 'at any place of the town, by sinking to the depth of 20 or 30 feet, an abundant supply of water can be procured, fit for all domestic purposes except washing'. But two years later Dr David Scott, aged forty-three, and Dr Adam Wiseman, aged 40, both died of typhus caught while visiting the poor. In 1847 the *Fifeshire Journal* noted 'with feelings of alarm and regret' that 'typhus fever is prevalent amongst the poorer classes of our population living in closes throughout the town. The inspector of the poor, and the medical attendant, both complain of the extreme filthiness in which these closes are kept', compounded by the lack of an adequate water supply. This outbreak claimed the life of another doctor, Andrew Mackie, aged thirty, who as medical officer to the Parochial Board 'had to visit many of the most wretched hovels in the place, and had to face disease, aggravated by all the evils that never fail to accompany filth and poverty'. His younger brother Archibald, also a doctor in Cupar, caught typhus a few months later, but survived. In 1854 the town escaped the worst of the cholera epidemic.

But an increasing population meant more domestic and industrial waste, and epidemics continued to occur: scarlatina in 1861, smallpox in 1864 and 1881, measles in 1870, typhoid in 1880 and scarlet fever in 1882. In 1867, under pressure from health inspectors, the council sent off samples of water from a selection of public wells to analysts in Edinburgh and Glasgow. The analyst from Surgeon's Hall in Edinburgh was reported in the *Fifeshire Journal* to have stated that all the samples were 'impregnated with the products of the decomposition of animal matter of the nature of sewage, and such as may be derived from house cesspools, surface or imperfect town drainage', and he was 'confident that the daily use of such water will predispose the members of the community to attacks of illness'. It was recommended that all public wells should be closed. A debate then began about whether a public water supply was desirable, and if so, where a reservoir should be built. In 1874 an engineer looked at twelve sites and chose Clatto (south-east of Cults), as having enough volume of water, and being high enough above the town. But the cost of the reservoir and its associated pipe-work was high, and caused a public outcry. There were several meetings held to try to stop the scheme, but at the end of 1876 the new system was turned on, and Cupar was raised 'high in the sanitary scale of towns'.

However, the provision of clean water did not solve all public health problems. In 1880, during a typhoid scare, the *Fifeshire Journal* commented that 'in many places ... the piggeries are too near the bed-rooms, and the manure heaps too contiguous to the dwelling-places'. Carbolic acid was being poured into gutters and drains to keep infection at bay. It was 1906 before a drainage system was installed, and a sewage works built on the Eden below Tailabout Farm.

In 1866 Alexander Adamson of South Callange left his estate in trust for the building of a hospital. The 'Adamson Institution' was opened in 1877 in Bridgend, Ceres, just within the parish of Cupar. However, after problems with the distance from Cupar, and the running costs, in 1895 it was leased, and six years later sold. It became Alwyn House, a training centre for blind people. Meanwhile the Adamson Trust continued, and in 1901 joined with the Cupar Sick Poor Association to plan a new hospital for Cupar. Funds were augmented by the proceeds of a bazaar to raise money for a permanent memorial to those members of the Fife and Forfar Yeomanry who died in the Boer War. The Adamson Hospital in Bank Street was opened in 1904, with seven beds in three wards.

Cupar in the nineteenth century lay at 'the centre of a large district of country, dotted by numerous villages and a multitude of fertile farms, the wants of whose inhabitants are to a great extent supplied by the shopkeepers and tradesmen of the burgh; and this accounts for the number and respectability of the various places of business'. Cupar on the eve of the First World War was a thriving town. Its economic base had not changed much, nor had its townscape, but its residents were now provided with a range of public services, and could join a growing number of charitable, social, cultural, sporting and recreational organisations.

Notes

1. *Third Statistical Account*, 42.
2. Some of Burton's equipment and examples of his work can be seen in the Fife Folk Museum, Ceres.
3. Campbell, *Notes By the Way*, 66.
4. The returns for 1841 do not survive. 'Professional' includes financial, managerial and clerical; 'building trades' comprises masons, slaters, glaziers, plasterers and painters – there is of course some overlap with woodworking; 'clothing' includes hats and shoes; 'food and drink' includes bakers, confectioners, butchers, grocers, tea dealers, vintners and spirit dealers. 'Transport' includes hotels and their male staff, carriers, carters, railway staff etc.; 'printing' includes bookbinding and bookselling.
5. Rodger, *The Kingdom of Fife Calotyped*.
6. Govan, *Notes of a Communication to the Fifeshire Literary, Scientific and Antiquarian Society*, 10–11.
7. Examples include Weston House; 1 The Barony; Marybank, *c.*1830; and the Relief Chapel in Provost Wynd, 1830.
8. A Relief congregation was established in 1770, and built a church in 1772 at West Port, but it was replaced in 1849, became a cinema in the 1920s, then a

bingo hall, and was demolished and replaced by the Job Centre. The Burghers had a chapel on Burnside, with a surviving Session House.

9. A forceful character who took a leading part in the Disruption, he is credited with persuading the railway company to build a bridge rather than a level crossing.

10. Accounts as to how it got on top of Tarvit hill vary, but one is that the owner of the land wanted to mark the spot where the truce was signed between Mary of Guise's forces and the Lords of the Congregation in 1559. The new plinth was designed by Mr Simpson, drawing master. The original unicorn was destroyed by a lorry in the 1980s.

12

Cupar 1914 to the Present Day

In 1915 Cupar's economy still involved trade in grain, flax-spinning, dyeing, tanning and malting. But times were changing. The U-boat campaigns of the First World War highlighted the danger of over-reliance on imports. Just as the Forestry Commission was established to promote home-grown timber, so the Government tried to encourage the growing of beet sugar. Cupar was pivotal in this strategy. After the British Sugar (Subsidy) Act of 1925 the industry took off, and by 1928 there were eighteen factories, though only one of them was in Scotland. Built in 1926 by the Second Anglo-Scottish Beet Sugar Corporation Ltd, the plant was located near Cupar because of good supplies of fresh water, and road and rail links. But it was not close to the main growing areas. Only about 30 per cent of the beet it processed came from Fife, 17 per cent from Angus, and the rest from as far north as the Black Isle, and as far south as Northumberland. The demand for labour was greater than was available locally, so there was an influx of families from the depressed industrial areas of West Scotland. This made Cupar's existing housing shortage worse.

In 1936 the sugar producers were semi-nationalised, and forced to amalgamate into the British Sugar Corporation. In 1946 the Cupar factory employed about 500 people during the season (October to December). It took 7 tons of beet, 1 ton of coal and 6 hundredweight of limestone to make 1 ton of sugar. From 1930, between May and September, some cane sugar from the West Indies was refined, helping to extend employment and reduce overheads, but this stopped during the Second World War. In 1964 the plant was flourishing, and a giant silo was built, which still dominates the landscape (Plate 16b). Soon afterwards, however, things began to go wrong. The price for raw beet was reduced, and there were suspicions that modernisation of the factory was being delayed until it would be uneconomic, and that production was being reduced to appease France, a major beet grower and processor, in the run-up to Britain joining the Common Market. Despite strenuous local efforts the factory closed at the end of 1971, just before a substantial rise in world sugar prices.

In 1952 the *Third Statistical Account* reported that 'factories and mills provide a welcome sheet-anchor to the economy, and offer hope of stemming the drift of population and general decay of the social structure'. Leadbetter's linen factory closed in 1926, Honeyman's in 1958. Stenhouse stopped weaving in 1960, but made flags until fairly recently. St James' Fair, the longest-surviving of the eight medieval fairs, was held for the last time in 1958. Weekly cattle markets, first held in the Crossgate, then moved to the Fluthers, had been provided with purpose-built premises in Station Road in 1880. The final closure of this market in 1993 was symbolic of changing times in agriculture at the end of the twentieth century. The 1950s had seen great efforts to maximise production and land-use, in reaction to the reliance on imports which had been highlighted by the Second World War. But gradually this effort became uneconomic. There was increasing reliance on chemicals and machinery rather than manual labour, and economies of scale, with small farms absorbed into larger units. Farming became increasingly mechanised and the countryside correspondingly lost population.

Many of Fife's railway lines disappeared between the 1920s and 1960s, giving Cupar's direct north–south rail link an increased importance, particularly as St Andrews lost its branch line. A motorway now takes long-distance traffic north from the Queensferry crossing, and traffic from south Fife to Dundee crosses the Howe of Fife. But Cupar is still the centre of a local road network. A bypass was first proposed in 1946, but the land was later built on. With ever-increasing car ownership, and the growth of St Andrews as a tourist destination, Cupar's town centre suffers from severe traffic congestion. Station Road has been widened to divert some traffic from the centre, but the problem is far from being solved. The town has fewer hotels, though there are several in the surrounding area, reflecting increased car travel. The surviving public houses are a far cry from the coaching inns of the eighteenth and nineteenth centuries. Some of those which have not survived are remembered in names such as Cross Keys Close and Bell Close.

In 1927 a transatlantic wireless station was established at Kemback, and five years later moved to Cairngreen, on the Pitscottie road. During the Second World War a signals station was established at Hawklaw, which continued as one of two outposts in Scotland of GCHQ at Cheltenham, eavesdropping on international communications. It closed in 1988.

As well as changes in agriculture, the twentieth century saw a move from manufacturing to servicing. Blacksmiths, for example, often gradually converted their skills and premises to motor repairs, and shops increasingly retailed goods bought in rather than made in their own back premises. There are still two clock and watch repairers and an upholsterer in Cupar, but no longer a saddler. With so much car ownership, specialist craftsmen and dealers are increasingly setting up in the countryside where space is cheaper.

During the first half of the century employment for men probably changed less than that for women. In the 1950s growth areas included legal services, local government employment and shops. The *Third Statistical Account* noted that 'Friday and Saturday are shopping days for country people, with Friday becoming increasingly popular owing to the more crowded conditions of the buses on Saturday'. This reminds us of the rigid hours most people worked, in contrast to the more flexible working patterns of today. In 1960 the county council was the largest employer in the town. Other major employers were the two printing works, the laundry, various depots, and facilities such as the gas-works. Cupar had seven banks and one building society, four accountants, two architects, a surveyor and an auctioneer. There were ten grocers, two greengrocers, eight bakers, seven confectioners, six butchers, three fishmongers, five drapers and a 'fancy repository', four tailors and clothiers, three ladies and children's outfitters, three shoe shops, three tobacconists, two dairies, two newsagents and a bookseller. To serve the surrounding area there were eight motor engineers, six agricultural engineers, three builders, three plumbers, two slaters and plasterers, six joiners and two haulage contractors. There were only six public houses, and four hotels. But there were still jobs which have now disappeared completely, such as tank-maker and horse-slaughterer. Since then the number of shops has declined, though there are probably more people employed in building and related trades. But the biggest change must be the number of people living in the town who now travel to work elsewhere.

Cupar is still a centre for legal services, and for banking. In 1958 the National Bank merged with the Commercial and in 1969 the National & Commercial merged with the Royal and the British Linen with the Bank of Scotland, leaving Cupar with three long-established banks (Bank of Scotland, Royal Bank and Clydesdale), plus the Trustee Savings Bank, which had taken over the Cupar Savings Bank (now Lloyds TSB).

The number of churches decreased over the century. In 1929 when most of the Free Church rejoined the Church of Scotland, the Baptists moved from Provost Wynd to the Bonnygate church. In 1937 the parish charge was reduced from two ministers to one. The year 1951 saw the closure of St Michael's, which became the assembly hall of Bell Baxter School. The century did however see the building of one new church. St Columba's Roman Catholic Church in Kirkgate, designed by Peter Whiston, opened in 1965 to serve the increasing numbers of Roman Catholics moving to Fife to work in the mining industry (Plate 16c).

After the First World War Cupar, as the county town, built a grander War Memorial than anywhere else in Fife (Plate 16a), on an impressive site, originally intended for the prison. The statue is by HS Gamley of Edinburgh, the rest of the monument designed by John Kinross. Opened by Sir Douglas Haig in 1922, it commemorates Cupar's 189 dead, a figure which must have had a devastating effect on the community.[1] The following year the bandstand was built in the Haugh Park. In about 1925 the Tontine Hotel was demolished to make way for an extension to County Buildings. Gradually almost the whole of the west side of St Catherine Street was taken over for council offices, and in 1947 further offices were built in Waterend Road. In 1937 the police moved to a building behind the east end of County Buildings (now the headquarters for Fife Museums East). This was replaced in 1963 by a spacious new building in Carslogie Road. In 1953 it was claimed that the 'bare walls, primitive seating ... poor acoustics, and ... ill-planned platform' of the Corn Exchange, 'compare unfavourably with what may be found in most towns of a like size'. But a replacement would have been too expensive for the shareholders. In 1961 the Town Council bought it for £4,000; it reopened in 1967 after extensive alterations, and is the main public hall in Cupar.

After the First World War came the realisation that poor health was being caused by poor housing, particularly in the dark and damp closes. The Scottish Housing Act of 1919 offered subsidies to local authorities as an incentive to provide new, and more sanitary, housing. But although it was recognised that Cupar had a housing problem, the local authority was slow to act. In 1926 they erected fifty temporary steel houses (prefabs), followed by twenty-four houses in Balgarvie Road in 1929 and 12 in Bishopgate in 1931, eventually rehousing about 300 families, but this was 'quite insufficient' to replace inadequate town-centre housing. The 1930s saw few distinctive private houses, just a pair in Bowling Green Road, built c.1935, with art deco detail, and Firbank, Brighton Road, built in 1936, but now with a pitched roof.

A report in 1946 admitted that Cupar's housing stock was of poor quality and insufficient to meet demand. Another 330 council houses were constructed, as well as private housing estates. There were those who advocated wholesale modernisation. Much more has been built since, to ever increasing standards. The author of the *Third Statistical Account* suggested that: 'The housing problem of Cupar ... is not to be solved in a piecemeal fashion. A complete clear-out of derelict and semi-derelict property, some of it inhabited and some uninhabited, is long overdue, together with a replanning of the old town and a long-term scheme for replacing eighteenth and nineteenth century houses by dwellings with modern facilities.' Today some would like to make similar drastic changes for the sake of traffic management. But the town centre survived, perhaps by luck more than by design. Perhaps it is time to revitalise it by the renovation of more properties for housing. It also deserves to be appreciated for the survival of its medieval town plan, and the style and quality of many of its eighteenth- and nineteenth-century buildings.

Bell Baxter High School expanded again in 1929, after the school had been handed over from its trustees to the Education Authority. In 1932 the Castlehill buildings, which had been further extended to the east in 1908, became primary only, and Kirkgate (which had been extended in 1881) became part of Bell Baxter. In 1975 Castlehill school moved to a new building on the Ceres Road. The *Third Statistical Account* reported that for many years Bell Baxter had run 'a series of continuation classes dealing with such practical subjects as plumbing, welding, baking etc. Of some significance are the agricultural classes, which qualify for a diploma'. These moved to a Nissen hut, then in 1953 Elmwood House was bought by Fife County Council. Day-release classes started in 1956, and in 1960 the Agricultural Training Centre was rapidly expanding. Farmland was purchased in 1962, with more added in 1971. In 1971 new buildings were opened on the Elmwood site, and a golf course built in 1995.

Social and cultural organisations continued to flourish. In the 1920s these included the Choral Union (renamed the Choral Association in 1947), the Amateur Operatic Society, a Burns Club, a Literary and Debating Society and three masonic lodges. In the 1950s there was an Amateur Orchestral Society. In 1960 there was a Pipe Band and a Silver Band, and two cinemas, both in former church buildings, the Regal in South Union Street and La Scala at the West Port.

JC Duffus, born in Cupar, had made a successful career in the jute industry, spending many years in Calcutta before settling near London. In 1911 he bought Bonvil Park and gave it to the town with an endowment, and it was renamed Duffus Park in his memory. In 1925 he bought extra adjoining land for a football pitch. At the time the bowling green was at Eden Park, but in 1946 Duffus's sister donated the present bowling green at Duffus Park. In 1960 there were football, rugby and cricket clubs, bowling greens at both ends of the town, and the golf course.

Some county council departments were moved to Kirkcaldy in 1919. The Local Government (Scotland) Act of 1929 abolished Parish Councils, and transferred many of the functions of the smaller burghs to the county. This increase in governance was financed by an increase in local taxation, based on property values, although there was a contribution from central government. According to the *Third Statistical Account* there was growing questioning of Cupar's position as the county town, with Kirkcaldy claiming 'its intrinsic importance, its much larger labour force, its proximity to the main centres of population, its greater potentialites for expansion'. Cupar, on the other hand, apart from history, offered 'extensive and generally commodious premises, presumably less vulnerability to air attack, and, by no means least important, just that degree of remoteness from the hectic, industrial scene that is often an advantage for the dispassionate consideration of long-term policies'. After the Second World War, Kirkcaldy seems to have dropped its claims, though eventually the whole question became irrelevant with the abolition of burghs and the county council in 1975, to be replaced by three District Councils, one based in Cupar, one in Kirkcaldy and one in Dunfermline, and a Regional Council based in the new town of Glenrothes. That system was replaced in 1996 by a single-tier Fife Council, in new buildings at Glenrothes. But whatever the name of the council, the offices which have grown up around county buildings in Cupar are still the home of local government officials.

Public services have continued to improve. In 1926 the supply provided by the Fife Electric Power Company was extended to Cupar. Three years later the Garliebank reservoir was built and Clatto reservoir improved. The end of an era, however, was marked by the abolition of the post of town bellringer, and the ringing of the curfew bell, in 1938. In 1946 the Eden was said to be 'contaminated by domestic sewage and industrial waste', and a new and expanded plant on the same site was opened in 1969.

Despite the many changes experienced during the twentieth century, Cupar still has a viable economic base. For a long time its footprint was expanding without its population growing. Expansion was not only for housing purposes shops and industrial premises are increasingly moving out of the congested town centre. The silo of the former sugar beet factory now stands between an industrial estate and a trading estate. Today, however, the town is expanding in population as well as buildings and roads, and is once again being seen as a nice little town to retire to, or from which to commute to work elsewhere.

Note

1. It cost between £6,000 and £7,000. Haig, a Fifer, had been given the freedom of Cupar in 1919. The flanking pillars were added after the Second World War, commemorating the fifty-one who died in that conflict, and these were unveiled by the Earl of Elgin in 1950.

13

Conclusions

Cupar seems to have been an important place since the time of the Picts. In the medieval period it flourished, exporting woollen cloth, wool and hides through its outport in the Eden estuary. There followed two centuries in which the town became less active in overseas trade. Increasingly under threat from newer burghs, particularly those on the coast, the town survived because it was a regional market centre, and a focal point for administrative and legal services. Cupar probably grew faster during the eighteenth century than at any other time in its history, but nevertheless by 1820 was far less important within Scotland, and even within Fife, than it had been in 1700. No longer able to rely on its geographical position and its status as a royal burgh, Cupar evolved, whether by accident or design, into a centre of legal and financial services, education, culture and leisure rather than of manufacturing industry.

Cupar was not an industrial town, a port or a major regional centre, but it was a market and county town, and, it could be argued, a 'leisure town'. McInnes has identified a number of features which contribute to the definition of a leisure town. These include good transport links to bring in cheap and plentiful goods; being a county town which attracted gentry, and school pupils, from a wide area; being a religious centre, particularly for the new non-conformist churches; having a town council with commercial acumen; the leading role played by innkeepers; and the presence of specialist tradesmen such as booksellers.[1] Cupar does not fit all his criteria, having no public water supply or hospital (but this is true of most Scottish towns of a similar size). Few developments were led by the town council, though in general it encouraged progress. Other slightly larger towns such as Dumfries or Inverness probably come closer to McInnes's definition. Cupar, however, certainly had an architectural renaissance. By 1820 it had several planned suburbs, a new street with new public buildings, commercial offices and a number of private villas. And with them came gardens, and public walks laid out for the middle classes to promenade. The Mote Hill today is still evocative of its Georgian heyday.

Everitt has highlighted the importance during the eighteenth century of English county towns, which were entrepots, business centres, regional shopping centres, professional and entrepreneurial centres, and, as a result of these functions, centres of leisure. Many, however, were in decline by the 1820s as improved transport diminished their role. Cupar seems closer to this more specific model. As the county town, Cupar saw economic diversification, mainly into service industries. As a travel town it had great inns which were central to the life of the town, providing dancing and dining space and catering facilities for almost all social events held by or for the elite. They also provided rooms for use by travelling salesmen or for businessmen to meet on neutral territory. Early inns were built in the central market-place. With the coaching era some moved out of town centres to gain more space or easier access.[2] Cupar by 1811 had a new coaching inn next door to the County Buildings. Like many towns of its size, Cupar never had purpose-built assembly rooms, but as these sometimes killed off inns, this may have been deliberate, leaving inns free to exploit the commercial potential of the leisure revolution.

County towns by their nature became centres of fashionable culture. The development of leisure activities and facilities can be clearly charted, and by 1820 Cupar had races and hunt balls, a coffee house, public walks ('promenades'), a theatre, music and dancing, booksellers and libraries, street and pavement improvements, street cleaning and lighting, and a building revolution, with gentry and professionals leading the way in private developments. Cupar also fulfilled another criterion, by having a larger proportion of middle-class residents than industrial towns. The experience of Cupar reflects, over a shorter time and on a reduced scale, the cultural development of larger towns such as Edinburgh. Its nearest rivals in Fife were Dunfermline and Kirkcaldy; neither had a theatre or racecourse, though Kirkcaldy did have assembly rooms.

But although much has been written about the dramatic growth of towns between 1760 and the 1820s, the assumption has been that growth continued after that date, as industrialisation took off. This is certainly true for most larger towns, but for many smaller towns in England, including some county towns, this was not the case. A study of Ashbourne, in Derbyshire, has demonstrated that with improvements in transport, small country towns with no industrial development declined after 1815. Like Cupar, Ashbourne had a bowling green, horse races, a theatre, visiting dancing masters, but no purpose-built assembly rooms. And although coaching traffic continued to increase, the growth of industrial towns and the ease of access to major conurbations, combined with a movement of the elite from town houses to suburban villas, all contributed to the decline of many small communities which had developed all the trappings of a fashionable

Georgian town within the previous fifty years. Cupar, similarly, did not develop as an industrial centre, and therefore declined after 1820. While its population continued to increase until 1851, it had lost its dynamism, and this is reflected in the conservatism of its architecture between 1820 and 1860.

At the beginning of the eighteenth century most inhabitants lived close together and attended the same school, reinforcing social bonds across a range of income and occupational groups. By the 1820s, however, there was an increasing financial and social divide between areas of housing, and between the academy and the cheaper private schools. By the 1820s there was a perceived conflict between educating the working classes (and females) into practicality and subservience, and the danger of teaching them to think for themselves. 'It was far easier to teach people to read than subsequently to direct their reading'.[3] Although inventories demonstrate an increase in book ownership, it is notable that this is among the professionals and retired people, and not the merchant class. Retired people, especially those who had served in the armed forces or the colonies, brought to Cupar a wider view of the world, as did newspapers and travel literature. More professionals were leaving the town for at least part of their training, and more non-local professionals were moving in.

The early nineteenth century also saw a changing relationship between town, church and county. The gentry throughout Britain were developing a taste for urban life, but this led to increased social zoning, so that the pleasures of the gentry need not be disturbed by the common people. It is significant that Cupar races moved out to Uthrogle, and after a few years entry to the stand was by ticket. Church membership increasingly reflected class divisions. Many of the gentry and professionals attended the episcopal church, which revived in the early nineteenth century. Many of the retired army officers and colonials were episcopalian, as were some other incomers, including several of the innkeepers.[4] Many tradesmen, on the other hand, belonged to the seceding congregations which had grown up during the second half of the eighteenth century. The social distinctions which were once reflected in which pew one rented in the parish church were now reflected in which church one attended.[5] The decline of the power of the established church perhaps also encouraged the growth of other aspects of urban life, including an increase in drinking and immorality.

There was a growth of clubs of many types, but the majority for which there is evidence surviving were exclusive to the 'middling sort', and helped provide a collective identity. But at the same time organisations such as the Volunteers, and perhaps masonic lodges, allowed townspeople to act together within a formalised structure in which each man knew his place, but had a common bond of membership and participation. Most of those for whom there is evidence in Cupar were members of the 'middling sort'. There is some debate about how this group should be defined, and it is impossible to categorise people completely by occupation. There was no clear divide between gentry and professionals, or between merchants and tradesmen. Urban society in general, however, became increasingly distinct, as more and more urban dwellers were cut off from their agricultural roots, and relied on earned income to buy food. Distribution trades increased, because increased spending power and better road transport led to a growth in demand. There was an increase in specialisations at the luxury end of trades, such as confectioners, perfumers and watchmakers.

By 1820 the women of Cupar seem to have lost few rights or freedoms, a reasonable number were receiving education, and they do not seem to have been formally excluded from any occupations they had pursued at the beginning of the century. Most single women by the 1820s, according to the available evidence, were working as teachers, milliners or mantua-makers, or running inns or lodging houses.

The landed gentry gradually lost what control they once exercised within the town, concentrating instead on county administration and politics, or devoting themselves to improving their estates. The void created by this and the declining influence of the church was filled by lawyers and innkeepers. All towns in the eighteenth century saw the development of the professional classes, especially lawyers. But because in Cupar lawyers were able to serve on the town council, and took over from merchants in the financial service industries, they seem to have become particularly dominant. And though their numbers fell after a peak in the second decade of the nineteenth century, those who remained seem to have held on to both financial and political power. Despite some financial setbacks (Appendices 3 and 4), writers made a lasting impact on the political, economic and architectural development of Cupar.

All county and leisure towns in Britain attracted numbers of what have been called 'pseudo-gentry' or 'town-based gentry', the group usually described in Cupar as 'residenters'. These were people who lived off savings or investments, had no land to manage, and chose to live in an urban environment and enjoy all the facilities it offered. They were employers of servants and purchasers of consumer goods, and therefore major contributors to the economy of the town, and their presence led to the development of social and cultural activities, even in quite small towns. 'Military service, colonial administration and migration to the plantation economies could produce men of considerable wealth who ... came home to enjoy retirement and the modest comforts of life in a country town like Cupar.'[6] One example is Sir George Campbell of Edenwood, older brother of John Campbell, who went to India as an assistant surgeon in the East India Company. After about twenty-five years he returned to Cupar, married Andrew Christie's daughter, built a country house, and took an active part in county politics for the next thirty years. Added to such people were the country gentry who seem to have spent much of the year in their new, elegant town houses or suburban villas.

The long eighteenth century saw a change to more 'civilised' behaviour and values. When the hangman died in the 1750s he was not replaced, and cock-fighting was banned at the school from 1805. Travel and newspapers led to greater outside influences, and conformity to national norms, and the enjoyment of leisure became more acceptable. A corollary of this was 'middle-class efforts to influence working-class culture and values'; this began in the 1790s, but intensified from the 1820s.[7] All over Britain were founded Mechanics Institutions, Temperance Societies and Savings Banks. In Cupar, a Savings Bank was established in 1815. The Bible Society of Fife and Kinross Shires, established 1812, had numerous gentry as vice-presidents, and a committee of all the ministers 'of whatever denomination'.[8] But, at the same time, more rigid social divisions seem to have led to less sympathy for the poor (or at least those who did not respond to middle-class attempts to organise them), to debate over the need to educate them, and to physical separation in housing and education.

But why did Cupar not continue to develop after the 1820s? The first reason suggested in Chapter 4 was lack of capital, or perhaps lack of entrepreneurs. Some industrial development inevitably moved to larger towns such as Kirkcaldy or Dundee, which had a larger labour-force, and which were ports with easier access to raw materials. Travel to larger centres of population became faster and more comfortable. The coming of the railway in 1848 had been eagerly anticipated as the saving of the town, because raw materials would be able to be imported more cheaply and finished goods exported. But instead Cupar lost its passing trade, and much of its importance as a market centre. Forfar, however, managed to continue to develop its linen industry, and there is no clear explanation as to why Cupar did not.

But a town can fail to grow but still remain prosperous – in Cupar's case because of the presence of the sheriff court and the large number of writers, who continued to control both financial services and the town council for much of the nineteenth century. The patronage brought to the town by its various MPs provided posts in the East India Company for the sons of minor gentry and writers. Many of the sons of those who presided over Cupar's heyday left for the colonies and never returned. Andrew Christie, for example, had one son who stayed in Cupar as a writer, but three who went to India. George Aitken had one son who stayed in his father's business, but two who died young in India. As the town failed to develop, the colonies remained attractive to young men of the next generation, for whom there was a wider range of occupations on offer in a greater number of places around the world, and few returned.[9]

The effect of the growth of Dundee, and to a lesser extent of Kirkcaldy, has already been demonstrated. But there was another local factor which possibly represented the most serious blow to Cupar's prospects. This was the renaissance of St Andrews, only nine miles away, which had been in decline since the Reformation. During Cupar's heyday in the late eighteenth and early nineteenth century, St Andrews had passed its lowest ebb, but its revival was initially slow, and the 'New Town' of 1810 got no further than a Tontine Hotel and hot and cold sea-water baths. In 1842, however, Hugh Lyon Playfair, who had retired from the Indian Army in 1834, was elected provost of St Andrews, and the next twenty years saw a programme of street-paving, laying out walks, improving the harbour, building new streets such as Bell Street and Queen's Gardens, and developing Madras College. With all these new facilities, and the opening of the railway line in 1852, St Andrews attracted not only holidaymakers, but more importantly the sort of wealthy retired people who had helped to make Cupar what it was. The revival of the university was the final straw, creating a strong cultural centre which Cupar could not hope to emulate.

Towns only thrive if people want to live in them, and people want to invest money in them, which creates work for those who live there. Cupar may not have turned into another Kirkcaldy, but it is still here, and people still choose to live here. And the reasons lie not just in its geographical position, but in its history. Once it lost its rich retirees to St Andrews, what was Cupar left with? It was back where it had been in 1700 and before: a county town, with markets, fairs and a sheriff court. During the nineteenth century an increasing system of county organisation was necessary, and this was based in Cupar. Roads had to be planned and managed, as did police, licensing and poor relief. The later nineteenth and early twentieth century saw a reduction in the number of shops, and the gradual disappearance of a dye-works, three small breweries, a flax factory, a linen factory, two carriage works, three tinsmiths, a cooperage, a snuff-mill and an aerated water factory. The town became much less self-sufficient, but this was true of most small towns.

In the 1950s agriculture was still the mainstay of the Fife economy, but was employing fewer and fewer people, which led to depopulation of the countryside, and the closure of village shops and schools. Even the very optimistic writer of the *Third Statistical Account* realised that Cupar's success 'owes much to the historical fact of being the county town, and to the perhaps fortuitous decision to open the sugar beet factory on its outskirts'. The real mainstay of the economy in the 1950s was the County Council, and Cupar's position at the centre of a road network. The town's continued existence and relative prosperity today can therefore be traced back to the establishment of a sheriff court in the early thirteenth century.

But does this also explain why the town did not grow in the later nineteenth century. Did its legal and administrative basis provide a safety-net? However bad the economy gets, however much political upheaval there is, the law goes on, and lawyers remain in employment. Does such an economic safety-net stifle development? If we look at what happened to Scotland's other county towns, we can see that many fared worse than Cupar. There are thirty-three towns in Scotland which have been at some time or other classified as county towns. Of these, only eight – Aberdeen, Ayr, Edinburgh, Inverness, Lanark, Perth, Renfrew and Stirling – have done better than Cupar. The rest have much the same history as Cupar of failing to develop industrially in the nineteenth century, and subsequently declining or stagnating.

Whatever the future may hold, Cupar should be proud of its history and status. The war memorial says a lot about Cupar's self-confidence and civic pride. The grandest war memorial in Fife, it is a dominant feature in the townscape, joining with many other fine public and private buildings to mark the enduring legacy of Cupar's long history as the administrative, legal, financial, cultural and social centre of east Fife.

Notes

1. McInnes, 'The emergence of a leisure town: Shrewsbury 1660–1760'.
2. Coaching inns began to decline after the coming of railways (1847 in Cupar), and the erection of public buildings such as corn exchanges (1862 in Cupar) and town halls.
3. Porter, *English Society*, 168.
4. GD26/10/128; the subscription list for the building of the chapel in St Catherine Street, 18 Aug 1817, contains a list of names of gentry and town elite, including a donation from the town council itself, presumably either because a majority were episcopalian, or in order to curry favour with the gentry. Unfortunately, there are no surviving registers of births, marriages and deaths in public collections from Cupar episcopal congregation, which might have helped define who the episcopalians in the town were.
5. A case in the burgh court in 1761 illustrates the importance of church seats. During the summer absence of the Earl of Crawford's family the kirk session had re-let their seats to a country gentleman, but a local doctor, Dr Robert Menzies, had broken into the church, seized possession of the pew, and in order to stop anyone else sitting there 'put into the said seat a poor man with a cancered leg and most nauseous smell'.
6. Nenadic, 'Urban Middle Class', 115–16.
7. The evangelical campaign for reform of public morals, which started in England in the 1790s, became linked with public support for Queen Caroline as a symbol of domestic virtue in conflict with a licentious husband.
8. *Dundee Advertiser*, 18 Sept 1812; 'Report of the Bible Society of Fife and Kinross Shires, for the year commencing 27th August 1816, and ending 27th August, 1817'.

9. The same is true of most small towns. Go into any Fife cemetery and you will
   see rows of gravestones of the mid to late nineteenth century recording deaths
   of young men building railways in South America, governing India, or fighting
   in South Africa.

Notes on Sources

General

Primary: NAS CS96/1736, account book of James Wilson; StAU B13/7–13, burgh court records; St AU B13/14, town council minutes; StAU msCS479.A8, account book of Lady Elizabeth Anstruther (which covers most of her expenditure between 1768 and 1804 – everything from £67 7s to David Martin for a framed portrait of her brother, to mundane items such as mouse traps and corn plasters); inventories (Appendix 4).

Printed primary: *Extracts from the Records of the Convention of the Royal Burghs of Scotland*; Lamont, *Diary*; *New Statistical Account of Scotland*, vol. IX; *The Statistical Account of Scotland*, vol. X.

Secondary: Borsay, *English Urban Renaissance*; Corfield, *Impact of English towns*; Earle, *English Middle Class*; Hardcastle, *Life of Lord Campbell*; Houston, *Social Change*; Innes, *Historical Notes*; Keddie, *Three Generations*; Leighton, *History of Fife*; Porter, *English Society in the Eighteenth Century*; Thomson, *Agriculture of Fife*; Wood, *Descriptive Account*.

1. Introduction

Secondary: Dewdney, 'Changes in population distribution in Fife 1755–1951'; Gifford, *The Buildings of Scotland: Fife (introduction)*; Kyd, *Scottish Population Statistics*; McNeill & MacQueen, *Atlas of Scottish History to 1707*; Pryde, *Burghs of Scotland*; *Statistical Account of Scotland*, vol. I, *General*, and vol. X, *Fife* (introduction).

2. Medieval Cupar

Primary: NLS Adv MS 29.4.2, f.212r; StAU B13/14/8 (discussion in 1813 about reasserting the town's rights to the port of Motray [also B13/22/1]).

Printed primary: *Acts of the Parliaments of Scotland*; Bower, *Scotichronicon* (v, 403, death of Queen Margaret; vii, 97, Bullock appointed keeper of castle; vii, 117, 127, 135, 137, events at castle 1336–7; viii, 75, fire in 1410); *Calendar of documents relating to Scotland* (ii, 165, appointment of Walter de Camehou); *Calendar of Scottish Supplications to Rome 1418–1422*; *Calendar of State Papers Scotland, vi*; *Charters of the Royal Burgh of Cupar*; *Documents Illustrative of the History of Scotland*; *Exchequer Rolls of Scotland*; *Laing Charters*; *Liber cartarum prioratus Sancti Andree in Scotia*; *Regesta Regum Scotorum*; *Registrum Magni Sigilli*; *Rotuli Scotiae* (i, 409b, 536b, 542a, 544a, 545b, 556a, supplies sent to castle); *Sheriff Court Book of Fife* (introduction); *Treasurer's Accounts*, v, 414 (purchase from Cupar goldsmith).

Secondary: Brown, *Wars of Scotland*; Colvin, *History of the King's Works*; Cowan & Easson, *Medieval Religious Houses*; Cowan, Mackay & Macquarrie, *Knights of St John of Jerusalem*; Ditchburn, 'Trade with Northern Europe'; Ewan, *Townlife in Fourteenth-Century Scotland*; Fawcett, *Scottish Medieval Churches*; Hall & King, 'Field Survey at the site of St Christopher's Church'; Porteous, *Town Council Seals of Scotland*; Simpson & Stevenson, *Historic Cupar*; Stell, 'Urban Buildings'; Stevenson, 'Trade with the South, 1070–1513'; Verschuur, 'Merchants and craftsmen in sixteenth-century Perth'; Webster, 'Scotland without a king, 1329–1341'.

3. Cupar in the Early-Modern Period

Primary: *Extracts from the Records of the Convention of Royal Burghs,* iii (1616 fire); *Darien Papers ... 1695–1700*; *Ecclesiastical Records* (witch trials); NAS CC20/6/2 (testament of David Clephane of Carslogie); NAS E69/10/2 (Hearth Tax, Cupar, Kirkcaldy and St Andrews presbyteries, 2 March 1694); *Register of the Privy Council*, 3rd ser, iv, 229, 238, 580; v, 50–51, 159, 195, 265 (conventicles), v, passim, vi, 4 (billeting of troops, and reaction to murder of Sharp); *RPC*, 3rd series (vii, 234, 273–74, 542, 597; local politics, 1680s; xv, 56–57, xvi, 522; complaints about cost of quartering troops).

Secondary: Chambers, *Domestic Annals* (1669 fire); Devine, 'Urbanisation'; Dingwall, 'Social and economic structure of Edinburgh' (Hearth Tax data); Dow, *Cromwellian Scotland*; Houston & Whyte, *Scottish Society*; Lynch, 'Urbanisation and urban networks'; Lynch, 'Whatever happened to the mediaeval burgh?'; Lynch, 'Continuity and change in urban society'; Lynch, 'The Crown and the Burghs 1500–1625'; Macdonald, *Witches of Fife*; McNeill & MacQueen, *Atlas of Scottish History*; Martin, 'Towns and villages'; Oram, 'From

the Union of the Crowns to the Union of the Parliaments'; Scott, *Fasti*;
Stevenson, 'Burghs and the Scottish Revolution'; Whyte, 'Urbanization
in eighteenth-century Scotland'; Whyte, 'Urbanisation in early-modern
Scotland' (24–9 and Table 2, 1639 population figures); Whyte, *Scotland
before the Industrial Revolution*.

4. The Economy

Primary: BS Private Letter Books, 1802 no. 1 and 1809 no, 4; BS 1/
288/17 'Business peculiar to the agencies', Cupar, 1812–14 passim; DU
ms15/154, memoir of George Moon; Loch, *Essays on trade*; NAS E326/
4/6 (Shop Tax); NAS NG1/42, Records of Board of Trustees; NG1/64/
38, 'Minutes of evidence taken before the Select Committee of the
House of Lords', 1823; NAS GD242/40/9, Shepherd & Wedderburn;
NLS ms6727; 6734, 6749, 6756, 6764, 6773 , 6784; papers of William
Wilson & Son, tartan manufacturers, Bannockburn; StAU Ch2/82/6;
StAU ms36929/5/89, 'Articles for erecting a manufactory att Couper
in Fiffe 1727'; *Scots Magazine*, 1806, 316 (establishment of Fife Fire
Insurance Co.).

Secondary: Boase, *Banking in Dundee*, Cameron, *Bank of Scotland*;
Campbell, *Scotland since 1707*; Checkland, *Scottish Banking*; Doughty,
Tullis Press; Durie, *Scottish Linen Industry*; Fraser, *Conflict and Class*;
Haldane, *Three Centuries of Scottish Posts*; Hamilton, *Economic
History*; Jesperson, 'Watermills on the river Eden'; Jesperson, *Water
mills of the River Eden* (StAU msDA880.E4J4–7); Ketelbey, *Tullis
Russell*; Lenman, *Economic History*; Livingstone, *Flax and Linen*;
Lythe & Butt, *Economic History of Scotland*; Malcolm, *British Linen
Bank*; Martin & Martin, 'Vernacular pottery manufacture' (brick-
works); Munn, *Scottish Provincial Banking Companies*; Saville, *Bank
of Scotland*; Silver, *Roads of Fife*; Steel, 'linen industry of Fife'; Whatley,
Industrial Revolution in Scotland; Whatley, *Onwards from Osnaburghs*
(history of Don & Low, Forfar).

5. The World of Work

The figures from the database, on which graphs are based, can be
found in Appendix 3 (men who had two or more occupations have
been counted under each).

Primary: Connolly, *Biographical Dictionary of eminent men of Fife*;
NAS AD14/16/32, 19 Oct 1816 (Christian Robbie); NAS AD14/23/
162, /25/70 (references to women at spinning mills); NAS E326/5 and
6/passim (Servant Taxes), E326/7/passim (Cart Tax); NAS GD82/43/
indentures 1740 (indenture of George Makgill); NAS SC20/50/1, p493

(Jean Tod's legacy); NLS, ms200 (Fife Chapman Society); StAU B13/12/2, 15 Mar 1749, 1–24 and B13/18/2, 29 Nov 1751 (prosecution of James Bell, glover); StAU B13/18, guildry records; Scott, *Fasti*.

Secondary: Clark, 'Introduction: English country towns 1500–1800'; Devine, 'The Merchant Class'; Dingwall, *Late Seventeenth-century Edinburgh*; Dingwall, *Physicians, Surgeons and Apothecaries*; Everitt, 'English Urban Inn'; Fraser, *Conflict and Class*; Fulton, 'John Moore'; Gibson, *Extracts from the Records of Dysart*; Hendry, *Cupar Doctors*; Hill, *Servants*; McLaren, 'Patronage and Professionalism'; Murray, *Scottish Handloom Weavers*; Rendall, *Women in an Industrialising Society*; Sharpe, *Adapting to Capitalism*; Sanderson, *Women and work in eighteenth century Edinburgh*; Smith, *Nine Trades of Dundee*; Smith, *United Trades of Dundee*; Stephen, *Story of Inverkeithing and Rosyth*; Strawhorn, *History of Irvine*; Turner, *Anatomical Memoirs of John Goodsir*; Whatley, 'Women and the economic transformation of Scotland'.

6. Buildings and Townscape

Primary: Bettesworth & Hitch, *Builder's Dictionary*; Fife 1/1/1/3–7, and 1/11/1 (building of St Catherine St); Groome, *Ordnance Gazetteer*; *Instructions to the Constables* (courtesy of Sonia Anderson); Johnson, *Journey to the Western Islands* (quote p2); NAS GD26/10/128 (subscription for episcopal chapel); Pococke, *Tours in Scotland*, ii, 265; *Sasine Abridgements*; Topham, *Edinburgh life*.

Secondary: Aston & Bond, *Landscape of Towns*; Carter & Pittock, *Aberdeen and the Enlightenment*; Clark, 'Introduction'; Gifford, *Buildings of Scotland: Fife*; Gow, 'The Edinburgh Villa' (quote p37); Harley, *Dalgairn*; Lindsay, *Georgian Edinburgh*; Lockhart, 'Planned village development'; McDowall, *History of Dumfries*; McWilliam, *Scottish Townscape*; Martin & Martin, 'Vernacular pottery manufacture' (brick-works); Naismith, *Scotland's Towns* (plans of other burghs); Pride, *Kingdom of Fife*; Rodger, 'Evolution of Scottish town planning'; RCAHMS, *Tolbooths and Town-houses*; Shvidkovsky, 'Classical Edinburgh and Russian town-planning'; Stell, 'Urban buildings'; Walker, *Rudiments of Architecture*.

7. Material Culture

Primary: testaments and inventories, see Appendix 4; Boswell, *Tour to the Hebrides*; Gurney, *Notes on a visit made to some of the Prisons in Scotland*; Home, *Sketches of the History of Man*; Loudon, *Encyclopaedia of cottage, farm and villa architecture*; StAU ms36929,

Cheape of Rossie Papers, box VIII/298 (purchases at roup); Somerville, *My Own Life and Times*.

Secondary: Bayne-Powell, *Housekeeping in the Eighteenth Century*; Bremner, *Industries of Scotland*; Edwards, *Eighteenth-century furniture*; Emmerson, *British Teapots*; Gilbert, *English Vernacular Furniture*; Gloag, *Social History of Furniture Design*; Gow, *Scottish Interior*; Gow, 'The Dining Room'; Hatcher & Barker, *History of British Pewter*; Jones, 'The Hall and Lobby'; Jones, 'Box Beds in Eastern Scotland'; Laing, *Lighting*; Lubar & Kingery, *History from Things*; Lucie-Smith, *Furniture*; McKendrick, 'Home demand and economic growth'; McKendrick, 'Consumer revolution in eighteenth-century England'; McKendrick, 'Josiah Wedgwood and the commercialization of the Potteries'; McVeigh, *Scottish East Coast Potteries*; Martin & Martin, 'Vernacular pottery manufacture'; Nenadic, 'Domestic culture'; Nenadic, 'Print collecting and popular culture'; Nenadic, 'The Enlightenment in Scotland and the popular passion for portraits'; Sprott, *Farming*; Steel, 'Linen industry of Fife'; Tarrant, 'The Bedroom'; Tarrant, *Going to Bed*; Thornton, *Authentic Decor*; de Vries, 'Between purchasing power and the world of goods'; Warrack, *Domestic Life in Scotland*; Weatherill, *Consumer Behaviour*; Wells-Cole, *Historic Paper Hangings*; Wood, *Scottish Pewter-Ware*; Wright, *Clean and Decent*.

8. Literacy and Leisure

Primary: Fife Hunt Minute Book, 1826–54, courtesy of the Secretary; NAS CC20/3/7 (John Ewan's legal action); NAS GD26/5/570 box 1, cash book 1823–27 of James Kyd, writer; GD26/5/726/5 Lady Leven's 'school of industry'; GD26/12/33 (racecourse); NAS GD26/13/639 (letter George Boes to Earl of Leven, 20 Apr 1756); GD164/897, petition of Alexander McNab to the owners of Tontine, Sept 1828; NAS RH9/1/121 (record of fees received, Cupar gammar school); NLS ms200, Acts of the Fife Chapman Society, 1797; NLS 1948.63(22) (Cupar Library, laws and catalogue, 1813 and 1818); StAU B13/11/1, B13/12/2, B13/13/1, bonds of caution in lawburrows; Sinclair, *Analysis of the Statistical Account*, i, 126–28; Topham, *Edinburgh Life*; Wiseman, *The Arithmetician's Text-Book*.

Secondary: Anderson, *Education and the Scottish People*; Anderson, *Old Libraries of Fife*; Babington, *Fife Fox-Hounds*; Bain, *Education in Stirlingshire*; Bain, *Patterns of Error*; Beale, *Burgh and Parochial Schools of Fife*; Borsay, 'The rise of the promenade'; Borsay, '"All the town's a stage"'; Cameron, *Prisons and Punishment*; Campbell, *Fifeshire Journal*; Chalkin, *Provincial Towns of Georgian England*; Clark, 'Introduction'; Clark, 'Small towns in England 1550–1850';

Colley, *Britons*; Cox, *History of Gardening*; Devine, 'Urbanisation'; Everitt, 'The English Urban Inn'; Fittis, *Sports and Pastimes;* Fraser, 'Developments in Leisure'; Gardiner, *Man in the Clouds*; Gibson, *Education in Scotland*; Grant, *History of Burgh Schools of Scotland*; Houston, *Scottish Literacy*; Jessop, *Education in Angus*; Johnson, *Music and Society in Lowland Scotland*; Kelsall, *Scottish Lifestyle*; Low, *Fifty Years with John Company*; Mair, *Stirling*; Martin, 'racecourse stand', Moffat, *Kelsae*; Nenadic, 'Domestic culture'; Plumb, *Commercialisation of Leisure*; Reed, 'Cultural role of small towns in England'; Robertson, *History of the Dundee Theatre*; Scotland, *History of Scottish Education, vol 1;* Tranter, 'Schooling and literacy in early nineteenth century Scotland'; Tressider, 'Coronation Day celebrations in English towns'; Whatley, 'Royal Day, People's Day'.

9. Local and National Politics

Primary: The sett, printed for the Convention of Royal Burghs in 1721, can be found in various sources, including StAU B13/14/3; Rothes's story, 1720s in NA SP54/9/105 (1715 proclamation), SP54/13,14 (letters from Dundas to the King); SP54/13/119, 'Extracts of Letters from the Earl of Rothes relating to some tumultuous Proceedings at Coupar in Fife'; NAS CS226/2213, Magistrates of Cupar v. Thos Robertson, 1783–84; NAS CS230 M3/4 (legal disputes, 1760s); NAS CS234 R4/1 (disputed election of town clerk, 1759); NAS GD20/7/222 (United Scotsmen); NAS JC26/294 (United Scotsmen); *Report from the Select Committee to whom the several petitions from the Royal Burghs of Scotland ...;* Scots Magazine, Dec 1767, Mar 1768 (1760s political unrest); Sinclair, *Correspondence of Sir John Sinclair; A Vindication of the Action of Declarator ...* (anti-Rothes account, 1721).

Secondary: Brims, 'From Reformers to "Jacobins"'; Brown, 'Nothing but Strugalls and Corruption'; Brown & Mann, *History of the Scottish Parliament, vol. 2* (Rothes as a national figure); Colley, *Britons*; Cookson, *British Armed Nation*; Fergusson, *Letters of George Dempster*; Fraser, *Conflict and Class*; Fraser, 'Patterns of Protest'; Fry, *Patronage and Principle*; Fry, *Dundas Despotism*; Gauldie, *One Artful and Ambitious Individual*; Hayton, 'Traces of Party Politics in Early Eighteenth-Century Scottish Elections'; Lang, *Life of George Dempster*; Lenman, *Integration and Enlightenment*; Logue, *Popular Disturbances in Scotland*; Meikle, *Scotland and the French Revolution*; Murdoch, *The People Above*; Namier & Brooke, *History of Parliament: Commons, 1754–1790*; Nenadic, 'Political Reform and the "Ordering" of Middle-Class Protest'; Philips, *Correspondence of David Scott*; Riley, *Union of England and Scotland*; Sedgwick, *History of Parliament: Commons, 1715–1754*; Sellar, *Fife and Forfar Yeomanry*; Sunter, *Patronage and*

Politics; Warden, *Burgh Laws of Dundee*; Whatley, 'How tame were the Scottish Lowlanders?'; Whatley, 'The Union of 1707, integration and the Scottish burghs: the case of the 1720 food riots'; Whetstone, *Scottish County Government*.

10. Poor Relief, Social Control and Public Services

Primary: Fife 1/1/1, Minutes of Commissioners of Supply; NAS HR 31/, heritor's records; StAU B13/18/3, guildry records; StAU CH2/82 presbytery minutes *Instructions to the Constables* (private collection).

Secondary: Belof, 'women in seventeenth century Fife'; Brown, *Religion and Society*; Brown, 'Religion and Social Change'; Fraser, *Conflict and Class*; Gibson & Smout, *Prices, food and wages*; Hamilton, *Economic History*; Leneman & Mitchison, *Sin in the City*; Lindsay, *Scottish Poor Law*; Mitchison, *Old Poor Law in Scotland*; Mitchison, 'The Poor Law'; Mitchison, 'Who were the Poor in Scotland?'; Mitchison & Leneman, *Sexuality and Social Control*; Sharpe, *Adapting to Capitalism*; Thompson, *Customs in Common*; Whyte, *Scotland before the Industrial Revolution*.

11. Cupar *c.*1820–1914

Bruce, *The Railways of Fife*; Campbell, *Alexander Westwood*; Campbell, *Notes By the Way*; Campbell, *Whitehead and Burns*; Campbell, *Fifeshire Journal Press*; Campbell, *J & G Innes*; Doughty, *Tullis Press*; *Fife Herald*; *Fifeshire Journal*; Gifford, *Buildings of Scotland: Fife*; Govan, *Notes of a Communication to the Fifeshire Literary, Scientific and Antiquarian Society*; Groome, *Ordnance Gazetteer*; Martin, 'Pipemakers in the rest of Scotland'; *New Statistical Account*; Rodger, *The Kingdom of Fife Calotyped*; Silver, *Roads of Fife*; *Slater's Directories*; *Third Statistical Account*; *Westwood's Directory*.

12. Cupar 1914 to the Present Day

Fife Looks Ahead; Gifford, *Buildings of Scotland: Fife*; Haig, *A Scottish Tour*; Harley, 'The "Beet" Generation'; *Third Statistical Account*; *The Royal Burgh of Cupar, Official Guide* (1960); *Royal Burgh of Cupar, Sewage Purification Works Official Opening, 1969*; Spaven, *Fortress Scotland*; Turnbull, 'The Agricultural Tradition'.

13. Conclusions

Barry, 'Bourgeois collectivism?'; Borsay, *English Urban Renaissance*; Everitt, 'English urban inn'; Everitt, *Landscape and Community in England*; Hall, *White, Male and Middle Class*; Henstock, *Ashbourne*

1725–1825, vol.1; McInnes, 'The emergence of a leisure town'; Martin, 'Racecourse stand'; Morris, *Class and Class Consciousness*; Nenadic, 'Urban Middle Class'; Rendall, *Women in an Industrializing Society*; Whyte, 'Urbanization in eighteenth-century Scotland'.

Glossary

ashlar
Squared and dressed hewn stone used for building purposes.

bailie
The top councillors were provost, bailies (there were usually between two and four), treasurer and dean of guild. These 'magistrates' ran the town on a day-to-day basis.

barony
Land or lands controlled by a baron.

baxter
Baker.

bill
Written order to pay sum on given date to drawer or to named payee.

boll
Measure of capacity, in Scotland equal to 6 imperial bushels (48 gallons, 218 litres).

Bridewell
Reformatory, named after one which stood near St Bride's in London.

burgage
Tenure by which lands or tenements in burghs were held from a fue superior for an annual rent; the tenements held under that tenure.

burgess
Member of the core of craftsmen and merchants within a burgh, who had exclusive privileges within the burgh. Membership could be inherited, acquired by marriage to a burgess's daughter, or purchased.

cadger
Pedlar, small-scale itinerant salesman.

cess
Local tax, assessed on the value of property.

charter
Formal legal document, usually issued by the crown or a superior lord, detailing the properties, rights and obligations of the recipient.

clinkmill
Probably an early form of mill with a horizontal wheel.

Commissioners of Supply
Established in 1667. Landowners appointed initially to collect land tax from fellow landowners, but gradually acquiring other duties (outside burghs) such as maintenance of roads.

229

common good	The lands or other sources of income which were held and managed by a burgh on behalf of its inhabitants.
common herd	Herdsman paid by the town, and by the owners of the animals, to take urban cattle out to graze each day, guard them, and return them at night.
customer	Person employed by the burgh to collect its customs on goods coming in for sale.
deal	Plank of wood.
demesne	The portion of the lands of a barony or lordship kept in the lord's hands for the direct support of his household (from the Latin *mensa*, a table, i.e. the table lands).
dicht	Wipe clean.
diocese	Territory under the jurisdiction of a bishop.
dyke	Low wall of stone or turf.
feu	Grant of land rights. In exchange for an agreed sum and a continued fixed annual rent, a tenant bought the right to hold a property in perpetuity, and to bequeath or sell it (differing from English leasehold in not being time-limited, and the rent being fixed).
feuar	Individual who holds land in feu.
feuferme	Arrangement whereby property could be conveyed in return for an annual payment fixed in perpetuity. It preserved the fiction of the land being held from a superior lord, but the occupant had almost complete security in the property.
fiars	Price of grain legally fixed for the year in each county.
flesher	Butcher.
girnel	Storehouse.
grass meall	Fee paid to landowner for grazing an animal.
guildbrother	Member of the guildry.
guildry	Merchant guild, entered by family links or purchase, with exclusive rights to trade within the liberties of a burgh.
guinea	Gold coin worth 21 shillings (£1.05)
harling	Traditional coating for rubble stone walls in Scotland, whether high status or vernacular: both as a protection from the weather, and to create the impression of geometric mass. Formed from a mixture of usually local gravel bound with lime.

heritor	Landowner. Heritors in each parish were responsible for the upkeep of church and school, and payment to minister and schoolteacher.
infeft	Technical term for the process by which an individual is given possession of property or rights by a superior lord.
laigh	Low.
liberty	The area within which a burgh had exclusive trading rights. As more burghs were created, they inevitable impinged on the liberties of earlier ones.
loft	Gallery in a church.
mantua	Woman's loose gown. Mantua-maker means dressmaker.
merk	Medieval unit of account equivalent to 13 shillings and 4 pence or two-thirds of a Scots pound.
midden	Rubbish heap, whether domestic, agricultural or mixed.
mortcloth	A cloth (pall) hired to cover a coffin during the funeral.
multure	Fee paid to a miller in the form of a fixed percentage of the grain he ground.
mutchkin	Liquid measure equal to an English pint.
patronage	The right of appointment. The right of landowners to appoint ministers of the Church of Scotland had long been contentious, and eventually led to the Disruption in 1843.
postillion	Rider on one of the horses drawing a coach (when there is no coachman).
precentor	One who leads a congregation in singing.
provost	Chief magistrate of a burgh.
roup	Auction.
royal burgh	A burgh which paid taxes direct to the crown in exchange for the right to self-government, and whose rights included foreign trade.
sasine	Act of taking possession of a property, symbolised by the handing over of an object (e.g. a piece of turf from the land in question, etc.), and recorded in a document called a sasine.
seised	Granted a sasine.
sett	The constitution (or standing orders) of a town council

shambles	Slaughterhouse.
shuttles	Drawer or box used as shop till.
stent	Local tax, assessed on the value of landed property.
superior (feu superior)	Landowner from whom feuars have acquired their property and to whom they pay feu duty.
tack	Lease.
teind	The tenths of produce (in England, tithes) rendered by parishioners for the upkeep of the local priest and church.
tenement	Land or real property held of another by any form of tenure; in Scotland a large building let in portions to a number of tenants.
thackstane	Stone projecting from a chimneyhead to cover the top of the roof thatch and stop rain getting under it.
thirlage	The obligation on a holding or individual to have grain ground at a particular mill and to pay for the grinding.
tolbooth	The central administrative building of a burgh, usually combining council and court rooms, weigh house and prison.
tron	Public weigh beam.
vicar	A priest serving as deputy for a parson or rector of a parish, where the revenues and title of parson have been allocated as a stipend to another priest.
waulking	Fulling (processing woollen cloth).
waulkmills	Mills where woollen cloth was processed.
wort	Infusion of malt before it is fermented into beer.
writer	Lawyer, solicitor.

Appendix 1

Parish population figures and percentage increase or decrease, east Fife, 1755–1821

	1755	1790s	1755–90s		1801	1790s–1801		1811	1801–11		1821	1811–21		1755–1821	
			% +	% –		% +	% –		% +	% –		% +	% –	% +	% –
Anstruther E/W/Kilrenny	2833	2456		13	2309		6	2634	14		3013	14		6	
Auchtermuchty	1308	1439	10		2060	43		2403	17		2754	15		111	
Balmerino	565	703	24		786	12		921	17		965	5		71	
Cameron	1295	1165		10	1095		6	1005		8	1068	6			18
Carnbee	1293	1041		19	1083	4		1098	1		1048		5		19
Ceres	2540	2320		9	2352	1		2407	2		2840	18		12	
Collessie	989	949		4	930		2	954	3		1030	8		4	
Crail	2173	1710		21	1652		3	1600		3	1854	16			15
Creich	375	306		18	405	32		403		0.5	394		2	5	
Cults	449	534	19		699	31		766	10		853	11		90	
Cupar	2192	3702	69		4463	21		4758	7		5892	24		169	
Dairsie	469	540	15		550	2		553	0.5		589	7		26	
Dunino	598	383		36	326		15	294		10	343	17			43
Dunbog	255	235		8	232		1	185		20	176		5		31
Elie	642	620		3	730	18		886	21		966	9		50	
Falkland	1795	2198	22		2211	1		2317	5		2459	6		37	
Ferryport	621	875	41		920	5		1164	27		1461	26		135	
Flisk	318	331	4		300		9	318	6		301		5		5
Forgan	751	875	17		916	5		898		2	937	4		25	
Kembback	420	588	40		626	6		625		0.2	634	1		51	
Kettle	1621	1759	9		1889	7		1968	4		2046	4		26	
Kilconquhar	2131	2013		6	2005		0.5	2103	5		2317	10		9	
Kilmany	781	869	11		787		9	781		1	751		4		4
Kingsbarns	871	807		7	832	3		860	3		998	16		15	

(continued overleaf)

(Appendix 1 continued)

	1755	1790s	1755–90s % +	1755–90s % −	1801	1790s–1801 % +	1790s–1801 % −	1811	1801–11 % +	1801–11 % −	1821	1811–21 % +	1811–21 % −	1755–1821 % +	1755–1821 % −
Largo	1396	1913	37		1867		2	1973	6		2301	17		65	
Leuchars/Logie	2104	2045		3	2026		1	2041	1		2171	6		3	
Monimail	884	1101	25		1066		3	1160	9		1227	6		39	
Moonzie	249	171		31	201	18		183		9	209	14			16
Newburgh/Abdie	2194	2164			2659	23		2719	2		3024	11		39	
Newburn	438	456	4		412		10	428	4		398		7		9
Pittenweem	939	1157	23		1072		7	1096	2		1200	9		28	
St Andrews	4913	4335		12	4566	5		4692	3		5412	15		10	
St Monans	780	832	7		852	2		849		0.4	912	7		17	
Strathmiglo	1095	980		11	1629	66		1697	4		1842	9		68	
Total population	42,252	43,572			46,508			48,739			54,385				

Source: Webster's 1755 census, *Old Statistical Account*, and censuses. Totals for Leuchars and Logie have been merged because of boundary changes between them, Newburgh and Abdie because as Newburgh grew it spilled into Abdie, distorting the figures; Anstruther Easter, Anstruther Wester and Kilrenny have been merged for similar reasons.

234

Appendix 2

The financial elite of Cupar c.1790–c.1820

	Occupation	Floruit	Official Posts	Banks Posts	Insurance Companies	Industry	Volunteers/ Militia	Miscellaneous	Bank-rupt	Died
Adamson, Laurence	Minister	1794–1837		P/D, Fife Bank, 1808–12	D, Fife Ins Co, 1806–16			M, library, 1813, 1828; Subs, Hopetoun Mon; Subs, Academy 10 gns	1827	1837
Aitken, George	Writer, partner of A Christie*	1787–1830	Provost 1818–19, 1825–26	P, Fife Bank, cashier 1802–25			Major 1804, Col. 1815	Sh, theatre, 1812–25; Sec & Treas, Fife Hunt, 1808–26	1826	1831
Allan, David	Merchant, tobacconist, candlemaker	1785–1827		P, Cupar Bank, 1802–11e		Auchmuty 1811–23, tannery 1816–?				
Christie, Andrew	Writer, banker, partner of Geo Aitken	1783–1830	Treasurer 1797–1806, 1811, 1813	A 1797–1824 Brit Lin Bank		Sh, Balgonie Colliery 1811; Sh, Walkerton bleachfield 1811	Lieut 1804	Sh, theatre, 1812–25 Subs, Academy £50	1827	1831
Ferguson, John	Writer, merchant, banker, developer	1801–1824	Provost 1806–15	Cashier, Cupar Bank, 1802–10	D, Fife Ins Co, 1806–16	Auchmuty paper mill 1811–23; Balgonie Colliery 1811; Mill + bleachfield, Leslie, 1810; 1/3 brick-works 1814		M, library, 1811; Sh, theatre, 1812	1815	left town 1859 (c.78)
Horsburgh, Thomas	Writer, banker	1785–1829	Sheriff clerk 1797–death?	A, 1803–14 B Scot; A 1818; Brit Lin B	D, Fife Ins Co, 1806–28			Factor for Kemback and Fingask; Subs, Academy, 15 gns		1847
Inglis, Henry	Merchant, grocer	1783–1816	none	P Cupar Bank, 1802–11;10 shares Commercial Bank	S, Fife Ins Co					1816

(continued overleaf)

(Table continued)

	Occupation	Floruit	Official Posts	Banks Posts	Insurance Companies	Industry	Volunteers/ Militia	Miscellaneous	Bank-rupt	Died
Kyd, James	Writer, brick-maker	1790–1828	Bailie	Sh, Fife Bank	D & Sec, Fife Ins Co, 1806–28	Auchmuty paper mill 1811–23; Balgonie Colliery 1811; brick-works 1816–?		Factor to earl of Leven 1803–27; Sh, theatre, 1812–25; Hope St Trustee; Subs, Hopetoun Mon	1827	1838
Thomson Jr, James	Writer (trained under G Aitken)	1788–1830	Bailie, treasurer 1823	P, Fife Bank	D, Fife Ins Co, 1826–28		Lieut 1804, Capt 1807	Subs Hopetoun Mon Subs, Academy, 10 gns		1841
Tullis, Robert	Printer	1797–1831	Bailie, treasurer 1824; Chief constable		D, Fife Ins Co, 1812–28	Auchmuty Paper mill, 1811–23	Lieut 1812, Capt 1815	Sh theatre 1812–25; Subs, Hopetoun Mon		1831
Wilson, James	Writer (trained under A Christie)	1795–1830	Bailie	Sh, Fife Bank + Cupar Bank 1807–?; A, Commercial Bank, 1813 ?	D, Fife Ins Co, 1806–12	Brick-works 1807–?; Tontine Hotel; speculated w Aitken & Tod	Ensign 1803, Capt 1815	Preses library, 1828; M Coffee Room 1829	?	1851

A = agent; Acc = accountant; Cash = cashier; D = director; M = member; P = partner; Sec = secretary; Sh = shareholder; Subs = subscriber; Tr = treasurer; Trus = trustee (Hope Street Trustees were those who took over the development of St Catherine Street in 1815 after Ferguson got into financial difficulties). All except Henry Inglis and Robert Tullis were subscribers to Cupar Library. All except Henry Inglis, David Allan, Laurence Adamson (the editor) and Robert Tullis (the printer) subscribed to the 1803 edition of *Sibbald's History of Fife*.

Appendix 3

Occupational profile of Cupar, 1700–1829

	1700–09	1710–19	1720–29	1730–39	1740–49	1750–59	1760–69	1770–79	1780–89	1790–99	1800–09	1810–19
Writers	18	25	28	23	14	17	24	38	53	58	64	115
Doctors	9	7	10	8	6	7	11	9	7	6	9	15
Ministers and teachers	12	8	10	11	8	7	11	13	11	25	17	24
Merchants	44	33	46	45	41	36	55	56	47	69	98	106
Maltmen and brewers	78	69	77	55	45	34	35	29	18	20	14	18
Vintners and innkeepers	5	9	9	11	16	18	25	33	31	34	31	35
Dyers	10	6	11	6	9	9	14	12	6	1	3	3
Barbers and wig-makers	4	6	5	8	11	10	8	6	7	6	6	4
Smiths	17	21	15	18	13	11	24	20	28	38	35	4
Wrights	33	31	39	39	36	42	69	77	75	105	115	142
Weavers	54	57	70	63	75	72	111	92	124	195	177	188
Waulkers	8	7	5	6	7	5	6	7	5	5	3	4
Tailors	24	23	26	22	22	27	39	32	30	25	22	23
Shoemakers	14	15	16	18	20	21	31	34	32	34	36	46
Baxters	19	20	17	12	11	11	15	19	17	24	17	21
Millers and mealmakers	8	10	11	10	8	14	25	16	11	12	6	7
Fleshers	11	11	7	10	9	11	15	18	15	18	19	14
Total of above	368	358	402	365	351	352	518	511	517	675	672	807
Carriers, carters etc	5	8	10	18	12	13	17	20	27	37	43	51
Male servants	4	5	6	9	6	4	19	9	22	22	17	12
All occupations	391	395	446	419	420	423	629	623	657	827	866	1019

Source: author's thesis database.

Appendix 4

List of inventories used in Chapter 7

Most were attached to testaments: seventy-one from St Andrews commissary court; eleven from Cupar sheriff court (five because the heir was a minor, and six from after the sheriff court took over the administration of testaments); three from court of session records, listing the property of bankrupts; five from Cupar burgh court, when creditors applied for goods to be sold to pay debts. One was found among loose commmissary court papers within St Andrews burgh records.

	Occupation	Date	Source
John Thomson	Writer	1689	NAS CC20/4/15
William Mortimer	Merchant	1700	NAS CC20/2/8
Peter Birrell	Merchant	1701	NAS CC20/2/8; 4/16
John Malcolm	Writer	1709	NAS CC20/4/18
James Spens	Writer	1711	NAS CC20/4/17
Patrick Bruce	Gentleman, sheriff-depute	1719	NAS CC20/4/18
David Clephane	Gentleman	1721	NAS SC20/27/1(1)
Christian Smith	Widow of maltman	1723	StAU B13/12/1
David Muir	Brewer	1735	StAU B13/12/1
William Dick	Minister	1736	NAS SC20/27/1(2)
James Latto	Cadger	1739	StAU B13/12/1
Margaret Black	Widow of writer	1741	NAS CC20/6/21
Robert Philp	Maltman	1742	NAS CC20/6/21
James Oliphant	Vintner, merchant	1743	NAS SC20/27/1(3)
Thomas Robertson	Dyer	1744	NAS CC20/6/23
Andrew Gullan	Residenter	1747	NAS CC20/4/20
Margaret Peat	Wife of merchant	1747	NAS CC20/4/20
William Beveridge	Writer	1749	NAS SC20/27/1(4)
Thomas Thomson	Writer	1751	NAS CC20/6/30
James Mitchell	Maltman, brewer	1752	NAS CC20/4/21
John Mathie	Merchant, tobacconist	1754	NAS CC20/4/22; CC20/6/35
John Gordon	Merchant	1756	NAS CC20/4/22; CC20/6/34
Alexander Melville	Gent, provost, sheriff-sub	1756	NAS CC20/4/22
Jean Smith	Widow of wright	1757	NAS CC20/4/22
Jean Abercrombie	Widow of dyer	1758	NAS CC20/4/22
Patrick/Peter Henry Bruce	Captain (soldier?)	1758	NAS CC20/4/22
Thomas Thomson	Maltman, brewer	1759	NAS CC20/4/22
Elizabeth Duncan	Brewer, widow of smith	1760	NAS CC20/4/22
John Greig	Merchant, brewer	1760	NAS CC20/6/37
John Simson	Teacher	1760	NAS CC20/6/37
Robert Menteith	Dyer	1765	NAS CC20/6/42
Margaret Fernie	Widow of baxter	1766	NAS CC20/6/45
William Greig	Residenter	1766	NAS CC20/6/44
William Geddie	Merchant	1768	NAS CC20/6/46
John Brabiner	Merchant; tobacconist	1769	NAS CC20/6/46
Andrew Scott	Surgeon	1769	NAS CC20/6/46

(continued overleaf)

(Appendix 4 continued)

	Occupation	Date	Source
John Stark	Baxter	1769	NAS CC20/6/46
John Hislop	Vintner, innkeeper	1770	NAS CC20/4/23
Robert Ramsay	Brewer	1770	NAS CC20/4/24
John Innes	Weaver	1772	NAS CC20/4/23
David Sibbald	Merchant	1773	NAS CC20/6/51
John Anderson	Vintner, innkeeper	1775	NAS CC20/4/23
George Bethune	Physician, provost	1775	NAS CC20/4/24
Janet Melville	Widow of baxter	1776	NAS CC20/4/24
William Smibert	Soldier (Lieut, 26th Foot)	1776	NAS CC20/6/53
Katherine Millar	Widow of 'undertaker'	1778	NAS CC20/4/24
William Baldie	Wright	1779	NAS CC20/6/55
Primrose Rymer	Writer	1779	NAS CC20/4/24
James Hislop	Residenter, ex-surgeon	1783	NAS CC20/4/25
David Kirk	Smith	1783	NAS CC20/6/58
John Thomson	Merchant, provost	1783	NAS CC20/4/25
Robert Newlands	Weaver	1784	NAS CC20/4/25
Alexander Young	Merchant	1784	StAU B13/7/5
David Greig	Wright	1787	NAS CC20/6/61
Alexander Hay	Soldier (Royal Reg Foot)	1792	NAS CC20/6/64
Bartholomew Cockburn	Vintner	1795	NAS CC20/4/27
John Kilgour	Wright	1795	NAS CC20/4/27
John Stevenson	Writer	1795	NAS CC20/6/66
Thomas Falconer	Mason (architect)	1796	NAS CC20/6/68
Mary Anderson	Residenter, ex-innkeeper	1797	NAS CC20/6/69
Katherine Ross	Innkeeper	1797	NAS CC20/6/69
Jean Wright	Midwife, widow of merchant	1797	NAS CC20/6/68
William Watson	Glover	1801	StAU B13/7/5
Margaret Stewart	Residenter	1805	NAS CC20/4/28
Rachel Strachan	Residenter	1809	StAU B65/22/
Elizabeth Bell	Residenter	1812	NAS CC20/7/6
David Tod	Writer	1812	NAS CC20/7/5
David Wilkie	Minister of Cults	1812	NAS CC20/7/5
David Birrell	Manufacturer	1813	NAS CC20/7/7
Alexander Melville	Baker	1813	NAS CC20/4/29; CC20/7/5
Katherine Skene	Residenter	1813	NAS CC20/7/6
Isobel Stevenson	Widow of writer	1813	NAS CC20/7/6
Alexander Swan	Surgeon	1814	NAS CC20/7/6
Peter Gray	Militia sergeant	1815	NAS CC20/7/8
John Annan	Residenter	1816	NAS CC20/7/8
Alexander Low	Residenter	1817	NAS CC20/7/11
Henry Walker	Writer	1818	NAS CC20/7/10
William Cockburn	Cabinet-maker	1819	NAS CC20/7/13
Thomas Birrell	Residenter	1820	NAS SC20/50/1, 82–4, 88
Robert Guthrie	Merchant	1820	NAS CS96/359
Christian McPherson	Residenter, ex-teacher	1821	NAS CC20/7/13
John Anderson	Manufacturer	1822	NAS CC20/7/14
George Smith	Residenter, ex-farmer	1822	NAS CC20/7/14

(continued overleaf)

	Occupation	Date	Source
William Thomson	Merchant	1822	NAS CC20/7/14
Robert Wiseman	Teacher	1822	NAS SC20/50/1,
Betty Hugh	Merchant	1823	NAS SC20/50/1, 1–2, 8–9, 110–11
John Melville	Residenter	1823	NAS SC20/50/1, 294, 298
David Methven	Vintner, postmaster	1824	NAS SC20/50/1, 479–80, 488–94
John Smith	Baxter	1825	NAS SC20/50/1, 818–24
Robert Scott	Manufacturer	1826	NAS CS96/785
Andrew Christie	Writer and banker, provost	1827	NAS CS96/692/1

Bibliography

Manuscript Sources

Bank of Scotland (BS)
British Linen Company records (BL)
'Business Peculiar to the Agencies', Cupar, 1785–1816 (1/288/17)
Private Letter Books 1802–1814

Dundee University Archives (DU)
Memoir of George Moon (ms 15/154)

Fife County Records (Fife)
Minutes of Commissioners of Supply (1/1/1, 3–7).
'Minutes relative to the County Rooms' (1/11/1)

National Archives, Kew (NA)
State Papers (SP54/12/54; 54/13; 54/14; 54/38/37)

National Archives of Scotland (NAS)
Lord Advocate's Department (AD)
Commissary Court, St Andrews (CC20)
Court of Session (CS)
Exchequer (E)
Gifts and Deposits (GD) GD20, Crawford Priory Collection; GD26, Leven and Melville Papers; GD82, Makgill Charters; GD164, Rosslyn Muniments; GD242, Shepherd & Wedderburn WS
Heritors Records (HR)
Inland Revenue (IRS)
Court of Justiciary (JC)
Records of the Board of Trustees (NG)
Register House (RH)
Sheriff Court, Cupar (SC20)

National Library of Scotland (NLS)
Acts of the Fife Chapman Society, 1797 (ms200)
Correspondence of Henry Walker (writer, fl.1773–1818) (ms1074)
Papers of William Wilson and Son, tartan manufacturers,
     Bannockburn (ms6661–6798)

Royal Bank of Scotland (RBS)
Minutes of National Bank, 1, 1825–26

St Andrews University (StAU)
Anon, Cupar, burgh court (B13/7, 8, 9, 11, 12, 13)
Cupar, town council minutes (B13/14)
Cupar, trades records (B13/17)
Cupar, guildry records (B13/18)
Cupar, miscellaneous (B13/22)
St Andrews, miscellaneous (B65/22)
Cupar, presbytery minutes (CH2/82)
Cupar, minutes of Boston UP Church (CH3/66/1)
Account book of Lady Elizabeth Anstruther (msCS479.A8)
Tour through Scotland and the Borders of England made in the year
     1791 and 1792 (msDA855.A9T7)
Jesperson, A, Water mills of the River Eden, 4 vols, Cupar, 1948–50
     (msDA880.E4J4–7)
Leven and Melville factor's letter books 2, 4, 7 and 10
     (msDA880.F4B21)
St Andrews Hammermen Book (msDA890.S1H2)
Cheape of Rossie Papers (ms30488 and ms36929)

Printed primary sources

Accounts of the Lord High Treasurer of Scotland, T Dickson and
     J Balfour Paul (eds), 13 vols, Edinburgh, 1877–1916
Acts of the Parliaments of Scotland, T Thompson and C Innes (eds),
     Edinburgh, 1814–75
Anon, *Notes of a tour through the shires of Fife, Forfar, Perth and
     Stirling in 1800*, privately printed, 1898
Bettesworth, A, and C Hitch, *The Builder's Dictionary: or Gentleman
     and Architect's Companion ...*, 2 vols, 1734, reprinted Washington,
     1981
Boswell, J, *Journal of a Tour to the Hebrides with Samuel Johnson,
     LLD*, 1773, RW Chapman (ed.), Oxford, 1924
Bower, W, *Scotichronicon*, DER Watt (ed.), 9 vols, Aberdeen, 1987–98
*Calendar of documents relating to Scotland preserved in Her Majesty's
     Public Record Office, London*, J Bain (ed.), 9 vols, Edinburgh,
     1881–1986

Calendar of Scottish Supplications to Rome 1418–1422, E Lindsay and A Cameron (eds), SHS, Edinburgh, 1934

Calendar of Scottish Supplications to Rome 1428–1432, AI Dunlop and IB Cowan (eds), SHS, Edinburgh, 1970

Calendar of State Papers relating to Scotland ..., J Bain (ed.), 13 vols, Edinburgh, 1898–1969

Chambers, R, *Domestic Annals of Scotland*, 3rd edn, vol. III, Edinburgh and London, 1874

Chambers, R, *Domestic Annals of Scotland*, abridged edn, Edinburgh and London, 1885

Charters and other Muniments belonging to the Royal Burgh of Cupar, G Home (ed.), Cupar, 1882

Connolly, MF, *Biographical Dictionary of eminent men of Fife of past and present times ...*, Cupar and Edinburgh, 1866

Copy of minutes of election of Alexander Mair, deacon of tailors, 5 October 1768 (StAU TypBX.D68XM)

Copy of minutes of election of Henry Robertson junior, deacon of wrights, 5 October 1768 (StAU TypBX.D68X1)

The Darien Papers ... 1695–1700, J Burton (ed.), Edinburgh, 1849

Documents Illustrative of the History of Scotland ... [1286–1306], J Stevenson (ed.), 2 vols, Edinburgh, 1870

Ecclesiastical Records: Selections from the Minutes of the Presbyteries of St Andrews and Cupar, G Kinloch (ed.), Abbotsford Club, Edinburgh, 1837

The Exchequer Rolls of Scotland, J Stuart et al. (eds), 23 vols, Edinburgh, 1878–1908

Extracts from the records of the Convention of the Royal Burghs of Scotland, 1615–1676, Edinburgh, 1878

Extracts from the records of the Convention of the Royal Burghs of Scotland, 1677–1711, Edinburgh, 1880

Fife County Council, *Fife Looks Ahead: a regional survey of the county*, Edinburgh, 1946

Forsyth, R, *The Beauties of Scotland*, 5 vols, Edinburgh, 1805–08

Groome, FH, *Ordnance Gazetteer of Scotland*, 6 vols, London, 1894

Gurney, JJ, *Notes on a visit made to some of the Prisons in Scotland ... in company with Elizabeth Fry ...*, London, 1819

Hardcastle, Hon Mrs (ed.), *Life of John, Lord Campbell, Lord High Chancellor of Great Britain ...*, 2 vols, London, 1881

Home, H, Lord Kames, *Sketches of the history of man*, 2 vols, Edinburgh, 1774

Johnson, S, *A Dictionary of the English Language*, 3rd edn, Dublin, 1768

Johnson, S, *Journey to the Western Islands of Scotland, 1773*, RW Chapman (ed.), Oxford, 1924

Keddie, H, *Three Generations: the story of a middle-class Scottish family*, London, 1911

Kyd, JG, *Scottish Population Statistics, including Webster's Analysis of Population 1755*, Edinburgh, 1975

Lamont, J, *The Diary of John Lamont 1649–1672*, Edinburgh, 1810

Calendar of the Laing Charters, J Anderson (ed.), Edinburgh, 1899

Liber cartarum prioratus Sancti Andree in Scotia : e registro ipso in archivis baronum de Panmure hodie asservato, Edinburgh, 1841

Loch, D, *Essays on the trade, commerce, manufactures and fisheries of Scotland*, 3 vols, Edinburgh, 1778

Loudon, JC, *An Encyclopaedia of cottage, farm and villa architecture and furniture ...*, London, 1833

A New Gazetteer of Scotland, Edinburgh, 1817

New Statistical Account of Scotland, vol. IX, Fife-Kinross, Edinburgh and London, 1845

Philips, CH (ed.), *The Correspondence of David Scott Director and Chairman of the East India Company relating to Indian Affairs 1787–1805*, 2 vols, Royal Historical Society vols LXXV-LXXVI, London, 1951

Pigot and Co's New Commercial Directory of Scotland for 1825–6, London and Manchester

Pococke, R, *Tours in Scotland 1747, 1750, 1760*, DW Kemp (ed.), Edinburgh, 1887

Pryde, GS, *The burghs of Scotland: a critical list*, London, 1965

Regesta Regum Scotorum, v, The Acts of Robert I, AAM Duncan (ed.), Edinburgh, 1988

'Register containing the State and Condition of every Burgh within the Kingdome of Scotland in the year 1692' in *Miscellany of the Scottish Burgh Records Society* (Edinburgh, 1881), 49–157

Register of the Privy Council of Scotland, JH Burton et al. (eds), 38 vols in 3 series, Edinburgh, 1877–1970

Registrum Magni Sigilli Regum Scotorum, JM Thomson et al. (eds), 11 vols, Edinburgh, 1882–1914

Report from the Select Committee to whom the several petitions from the Royal Burghs of Scotland, during the years 1818, 1819, 1820, 1821, were referred: together with the minutes of evidence taken before the committee, printed 14 and 15 June 1821

Report of the Bible Society of Fife and Kinross Shires, for the year commencing 27th August, 1816 ..., Kirkcaldy, 1818

Report upon the boundaries of the several cities burghs and towns of Scotland ... 1832

Rodger, T, *The Kingdom of Fife Calotyped*, Cupar-Fife, 1861

Rotuli Scotiae in Turris Londinensis et in Domo Capitulari west-monasterieusi asservati, D MacPherson, J Caley and W Illingworth (eds), 2 vols, London, 1814–19

Sasine Abridgements, Fife, vol. 1 part 1,1781–1807; part 2, 1807–20

Scott, H, *Fasti Ecclesiae Scoticanae, vol. 5, Synods of Fife, and of Angus and Mearns*, Edinburgh, 1925

The Sheriff Court Book of Fife 1515–1522, WC Dickinson (ed.), SHS, Edinburgh, 1928

Sinclair, J, *Analysis of the Statistical Account of Scotland ...*, 2 vols, Edinburgh, 1825–1831

 The Correspondence of Sir John Sinclair, Bart, 2 vols, London, 1831

Somerville, T, *My Own Life and Times 1741–1814*, Edinburgh, 1861

The Statistical Account of Scotland: vol. 1, General, Wakefield, 1983

The Statistical Account of Scotland: vol. x, Fife, IR Grant and DJ Withrington (eds), Wakefield, 1978

The Third Statistical Account of Scotland, The County of Fife, A Smith (ed.), Edinburgh, 1952

Topham, E, *Edinburgh life in the eighteenth century: with an account of the fashions and amusements of society ...*, np, c.1900

A Vindication of the Action of Declarator concerning Burghal Privileges. Patrick Crombie Merchant and late Baillie of Coupar in Fife, etc, against Mr Robert Hay of Naughtoun, Sheriff-depute of Fife, and others: or, An Account of the Occasion of the Division which happen'd in the Town of Coupar, anent the Election of the Magistrates, at Michaelmas 1720 and hath greatly increas'd since, with several Instances of the sad Effects thereof. By a certain Gentleman, who is a true Lover of Liberty and Property, np, 1721 (StAU Typ BX.D21XA)

Walker, D (ed.), *The Rudiments of Architecture: or the Young Workman's Instructor...*, 2nd edn, Edinburgh, 1778, facsimile reprint, Whittinghame, 1992

Westwood's Directory for 1862, Cupar

Wiseman, R, *The Arithmetician's Text-Book in three parts ..., with an appendix on Gauging ...*, 2nd edn, Cupar-Fife, 1806

Wood, J, *Descriptive Account of the Principal Towns in Scotland*, Edinburgh, 1828

Maps

Ainslie J, inset plan of Cupar on *The Counties of Fife and Kinross with the Rivers Forth and Tay*, 1775

Gordon, J, 'Fyfe Shyre MDCXLII. Fifa Provincia Noviter delineata Auctore Jacobo Gordonio ...'; plan of Cupar inset at south-east corner

Ordnance Survey, 6" map, 1855/56

Wood, J, 'Plan of the town of Cupar' in *Town Atlas of Scotland 1818–1828*, Edinburgh, 1820

Newspapers, periodicals and almanacs

Dundee, Perth and Cupar Advertiser, or Perth, Fife and Angus Shires Intelligencer
Fife Herald
Fifeshire Journal
Gardiner's Miscellany
Rudiman's Weekly Mercury
Scots Magazine

Secondary Sources

Anderson, A, *The Old Libraries of Fife*, Fife County Library, Kirkcaldy, 1953

Anderson, RD, *Education and the Scottish People 1750–1918*, Oxford, 1995

Aston, M, and J Bond, *The Landscape of Towns*, London, 1976

Babington, Lieut-Col, *Records of the Fife Fox-Hounds*, Edinburgh and London, 1883

Bain, A, *Education in Stirlingshire from the Reformation to the Act of 1872*, London, 1965

  Patterns of Error: the teacher and external authority in Central Scotland, 1581–1861, Edinburgh, 1989

Barry, J, 'Bourgeois Collectivism? Urban association and the middling sort' in J Barry and C Brooks (eds), *The Middling Sort of People: culture, society and politics in England, 1550–1800*, London, 1994

Bayne-Powell, R, *Housekeeping in the Eighteenth Century*, London, 1956

Beale, JM (ed. DJ Withrington), *A History of the Burgh and Parochial Schools of Fife*, The Scottish Council for Research in Education, Edinburgh, 1983

Boase, CW, *A Century of Banking in Dundee*, 2nd edn, Edinburgh, 1867

Borsay, P, '"All the town's a stage": urban ritual and ceremony 1660–1800' in P Clark (ed.), *The Transformation of English Provincial Towns 1600–1800*, London, 1984

  The English Urban Renaissance, Culture and Society in the Provincial Town 1660–1770, Oxford 1989

  'The rise of the promenade: the social and cultural use of space in the English provincial town *c.*1660–1800', *British Journal for Eighteenth-Century Studies* 9, 1986

  'The English urban renaissance: the development of provincial urban culture *c.*1680–*c.* 1760' in P Borsay (ed.), *The Eighteenth-Century Town, a Reader in English Urban History, 1688–1820*, London 1990

Bremner, D, *Industries of Scotland*, Edinburgh, 1869

Brims, J, 'From Reformers to "Jacobins": The Scottish Association of the Friends of the People' in TM Devine (ed.), *Conflict and Stability in Scottish Society 1700–1850*, Edinburgh, 1990

Brown, CG, 'Religion and Social Change' in TM Devine and R Mitchison (eds), *People and Society in Scotland, vol. 1, 1760–1830*, Edinburgh, 1988

Religion and Society in Scotland since 1707, Edinburgh, 1997

Brown, DJ, ' "Nothing but Strugalls and Corruption": the Commons' elections for Scotland in 1774', *Parliamentary History 15*, 1996

Brown, K and A Mann (eds), *The History of the Scottish Parliament, vol. 2: Parliament and Politics in Scotland 1567–1707*, Edinburgh, 2005

Brown, M, *The Wars of Scotland, 1214–1371*, Edinburgh, 2004

Bruce, WS, *The Railways of Fife*, Perth, 1980

Cameron, A, *Bank of Scotland, 1695–1995, a very singular institution*, Edinburgh, 1995

Cameron, J, *Prisons and Punishment in Scotland from the Middle Ages to the Present*, Edinburgh, 1983

Campbell, A, *The Fifeshire Journal Press*, privately published, nd

The Firm of J & G Innes, privately published, nd

Campbell, A, *Notes By the Way*, Ayr, c.1890

The Press of Alexander Westwood (and Son), privately published, 1992

The Press of Whitehead and Burns, privately published, 1992

Campbell, RH and JB Dow, *A Source Book of Scottish Economic and Social History*, Oxford, 1968

Campbell, RH, *Scotland since 1707: the rise of an industrial society*, 2nd edn, Edinburgh, 1985

Campbell, RH, 'The Landed Classes' in TM Devine and R Mitchison (eds), *People and Society in Scotland, vol. 1, 1760–1830*, Edinburgh, 1988

Cant, RG, and IG Lindsay, *Old Elgin*, Elgin, 1946

Carter, JJ and Pittock, JH (eds), *Aberdeen and the Enlightenment*, Aberdeen, 1987

Chalklin, CW, *The Provincial Towns of Georgian England: a Study of the Building Process 1740–1820*, London, 1974

Checkland, SG, *Scottish Banking, A History, 1695–1973*, Glasgow and London, 1975

Clark, P, 'Introduction: English country towns 1500–1800' in P Clark (ed.) *Country towns in pre-industrial England*, Leicester, 1981

'Small towns in England 1550–1850' in P Clark (ed.), *Small towns in early modern Europe*, Cambridge, 1995

Colley, L, *Britons: forging the nation 1707–1837*, London, 1992

Colvin, HM, *The History of the King's Works*, i, London, 1963

Cookson, JE, *The British Armed Nation 1793–1815*, Oxford, 1997

Corfield, PJ, *The Impact of English towns 1700–1800*, Oxford, 1982

Power and the Professions in Britain 1700–1850, London and New York, 1995

'Defining urban work' in PJ Corfield and D Keene (eds), *Work in Towns 850–1850*, Leicester, 1990

Cowan, IB and DE Easson, *Medieval Religious Houses, Scotland*, 2nd edn, London, 1976

Cowan, IB, PHR Mackay, and A Macquarrie, *The Knights of St John of Jerusalem in Scotland*, SHS, Edinburgh, 1983

Cox, EHM, *A History of Gardening in Scotland*, London, 1935

Devine, TM, 'The Failure of Radical Reform in Scotland in the Late Eighteenth Century: the social and economic context' in TM Devine (ed.), *Conflict and Stability in Scottish Society 1700–1850*, Edinburgh, 1990

'The Making of Industrial and Urban Society' in R Mitchison (ed.), *Why Scottish History Matters*, revised edn, Edinburgh, 1997

'The Merchant Class of the larger Scottish Towns in the later seventeenth and early eighteenth centuries' in G Gordon and B Dicks (eds), *Scottish Urban History*, Aberdeen, 1983

'The Scottish Merchant Community, 1680–1740' in RH Campbell and AS Skinner (eds), *The Origins and Nature of the Scottish Enlightenment*, Edinburgh, 1982

'The Social Composition of the Business Class in the Larger Scottish Towns, 1680–1740' in TM Devine and D Dickson (eds), *Ireland and Scotland 1600–1850: parallels and contrasts in economic and social development*, Edinburgh, 1983

'Urbanisation' in TM Devine and R Mitchison (eds), *People and Society in Scotland, vol. 1, 1760–1830*, Edinburgh, 1988

'Urbanisation and the Civic Response: Glasgow 1800–30' in AJG Cummings and TM Devine (eds), *Industry, Business and Society in Scotland since 1700*, Edinburgh, 1994

Dewdney, JC, 'Changes in population distribution in the county of Fife 1755–1951', *Scottish Geographical Magazine* 17.1, 1955

Dingwall, HM, *Late Seventeenth-century Edinburgh: a demographic study*, Aldershot, 1994

Physicians, Surgeons and Apothecaries: medicine in seventeenth-century Edinburgh, East Linton, 1995

Ditchburn, D, 'Trade with Northern Europe, 1297–1540', in M Lynch, M Spearman and G Stell (eds), *The Scottish Medieval Town*, Edinburgh, 1988

Doughty, DW, *The Tullis Press Cupar, 1803–1849*, Abertay Historical Society publication no.12, Dundee, 1967

Dow, F, *Cromwellian Scotland, 1651–1660*, Edinburgh, 1979

Durie, A, *The British Linen Company 1745–1775*, SHS, Edinburgh, 1996
  The Scottish Linen Industry in the Eighteenth Century, Edinburgh, 1979
Earle, P, *The Making of the English Middle Class: Business, Society and Family Life in London, 1660–1730*, Berkeley, 1989
Edwards, CD, *Eighteenth-Century Furniture*, Manchester, 1996
Emmerson, R, *British teapots and tea drinking*, HMSO, London, 1992
Everitt, A, 'The English Urban Inn, 1560–1760' in Alan Everitt (ed.), *Perspectives in English Urban History, London*, 1973
  Landscape and Community in England, London, 1985
Ewan, E, *Townlife in Fourteenth-Century Scotland*, Edinburgh, 1990
Fawcett, R, *Scottish Medieval Churches, Architecture and Furnishings*, Stroud, 2002
Ferguson, W, 'Dingwall Burgh Politics and the Parliamentary Franchise in the Eighteenth Century', *Scottish Historical Review* XXXVIII, 126, 1959
Fergusson, J (ed.), *Letters of George Dempster to Sir Adam Ferguson 1756–1813*, London, 1934
Fittis, RS, *Sports and Pastimes of Scotland*, Paisley and London, 1891
Fraser, WH, *Conflict and Class: Scottish workers 1700–1838*, Edinburgh, 1988
  'Developments in Leisure' in WH Fraser and RJ Morris (eds), *People and Society in Scotland, vol. II, 1830–1914*, Edinburgh, 1990
  'Patterns of Protest' in TM Devine and R Mitchison (eds), *People and Society in Scotland, vol. I, 1760–1830*, Edinburgh, 1988
Fry, M, *The Dundas Despotism*, Edinburgh, 1992
  Patronage and Principle, Aberdeen, 1987
Fulton, HL, 'John Moore, the Medical Profession and the Glasgow Enlightenment' in RB Sher and A Hook (eds), *The Glasgow Enlightenment*, East Linton, 1995
Gardiner, L, *Man in the Clouds: the story of Vincenzo Lunardi*, Edinburgh, 1963
Gauldie, E, *One Artful and Ambitious Individual: Alexander Riddoch (1745–1822)*, Abertay Historical Society Publication no. 28, Dundee, 1989
Gibson, A, *Extracts from the Ancient Records of Dysart from 1533 to 1763*, np, 1865
Gibson, AJS and Smout, TC, *Prices, food and wages in Scotland 1550–1780*, Cambridge, 1995
Gibson, WJ, *Education in Scotland*, London, 1912
Gifford, J, *The Buildings of Scotland: Fife*, London, 1988
Gilbert, C, *English Vernacular Furniture 1750–1900*, Yale, 1991

Gloag, J, *A Social History of Furniture Design from* BC *1300 to* AD *1960*, London, 1966

Govan, J, *Notes of a Communication addresssed to the Fifeshire Literary, Scientific and Antiquarian Society*, Edinburgh, 1851

Gow, I, *The Scottish Interior*, Edinburgh, 1992

'The Dining Room' in A Carruthers (ed.), *The Scottish Home*, Edinburgh, 1996

'The Edinburgh Villa', *The Book of the Old Edinburgh Club*, NS, vol. I, 1991

Graham, HG, *The Social Life of Scotland in the Eighteenth Century*, 2 vols, 2nd edn, London, 1900

Grant, J, *History of the Burgh Schools of Scotland*, London and Glasgow, 1876

Haig, Lady, *A Scottish Tour*, Edinburgh, 1935

Haldane, ARB, *Three Centuries of Scottish Posts*, Edinburgh, 1971

Hall, C, *White, Male and Middle Class: explorations in feminism and history*, Oxford, 1992

Hall, WD and M King, Field Survey and Assessment at the former site of St Christopher's Parish Church, Cupar, *Tayside and Fife Archaeological Journal* 5, 1999

Hamilton, H, *An Economic History of Scotland in the Eighteenth Century*, Oxford, 1963

Harley, W, *Dalgairn: the Story of a House and its Garden*, Fife Folk Museum, 2004

'The "Beet" Generation', *History Scotland* 3.1, 2003

Hatcher, J and TC Barker, *A History of British Pewter*, London, 1974

Hayton, D, 'Traces of Party Politics in Early Eighteenth-Century Scottish Elections', *Parliamentary History*, 15, 1996

Hendry, D, *Cupar Doctors – and their families*, privately published, Cupar, 1992

Henstock, A (ed.), *A Georgian Country Town: Ashbourne 1725–1825, vol. 1: Fashionable Society*, Ashbourne, 1989

Hill, B, *Servants, English Domestics in the Eighteenth Century*, Oxford, 1996

Houston, RA, *Scottish Literacy and the Scottish Identity: illiteracy and society in Scotland and northern England 1600–1800*, Cambridge, 1985

Social Change in the Age of Enlightenment: Edinburgh 1660–1760, Oxford, 1994

'Women in the economy and society of Scotland, 1500–1800' in RA Houston and ID Whyte (eds), *Scottish Society 1500–1800*, Cambridge, 1989

Houston, R A and ID Whyte, *Scottish Society 1500–1800*, Cambridge, 1989

Innes, G, *Historical Notes and Reminiscences of Cupar*, Cupar, 1884

Jesperson, A, 'Watermills on the river Eden', *Proceedings of the Society of Antiquaries of Scotland* XCVII, 1963–64

Jessop, JC, *Education in Angus*, London, 1931

Johnson, D, *Music and Society in Lowland Scotland in the Eighteenth Century*, London, 1972

Jones, D, 'Box Beds in Eastern Scotland', *Regional Furniture* V, 1991
'The Hall and Lobby' in A Carruthers (ed.), *The Scottish Home*, Edinburgh, 1996

Kelsall, H and K, *Scottish Lifestyle 300 Years Ago: new light on Edinburgh and Border families*, Edinburgh, 1986

Ketelbey, CDM, *Tullis Russell 1809–1859*, Tullis Russell, Markinch, 1967

Kinchin, J, 'The Drawing Room' in A Carruthers (ed.), *The Scottish Home*, Edinburgh, 1996

Laing, A, *Lighting*, Victoria and Albert Museum, London, 1982

Lang, AM, *A Life of George Dempster, Scottish MP of Dunnichen (1732–1818)*, Lampeter, 1998

Leighton, JM, *History of the County of Fife*, 3 vols, Glasgow, 1840

Leneman, L (ed.), *Perspectives in Scottish Social History*, Aberdeen, 1988

Leneman, L and R Mitchison, *Sin in the City: sexuality and social control in urban Scotland 1660–1780*, Edinburgh, 1998

Lenman, B, *An economic history of modern Scotland 1660–1976*, London, 1977
Integration and Enlightenment: Scotland 1746–1832, Edinburgh, 1981

Lindsay, IG, *Georgian Edinburgh*, Edinburgh, 1973

Lindsay, J, *The Scottish poor law: its operation in the north-east from 1745 to 1845*, Ilfracombe, 1975

Livingstone, PK, *Flax and Linen in Fife through the centuries*, Kirkcaldy, 1952

Lockhart, DG, 'Planned Village Development in Scotland and Ireland, 1700–1850' in TM Devine and D Dickson (eds), *Ireland and Scotland 1600–1850: parallels and contrasts in economic and social development*, Edinburgh, 1983

Logue, K, *Popular Disturbances in Scotland 1780–1815*, Edinburgh, 1979

Low, U, *Fifty Years with John Company, from the letters of General Sir John Low of Clatto, Fife*, London, 1936

Lubar, S and Kingery, WD (eds), *History from Things: Essays on Material Culture*, Washington and London, 1993

Lucie-Smith, E, *Furniture: a Concise History*, London, 1979

Lynch, M, 'Continuity and change in urban society, 1500–1700' in RA Houston and ID Whyte (eds), *Scottish Society 1500–1800*, Cambridge, 1989

Lynch, M, 'The Crown and the Burghs 1500–1625' in M Lynch (ed.), *The Early Modern Town in Scotland*, London, 1987

'Introduction: Scottish Towns 1500–1700' in M Lynch (ed.), *The Early Modern Town in Scotland*, London, 1987

'Urbanisation and Urban Networks in Seventeenth Century Scotland: some further thoughts', *Scottish Economic and Social History*, 12, 1992

'Whatever happened to the mediaeval burgh? Some guidelines for sixteenth and seventeenth century historians', *Scottish Economic and Social History*, 4, 1984

Lythe, SGE and J Butt, *An Economic History of Scotland 1100–1939*, Glasgow and London, 1975

Macdonald, S, *The Witches of Fife: witch-hunting in a Scottish shire, 1560–1710*, East Linton, 2002

McDowall, W, *History of the Burgh of Dumfries*, 1906, reprinted Wakefield, 1972

McInnes, A, 'The emergence of a leisure town: Shrewsbury 1660–1760', *Past and Present*, 120, 1988

McKendrick, N, 'The Consumer Revolution in Eighteenth-century England' in N McKendrick, J Brewer and JH Plumb (eds), *The Birth of a Consumer Society: the Commercialization of Eighteenth-century England*, London, 1982

'Home Demand and Economic Growth: a new view of the role of women and children in the industrial revolution' in N McKendrick (ed.), *Historical Perspectives: Studies in English Thought and Society*, London, 1974

'Josiah Wedgwood and the Commercialization of the Potteries' in N McKendrick, J Brewer and JH Plumb (eds), *The Birth of a Consumer Society: the Commercialization of Eighteenth-century England*, London, 1982

MacLaren, AA, 'Patronage and Professionalism: the "Forgotten Middle Class", 1760–1860' in D McCrone, S Kendrick and P Straw (eds), *The Making of Scotland: Nation, Culture and Social Change*, Edinburgh, 1989

McNeill, PGB and HL MacQueen, (eds), *Atlas of Scottish History to 1707*, Edinburgh, 1996

McVeigh, P, *Scottish East Coast Potteries 1750–1840*, Edinburgh, 1979

McWilliam, C, *Scottish Townscape*, London, 1975

Mair, C, *Stirling, the Royal Burgh*, Edinburgh, 1990

Malcolm, CA, *The History of the British Linen Bank*, Edinburgh, 1950

Martin, CJM and PF de C Martin, 'Vernacular pottery manufacture in a nineteenth-century Scottish burgh: a kiln deposit from Cupar, Fife', *Tayside and Fife Archaeological Journal* 2, 1996

Martin, P, 'An early nineteenth century racecourse stand at Uthrogle, near Cupar, Fife', *Tayside and Fife Archaeological Journal* 5, 1999

'Pipemakers in the rest of Scotland' in *The Archaeology of the Clay Tobacco Pipe*, x, *Scotland*, P Davey (ed.), BAR British series 178, Oxford, 1987

'Towns and villages' in D Omand (ed.), *The Fife Book*, Edinburgh, 2000

Meikle, H, *Scotland and the French Revolution*, Glasgow, 1912

Millar, AH, *Fife: Pictorial and Historical*, 2 vols, Cupar, 1895

Mitchison, R, *The Old Poor Law in Scotland: the experience of poverty, 1574–1845*, Edinburgh, 2000

'The Poor Law' in TM Devine and R Mitchison (eds), *People and Society in Scotland, vol. 1, 1760–1830*, Edinburgh, 1988

'Who Were the Poor in Scotland?' in R Mitchison and P Roebuck (eds), *Economy and Society in Scotland and Ireland 1500–1939*, Edinburgh 1988

and L Leneman, *Sexuality and Social Control, Scotland 1660–1780*, Oxford, 1989

Moffat, A, *Kelsae: a history of Kelso from Earliest Times*, Edinburgh, 1985

Morris, RJ, *Class and Class Consciousness in the Industrial Revolution 1780–1850*, London, 1979

Munn, CW, *The Scottish Provincial Banking Companies, 1747–1864*, Edinburgh, 1981

Murdoch, AJ, *The People Above: Politics and Administration in Mid-Eighteenth-Century Scotland*, Edinburgh, 1980

'Politics and the People in the Burgh of Dumfries, 1758–1760', *Scottish Historical Review* LXX, 1991

Murray, N, *The Scottish Handloom Weavers 1790–1850: a Social History*, Edinburgh, 1978

Naismith, R, *The Story of Scotland's Towns*, Edinburgh, 1989

Namier, L and J Brooke, *History of Parliament: Commons, 1754–1790*, HMSO, London, 1964

Nenadic, S, 'The Enlightenment in Scotland and the popular passion for portraits', *British Journal for Eighteenth-Century Studies* 21.2, 1998

'Middle-rank consumers and domestic culture in Edinburgh and Glasgow 1720–1840', *Past and Present* 145, 1994

'Political Reform and the "Ordering" of Middle-Class Protest' in TM Devine (ed.) *Conflict and Stability in Scottish Society 1700–1850*, Edinburgh, 1990

'Print Collecting and Popular Culture in Eighteenth-Century Edinburgh', *History* 82 no. 266, 1997

Nenadic, S, 'The Rise of the Urban Middle Classes' in TM Devine and R Mitchison (eds), *People and Society in Scotland, vol. 1, 1760–1830*, Edinburgh, 1988

Oram, R, 'From the Union of the Crowns to the Union of the Parliaments: Fife 1603–1717', in D Omand (ed.), *The Fife Book*, Edinburgh, 2000

Pagan, T, *The Convention of the Royal Burghs of Scotland*, Glasgow, 1926

Plumb, JH, *The Commercialisation of Leisure in Eighteenth-century England*, Stenton Lecture 1972, University of Reading, 1973

Porteous, A, *The town council seals of Scotland ...*, Edinburgh, 1906

Porter, R, *English Society in the Eighteenth Century*, revised edn, London, 1990

Pride, G, *The Kingdom of Fife*, Edinburgh, 1990.

Pryde, GS, *Central and Local Government in Scotland since 1707*, Historical Association, General Series no. 45, London, 1960

RCAHMS, *Tolbooths and Town-houses, civic architecture in Scotland to 1833*, Edinburgh, 1996

Reed, M, 'The cultural role of small towns in England 1600–1800' in P Clark (ed.), *Small towns in early modern Europe*, Cambridge, 1995

Rendall, J, *Women in an Industrialising Society: England 1750–1880*, Oxford, 1990

Riley, PWJ, *The Union of England and Scotland: a study in Anglo-Scottish politics of the eighteenth century*, Manchester, 1978

Robertson, A, *History of the Dundee Theatre*, London, 1949

Rodger, RG, 'The Evolution of Scottish Town Planning' in G Gordon and B Dicks (eds), *Scottish Urban History*, Aberdeen, 1983

Sanderson, E, *Women and work in eighteenth century Edinburgh*, Basingstoke, 1996

Saville, R, *Bank of Scotland, a history 1695–1995*, Edinburgh, 1996

Scotland, J, *The history of Scottish Education, vol. 1, from the beginning to 1872*, London, 1969

Sedgwick, R, *History of Parliament: Commons, 1715–1754*, HMSO, 1970

Sellar, RJB, *The Fife and Forfar Yeomanry 1919–1956*, Edinburgh, 1960

Sharpe, P, *Adapting to Capitalism: working women in the English economy 1700–1850*, Basingstoke, 1995

Shvidkovsky, D, 'Classical Edinburgh and Russian Town-Planning of the late 18th and Early 19th Centuries: the Role of William Hastie (1755–1832)', *Architectural Heritage* II, (Scottish Architects Abroad), 1991

Sibbald, R, *The History, Ancient and Modern, of the Sheriffdoms of Fife and Kinross* ... [1710], new edition, L Adamson (ed.), Cupar, 1803

Silver, O, *The Roads of Fife*, Edinburgh, 1987

Simpson, AT and S Stevenson, *Historic Cupar; the Archaeological Implications of Development*, Scotish Burgh Survey, Glasgow, 1981

Smith, A, *The Wealth of Nations*, Penguin Classics edition, London, 1986

Smith, AM, *The Nine Trades of Dundee*, Abertay Historical Society Publications no. 35, Dundee, 1995

The Three United Trades of Dundee: masons, wrights and slaters, Abertay Historical Society Publications no. 26, Dundee, 1987

Smout, TC, *A History of the Scottish People 1560–1830*, London, 1969

Spaven, A, *Fortress Scotland: a guide to the military presence*, London, 1983

Sprott, G, *Farming*, NMS, Edinburgh, 1995

Stell, G, 'Urban Buildings' in M Lynch, M Spearman and G Stell (eds), *The Scottish Medieval Town*, Edinburgh, 1988

Stephen, W, *The Story of Inverkeithing and Rosyth*, Edinburgh, 1938

Stevenson, A, 'Trade with the South, 1070–1513', in M Lynch, M Spearman & G Stell, *The Scottish Mediaeval Town*, Edinburgh, 1988

Stevenson, D, 'The Burghs and the Scottish Revolution', in M Lynch (ed.), *The Early Modern Town in Scotland*, London, 1987

Strawhorn, J, *The History of Irvine: Royal Burgh and New Town*, Edinburgh, 1985

Sunter, RM, *Patronage and Politics in Scotland, 1707–1832*, Edinburgh, 1986

Tarrant, N, 'The Bedroom' in A Carruthers (ed.), *The Scottish Home*, Edinburgh, 1996

Tarrant, N, *Going to Bed*, NMS, Edinburgh, 1998

Thompson, EP, *Customs in Common*, London, 1991

Thomson, J, *General View of the Agriculture of Fife*, Edinburgh, 1800

Thornton, P, *Authentic Decor: the domestic interior 1620–1920*, London, 1984

Tranter, N, 'Schooling and literacy in Early Nineteenth Century Scotland: some additional evidence and its implications', *Scottish Economic and Social History* 17.1, 1997

Tressider, GA, 'Coronation day celebrations in English towns, 1685–1821: elite hegemony and local relations on a ceremonial occasion', *British Journal for Eighteenth-Century Studies* 15, 1992, 1–16

Turnbull, I, The Agricultural Tradition, in D Omand (ed.), *The Fife Book*, Edinburgh, 2000

Turner, W, *The Anatomical Memoirs of John Goodsir*, 2 vols, Edinburgh, 1868

Verschuur, M, 'Merchants and Craftsmen in Sixteenth-Century Perth', in M Lynch (ed.), *The Early Modern Town in Scotland*, London, 1987

de Vries, J, 'Between purchasing power and the world of goods: understanding the household economy in early modern Europe' in J Brewer and R Porter (eds), *Consumption and the World of Goods*, London and New York, 1993

Walker, JR, *Pre-Reformation Churches in Fifeshire*, Edinburgh, 1895

Warden, AJ, *Burgh Laws of Dundee, with the history, statutes and proceedings of the guild of merchants and fraternities of craftsmen*, London, 1872

Warrack, J, *Domestic Life in Scotland, 1488–1688*, London, 1920

Weatherill, L, *Consumer Behaviour and Material Culture in Britain 1660–1760*, London, 1988

Webster, B, 'Scotland without a King, 1329–1341' in *Medieval Scotland, Crown, Lordship and Community*, A Grant and K Stringer (eds), Edinburgh, 1993

Wells-Cole, A, *Historic Paper Hangings from Temple Newsam and other English Houses*, Leeds City Art Galleries, Leeds, 1983

Whatley, CA, 'How tame were the Scottish Lowlanders during the Eighteenth Century?' in TM Devine (ed.), *Conflict and Stability in Scottish Society 1700–1850*, Edinburgh, 1990

The Industrial Revolution in Scotland, Cambridge, 1997

Onwards from Osnaburghs: the rise and progress of a Scottish Textile Company Don and Low of Forfar, 1792–1992, Edinburgh, 1992

'Royal Day, People's Day: The Monarch's Birthday in Scotland, c.1660–1860' in R Mason and N Macdougall (eds), *People and Power in Scotland: essays in honour of TC Smout*, Edinburgh, 1992

'The Union of 1707, integration and the Scottish burghs: the case of the 1720 food riots', *Scottish Historical Review* LXXVIII.2, 1999

'Women and the economic transformation of Scotland c.1740–1830', *Scottish Economic and Social History* 14, 1994

Whetstone, A, *Scottish County Government in the Eighteenth and Nineteenth Centuries*, Edinburgh, 1981

Whyte, ID, *Scotland before the Industrial Revolution: an Economic and Social History c.1050–c.1750*, London, 1995

'Urbanisation in early modern Scotland: a preliminary analysis', *Scottish Economic and Social History* 9, 1989

Whyte, ID, 'Urbanisation in eighteenth-century Scotland' in TM Devine and JR Young (eds), *Eighteenth Century Scotland: New Perspectives*, East Linton, 1999

Wood, LI, *Scottish Pewter-ware and Pewterers*, Edinburgh, 1905

Wright, L, *Clean and Decent: the fascinating history of the bathroom and the water closet*, London, 1960

Theses

Belof, MM, 'The situation of women in seventeenth century Fife, as illustrated by the records of the church courts', unpublished MPhil thesis, StAU, 1989

Dingwall, H, 'The social and economic structure of Edinburgh in the late seventeenth century', PhD thesis, University of Edinburgh, 1989

Sanderson, E, 'Women and Work in Eighteenth Century Edinburgh', PhD thesis, University of Edinburgh, 1993

Steel, D, 'The linen industry of Fife in the later eighteenth and nineteenth centuries', unpublished PhD thesis, StAU, 1975.

Index

[dates are of birth and death, unless 'fl.' indicates dates of known activity]

Abbotshall, parish, 7, 45

Abdie, parish, Fig.1.1, 3, 7, 38, 234

Abercrombie, Jean (d.1757), widow of Peter Hutton (fl.1742–43), dyer, 239

Aberdeen, Map 1, 7, 10, 29–30, 42, 50–51, 91, 165, 184, 219

Aberlady, Map 1, 22

Abernethy, Map 2, 35

Adam, Robert (1728–92), architect, 105

Adamson, Alexander (d.1866) of South Callange, 204

Adamson, John (fl.1805–09), manufacturer, Burnside, 63

Adamson, Laurence (1767–1837), 2nd minister 1794, 1st minister 1825, joint author of *New Statistical Account*, m. 1795 Isobel, dau. of William Robertson, town clerk (qv), 47, 66, 113, 115, 131, 143, 235

Adamson, Misses (fl.1800–27), mantua-makers, milliners and teachers of dressmaking, sisters of Laurence (qv), 131

Adamson Hospital, Bank Street, 204

Adamson Institution (later Alwyn House), Bridgend, Ceres, 204

Aitken, George (1761–1831) of Todhall (Map 3), writer, bailie and provost, 97, 101, 165, 217, 235

Aitken, John (fl.1796–1822), weaver and manufacturer, Newtown, 158

Alexander III (r.1249–85), 10, 14

Alison, Helen (fl.1782), unmarried mother, 179

Allan, David (fl.1785–1827), merchant and tobacconist, Crossgate, 55–56, 63, 235

Anderson, Ebenezer (fl.1815–29), writer and banker, Bonnygate, partner and cashier, Fife Bank, sequestrated 1829, 48, 54, 63

Anderson, John (fl.1765–75), innkeeper, 72, 113, 240

Anderson, John (fl.1800–22), manufacturer, Cupar Mills, m. Ann dau. of David Allan (qv), 110, 118, 120, 122, 135, 241

Anderson, Mary (d.1797), residenter, former innkeeper, 73, 240

Anderson, Robert Rowand (1834–1921), architect, 195

Anderson, Thomas (fl.1797–1825), manufacturer, co-partner with James Carstairs (qv), William Anderson (qv) and George Hog (qv), Tarvit spinning mill, 48

Anderson, William (fl.1799–1817), manufacturer, co-partner with James Carstairs (qv), Thomas Anderson (qv) and George Hog (qv), Tarvit spinning mill, 48, 63

Anderson, Birrell & Co., linen manufacturers, 48

Annan, Map 1, 143

Annan, John (d.1816), residenter, 54, 240

Anstruther Easter, burgh and parish, Map 2, Fig.1.1, 3, 7, 29, 63, 192, 201, 233

Anstruther Wester, burgh and parish, Map 2, Fig.1.1, 3, 7, 201, 233

Anstruther, Lady Elizabeth, nee Maitland, 2nd dau. of 6th earl of Lauderdale, b. c.1714/19, 1739 m. (1) James Ogilvie of Inchmartin, Errol, Perthshire, at least 2 dau., ? 1 or 2 sons, m. (2) 1765 General Robert Anstruther of Balgarvie. After his death in 1767 she sold the estate and moved to Balgarvie House, Cupar, 54, 80, 84, 115–17, 125, 133, 135, 137–38, 174, 176

Applin, Richard (fl.1709–32), vintner (former soldier), 165

Arbroath, Map 1, 5, 7, 35, 63, 143

Arngask, Fig.2.1, 11

Arnot, Robert (1742–1820) of Chapel (SE of Kettlebridge), surgeon, partner of George Bethune (qv), councillor, 69

Arnot, Thomas (fl.1658–94), 2nd minister 1658–62, 1st minister 1690–94, 26

Arthur, Alexander (fl.1808–19), slater, 86, 88

Ashlar Wynd, Map 4, 91–92

Auchmuty, near Markinch, paper mill, Map 2, 50, 56, 134

Auchterderran, Map 2, 6

Auchtermuchty, burgh and parish, Map 2, Fig.1.1, 3, 7, 38, 45–47, 62–63, 68–69, 87, 104, 156–57, 233

Austin, Joseph (MP 1708–10), 163

Ayr, Map 1, 29, 138, 143, 219

Back Lebanon (*see also* Lebanon), 188, 202

Balbirnie Bridge, near Markinch (Map 2), 63

Balcarres, earl of, 31
Baldie, William (fl.1754–79), wright, 75,
    240
Baldinnie, Map 2, 201
Balfour, Sir Andrew (1630–94) of Denmylne
    (Map 2), 28
Balgarvie, Map 3, 19, 51, 137
Balgarvie House, 19, 92, 96, 98
Balgarvie Road, 197, 210
Balliol, Edward (fl.1296–1367), son of John
    (qv), 15
Balliol, John (r.1292–96), 10, 15
Balmerino, village and parish, Map 2, Fig.1.1,
    3, 38, 69, 87, 162, 233
Balmerino, Lord, 33
Balmerino Place (Bonnygate), 33
Bandstand, 210
Banff, Map 1, 138
Bank Street, Map 4, 197
Banks
    Bank of Scotland (1785–1814, 1963–
        present), 53–55, 64, 161, 197, 209
    British Linen Company/Bank (1792–1969),
        53–54, 56, 64, 189, 197, 209
    City of Glasgow Bank (1857–78), 189
    Clydesdale Bank (1840–present), 105, 189,
        197
    Commercial Bank (1810–1958), 54, 63–64,
        70, 98, 166, 189, 197, 209
    Cupar Bank (1802–11), 54–55, 63–64
    Cupar Savings Bank (est.1837), 197, 217
    Dundee Bank (est.1763), 54
    Fife Bank (1802–25), 54–56, 64
    National Bank (1825–1958), 63, 189, 197,
        209
    National & Commercial Bank (1958–69),
        209
    Royal Bank (c.1860 to present), 189, 197,
        209
    Savings and Loan Bank (est.1815), 56
    Trustee Savings Bank, 197, 209
    Union Bank, 197
Bannockburn, near Stirling (Map 1), 49
Barclay, Alexander (fl.1728–42), merchant,
    clerk to linen manufactory, 39, 62
Barclay, David (fl.1714–33), millmaster, m.
    Elizabeth Forster (qv), 82
Barclay, David (fl.1736–49), weaver, master-
    bleacher at linen manufactory, 62
Barclay, John (fl.1690s), surgeon, 35
Barnyards, near Kilconquhar (Map 2), 63
Barony, Map 4, Pl.14b,c, 33–34, 198, 204
Baxter, Sir David (1793–1872) of Kilmaron
    (Map 3), Dundee industrialist, 195
Baxter, Lady Elizabeth, wife of David (qv), 199
Baxter, James (fl.1711–32), surgeon-
    apothecary, 165
Baxter, John (fl.1764–80) of Leckiebank (Map
    2), provost, 155
Bayne, John (fl.1788–95), Latin master, came
    from Kirkcudbright, left for South Leith,
    130
Beath, parish, 6
Beith, Map 1, 42

Bell, Dr Andrew (1753–1832), b. St Andrews,
    educated St Andrews grammar school
    and university, episcopal clergyman, went
    to India 1787, bequeathed his estate for
    educational purposes in Fife, 198
Bell, Captain Charles (fl.1780–1801) of
    Pitblado (Map 3), 159
Bell, Elizabeth (fl.1763–1812), residenter, 240
Bell, Hay (fl.1783–88), partner in brick-works,
    architect of parish church, later living in
    Tobago, W Indies, son of Robert senior,
    merchant (qv), 104
Bell, James (fl.1729–89), glover, 70–71, 79,
    133
Bell, Robert senior (fl.1722–83), merchant,
    partner in brick-works, 39, 41
Bell, Thomas (fl.1776–1803), merchant and
    manufacturer, bailie, shareholder in Fife
    Bank, 46, 54
Bell Close, 208
Belhaven, port of Dunbar (Map 1), 22
Bellfield, Map 4, Pl.6b, 100, 111, 137
Bernham, David de (fl.1224–53), bishop of St
    Andrews, 16, 32
Berwick-upon-Tweed, Map 1, 10, 15
Bethune, Dr James (1664–1743) of Kingask
    (Map 3), physician, son of Dr James of
    Nether Tarvit, bro. of Thomas (qv), 139,
    151
Bethune, Dr George (c.1718–75), physician,
    partner of Robert Arnot (qv), provost and
    bailie, son of James (qv), 62, 68–69, 240
Bethune, Thomas (fl.1690s–1744) of Tarvit
    (bought Kilconquhar 1714, sold Tarvit
    1720), bro. of James (qv), 35, 148, 151
Beveridge, William (c.1716–49), writer, 67,
    112–13, 239
Bible Society of Fife and Kinross Shires, 217,
    219
Birrell, David (fl.1784–1813), weaver and
    manufacturer, partner in factory at
    Burnside with William Geddie (qv) and
    William Anderson (qv), 46, 54, 56, 63,
    240
Birrell Peter (fl.1692–1701), merchant, 39,
    239
Birrell, Thomas (d.1820), residenter, 240
Bishopgate, Map 4, 32, 93, 198, 210
Bishopgate House, Map 4, 100
Black, Margaret (fl.1724–41), widow of
    Andrew Glasford (d.1724), writer, 239
Blackness, port of Linlithgow (Map 1), 22
Blaireuk, 197
Blalowan, Map 4, 100, 183
Blebo Mills, Fig.4.2, 6, 48, 60
Board of Trustees for Fisheries and
    Manufactures in Scotland, 43–44, 63
Boarhills, Map 2, 192
Bobber Wynd, Map 4, 91, 183
Boes, George (c.1702–75), 2nd minister 1728,
    1st minister 1738, 139
Bogie, Mistress, Anna Turnbull (fl.1701–30),
    innkeeper, widow of James (fl. 1692–
    1700), brewer and merchant, 153, 179

Bonnygate, Map 4, Pl.4b, 8a, 19, 32, 55, 90–92, 100–01, 103, 188, 197–98
Bonvil Park, see Duffus Park
Bouch, Thomas (1822–80), engineer, 192
Bow Butts, 10, 92–93
Bowling Green Road, 210
Brabiner, John (c.1735–68), merchant and tobacconist, 39, 240
Braeheads, 93
Brechin, Map 1, 29, 46
Bridge Hill, across South Bridge, now cut into by the railway, 139, 177
Bridge Port, 20, 32
Brighton, see Cupar Muir
Brighton Road, 210
British Linen Company, 44
Broughty Ferry, Map 2, 192
Brown, Alexander (fl.1767–75), merchant, 41, 62
Bruce, Patrick (d.1719) of Bunzion, MP 1702–07, sheriff-depute, distant cousin of earl of Elgin, 90, 239
Bruce, Patrick (1726–58) of Bunzion, 239
Bruntshiels, Map 2, 201
Buckhaven, Map 2, 6
Bullock, William, 1333–39 keeper of Cupar Castle, 15
Bunzion (Lower), Map 3, 111, 113, 119–20, 135
Burgh Chambers, see Council House
Burn, William (1789–1870), architect, Edinburgh, 98, 105, 195
Burnside (see also Lady Burn and North Burnside), 104, 188, 195
Burntisland, Map 2, 6–7, 29–30, 83, 191–92
Burton, James (c.1815–c.1882), clay-pipe-maker, 188, 204

Cairngreen, Map 3, 208
Cairnie, Map 3, 101
Callange (North, South and Coaltown), Map 3, Fig.2.1, 11, 140, 204
Camehou, Walter de (fl.1293–1301), 15, 22
Cameron, parish, Fig.1.1, 3, 7, 233
Campbell, Douglas & Sellars, architects, 195
Campbell, Douglas & Stevenson, architects, 196
Campbell, John, (1779–1861), educated Cupar, then St Andrews University, moved to London and became Lord Chancellor and Baron Campbell of St Andrews, son of George (qv), 128–30, 138, 140, 142–44, 216
Campbell, George (c.1753–1824), 2nd minister 1773, 1st minister 1791, author of Old Statistical Account, 96, 107, 129
Campbell, George (1778–1855) of Edenwood, knighted 1833, son of George (qv) and brother of John (qv), m. (2) Margaret (1802–74), dau. of Andrew Christie (qv), 129, 142, 216
Campbell, Miss (fl.1795–1822), schoolmistress, 143
Campbell's Tower, Bonnygate, 198

Canongate, Edinburgh, tolbooth, 33
Carnbee, parish, Fig.1.1, 3, 87, 233
Carnegie, John (fl.1757–82), flesher, deacon, 179
Carnegie, Mrs, prob. Mary Lawson, wife of David (fl.1778–1817), carrier and horse-hirer, 84
Carslogie, Map 3, 51, 135
Carslogie Road, Map 4, Pl.15b, 197, 210
Carstairs, James sen. (1750–1836), writer, provost and bailie, 1765–67 apprentice to William Robertson (qv), town clerk 1784–1816, then joint with son, 48, 98
Carstairs, James (1788–1843), writer, town clerk from 1816 with father James (qv), 67
Cart Haugh, Map 4, 92, 99, 140, 144, 201, 210
Carters Society, 174
Castle, 9, 14–16
Castle Street, 195
Castlebank Road, Map 4, 198
Castlefield House, 197
Castlehill, Map 4, 14, 17, 32, 92, 96, 139–40, 185, 198, 211
Cattle Market, Station Road, 208
Cemetery, Ceres Road, 195, 197
Ceres, burgh and parish, Maps 2 and 3, Fig.1.1, 3, 35, 45–46, 62, 75, 87, 115, 140, 170, 233
Ceres Burn (Kemback Water), Fig.2.1, 11, 48
Ceres Road, 51, 198, 211
Chalmers, James (fl.1763–68), merchant, 39, 42
Chalmers, John (fl.1788–93), manufacturer, flax-dresser, 48
Chalmers, Isabel (fl.1710), unmarried mother, 184
Chalmers, Rev Dr Thomas (1780–1825), minister of Kilmany, later professor at St Andrews, then Edinburgh, played a leading role in the Disruption of 1843, 143, 184
Chance Inn (W of Craigrothie, Map 2), 46
Chancellor's House, Crossgate, Pl.3b, 34
Charles I (r.1625–49), 25
Charles II (r.1660–85), 26, 31
Charleton, Map 2, 59
Chippendale, Thomas junior (1749–1822/3), cabinet-maker, London, 63
Christie, Andrew (1765–1831) of Ferrybank, writer and banker, 1783 apprentice to Robert Johnston (qv), provost, bailie and treasurer, m. Margaret, dau. of Charles Dempster, banker, St Andrews, 56, 63, 67, 98, 101, 105, 109, 111, 114, 118–19, 122, 216–17, 235, 241
Christie, Charles (c.1800–70), son of Andrew (qv), Indian army officer, 56
Christieson, John, minister of Kemback 1672–73, then of Liff (Angus), prosecuted for holding conventicles, 26

Churches and congregations
    Baptist (est.1815, Kirkgate 1821, Provost
        Wynd 1847, Bonnygate 1929), 194–95,
        209
    Bonnygate Church (built 1865–66, United
        Presbyterian, then Baptist), Map 4, Pl.15c,
        195
    Boston (First Relief, then UP) Church
        (est.1770, rebuilt 1849), 173, 178,
        194–95, 204
    Burnside Chapel (Burgher), 1796, 194
    Congregational (Glassite), 194
    Episcopal Chapel (1820, St Catherine St),
        98, 105, 163, 194, 219
    Episcopal meeting room, Bonnygate, 26, 105
    Episcopal Church (1866, St James, St
        Catherine St), Map 4, 195
    Episcopal Sunday School, Castle Street, 195
    Free Church, South Union Street (c.1845–
        78), 195, 197
    Free Church, Bonnygate (1878, now St
        John's), Map 4, 195
    Parish church, pre-1415, 16
    Parish church, 1415–1785, Pl.1a,b,c,6a,
        Fig.2.2–4, 16–17, 32–33
    Parish church, 1785, Map 4, Pl.6a, 58, 94,
        123, 195
    Parish Sunday School (1878), Kirk Wynd,
        195
    Relief Chapel, Provost Wynd (1830–47),
        194–95, 204
    Roman Catholic mission (1864, Millgate),
        195
    St Columba's RC church (1965-present),
        Map 4, Pl.16c, 209
    St Michael's, West Port (1837–1951), Map
        4, 195, 209
    Secession Church (b.1794–96), Burnside,
        178
    United Associate, 178, 194
Cinemas, 211
Clark, Isobel (fl.1724), dau. of James, town
    officer, servant to John Arnot (fl.1720–62),
    surgeon-apothecary, 83
Clarkson, John (fl.1779–1806), dancing-
    master, 135
Clarty Wynd, 92
Clatto, Map 2, reservoir, 203, 212
Cleish, Map 2, 46
Clephane, David (d.1721) of Carslogie, 38,
    239
Clephane, George (fl.1698–1730) of Carslogie,
    merchant, 179
Clerk, John (fl.1701–51), merchant and
    vintner, bailie, 151
Coaltown of Balgonie (S of Markinch, Map
    2), 98
Cockburn, Bartholomew (fl.1763–95),
    vintner and innkeeper, Blue Bell, m. Mary
    Anderson, dau. of John Anderson (qv),
    72–73, 240
Cockburn, Mrs, Mary Nisbet (fl.1792–1825),
    innkeeper, widow of Bartholomew (qv),
    73

Cockburn, William (1764–1819), cabinet-
    maker, son of Batholomew (qv), 75, 111,
    125, 240
Coffee House/Room, 116, 133, 136, 142–44
Colinsburgh, Map 2, 59
Collessie, parish, Fig.1.1, 3, 233
Commissioners of Supply, 105, 160, 166, 172,
    176–77, 202
Common Braes, 58, 92
Common herd, 31, 58
Connolly, Erskine (1796–1843), bookseller,
    St Catherine Street, brother of Matthew
    (qv), 143
Connolly, Matthew Forster (1789–1877),
    writer and bank agent, Anstruther, 200
Constables, 93–94, 103–04, 141, 177, 182
Convention of Royal Burghs, 31–32, 44, 97,
    152, 160–61
Corn Exchange, Pl.15a, 196, 210
Correction House, 176–77
Council House, Pl.10c, 94, 98. 122, 160
County Buildings, Pl.9c, 97–98, 139, 160, 200,
    210, 214
Cow (or Common) Bridge, 31
Cowdenbeath, Map 2, 6
Crail, burgh and parish, Maps 1 and 2,
    Fig.1.1, 1, 4, 7, 10, 12, 23, 29, 35, 46,
    62–63, 68, 87, 201, 233
Crawford, earls of, 33, 69, 139, 166, 219
Crawford Priory, Map 3, 119, 166
Creich, parish, Fig.1.1, 3, 87, 233
Crombie, Patrick (fl.1699–1741), merchant,
    bailie and treasurer, his mother Beatrice
    was the sister of James Wedderburne (qv),
    151
Cromwell, Oliver (1599–1658), 26
Cross, The, Map 4, 32, 99
Cross Keys Close, 208
Cross Macduff, Fig.2.1, 11
Crossgate, Map 4, Pl.4a, 7c, 19–20, 32, 91,
    104, 136–37, 182, 197, 199, 208
Crossgate House, Pl.11a, 100
Culbert, James (fl.1800), merchant, 42
Culross, Map 1, 7
Cults, kirkton and parish, Map 3, Fig.1.1, 3,
    170, 233
Cults Mill, Fig.4.2, 48
Cunzie Neuk, narrowest part of Bonnygate,
    near Cross, 91
Cupar
    burgh arms, Fig.2.5, 22, 33
    county town, 1
    name, meaning of, 1
    royal burgh, 1, 10
Cupar, clubs and societies
    Amateur Musical Association (est.1865),
        201
    Amateur Operatic Society, 211
    Amateur Orchestral Society, 211
    Benevolent Society, 53, 174
    Bowling Club (est.1859), 201
    Burns Club, 211
    Choral Society, 201
    Choral Union/Association, 211

Cupar, clubs and societies (*cont.*)
  Conservative Association (est.1879), 202
  Cricket Club (est.1833), 201
  Curling Club (est. by 1822), 201
  Golf Club (est.1856), 201
  Horticultural Society (est.1820), 137
  Ladies Society, 202
  Lawn Tennis Club (est.1882), 201
  Liberal Association (est.1879), 202
  Literary and Debating Society, 211
  Philharmonic Society (est.1853), 201
  Phrenological Society (est.1835), 200–01
  Pipe Band, 211
  Sick Poor Association, 204
  Silver Band, 211
Cupar Gas Company (est.1830), 202
Cupar Mills, Fig.4.2, 48, 57, 78, 118, 120,
  135, 187–88
Cupar Muir, Map 3, 57, 59, 188
Cupar Races, 34, 136, 138–41, 215
Cupar Volunteers (est.1797), 56, 136, 140,
  144, 159, 166, 172, 215

Dairsie, village and parish, Map 3, Fig.1.1, 3,
  170, 199, 233
Dairsie Mill, Fig.4.2,
Dalgairn, Map 3, 101, 105
Dalkeith, Map 1, 30, 42
David I (r.1124–53), 10
David II (r.1329–71), 11, 15, 19, 21
Davidson, James (d.1770), merchant, 40
Davidson, Mrs (fl.1768–73), wife of James
  Davidson (fl.1766–1812), merchant, 84
Dead Wynd, *see* Short Lane
Dempster, George (1732–1818) of Dunnichen,
  MP 1761–90, Director of E India Co.,
  interested in industry, agriculture, fisheries,
  and the building of lighthouses, 155–56,
  163–66
Dempster, Dr James (fl.1792–1843), physician,
  druggist, house painter, and organiser of
  illuminations, MD Edinburgh, 68, 144
Denmuir, Map 2, 34
Dick, William (fl. 1701–36), 1st minister
  1702, m. (2) Isobel Mackgill (d.1787)
  of Rankeilour (their dau. Margaret,
  heiress of Rankeilour, m. 1767 Capt Hon.
  Frederick Lewis Maitland RN (qv)), 110,
  116, 119, 132–33, 141, 239
Dingwall, Map 1, 166
Dingwall, John, tenant, Ramornie Mill, ? later
  lint-miller, Tarvit Mill, 105
Dingwall, Walter (fl.1802–45), saddler, Hope
  Street Trustee, Director of Fife Fire
  Insurance Co., 105
Don, William, linen manufacturer, Forfar, 60
Douglas, Andrew (fl.1725–50), merchant,
  involved with linen manufactory and
  bleachfield, 39, 62
Douglas, John (fl.1730–c.1778), architect,
  Edinburgh, 104
Douglas, George (fl.1715–33), merchant, 165
Drummond, William (1792–1867), writer,
  agent for Commercial Bank, 67

Duffus, J. C. (fl.1873–1927), jute merchant,
  Dundee, later businessman, London,
  donor of park, 211
Duffus Park, Carslogie Road, 211
Dumbarton, Map 1, 12
Dumfries, Map 1, 29–30, 42, 67, 138, 143,
  165, 185, 213
Dunbar, Map 1, 22, 29, 165
Dunbog, parish, Fig.1.1, 3, 87, 233
Duncan, Elizabeth (fl.1737–60), brewer, widow
  of John Smith (d.1742), smith, 119, 239
Duncan, Miss, of Edengrove, 199
Duncan, Robert (fl.1792–1804), merchant,
  40, 42
Duncan Institute, *see* Libraries
Dundas, Robert (1685–1753), Lord Arniston,
  152–53
Dundas, Henry (1742–1811), viscount
  Melville, 55, 66, 164
Dundee, Map 1, 1–2, 4, 12–13, 23, 29–30, 32,
  37–38, 41–42, 46–47, 49–55, 57, 61, 63,
  74, 79, 81, 83, 86–87, 89, 93, 96, 135,
  143, 145, 150, 156–57, 163, 165, 184,
  187, 191, 208, 217–18
Dunfermline, burgh and parish, Maps 1 and
  2, 1, 4–6, 11, 21, 45, 63, 79, 83, 91, 105,
  134, 165, 189, 212, 214
Dunicher (Dunikier) Law, Fig.2.1, 11
Dunino, parish, Fig.1.1, 3, 87, 233
Duns, Map 1, 42
Dysart, Map 2, 5–7, 29–30, 45, 63, 83,
  165–66

Earlsferry, Map 2, 7, 216
East India Company, 6, 150, 156, 164, 217
East Port, 33, 92
East Road, Map 4, Pl.12c, 51
East Toll, 96
Eden, estuary and 'port', Map 2, 12–13, 22,
  50, 213
  river, 1, 11, 31–32, 50, 57, 96–97, 105, 137,
  183, 194, 201, 204, 212
Eden Park, 197, 211
Eden Place, 197
Edinburgh, Map 1, 1, 10, 22, 28–30, 35,
  37–38, 41–42, 50–52, 55, 62–63, 66–67,
  69, 73–74, 77–78, 81–83, 87, 91, 99–101,
  111, 114, 116–18, 134–35, 140, 145,
  147–48, 154, 156, 165, 175–77, 182, 184,
  190, 192, 203, 219
Edward I (r.1272–1307), king of England,
  10, 15
Edward II (r.1307–27), king of England, 15
Edward III (r.1327–77), king of England, 15
Elder, John, poss. young writer (1787 clerk to
  George Aitken (qv), 1788 clerk to Robert
  Stark), 164
Elder, Thomas (fl.1753–71), servant to flesher,
  179
Elgin, Map 1, 22, 29, 35, 143, 185
Elgin, earl of, 212
Elie, burgh and parish, Map 2, Fig.1.1, 3, 7,
  35, 62–63, 233
Elmwood College, Carslogie Road, 211

English School, *see* Schools, Grammar School
Epidemics, 20, 27–28, 183, 203
Erskine, James, bro. of William (qv), 152
Erskine, William (1691–1754) of Torrie,
      soldier, MP 1722–27, bro. of James (qv),
      152, 163
Ewan, John (fl.1793), private teacher, 129

Falconer, Thomas (fl.1788–96), mason,
      architect, 240
Falkirk, Map 1, 42
Falkland, burgh and parish, Map 2, Fig.1.1, 1,
      3, 10, 16, 31, 45–47, 51, 62–63, 67, 87,
      119, 233
Farmer, David (fl.1760–79), day-labourer and
      miller, 87
Farquharson, James (fl.1766–95), brewer,
      184
Ferguson, James (fl.1771–92), bleaching-
      master (and millwright?), 44
Ferguson, John (fl.1801–24) of Stronvar,
      writer, merchant banker and developer,
      provost, m. 1807 Ann, dau. of Robert
      Geddie (qv), Fig.4.6, 52–53, 55–56, 64,
      96–98, 104–05, 134, 148, 235
Fernie of Fernie (Map 3), arms and effigy of,
      Pl.1b, Fig.2.4, 17
Fernie, Margaret (d.1766), widow of William
      Lees (fl.1717–33), baxter, 239
Fernie, Robert (d.1824), merchant, 40
Ferrybank (now Ferrymuir), Map 3, 101, 109,
      137
Ferryport-on-Craig, parish, Fig.1.1, 4, 7, 38,
      87, 233, *see also* Tayport
Fife, earls of, 9–10, 14–16
      Duncan, earl of, 15–17
Fife Agricultural Society (est.1821), 200
Fife Chapman Society, 80, 133
Fife Chirugico-Medical Society (est.1825), 69
Fife Council, 212
Fife County Council (1889–1975), 192, 202,
      209, 211
Fife Electric Power Company, 212
Fife and Forfar Yeomanry, 204
Fife Foxhounds (est.1805), 139
Fife Hunt (est.1780), 136, 138–39, 160
Fife Regional Council, 212
Fifeshire Agricultural Association (est.1834),
      200
Fifeshire Journal Press (1834–89), 199–200
Fifeshire Literary, Scientific and Antiquarian
      Society (est.1830s), 200
Fifeshire Medical Association (est.1882), 201
Fifeshire Militia, 144, 157–59, 166, 171, 196
Findhorn, Map 1, 22
Finlay, Maurice (fl.1802–17), mason, deacon
      of wrights, Pl.9b
Fire, 16, 23, 32, 58, 170
Fire engine, purchase of, 157, 166, 183
Fleming, William (fl.1815–26), merchant,
      agent for Commercial Bank, 48
Flisk, parish, Fig.1.1, 3, 233
Fluthers, Map 4, 93, 99, 194, 201, 208
Fogage Wynd, *see* North Union Street

Forfar, Map 1, 5, 7, 13, 60, 63, 77, 143, 145,
      150, 165, 217
Forgan, parish, Fig.1.1, 3, 233
Forres, Map 1, 22
Forster, Elizabeth, millmistress, widow of
      David Barclay (d.1733), miller, 82
Fort Augustus, Map 1, 86
Fort George, Map 1, 86
Fort William, Map 1, 86
Forth Bridge, 192
Forth and Clyde Canal, 37
Forthar, Map 2, 46
Foulis, John (fl.1762–76), merchant and
      stampmaster, 44, 154
Frazer, Peter (c.1760–1831), flesher, 106
Free Gardeners, 202
Friary, Dominican (Blackfriars), 13, 17
Front Lebanon (*see also* Lebanon), Map 4,
      103, 187
Fry, Elizabeth (1780–1845), Quaker,
      campaigner for prison reform, 122

Galloway, John (fl.1801–33), merchant,
      seedsman, 63
Gamley, H S (1865–1928), sculptor,
      Edinburgh, 210
Gaol, New (1844–89), Castlebank Road,
      195–96
Gaol, Old, Map 4, Pl.9b, 96–97, 104–05, 160
Garlie Bank, Map 3, 22, reservoir, 212
Geddie, Robert (fl.1760–1820), merchant and
      banker, bailie, agent for Bank of Scotland,
      part-owner of brick-works, son of a
      maltman, nephew of William, merchant
      (qv), 41, 48, 55, 63–64, 155
Geddie, William (fl.1716–68), merchant, bailie,
      active member of guildry, 39, 239
Geddie, William (fl.1796–1803), merchant and
      manufacturer, part-owner of brick-works,
      63
George, Thomas (fl.1772–1814), merchant,
      bailie, 42
Gibb, Harry (fl.1813–25), tenant farmer (Balass,
      just E of Cupar) then auctioneer, grandfather
      of Henrietta Keddie (qv), 84, 128, 135
Gladney (Ceres), Map 3, 4
Glasford, Andrew (fl.1690–1710), writer,
      bailie, 67
Glasgow, Map 1, 29–30, 37–38, 41–42,
      45–46, 55, 63, 148, 157, 165, 203
Glass, Miss (fl.1778–1800), schoolmistress, 143
Glenday, Alexander (fl.1796–1848),
      manufacturer, Lebanon, 187
Glenrothes, Map 2, 212
Goodfellow, Janet (fl.1759), maidservant to
      family of sheriff-clerk, 166
Goodsir, Alexander (fl.1802–27),
      manufacturer, Lebanon, developer of 12
      houses in Castlefield, 63
Goodsir, Adamson & Co, 46, 63
Gordon, John (fl.1739–56), merchant, 39, 239
Gourdon, Map 1, 22
Gow, Nathaniel (1763–1831), fiddle player,
      son of Niel (qv), 136, 144

Gow, Niel (1727–1807), fiddle player and composer, 144

Grace, Charles (1757–1814), surgeon, bailie, 1776 apprentice to Henry Young surgeon, 1796 MD St Andrews, 68–69, 176, 178–79, 184

Grace, Charles (1786–1858), physician, LRCSE 1806, MD St Andrews 1814, son of Charles (qv), m. (2) Magdalen (b.1792), dau. of George Campbell, minister (qv), 69, 87

Graham, James Gillespie (1777–1855), architect, Pls.9b,9c, 104

Graham, Dr James Moore (1784–1865), surgeon, Irish, came to Fife 1814, lived at 1 Barony, 1836–51 joint owner of *Fifeshire Journal*, m. (3) Mary (1798–1882), dau. of Andrew Christie (qv), 200

Granton, harbour and ferry point (W of Leith, Map 1), 192

Gray, George (fl.1775–88), rector of grammar school, 129–30

Gray, John (1724–1811) of Paddington Green, prob. son of William Gray (schoolmaster, Cupar, 1709–37), 53, 63, 131, 143, 172

Gray, Miss (fl.1774–80), mantua-maker, 84

Gray, Peter (d.1815), soldier, 54, 240

Greenock, Map 1, 42

Gregory, William (fl.1724–67), merchant, 90

Greig, Ann (fl.1822–26), schoolmistress, 135, 143

Greig, David (fl.1782–87), wright, 75, 240

Greig, John (c.1705–61), merchant and brewer, bailie, 239

Greig, Mr, prob. John (fl.1722–61), merchant and brewer, later bailie, m. Janet Crombie (poss. dau. of Patrick (qv)), 152

Greig, William residenter, prob. retired apothecary and bailie (fl.1702–66), 239

Greigston, Map 2, 201

Guardbridge, Map 2, 12

Gullan, Andrew (d.1747), residenter, 239

Gurney, Joseph (1788–1847), Quaker, prison reformer, 122

Guthrie, Robert (fl.1796–1826), merchant and maufacturer, bankrupt 1818 and 1820, 40–42, 122, 241

Hacket, Sir James (d.1705) of Pitfirrane, provost of Dunfermline, 179

Hackston, David (d.1680) of Rathillet (Map 2), Pl.2c, 26

Haddington, Map 1, 22, 29, 165–66

Haig, Field Marshal Earl Douglas (1861–1928), 210

Haig, William, distiller, Guardbridge, 12

Hain, Andrew (fl.1818–30), merchant, haberdasher and draper, 42

Haldane, Patrick (c.1683–1769), MP 1715–22, provost of St Andrews, 163

Hall, James (fl.1780–94), private teacher, 1780 excommunicated for fornication, 184

Hamilton, Map 1, 30, 42

Hastie, William (c.1755–1832), architect, 106

Hawick, Map 1, 42

Hawklaw, Map 3, signals station, 208

Hay, Captain Alexander (fl. 1785–92), soldier, 110, 120, 240

Hay, Laurence (d.1681), Covenanter, Pl.2c, 26

Hay, Robert (fl.1719–23) of Naughton (Map 2), sheriff-depute, 151, 153

Hay Fleming, David, historian, St Andrews, 200

Heggie, Isobel (fl.1623), wife of builder of Preston Lodge, 34

Henderson, Walter (1752–1815), bookseller and stationer, 54

Hepburn, James (fl.1699–1729), maltman, councillor, 165

High Street, *see* Crossgate

Hill, James (fl.1774–98), bleacher, bailie, 44

Hill Street, Map 4, 197

Hilton, Map 3, 101, 105, 144

Hislop, James (d.1783), retired surgeon, son of John (qv), 69, 240

Hislop, John (fl.1754–70), officer of excise and innkeeper, 72, 240

Hog, George (fl.1799), wright, Tarvit Mill, 'late of Dundee', 48

Honeyman, John (c.1800–79), linen manufacturer, est. power-loom factory (1871–1958), South Bridge, 187–88, 208

Hood Park, west of Cart Haugh, 201

Hope, Sir John (1766–1823) of Rankeilour (Maps 2 and 3), became earl of Hopetoun 1816, portrait by Raeburn in County Buildings, 105, 119, 126

Hope, John (fl.1791) of Craighall, 139

Hope, Thomas (d.1771) of Rankeilour (Maps 2 and 3), member of the Board of Trustees, leading member of the Honourable Society of Improvers, 43

Hope, Sir William (fl.1701) of Craighall, 179

Hope Street, *see* St Catherine Street

Hope Street Trustees, 98

Horsburgh, Major James (c.1730–1804) of Mayfield, 159

Horsburgh, Thomas (1760–1847) of Lathockar (Map 2), writer, banker and sheriff clerk (succeeded father 1797), bailie, Pl.11a, 55, 64, 98, 100–01, 103, 106, 157, 165–66, 235

Hospital Mill, Fig.4.2, 43, 48–49

Hotels, *see* Inns

Howe of Fife, plain of river Eden, W of Cupar, 1, 190, 208

Howie, John (1820–90), sculptor, Ceres, 197

Hugh, Betty (fl.1792–1823), merchant, 40–42, 54, 241

Hutchison, Robert (c.1769–1845), mason, from Coaltown of Balgonie, Pl.10c, 98

Inglis, Henry (fl.1783–1816), merchant, grocer, 40, 54–55, 235

Inglis, John (fl.1785–1825) of Colluthie, baxter and miller, feued town mills 1791, son of John of Hospital Mill, 77

Innes, John (fl.1733–72), weaver, 240
Innes, John (1840–1901), printer and publisher, 200
Innes, J & G (1892-present), printers, publishers and booksellers, 200
Inns and Hotels
Blue Bell, corner of Crossgate and South Bridge, 52, 72, 122, 137
Crown, Crossgate, 136–37, 140
George (rebuilding of Crown), Crossgate, 137
Royal, St Catherine St, Pl.14d, Fig.11.5, 105, 192–94
Tontine, St Catherine St, Pl.10a, Fig.11.4, 52, 63, 98, 105, 137, 144, 158, 183, 192–93, 195, 210, 214
Insurance Companies
Edinburgh Life Assurance Co., 54
Fife Fire Insurance Company (1806–34), Pl.10b, 54, 56, 64, 98, 166, 183
Scottish Union Assurance Co., 54
Inverbervie, Map 1, 22
Inverkeithing, Map 2, 1, 10, 12, 50, 87, 165–66
Inverness, Map 1, 29, 143, 213, 219
Irvine, Map 1, 29, 42, 143, 165, 185

Jack, William (fl.1778–1824), merchant, bailie, Hope Street Trustee, 105
James I (r.1406–37), 11–12
James VI and I (r.1567–1625), 17, 25
James VII and II (r.1685–88), 26
Jedburgh, Map 1, 29, 42, 138
Johnston, George (fl.1749–84), writer, later sheriff-substitute, bailie, 105
Johnston, Robert (1752–1812) of Kedlock (Map 3), writer, bailie and treasurer, son of George (qv), 101
Justices of the Peace, 67, 105, 153, 160, 166, 172

Keddie, Henrietta (1827–1914), schoolteacher, later wrote novels under the name Sarah Tytler, dau. of Philip (qv) and Mary (dau. of Harry Gibb (qv)), 52, 63, 116–17, 120, 125–26, 129, 131, 133, 135–36, 139, 142–43
Keddie, Philip (fl.1811–24), writer, 1811–12 apprentice to James Webster (qv), father of Henrietta (qv), 84
Kelso, Map 1, 42, 135, 138, 143
Kelty, Map 2, 6
Kemback, village and parish, Map 3, Fig.1.1, 3, 87, 170, 208, 233
Kemback Water, see Ceres Burn
Kennoway, Map 2, 35, 41, 46, 52
Kettle, parish, Fig.1.1, 3, 45, 47, 62, 87, 233
Kilconquhar, village and parish, Map 2, Fig.1.1, 3, 7, 68, 199
Kilgour, John (d.1795), wright, 240
Kilmany, parish, Fig.1.1, 3, 38, 170, 233
Kilmarnock, Map 1, 143
Kilrenny, burgh and parish, Map 2, Fig.1.1, 3, 7, 233

Kinghorn, Map 2,, 1, 10, 46, 48, 51, 101, 174
Kingsbarns, village and parish, Map 2, Fig.1.1, 3, 7, 63, 233
Kinross, Map 2, 55, 105
Kinross, John (1855–1931), architect, 210
Kirk, David (fl.1770–83), smith, Newbigging of Carslogie, 240
Kirk Wynd, Map 4, Pl.8b, 91, 99–100, 195
Kirkcaldy, Maps 1 and 2, 2, 4–7, 13, 29–30, 35, 45–46, 49–51, 55, 57, 61, 63–64, 87, 101, 117, 134, 166, 187, 189–90, 200, 211–12, 214, 217–18
Kirkgate, Map 4, 17, 19, 92, 187, 197, 209
Kirriemuir, Map 1, 55, 63
Knights Templar, 19
Knox Cottages, South Road, 202
Kyd, James (fl.1790–1838) of New Gilston (Map 2), writer, bailie, 1790–92 apprentice to Robert Johnston (qv), factor to Earl of Leven & Melville, son of a cooper and bro. of William (qv), Pl.10b, 56, 67, 98, 101, 105, 236
Kyd, William (fl.1805–30), merchant and linen manufacturer, Hospital Mill, bankrupt 1816 and 1826, son of a cooper and bro. of James (qv), 46

Lady Burn, Map 4, 1, 22, 32, 48, 89, 91–93, 96, 103, 140, 183, 201
Lady Wynd, Map 4, 32, 50, 91–92, 104
Ladybank, Map 2, 191
Ladyinch, junction of Carslogie and Balgarvie Roads, Pl.11b, 22, 100, 111, 201
Lanark (SE of Hamilton, Map 1), 219
Landale, George (fl.1809–10), manufacturer, 63
Largo, burgh (Upper and Lower) and parish, Map 2, Fig.1.1, 3, 11, 41, 46–47, 190, 192, 234
Latin School, see Schools, Grammar School
Latto, James (fl.1701–39), cadger, 239
Leadbetter, McCaull & Co (1864–1926), power-loom factory, Front Lebanon, 187–88, 208
Lebanon, 93, 104
Lebanon Mill, Fig.4.2, 49
Leckie (or Thomson), Janet (fl.1768), brothel-keeper, 180
Leith, Map 1, 22, 42, 46, 143
Leslie, Map 2, 28, 63
Leslie, family, see Rothes
Leslie, Charles (d.1769), MP 1722, army officer, bro. of earl of Rothes, 152, 163
Letham, Maps 2 and 3, 62, 136
Leuchars, village and parish, Map 2, Fig.1.1, 3, 7, 15, 22, 45, 47, 62–63, 67, 157, 192, 234
Leven, Map 2, 6, 35, 46, 48, 50, 69, 166, 192
Leven, river, Fig.2.1, 11
Leven and Melville, earls of, 151, 162
David Melville, 6th earl of and 5th earl of Melville (1722–1802, inherited 1754), 139, 155

Alexander (1749–1820), 7th and 6th earl, 119, 134
Jane, countess of, 131
David (1785–1860), 8th and 7th earl, 136
Liberty of Cupar, Fig.2.1, 11, 38
Libraries
Castlehill, 198–99
Coffee and Reading Room, 199
Duncan Institute, Fig.11.6, 196–97, 199–200
New Reading Room, 199
Subscription, 134
Lindsay, Sir David (1490–c.1567) of the Mount, poet, moralist and reformer, attended St Andrews university 1505–09, 1544–46 represented Cupar in Parliament, 16
Lindsay of the Byres, family of, 35
Linktown, Kirkcaldy (Maps 1 and 2), 4, 166
Linlithgow, Map 1, 22, 29–30, 165
Lochgelly, Map 2, 6, 37
Logie, estate and parish, Map 3, Fig.1.1, 3, 33, 90, 170, 234
Lords of the Congregation, 22–23, 205
Lorimer, Betty (fl.1768), unmarried mother, 179
Lossiemouth, Map 1, 22
Low, Alexander (fl.1784–1817) of Pittencrieff, residenter, developer of Newtown, 92–93, 240
Lowstown, see Newtown
Lunardi, Vincenzo (1759–1806), balloonist, 140, 171
Lundie, Alexander (fl.1686–89), 1st minister, 26
Lundy, John, pupil at Cupar grammar school 1654, 34
Lydox Mill, Fig.4.2, 48

Mackie, Dr Andrew (1815–47), physician, surgeon and druggist, 1841 bought Edenbank House, off Crossgate, 203
Mackie, Dr Archibald (1823–79, surgeon and physician, Edenbank House, then 1875 Bellfield, 203
Mackintosh, Robert of Auchintully, 155, 164
McNab, Alexander (fl.1810–49), innkeeper, coach-maker and coach-operator, Crown Inn, then Tontine Inn, m. Marjory Wiseman, prob. sister of Robert (qv), 52, 63
McPherson, Ann (fl.1808–26), schoolmistress, sister of Christian (qv) and Euphemia (qv), 131, 143
McPherson, Christian (fl.1803–21), residenter, former teacher, m. to Peter Barclay, minister of Kettle, sister of Ann (qv) and Euphemia (qv), 131, 143, 241
McPherson, Euphemia (fl.1795–1803), schoolmistress, sister of Ann (qv) and Christian (qv), 131, 143
Magus Muir, Map 3, 26

Maitland, Captain the Honourable Frederick Lewis (1730–86), bro. of Lady Elizabeth Anstruther (qv), m. Margaret Dick of Rankeilour, dau. of William (qv), 166
Maitland, Admiral Frederick Lewis (1777–1839), son of Capt. Hon. F. L. Maitland (qv), commander of HMS Bellerephon, to whom Napoleon surrendered in 1815, bought Lindores, 134
Maitland-Makgill-Crichton, David (1801–51) of (Nether) Rankeilour (Maps 2 and 3), 195, 197, 205
Makgill, George (fl.1740–69) of Kemback, physician, 68
Makgill, John (fl.1654–62), 1st minister, 26
Malcolm, John (c.1648–1709) of Foxton (Map 3), writer, bailie, 67, 239
Marathon House, Bonnygate, Map 4, Pl.3c, 100, 110
Margaret (d.1275), wife of Alexander III (qv), 14
Markinch, Map 2, 35, 41, 45, 50, 63, 134
Martin, Alexander (fl.1815–30), land-surveyor, d.1842 in New York, 100
Mary of Guise (1515–60), queen regent, mother of Mary, Queen of Scots, 22–23, 205
Marybank, East Burnside, 197, 204
Maryfauld, 16
Masonic Hall, Bonnygate, 196
Masonic Lodges, 136, 144, 211
Matthew, Christian (fl.1768), unmarried mother, 179
Mathie, John (fl.1748–54), merchant and tobacconist, 39, 42, 239
Maxwell, Catherine (fl.1775), threadmaker, 63
Melville, Maps 2 and 3, 151, 190
Melville, family, see Leven and Melville
Melville, Alexander (c.1704–56) of Balgarvie, sheriff-substitute, provost, nephew of David earl of Leven & Melville, 62, 113, 132, 141, 239
Melville, Alexander (fl.1774–1813), baxter, 54, 77, 111, 240
Melville, David (fl.1793–1833), weaver, manufacturer, stampmaster from 1801, bankrupt 1803, 46, 48
Melville, Janet (d.1776), widow of William Peage (fl.1702–42), baxter, 240
Melville, John (d.1823), residenter, 241
Menteith, Robert (fl.1750–65), dyer, 239
Menzies, Dr Robert (fl.1760–1810) of Dura, physician, MD (St Andrews 1760), 68, 219
Mercat Cross, Fig.3.1, 19, 33, 182, 197, 205
Mercer, Mr, architect, St Andrews, 104
Methil, Map 2, 6, 35
Methven, David (c.1744–1824), vintner, postmaster, entertained Lunardi (qv), 119, 132, 144, 241
Methven, John, pottery manufacturer, Kirkcaldy, 125

Methven, Robert (fl.1793–1837), writer, procurator fiscal, bailie, 1793 apprentice to Andrew Christie (qv), 164

Middleton, Abraham (fl.1825–32), plumber, 86, 88

Millar, Katherine (d.1778), widow of Thomas Young (fl.1770), undertaker, 240

Millgate, Map 4, Pl.14a

Millie, William (d.1811), shoemaker, 54

Mills, Fig.4.2, 10, 13, 16, 77–78

Milnathort, Fig.2.1, 11

Milne, John (1822–1904), architect, St Andrews, 199

Mitchell, Alexander (fl.1797–1825), weaver and manufacturer, 56

Mitchell, David (fl.1811–29), accountant, 1804–10 merchant's clerk in London, 1817 in Commercial Bank, 70

Mitchell, James (fl.1699–1751), maltman and brewer, 109, 239

Moffat, Dr James Wemyss (fl.1825), surgeon and accoucheur, formerly of East India Co., 70, 176

Monifieth, Map 1, 138

Monimail, parish, Fig.1.1, 3, 128, 170, 234

Montrose, Map 1, 29, 35, 42, 101, 138, 165–66, 184

Moon, George (fl.1814–36), linen manufacturer, Russell's Mill, 48, 60, 187

Moonzie, parish, Fig.1.1, 3, 38, 68, 170, 234

Morris, William (fl.1780–1801), weaver, 143

Morrison, Sir George (17th c.) of Dairsie, 33–34

Morrison, William Maxwell (fl.1786–97) of Naughton (Map 2) (and Bellfield), advocate, provost, 99

Mortimer, William (fl.1694–1700), merchant and brewer, bailie, 39, 239

Mote Hill, Map 4, Pl.12a, 10, 14, 19, 91, 105, 140, 160, 213

Motray, burn/port of, Map 2, 12–13, 22, 50

Mount Lebanon, 93

Mouse Wynd, see South Union Street,

Muir, David (fl.1721–35), brewer and maltman, 239

Munro, Robert (c.1730–78), vintner and innkeeper, bailie and treasurer, 7

Murray, Andrew (fl.1336–38), 15

Nairne, J. T., portrait painter, 119

New Inn, Map 2, 52, 190

Newburgh, burgh and parish, Map 2, Fig.1.1, 3, 7, 35, 38, 45, 47, 50–51, 106, 119, 149, 162, 234

Newburn, parish, Fig.1.1, 3, 234

Newhaven, fishing and ferry harbour just west of Leith (Map 1), 55, 190

Newlands, Robert (fl.1754–83), weaver and manufacturer, 240

Newport, Map 2, 3, 52, 191

Newspapers, 6, 59, 133–34, 142, 163, 183, 199–200

Newtown, Map 4, Pl.7b, 92–93, 103–04

Nicholas (fl.1357), rector of Cupar grammar school, 19

North Burnside, Map 4, Pl.7a,7b, 92

North East Fife District Council, 212

North Union Street, Map 4, 194

Oliphant, James (fl.1693–1743), merchant and vintner, bailie, 42, 109, 165, 239

Orr, John Cunningham (1827–80), printer and publisher 1857–69, 200

Osburn, Helen (fl.1724–56), millmistress and brewer, widow of William Sibbald (fl.1714–39), writer and brewer, 83

Pagan, William (1803–69), writer, bailie, 1836–51 joint owner of Fifeshire Journal, 67, 105, 200

Paisley, Map 1, 42

Paterson, George (d.1789), architect, 104

Pathhead, Kirkcaldy (Map 2), 166

Pearson, Patrick (fl. 1791–1825), writer, 1791 apprentice to George Aitken (qv), later worked in Edinburgh, Hope Street Trustee, 105

Peat, Margaret (d.1747), wife of James Williamson (c.1715–72), merchant, 39, 239

Peddie & Kinnear, architects, 195

Peebles, Map 1, 12

Perth, Maps 1 and 2, 7, 10, 12, 15, 27, 29, 32, 35, 42, 46–47, 51, 63, 74, 79, 87, 138, 143, 145, 150–51, 156, 163, 165, 191, 219

Pettycur, Map 2, 52

Philp, Robert (fl.1724–42), maltman and brewer, 72, 239

Pitcairne, Archibald (1652–1713), physician, Edinburgh, 28

Pitlessie, Maps 2 and 3, 38

Pitlour, Map 2, 115, 124

Pitscottie Road, Map 4, Pl.12c, 32, 51

Pittenweem, burgh and parish, Map 2, Fig.1.1, 2–3, 7, 13, 35, 62–63, 87, 106, 164–65, 201, 234

Pittilloch (or Pitulloch), Andrew (d.1681), Covenanter, Pl.2c, 26

Player, Samuel (fl.1800–48), vintner and innkeeper, Blue Bell Inn, 52

Playfair, Hugh Lyon (1786–1861), provost of St Andrews, 218

Playfield, 16

Pleasance, South Road, 92

Police Station, 210

Port Glasgow, Map 1, 42

Preston, James (fl.1690–1710) of Denbrae (Nether Kedlock, Map 3), uncle of Sir John of Prestonhall (qv), 34

Preston, James (fl.1777–78), merchant and linen dealer, 63

Preston, Sir John (fl.1694–1717) of Prestonhall, part of Jacobite council 1715–16, 34, 179

Preston, Sir Robert (c.1705–91), second minister 1758, first minister 1775, 1758–91 lived in Preston Lodge, 1782 inherited baronetcy of Airdrie (Map 2), Pl.3a, 100

Preston Lodge, Map 4, Pl.3a, 34, 100

Prestonhall, Map 3, 101, 179

Prinlaws, Leslie (Map 2), 56

Prison, *see* Gaol or Tolbooth

Provost Wynd, Map 4, Pl.8c, 91–92, 197

Railways, 191–92, 194, 208, 217–18

Railway Place, Map 4, 194

Ramsay, Allan (1686–1758), poet, 134

Ramsay, Robert (fl.1760–70), brewer, 240

Rankeilour, Maps 2 and 3, 137

Rattray, David (fl.1757–1825), musician, 136

Rattray, David jun. (c.1778–1843), musician, 136

Reekie, James (fl.1781–1820), wright (plasterer), 54

Reid, Alexander , architect, Edinburgh, 104

Renfrew (between Glasgow and Port Glasgow, Map 1), 219

Riddell, John (fl.1729–41) of Grange, bleachfield operator, 43, 62

Rigg, James (1707–62) of Tarvit, physician and surgeon, 68

Rigg, James Home (1783–1862) of Tarvit, son of Patrick (qv), c.1805 built Tarvit House, 165, 174, 195

Rigg, Patrick/Peter (1739–1801) of Tarvit, son of James (qv), 164, 167, 179

Rigg, William (1677–1740), surgeon apothecary, bailie, 151

Riggs Place, Map 4, 140, 194

Riggs Row, 92, 104

Ritchie, Mary (fl.1762), servant to John Carnegie (qv), 179

Robbie, Christian (fl.1816), dau. of James (fl.1783–1820), innkeeper, 82

Robert I (Robert Bruce) (r.1306–29), 10, 15

Robert II (Robert Stewart) (b.1316, r.1371–90), 11, 15

Robert III (r.1390–1406), 12

Robertson (Donovan), Rachel (fl.1813–37), tinsmith, widow of John Robertson (fl.1788–1808), smith and nail-maker, 75

Robertson, Thomas (fl.1709–44), dyer, bailie and treasurer, 239

Robertson, Thomas (fl.1761–84, writer, town clerk, councillor, son of William (qv), 150, 178, 184

Robertson, William (c.1714–83) of Middlefield (Map 3), writer, 1730 apprentice to John Annan (fl. 1712–39), town clerk from 1759, bailie and treasurer, 1761–77 factor to earl of Crawford, m. (3) Isobel Stevenson (qv), sister of John, writer (qv.), 53, 101, 150

Rose Terrace, Bank Street, 197

Rosemount Cottage, Riggs Place, Pl.11c, 100

Rosevale, Bank Street, 197

Ross (Smith), Katherine (fl.1784–97), innkeeper, 1797, widow of John Ross (fl.1775–84) innkeeper, 72, 240

Rossie, Map 2, 115

Rothes, earls of, 28, 33–35, 162, 164, 166
6th earl, 28
John Leslie (1630–81), 7th earl and 1st duke, 28
John Leslie, (1679–1722), 9th earl, 148, 150–52
John Leslie (1698–1767), 10th earl, 152–54

Roxburgh, Map 1, 10

Royal Arch Chapter, 137, 144

Royal burghs, 1, 7, 10, 28–30, 145–47, 161

Russel, John (fl.1808–36) of Middlefield (Map 3), writer, 1808–10 apprentice to Jas Kyd (qv), 1812–17 clerk to Andrew Christie (qv), 165

Russell's Mill, Fig.4.2, 48, 60, 89, 187

Rutherford, David (fl.1701–28), merchant, one of managers of linen manufactory, 62

Rymer, Primrose (c.1737–79), writer, bailie, 1756 apprentice to Alexander Black (fl. 1741–65), billet-master (1771–77), 67, 240

St Andrews, Maps 1 and 2, 1–2, 4–7, 10–13, 15–17, 21, 27, 29–32, 35, 46, 51, 61, 63, 65, 68–69, 75, 87, 103, 105, 145, 150, 163–65, 172, 189–90, 192, 201, 208, 218

St Andrews and St Leonards, parish, Fig.1.1, 3, 7, 45, 234

St Catherine's Haugh, 19

St Catherine Street, Map 4, Pls.9c, 10a,b, 14d, 43, 56, 93, 96, 101, 104–05, 125, 137, 143, 160, 163, 197, 210

St James Fair, 208

St James Yards, 16, 202

St Monans, burgh and parish, Map 2, Fig.1.1, 3, 35, 63, 234

Saints, dedications to
St Andrew, 16, 23
St Catherine of Sienna, 16–17, 105
St Christopher, 16, 22–23, 35
St Columba, 16, 23
St James, 16, 104
St Margaret, Dunfermline, 21
St Mary (Our Lady), 16, 23
St Michael, 16–17, 22, 32, 35

Salisbury, James (fl.c.1774–c.1800), architect, Edinburgh, 104

Schools
Academy (est.1823), Fig.8.1, 66, 95, 130–31, 135, 141, 175
Baxter Educational Institution for Young Ladies, 199
Bell-Baxter High School, 199, 209, 211
Castlehill Primary School, 211
Grammar School, Pl.9a, 19, 33–35, 66, 95–96, 104, 127–30, 135, 140–41, 154, 174–75
Kirkgate School, Fig.11.7, 198, 211
Madras Academy, 198–99

Scoonie, parish around Leven, Map 2, 166

Scott, Dr Andrew (fl.1752–69), surgeon, bailie, m. Margaret Arnot, prob. sister of Robert (qv), 69, 132, 170, 240

Scott, David (1746–1805) of Duninald, MP 1796–1805, Director of E India Co., related to Hopes of Rankeilour, 164

Scott, Dr David (1795–1838), physician, surgeon and accoucheur, 203

Scott, Janet (fl.1822), midwife, prob. wife of James Edie (1813–25), merchant (grocer), 69

Scott, Robert (fl.1809–29), merchant and manufacturer, Lebanon, bankrupt 1826, 46, 241

Scott, William (fl.1593–1642), minister of Cupar 1604–42, built spire of church, left money for education of poor children, lived at Bellfield, wrote *Apologetical Narration of the State and Government of the Kirk of Scotland* (Wodrow Society 1846), 17, 32

Seggie, Map 3, 12, 22, 162

Selkirk, Map 1, 77, 143

Sewage Works, Tailabout, 204, 212

Sharp, James, 1661–79 archbishop of St Andrews, 26

Sheriff Court of Fife
  Cupar (from 1213), 1, 9–10, 67, 97, 163, 188, 195, 217–18
  Dunfermline (from 1811), 1, 189
  Kirkcaldy (from 1732), 1

Shetland, fishermen from, 172

Short Lane, Map 4, 91, 194

Sibbald, David (17th c.) of Letham, 34

Sibbald, David (fl.1753–73), merchant, 40, 129, 142, 240

Sibbald, Sir Robert (1641–1722) of (Over) Rankeilour (Maps 2 and 3), 28

Simpson, Mr (fl.1897), drawing-master, 205

Simson, John (fl.1737–60), teacher, came from St Andrews grammar school, 239

Skene, Katharine (d.1813), residenter, 110, 114, 119–20, 124, 132, 141, 240

Skinners Steps, Map 4, 93, 188, 198

Smibert, William (d.1776) of Lochmalony (Map 2), soldier, m. Helen dau. of Dr James Bethune (qv), 132, 240

Smith, Alexander (fl.1788–1806), writer, 1801 in sheriff clerk's office, 184

Smith, Christian (d.1723), widow of Arthur Millar (fl.1694–1722), maltman and brewer, 239

Smith, George (d.1822), residenter in Lebanon, former farmer at Kinnaird (near Lydox Mill (qv)), 241

Smith, James (fl.1794–1820), weaver and manufacturer, 105

Smith, Jean (d.1757), widow of Robert Baldie (fl.1703–41), wright, 239

Smith, John, probably writer (fl.1699–1727), 165

Smith, John (c.1782–1825), baxter, 54, 77, 111, 120, 241

Smith, William (c.1777–1853), weaver and manufacturer, 1814 bought Russell's Mill, later moved to Cupar Mills, Hope Street Trustee, partner in Fife Fire Insurance Co., 46, 48, 105, 187–88

Snuffmill Park, *see* Lebanon

Society of Gardners, 174

Soldiers, quartering of, 26, 31, 156–60, 171, 179, 181, 183

South Bridge, Map 4, 20, 32, 91, 137, 187, 194

South Road, Map 4, 51, 93, 99, 140, 194, 197

South Toll, at junction of South Road and Ceres Road, Pl.12b, 92

South Union Street, Map 4, 92, 194, 197

Southfield (behind South Toll), 197

Spens, James (fl.1691–1711) of Letham, writer, 67, 239

Springfield, Maps 2 and 3, 4, 46

Stables, Alexander (fl.1822–29), plain and ornamental painter, and paper-hanger, 126

Staig, James (fl.1808–23), merchant, painter, gilder, and paper-hanger, 71, 125–26

Star, Map 2, 46

Stark, John (c.1704–69), deacon of baxters, 77, 240

Station Road, Map 4, 187, 208

Stenhouse, David (1819–83), linen manufacturer, 187

Stenhouse & Westwater (1866–1960), power-loom weavers, Station Road, 187–88, 208

Stevenson, John (fl.1770–95) of Kinnaird, writer, 67, 113, 120, 132, 179–80, 184, 240

Stevenson, Isobel (fl.1784–1813), widow of William Robertson (qv), sister of John (qv), 240

Stewart, Margaret (fl.1791–1805), residenter, 240

Stewart, Marjory (fl.1716), unmarried mother, 184

Stirling, Map 1, 10, 29, 42, 139, 165, 219

Strachan, Rachel (fl.1798–1809), residenter, 240

Stratheden Foundry, Cupar Mills, 188

Strathkinness, Map 2, 46

Strathmiglo, burgh and parish, Map 2, Fig.1.1, 3, 7, 69, 156, 234

Struthers, Maps 2 and 3, 35

Sugar-beet factory, Pl.16b, 207, 212

Swan, Alexander (fl.1803–14), surgeon, 132, 240

Tailabout Mill/Farm, Fig.4.2, 188, 201, 204

Tain, Map 1, 33, 143

Tarvit (Nether), Map 3, 32, 148, 201
  Hill, 22, 197, 205
  Hill of (Wemysshall), Map 3, 100
  Mill, Fig.4.2, 48
  St Michael of, parish, 7, 22–23, 32
  Street, 103

Tay Bridge, 192

Tayport, Map 2, 4, 35, 63, 138, 192

Templehill, 19

Theatre, Pl.9a, 135

Thomastoun Mill, Fig.4.2, 188, 201

Thomson, Alexander (fl.1812–37), brewer, 50

Thomson, James junior (c.1768–1841), writer, bailie, 1788–89 apprentice to Robert Stark (fl.1768–98), 1790 clerk to George Aitken (qv), 236

Thomson, John (d.1689), writer, 67, 239

Thomson, John (c.1704–83), merchant, bailie and provost, 39, 240

Thomson, Thomas (fl.1734–51), writer, 67, 239

Thomson, Thomas (fl.1735–59), maltman and brewer, 239

Thomson, Thomas (fl.1778–79), tailor, St Andrews, 87

Thomson, William (fl.1810–22), merchant, draper, bailie, 40, 42, 241

Thornton, Map 2, 101, 192

Tod, David (c.1776–1812), writer, 1790 apprentice to Robert Johnston (qv), 1805 deputy to town clerk James Carstairs sen. (qv), in partnership with George Aitken (qv), 54, 67, 111, 132, 240

Tod, James (fl.1754–81), surgeon, bailie and treasurer, son of George, maltman, 166, 179

Tod, Jean, servant to David Methven (qv), 81

Tolbooth, Fig.3.1, 10, 19–20, 26, 33, 58, 89, 94, 96, 149, 152–54, 159, 161, 177

Tollhouses, Pls12b,12c, 51

Town House, see Council House

Tron, Fig.3.1, 12, 20, 23, 33

Tullis, George Smith (1805–48), son of Robert (qv), printer and publisher, 199–200

Tullis, Robert (1775–1831), printer, publisher and paper-maker, bailie and treasurer, 50, 56, 120, 133–34, 143, 177, 199, 236

Tullis, Robert (c.1842–1936), son of George (qv), printer and publisher, 200

Turnpike Trustees, 166, 172, 192, 202

Turpie, John (fl.1825), tailor, habit & pelisse-maker, 87

United Scotsmen, Society of, 157–59, 164

Uthrogle, Map 3, 139, 201, 214

Victoria Bridge, Station Road, 194

Walker, Henry (fl.1773–1818) of Pittencrieff, writer, bailie and treasurer, 1773–76 apprentice to William Robertson (qv), brother of John (qv), 54, 66–67, 100, 111, 120, 132–33, 141, 240

Walker, John (fl.1802–33), manufacturer, Blebo Mill, brother of Henry (qv), m. Margaret, dau. of Harry Gibb (qv), 48, 60

Walker, Thomas (fl.1813–20), writer in Edinburgh but with strong Cupar connections, 98, 105

Walkerton Haugh bleachfield (on river W of Leslie, Map 2), 56

War Memorial, Map 4, Pl.16a, 209–10, 212, 219

Wardlaw, Henry (fl.1404–40), bishop of St Andrews, 16

Waterend Road, Map 4, 50, 188, 210

Watson, James (fl.1822–27), merchant, haberdasher and draper (d.1846 Sydney, Australia), 40, 42

Watson, William (fl.1751–1801), glover, 240

Webster, James (fl.1801–55), writer, bailie and treasurer, 1800–03 apprentice to James Thomson senior (fl.1766–1830), partner in Fife Bank, 91

Webster, John (fl.1765–91), merchant, 63

Wedderburne, James (1635–90), minister of Moonzie 1659–62, prosecuted for holding conventicles, 26

Well Close, between Newtown and N Burnside, 103

Well Tower, 32

Wemyss, burgh (West) and parish, Map 2, 6, 35

Wemysshall (Hill of Tarvit), Map 3, 100

West Port, Map 4, 32, 92, 199

Westfield, Map 4, 100, 197

Weston House, 197, 204

Westwood, Alexander (1813–1906), printer and publisher, 200

Whiston, Peter (1912–99), architect, 209

White, William (fl.1797–1837), wright, deacon, fireman, 157

Whitehead and Burns (1849–57), printers and publishers, 200

Wilkie, Alexander (fl.1787–1800), stampmaster, dismissed for drunkenness 1800, Fig.4.1, 44, 63

Wilkie, David (d.1812), minister of Cults, 54, 111, 240

Wilkie, David (1785–1841), artist, son of David (qv), attended Kettle parish school, Cupar grammar school 1798–99, then Trustees Academy, Edinburgh, 38, 101, 119, 126

Williamson, David (fl.1731–62), merchant, 39

Williamson, James (fl.1623), builder of Preston Lodge, 34

Wilson, James (fl.1795–1830), writer and banker, bailie, 1795–696 apprentice to Robert Johnson (qv), 1797–1801 clerk to Andrew Christie (qv), Fig.4.6, 49, 52–56, 60, 64, 136, 138, 143, 236

Wilson, Robert (fl.1783–1804), merchant, son of a tanner, 144

Winthank House, Kirk Wynd, 100

Wiseman, Dr Adam (1797–1838), physician, son of Robert (qv), 203

Wiseman, Marcia (fl.1793–1801), threadmaker, dau. of Robert (qv), 63

Wiseman, Robert (c.1750–1822), English master, built Bishopgate House c.1810, 60, 100, 111, 128, 133, 143, 175, 241

Wiseman, Dr Robert (1799–1876), LRCSE 1822, 1831 became editor of Fife Herald, 1833 elected to town council, returned to medicine after death of brother Adam (qv), son of Robert (qv)

Wishart, Robert (c.1240–1316), bishop of
Glasgow, 15
Woodhaven, Map 2, 51
Wright, Jean (fl.1785–97), midwife, widow of
Henry Lethangie (fl.1762–86), merchant,
63, 69, 83, 111, 122, 240

Yeaman, George, merchant, Dundee, MP
1710–15, 163
Young, Alexander (c.1707–84), weaver, later
merchant and co-partner in tannery, 40,
63, 240

Young, David (fl.1784–1820), merchant,
106
Young, Dr Henry (fl.1774–88), surgeon,
178
Young, John (fl.1802–25), merchant, 106
Young, William (fl.1760–1809), merchant,
bailie and treasurer, bankrupt 1798,
son of Alexander (qv), bro. of John (qv),
42
Young and Trotter, Edinburgh, 41, 62